"An exceptional story, because it captures – lucidly and honestly – the life, travails and triumphs of an exceptional man. Combining the focus of a former artilleryman with the drive of an entrepreneur and the soul of a philanthropist, Abraham George takes us on a voyage that is as much self-discovery as it is a feast for the intellect. His prognosis is informed and dispassionate, his conclusions inescapable. This is a story that must be read both by those who love India and by those who wish to understand the country."

— Ravindra Kumar, Editor and Managing Director
The Statesman, Kolkata.

"A moving story through self-discovery about bringing differences in the lives of millions residing in rural India through institutions built on the pillars of commitment, integrity, honesty and perseverance. Through his sensitivity and an eye for detailing, the author reminds the reader about the "unfinished agenda" in the largest democracy even after more than five decades of independence and more than one decade of liberalization."

— Verghese Kurien
Founder, National Dairy Development Board, and
Father of the "White Revolution" in India
Anand, Gujarat

"Born in India, educated in the West, accomplished his fortune in the United States, Abraham George is applying his meticulous mind, humane insights and compassionate drive to rural India – the often forgotten home for 650 million human beings. This book, India Untouched, takes the reader on a journey into a world of despair, cruelty, disease, and illiteracy and shows what an aroused populace can do about them. George and his Foundation are about solutions, institution building and lifting up the "Untouchables" so they, with other exploited castes, can start to fulfill their life's possibilities spiritually, materially, civically and through good governance. Pretty remarkable story of what one man can accomplish with vision and determination."

— Ralph Nader
Consumer Advocate and Environmentalist
Washington, D.C.

India
Untouched

Other Books by Abraham George

Lead Poisoning Prevention and Treatment: Implementing a National Program in Developing Countries, ed., Proceedings of International Conference on Lead Poisoning, 1999.

Protecting Shareholder Value: A Guide to Managing Financial Market Risk, Irvin Professional Publishing, 1996.

International Finance Handbook, A. George and I. Giddy, eds., 2 volumes, John Wiley and Sons, 1985.

Foreign Exchange Management and the Multinational Corporation, Holt, Reinhart and Winston, 1976.

India
Untouched
The Forgotten Face of Rural Poverty

Abraham M. George

THE WRITERS' COLLECTIVE

Independent Books for Independent Readers

Cover Design: Barbara Hodge
Book Design: Day to Day Enterprises

ISBN-13: 978-1-59411-122-8
ISBN-10: 1-59411-122-7

Library of Congress Control Number: 2004095498

Printed in the United States of America

Published by The Writers' Collective ✦ Cranston, Rhode Island

To

Mariam, Ajit, Vivek, Ammachi and Achachan

for everything you are to me.

CONTENTS

FOREWORD

India recently had a stunning election, with incumbents across the country thrown out, largely by rural voters. Rural Indians, who make up the country's majority, clearly told the cities and the government that they were not happy with the direction of events. I think I can explain what happened, but first I have to tell you about this wild typing race I recently had with an eight-year-old Indian girl at a village school.

The Shanti Bhavan school sits on a once-scorpion-infested bluff about an hour's drive - and ten centuries - from Bangalore, India's Silicon Valley. The students are mostly "untouchables" (the lowest caste in India), who are not supposed to even get near Indians of a higher caste for fear they will pollute the air others breathe. The Shanti Bhavan school was started by Abraham George, one of those brainy Indians who made it big in high-tech America. He came back to India with a single mission: to start a privately financed boarding school that would take India's most deprived children and prove that if you gave them access to the same technologies and education that have enabled other Indians to thrive in globalization, they could, too.

I visited Mr. George's school last February, and he took me to a classroom where eight-year-olds were learning to use Microsoft Word and Excel. They were having a computer speed-typing lesson, so I challenged the fastest typist to a race. She left me in the dust - to the cheering delight of her classmates. And dust is an appropriate word, because a drought in this area of southern India has left dust everywhere.

"These kids - their parents are ragpickers, coolies and quarry laborers," the school's principal, Lalita Law, told me. "They come from homes below the poverty line, and from the lowest caste of untouchables, who are supposed to be fulfilling their destiny and left where they are, according to the unwritten laws of Indian society. We get these children at age four. They don't know what it is to have a drink of clean water. They bathe in filthy gutter water - if they are lucky to have a gutter near where they live. Our goal is to give them a world-class education so they can aspire to careers and professions that would have been totally beyond their reach, and have been so for generations."

After our little typing race I asked the eight-year-olds what they wanted to be. Their answers were: "an astronaut," "a doctor," "a pediatrician," "a poetess," "physics and chemistry," "a scientist and an astronaut," "a surgeon," "a detective," "an author." Looking at these kids, Mr. George said, "They are the ones who have to do well for India to succeed."

And that brings us to the lesson of India's election: the broad globalization strategy that India opted for in the early 1990's has succeeded in unlocking the country's incredible brainpower and stimulating sustained growth, which is the best antipoverty program. I think many Indians understand that retreating from their globalizing strategy now would be a disaster and result in India's neighborhood rival, China, leaving India in the dust. But the key to spreading the benefits of globalization across a big society is not about more Internet. It is about getting your fundamentals right: good governance, good education.

India's problem is not too much globalization, but too little good governance. Local government in India - basic democracy - is so unresponsive and so corrupted it can't deliver services and education to rural Indians. As an Indian political journalist, Krishna Prasad, told me: "The average Indian voter is not saying, 'No more reforms,' as the left wants to believe, but, 'More reforms, please' - genuine reforms, reforms that do not just impact the cities and towns, but ones which percolate down to the grass roots as well."

India needs a political reform revolution to go with its economic one. "With prosperity coming to a few, the great majority are simply spectators to this drama," said Mr. George. "The country is governed poorly, with corruption and heavy bureaucracy at all levels. I am a great advocate of technology and globalization, but we must find a way to channel their benefits to the rural poor. What is happening today will not succeed because we are relying on a corrupt and socially unfair system."

If there is one thing I have learned about this new era of globalization that we are entering into it is this: All of the inputs, to do good or ill, will increasingly be available to more and more people. What will distinguish who does what with them will be imagination. That you cannot download. You have to upload it, the old-fashioned way, through teachers, parents, role-models and culture. Abraham George has precisely the kind of imagination that we should all want to emulate and, I certainly hope he will be a role model for many others in his native country and around the world.

Thomas L. Friedman
Foreign Affairs Columnist
The New York Times

PREFACE

IN THIS BOOK, I will try to tell the story of rural India from my personal experiences of working among the poor in the villages of Tamil Nadu and Karnataka in South India for the past eight years. The backdrop is the day-to-day lives of a great majority of Indians who live in the villages, mostly untouched by the rapid economic progress that has been occurring in every city across the country since reforms were introduced in 1991. The euphoria behind gains in foreign investment, export revenues, foreign exchange reserves and technology-based services has masked the deplorable conditions faced by the rural population. The widening gap between the haves and have-nots, and the ever increasing numbers of poor people, illustrate a story of broken promises by the rulers of India. It must be told candidly and honestly, not to indict anyone or any group, but to seek solutions that would reduce the hardships faced by hundreds of millions of people in this great nation.

When I left India for America in the late 1960s, the country was still struggling to cope with the difficulties it had confronted since gaining independence some 20 years earlier. A quarter-century later, I returned to a new India that was beginning to show the promise of prosperity for some in the industrial sectors. I had come to start a charitable foundation to educate a few children from socially and economically deprived families, especially among the "untouchables." Since then, my work has drawn me into several connected areas, each one dealing directly or indirectly with issues of poverty and sustainable development. It is those experiences that I want to share with the hope that the lessons I have learned would offer different perspectives and insights into some of the critical problems facing India today.

India is a land of great beauty, contrasts, and contradictions. For more than 4,000 years, its ancient civilization absorbed the values of every invader, suffered with grace every natural disaster, and accommodated the complexities of a multi-religious and multi-cultural society. Today, in the face of globalization and a powerful technological revolution engulfing much of the world, India is reaching out to these forces to satisfy the needs of its one billion plus population. The changes that have taken place in the country over the past decade have been profound, bringing opportunities and hope to millions of people. Yet, there exists two different Indias – one reaping the fruits of change and the other enduring eternal adversity.

While urban India is beginning to benefit from the economic liberalization measures being instituted, much of the rural population has been left behind. The 650 million or so people living in over 500,000 Indian villages are simply spectators to the drama being played out in the cities, and there is little hope that their lives will be any better in the foreseeable future. Despite the lofty ideals and goals constantly pronounced by the country's leaders, the truth is that rural India is simply the bread basket for the rest of the nation, to be used and exploited. If there is to be any justice and respect for human rights, it is the plight of the poor, especially the social underclass, that needs to be addressed. This book is about what can and must be done to bring about economic prosperity and social justice for all Indians.

India has had many notable successes during the past half century, especially in agriculture and information technology, but this book is not about those advances. Instead, it examines critically the broader policies and practices successive governments have employed, and which still continue, but have not yielded the desired results for the poor. The focus of the book is not on personalities but on issues and solutions. I have avoided discussing or taking sides in politics, except in elaborating policies and events that have had a major impact on the nation. The social work being carried out by our foundation has given me firsthand knowledge of the present government system and its many shortcomings in dealing with the problems faced by the poor. It has also put me in constant touch with the poor villagers in the Dharmapuri District of Tamil Nadu. In discussing their problems and by offering alternative solutions, I hope readers will be motivated to evaluate the premises under which present policies are being executed.

Honest efforts to overcome the problems of rural India have been mired in a swamp of obstacles ranging from poor planning and public governance to thousands of years of traditions, beliefs and unjust social hierarchies and practices. For more than 50 years, successive governments have initiated various programs to deal with poverty, but they have not made any major dent in the economic and social status of hundreds of millions.

Having been raised in India, and subsequently educated in the West where I have run businesses, I have now come full circle. My strong desire to demonstrate a successful model for solving some of the perennial problems of rural India stems from my life experiences in two worlds. My dual advantage as an outsider looking in, and as an insider working within the system, I believe, gives me a unique perspective from which to analyze these issues with a fresh and unbiased focus.

My attempt in socioeconomic reform is documented here in a series of interwoven essays that contradict the generally held assumption that rural poverty in India is beyond redemption. The book addresses several issues: education, economic development, social justice, healthcare, environment, free press, art and culture, and ethics. The underlying contention is that only through a determined and sustainable effort by the government, supported by non-governmental organizations, international agencies, and philanthropic institutions, and with active participation by the private sector, can the social and economic problems faced by the rural population in India be effectively tackled. This would require embracing new ideas that are a departure from the traditional ways of dealing with rural poverty. I have attempted to present some of the ideas that have evolved from our foundation's work in India.

In discussing each of the topics, I have also related my experiences, offering some realism to the subject being considered. Although I have avoided naming most of the individuals involved, all the narrated incidents are real and accurate. I have learned many lessons from those events, some of them frustrating and painful. It is my hope that they will provide some of the necessary understanding and insight to succeed in a complex environment involving many players – government, international agencies, private sector, non-governmental organizations, and beneficiaries.

If peace and tranquility are to prevail, India cannot go on much longer ignoring the plight of millions of poor people. A free and democratic India offers great promise, but only if it can mobilize its human resources to work as one people for the common good. It must turn despair into hope and promises into reality. With sound policies and their effective implementation, India can achieve prosperity and security, and assure social justice, equality and human rights for all its people. The unanswered question is whether India's leaders and policymakers can be persuaded by a participatory public to alter priorities, policies and practices to benefit all its citizens, both rich and poor.

I am thankful to all those in The George Foundation who strive every day to carry out its humanitarian mission. I must express my appreciation to the many well-wishers and supporters who have stood by me through the years. Finally, with humility, I thank the many poor people who have allowed me into their lives.

Acknowledgements

My sincere thanks to Martin Pope, Robert Hawkins, William Schroth and Laura Nader for reading the early versions of the manuscript, and making several suggestions to improve it.

I wish to express my appreciation to my editor, Bonnie Hearn Hill, and to everyone who helped bring the book together, including my colleagues at The George Foundation who provided much valuable insight.

A special thank you goes to The New York Times Company for their generous permission to use an adaptation of an Op-Ed piece for this book's foreword, written by their Foreign Affairs columnist Thomas Friedman.

Finally, I am grateful to my sons Ajit and Vivek, who have been great sounding boards.

Chapter 1

A Long-Awaited Journey

THE EARLY YEARS

I was born and brought up in the seaside town of Trivandrum in the coastal state of Kerala, at the southwestern tip of India. My memories of youth are still poignantly filled with the natural beauty of my home state. Kerala is renowned for its scenic backwaters, paddy fields and lush plantations. An intricate network of lagoons, lakes, canals, estuaries and the deltas of 44 rivers interweaves the landscape and connects to the Arabian Sea. Through the centuries, several of the world's major religions have made a home in this state, and people go about their lives not seriously worrying about their differences.

Visitors often come away with fond memories of the traditional Kathakali dance, celebrated boat races, exotic elephant festivals and ancient Ayurvedic medicine. The literacy rate and the percentage of college graduates are both higher here than in any other state.

As a young man, I was attracted by the discipline and glamour of the military and opted to join the officers' training. My first posting in 1966 was to the North-East Frontier that borders China at the Sela mountain passage 14,000 feet above sea level through which the Chinese army had marched in its invasion of India. During my years in the army, I learned much about loyalty, leadership, teamwork and discipline. There is, I suppose, a stage in everyone's life that has a greater impact on his future than all others. For me, it was these army experiences that helped shape much of my outlook on life. I also realized that, while I admired the dedication and values with which the military functioned, it was not a lifetime career I wished to pursue. I felt there were other opportunities out there, possibilities for a future where I could apply what I had learned from the army.

In the third year of my service, I suffered a hearing disability that continues to plague me. At the time, doctors in India were not trained to handle my medical problem as it needed specialized surgery. Fortunately, my mother was already in America teaching physics and working for NASA as a research scientist. I knew my mother's position provided me the opportunity to go to America where I could have my surgery done and then embark on a new life. After considerable effort, I managed to persuade the Indian army command to give me a medical discharge. A new chapter in my life had begun.

A NEW LIFE IN AMERICA

The transition from India to America was a startling, nearly overwhelming one. I joined my mother in Alabama during the heyday of segregationist Governor George Wallace. I felt I had gone to another world, not simply another country. Most of it was very foreign to me, so different from India and the life I had known. I think all immigrants to America experience an initial period of bewilderment, mixed with surprise and awe. I was exhilarated by what lay ahead of me and wanted to avail of every opportunity.

In America, as a graduate student, I specialized in developmental economics and finance with the hope that one day I would be able to make a contribution to India or one of the impoverished African nations. I was working part time for the Singer Company to meet the expenses toward my studies. As a young man too idealistic about what he should be doing with his life, I asked the management of the company to remove my name from its records after I had left so that I would never be identified with a profit-making institution.

My attempt to join the World Bank failed, and soon after completing my doctoral work I decided to enter the teaching profession. But teaching was not sufficiently gratifying, and I wanted to go out and do for myself what I was preaching to my students. That was when Chemical Bank, now part of JPMorgan Chase, offered me a job as an officer. It was time for me to put aside my idealism, work for a prestigious bank, and save enough money over the years to do something for humanitarian causes.

I had worked for Chemical Bank for only two years when I decided to start a company offering computerized systems to large multinational corporations to enable them to deal with their international financial risks. It was several years before my business became somewhat profitable, but when personal computers came along, we migrated our software to this new environment with great success. As I began to make money, I dreamt of the day when I would save enough to pursue work for the poor.

I had been away from India for too long, and consequently, my impressions about the country hadn't kept up with the changes that had taken place during the interim. Moreover, my experience in the Indian army had insulated me from civilian life. I had seen the poor living conditions of the tribal people in the Northeast frontiers of India, but it had not really raised sufficient awareness in me about the widespread poverty throughout the country. I had read that a great majority of Indians, especially in rural areas, were very poor, but their lives were too distant for someone like me who had been brought up in a middle-class family in a fairly prosperous town in Kerala. My social conscience was raised only when I began to read and watch on American television about the lives of the poor and the social injustice of the caste system in India.

By 1995, after 25 years in America, I felt I had accomplished what I had set out to do in my professional business career. I had not lost my youthful idealism; it had been buried, perhaps for awhile, but I felt there were more important things to accomplish than success in business. I had built a company from the ground up and would soon sell it to a large multinational firm, thereby concluding another chapter of my life. It was time for me to pursue what I had originally set out to do, to work full-time in the nonprofit sector.

What I knew about the hardships faced by the poor in India and elsewhere had affected me emotionally. I always believed that, after accomplishing my professional goals, I would turn towards nonprofit work in developing nations. While I was most interested in India, it mattered less to me which country I worked in as long as my efforts would make a difference and help alleviate the poverty and suffering that was pervasive worldwide.

THE BIRTH OF THE GEORGE FOUNDATION

It was during this time that my good friend Angeline Nair decided to return to India and settle down in Bangalore after spending nearly 20 years in America. She and I shared similar interests in social service and had worked together in the United States to provide a better education to African-American inner-city children who came from underprivileged and broken households. Angeline and I spent a lot of time discussing the ills that the poor of India faced and the sheer lack of hope to change their fates. The more we talked, the more we realized we had a duty and an opportunity to do something about it. She promised to help me start a foundation in India that eventually became The George Foundation.

It was in January 1995 that I went back to India after a long absence. I returned with the goal of reducing the injustices and inequalities I had observed and learned about from the media and many published works. I had a renewed sense of purpose and a lifetime of experience to undertake what I thought was a social obligation. Money, I had decided, was not an end but a means to an end. I had been professionally and financially successful, because of the opportunities that I had seized in my lifetime. But it was only the luck of my birth that allowed me these opportunities. I felt it was not fair for me to enjoy selfishly the fruits of my success when many others had never had a chance. It was my duty to do something about this inequity.

I took the journey with my 12-year-old son, Vivek, who had not seen much of India until then. I had spoken to him at length about the great landscapes of India – the majestic Himalayan mountains in the north and the plains and plateaus that cover much of the country. We talked about some of India's great souls – Buddha, Gandhi, Tagore and Vivekananda – as I wanted him to be proud of his heritage. Vivek was worried about how he would be treated by the people he would be meeting, but I assured him of the hospitality and the caring he could expect.

We decided we would tour India for two weeks, visiting my old haunts, showing my son parts of the country that had personal significance to me. We landed in Delhi on a January morning only to find the city covered by a thick fog. As the day proceeded, the air did not seem to clear, and we inquired whether Delhi was usually that foggy. It wasn't fog, we were told, but smog. Delhi was then one of the most air-polluted cities in India.

I had expected to see lots of changes and signs of real development. Three years had passed since new economic reforms had been introduced by the government. Yes, the city was more crowded, with more cars and other vehicles. Perhaps there were a few more buildings. But real sustainable development? I saw little signs of meaningful progress in Delhi. The same was true of every other city we visited; India had grown, but not necessarily the way I had hoped. My home town of Trivandrum, once a beautiful and fairly quiet place, was now congested with people, vehicles, houses and shops. The quality of life had not improved noticeably for the middle class, but people seemed busier. In some ways, life in Trivandrum had probably deteriorated for most people, except for those who left to work in the Middle East and had returned with considerable savings.

Angeline had organized a meeting with several prominent individuals of Bangalore society, like-minded individuals who believed in the need for social service. I found an extraordinarily talented young man, Jude Devdas, who would soon head all of the foundation's activities in India. Over the years, he has proved himself to be one of the most determined and hardworking individuals I have ever met. He oversees and coordinates every project we run and closely works with me to manage the finances of the foundation. His commitment, honesty and loyalty have been beyond measure. This meeting was the birth of The George Foundation, a nonprofit charitable trust that would work toward addressing some of the most persistent problems in Indian society, especially with regard to the poor.[1] It was the turning point in my life and in my professional interests. The sale of my company in America soon followed; I was now committed to humanitarian work in India.

Starting a nonprofit organization is no easier than starting a profit-focused company. If anything, this stage of my life was even more difficult than running a company, at least emotionally. My wife, children, parents and siblings all lived in the United States. America was my home just as much as India was, and I would not abandon one for the other. I would be forced to shuttle back and forth between the two countries and work through the phone and email to keep The George Foundation functioning smoothly. I had also decided to start a new company in America, both to keep myself busy while in the United States and to help gain additional funds for the undertaking in India.

My primary interest was in poor children, and I had learned that the main problem facing them was lack of access to anything resembling quality education. I felt that Indian society had long given up on these children, and there was no real hope for them to rise beyond their meager beginnings. Many people probably believe these children are simply incapable of doing anything better. Hence, the initial idea was to start a primary school in a rural village. It would be a world-class boarding institution for children from the poorest homes and for those belonging mostly to the lowest castes, mainly the "untouchables."

The school could not just be a holding pen designed to keep the kids in place until they assumed their lifelong roles as servants and workers to the rich. Instead, I was determined that it would be one of the best in India, a school that normally only the children of the richest families could afford. I would give these children the same opportunities as the children of the wealthy and powerful. As far as I knew, it was a model no one else had embarked upon in India. It was to be named Shanti Bhavan, Haven of Peace.

There are certain advantages to working in India, and one of them is that the cost of many things is much less than it might be in the United States. The initial estimate for Shanti Bhavan was roughly $200,000 dollars to build the school and then a few thousand dollars more each year to run and maintain it. However, as my plans for this educational institution widened, those estimates increased manifold. It was going to be a costly project that I would be funding nearly entirely on my own. But my course was set, and my commitment to the Shanti Bhavan concept was unshakeable; I was determined to make it a reality.

Shanti Bhavan was only the first step in our humanitarian work in India. When I started The George Foundation, there was no plan to go beyond Shanti Bhavan. Yet, there is so much to be done, so many difficulties that plague the nation. Social work in India is like emotional quicksand; once you take a step into it, you are pulled in deeper by all the other issues surrounding poverty. Many interrelated problems faced by the poor came to my attention. I knew I couldn't stop with just Shanti Bhavan.

Lead poisoning prevention became the next target on the agenda of the foundation. We realized that children in urban areas were being poisoned by lead in the air from vehicle exhaust and through many other pathways. Increased lead levels in the blood interfere with brain development in children, especially those with nutritional deficiencies, and cause many neurological problems. Lead poisoning was affecting over one hundred million children in India's cities, and yet, there was little or no awareness among the public. We took up the mantle of lead poisoning prevention and, by the year 2000, were successful in persuading the oil refiners to remove lead from gasoline throughout the country.

With our work in education and the environment, we opened ourselves to new projects. Soon we realized that basic health care and other key social necessities for the poor needed to be addressed. A rural hospital and community center catering to some 20 villages was established, and we also started "co-managing" four government-run primary health centers that serve a population of more than 150,000 people. Projects in farming and land ownership for women, promotion of the arts, and a school of journalism were all added to the list of important issues we felt we should work on.

While on the surface these projects seem diverse, they have the interrelated aspect of sustainable development, social justice and the strengthening of democratic institutions. It is my experience in these areas and the issues surrounding them that I have attempted to describe in this book. In doing so, I have tried to provide solutions that we have found effective with our own initiatives. While the projects we have undertaken are limited in scope and cover only a relatively small population, the lessons we have learned might prepare others to overcome the obstacles they might encounter. I have also openly expressed some of my impressions about India from my somewhat unique vantage point – the views of someone of Indian origin who has spent much of his adult life abroad and has now returned to do social work in rural India.

Many of my Indian friends in America cautioned me about the work I was planning to undertake, explaining that the obstacles were too big, and I would only have frustrations. Some of them told me about their horrendous experiences at the hands of government officials who purportedly created bureaucratic hurdles to extract money for simple legitimate requests. I was not deterred by any of those words of caution, though it became obvious to me that, if I were to succeed with honest work, I must avoid government involvement in whatever I planned to do in India. I decided on some very basic principles to follow, not too different from what is practiced in every good enterprise.

Regardless of the charitable nature of the projects I planned for in India, they would be run with business-like efficiency and accountability. Performance would be demanded of all employees in the foundation, and everyone would be encouraged to meet the high standards we set for ourselves. The power of money would only be used to accomplish our humanitarian goals and never for any undue advantage. To avoid real or perceived conflict of interest, I would not take up any business opportunity in India for personal gain. The foundation would adhere to the highest principles of professionalism and ethics in all its work. Finally, no individual in the foundation, especially myself, should seek personal recognition or reward for our work, except for the satisfaction we derive from getting things done and improving the lives of poor people.

LEARNING ABOUT POVERTY

I was naive enough, perhaps even foolhardy, to believe that one private individual could make an appreciable impact on a multitude of age-old problems. But I was convinced that together with inspired and talented co-workers, we could make a meaningful difference, and I proceeded on that principle. If we could lead the way in some areas, then others would follow and multiply whatever success we could achieve. The road we have embarked upon as The George Foundation, the goals and ambitions we have set out for ourselves, and our accomplishments and failures are part of the story I wish to tell. These past years were filled with extremes – moments of great joy, immense frustration and profound sadness. We have also faced much adversity on the path toward social welfare and reform. Hardly a day passes without a major incident or obstacle to overcome.

The first tragic event came during the initial year of recruitment for Shanti Bhavan. Lalita Law, the principal of the school, and social workers from The George Foundation combed distant villages in search of children to start their education at the school. This process was a long and arduous one because parents were dubious of our intentions. Still, some were willing to trust us and trust that our intentions for their children were genuine and good-hearted. Among those parents was a single mother, an attractive young woman whose son was four years old.

Her son, Vijay, was tested by our selection team, and Lalita decided that he should be admitted into Shanti Bhavan. However, he still had to be given a physical, and a date was set for him. The agreed date came, but Vijay did not come to the school for his test. At first we were worried that his mother had had second thoughts like other parents, but we were still hopeful.

Lalita decided she would go in search of Vijay and his mother, at least to find out why she decided not to let her son attend Shanti Bhavan. She went to the village only to find the hut empty and no sign of it having been lived in for some time. The villagers offered no information and were oddly silent about the whereabouts of both Vijay and his mother. But Lalita was persistent. She went back two weeks later and still could not find any sign of either mother or child. Finally, on her third visit to the village an old woman told her to go to the nearby Victoria Hospital where she would find what she was looking for.

Determined to uncover what had transpired, Lalita immediately made her way to the hospital. There she was greeted with a gruesome sight; Vijay was in a hospital bed with severe burns covering much of his body. While he would survive his injuries, he was horribly scarred. Only then, after asking one of the local doctors, was she told what had happened.

Vijay's mother had been lured by some men who came to the village claiming to be hiring servants to work in the Middle East. This was not an uncommon practice; the wealthy of the Middle East often hired cheap, menial labor in India. Even meager pay would seem like true wealth compared to the squalor they were resigned to live within their village. Desperate for a new life, Vijay's mother went with the men in their jeep.

Whether or not the men were truly hiring for a Middle East employer, they had no such intentions toward Vijay's mother. Instead, once she was away from the village, they proceeded to gang-rape her. This continued for days. When they were finished with her they dumped her at a nearby village. Such brutality is not uncommon in the poor villages of India.

The nightmare, however, was far from over for Vijay's mother when she returned home. Instead of sympathetic friends and neighbors, she received scorn and outrage. The villagers accused her of being a flirt, of inciting the men and bringing sexual attention to herself. They also brought up the past, once again blaming her for her husband's departure some years earlier. They ostracized her and cut her off from the community. She was a non-entity, a wanton woman who had brought this upon herself. There was no pity, no kindness, no sympathy, and no justice.

Life had no hope; there was no meaning to her existence anymore. She simply wanted an escape from it all. Unable to bear the burden any longer, the young mother poured kerosene over herself and set herself on fire. But Vijay was nearby when she decided to take her own life, and he rushed to grab her, perhaps to put out the flames. As his mother burned, so did Vijay from the raging fire. Luckily he escaped with his life but bore the scars of his desperate attempt.

Although Shanti Bhavan was not equipped to deal with such cases, I felt we had to make an exception. We decided to admit him into the school and treat his injuries, both physical and mental. Both plastic surgery and therapy were employed to help him recover. It has been a hard road for Vijay, but he has walked it well.

Back in New Jersey, I was busy balancing time between my company affairs and the activities of the foundation in India. Then as now, my daily routine started with an early morning call to India that usually lasted an hour or more, before I rushed off to the office. During working hours, I would take some time off to reply to emails and send new instructions to my key staff at the foundation.

The day would end with another set of phone calls. I wanted to be sure that, regardless of my physical absence in America, no one in the foundation would feel that I was not readily available to guide them when needed. My constant fear was that something terrible might happen one day, and I would not be able to do anything about it.

One night, my sleep was broken by the harsh ringing of the telephone. A quick glance at the bleary red digits of the clock told me it was well past two in the morning in New Jersey. It could only be bad news. It had to be a problem in India, an emergency at the foundation. I was most afraid that something serious had happened to one of my trusted people.

Reaching over my wife, Mariam, who was still fast asleep, I fumbled in the darkness for the phone, already having mentally braced myself for the worst. In the short time since I had started Shanti Bhavan, we had met with several setbacks. I was learning quickly that the project we had undertaken was more difficult than I had first thought. But with those setbacks came a perceptive understanding of the conditions and a certain emotional fortitude. With each problem successfully beaten, I felt a greater reserve of strength.

On the other end of the line was a panicked Lalita. She was speaking so quickly that I could not understand half of what she was saying. "Calm down, Lalita," I said, urging her to take a breath and tell me what was going on.

Slowly, Lalita began anew, explaining what had occurred. A rough looking man, probably in his early forties, had shown up at her home that morning when she returned from Shanti Bhavan. He had demanded the return of Sheena, a nine-year-old student at Shanti Bhavan. He told Lalita that Sheena's mother, his first wife, had committed suicide along with his second wife a day before. The man (call him Karin) demanded that Sheena come with him for two days of burial and prayer.

Lalita asked Karin whether the police had investigated the matter and if it had been officially ruled a suicide. Karin became belligerent and angrily replied that the police had already confirmed the deaths as suicides the night before. How could the police declare two deaths as suicides in just one evening of investigation, she thought. Once again, he demanded that Sheena return with him for the proper ceremony. Suspicious, Lalita replied that she would arrange to have the child brought over, but that Sheena could not stay overnight with him. Sheena had earlier told Lalita about family incidents that led Lalita to believe sexual abuse was taking place at the home.

Lalita's response only infuriated Karin further, and belligerence turned into out and out threats. He told Lalita that she'd better watch out and that he would take care of her. A courageous and competent woman, Lalita was still unnerved. Violence against women in India is a serious problem, especially in families, and in rural areas the authorities are less aggressive about investigating and prosecuting such cases. Lalita knew there could be real trouble against her and the foundation.

This was danger of a kind we had not faced before. We had dealt with crooked bankers and dishonest landowners, corrupt political officials and hostile police, but not a domestic issue of this type. I was sure there was more to the story of the two dead wives than Karin had related, and I feared for the safety of both Lalita and Sheena.

I instructed Lalita to speak to Jude Devdas, the CEO of the foundation, who would arrange to have Frank (one of the top employees of Shanti Bhavan) take Sheena to Karin's home for the burial ceremony and prayers, but to stay in her presence while the rituals were being performed. He was to then bring her back to Shanti Bhavan. We were not willing to let Karin keep Sheena overnight, at least without knowing more about what was really going on. I also told Lalita that she should go to Karin's house, with two senior staff members, to find out more. We needed to know quickly what the real story was.

Frank took Sheena to her home and Lalita, with the entourage from Shanti Bhavan, arrived in the evening. There were two women at the home, apparently relatives of Karin's, and they proceeded to berate Lalita for her unwillingness to leave Sheena in Karin's care. Initially, the scene was chaotic, but Lalita managed to calm them down long enough to ask some questions. The two dead wives were 40 and 15 years old. The older one had claimed to be Sheena's aunt, however, it was revealed that the older woman was Sheena's mother. Why she had lied about her identity was a mystery. The 15-year-old, a girl barely out of her adolescence, was Karin's own niece as well as his second wife.

The questioning led to another round of arguments; both Karin and his two female relatives told Lalita that Sheena should be left with them for a few days. They argued that because Sheena's mother was dead, her place was now with them at home. Though tensions mounted, Lalita stood fast and explained, as calmly as possible, that she could not relinquish Sheena to anyone but an official guardian. After all, Karin was not Sheena's father. She simply did not have the authority to do so. While this did not sit well with either of the two women or Karin, the point was made. Sheena was coming back with Frank. Lalita left with her senior staff, while Frank waited until the ceremony was done. Finally, Sheena returned to Shanti Bhavan under his escort after an arduous day and night.

The matter was far from over, however. Karin continued to try to have Sheena turned over to his custody. The reasons for his insistence were varied, but we believed he intended to make Sheena (a nine-year-old girl) his next wife. The risks were high and in such situations, turning to the police is not an option; they simply would not protect either us or Sheena. There is no government institution that would effectively intervene in support of the child's interest. The threats mounted from Karin's side and we were left in a dangerous position. For a while, we arranged special protection for Lalita.

We had to balance Sheena's safety with the overall interests of the school. I feared Karin might resort to violence against Lalita. There was no easy or immediate answer. Finally, we offered to hire a lawyer for Karin so that he could officially attempt to gain custody of Sheena. In turn, we also hired a different lawyer to counter Karin's claims of custody in the interest of the child. I felt if the process was taken to the courts, Karin would be appeased, while we retained custody of Sheena. It was a dangerous gambit, but our options were slim.

We have been able to drag out the matter for three years now, keeping Sheena away from Karin. But with constant threats, it is not certain how long we can hold out without any support from the community or the government. Moreover, Karin and his sisters are turning up at Shanti Bhavan periodically and showering Sheena with beautiful clothes and gold ornaments. Sheena is being swayed by all those expressions of affection. If she will not cooperate with us as she grows older, we may not be able to do much for her.

This hurdle was just one of many I had to tackle in my new life in a world I had hardly known before. It is one thing to be idealistic with a desire to help others, but now I was confronted with the realities of very complex situations characterized by poverty, ignorance, and unjust social norms. Yet this was the life I had slowly but surely been building toward through the years. Regardless of the trials and tribulations we had to go through in accomplishing a long cherished ideal, I was savoring the new challenges we had in front of us.

The stories of Sheena and Vijay illustrate just some of the troubles that are not uncommon to slum dwellers or villagers but are a symptom of the hardship of rural life in India. Poverty, crime and ill-health are not the only difficulties millions of rural people have to overcome; a majority of them are victims of caste- and gender-based discrimination. If the foundation was to tackle these problems, I needed a better understanding of what was going on in the nearby villages. For a start, I chose to conduct a series of interviews in the hope of gaining some insight into the hearts and minds of the underprivileged in rural India.

Chapter 2

GETTING TO KNOW INDIA

REALITIES OF RURAL LIFE

I asked Lalita and Nagaraj, a social worker, to accompany me on my visits to the villages. Our social workers had already arranged for me to meet different groups of people – single women, ragpickers, village elders, a school headmaster, government officials – anyone who could provide me with a true picture of village life. The jeep first drove into Baliganapalli, the village next to Shanti Bhavan. People crowded around out of curiosity, and a fairly prosperous-looking man emerged from an assembled group of village authorities and introduced himself as an elder. He smiled his welcome and proudly introduced his young daughter, Banu, an engineering college student who was to be my translator.

We were led into the Panchayat (the local governing body) office, a small room with dirty walls and a concrete roof. Cobwebs festooned the ceiling. The steel frames of the bright blue painted doors and windows complemented an old steel Godrej cupboard. A crumpled wad of paper and jute string lay in the dirt under the cupboard while two clean grass brooms were propped against it. A straw mat partially covered the holes in the cement floor. The room was furnished with an ancient stained wooden table, a blackboard resting on a rickety chair frame, a few plastic chairs, and smooth planks piled up against the wall. Panchayat statistics painted in white on a blue bulletin board were the room's main functional decoration.

A group of schoolchildren silently stared from the tiny courtyard of the village school next door. As we took our seats, I was aware of the buzz of voices, the calls of crows in the huge banyan tree nearby, and the dust blowing into the room. Four women surrounded by a host of onlookers entered the room. Their tattered and faded saris contrasted starkly with the stylish salwar khameez (comfortable women's attire) worn by the translator, who was from the same village. The gap between the haves and have-nots was obvious.

The women to be interviewed were single and varied in age from 20 to 40. They appeared to be apprehensive of this novel experience of being interviewed by a man. They had heard of The George Foundation and Shanti Bhavan so they were expecting some sort of help. I persuaded them to sit and reassured them that I only wanted to understand their way of life. They were also told there would be no handouts but that their stories might help others.

The women reacted with submissive compliance, the first indication that something was not quite right. I took their wariness as natural for secluded rural women being interviewed by a man. I had Lalita take notes and the young girl translate, and I hoped their presence would help put the women at ease. But I could sense that they were worried about the village officials listening in from outside. I asked Nagaraj to tell everyone to keep away.

I asked them to tell me whatever they could about their lives. Manju was the youngest, 20 years old. She said she fell in love with a local boy when she was studying in the seventh grade and married him. The man was an alcoholic and used to beat her. He married someone else after a while and went away. Manju married again and though her second husband now lived in the same village, he had nothing to do with her or their ten-month-old baby.

Manju lived with her parents and her younger brother. She did not want to make another mistake by marrying a third time. Her father was a coolie (menial laborer) and was an alcoholic. When he drank, he would blame his daughter for his misfortunes. Her mother had asked his employer not to pay him until the end of the month so he wouldn't buy drinks. Manju worked for a landlord in the field, beginning the day at 8:30 a.m. and ending at 5:30 p.m., six days a week. When she got home she would feed her baby, then cook and do housework.

Her parents wanted her to live independently, but she did not have the financial means to do so. She said that even if she were to find the means to stay in another part of the village, she would not be allowed to live there. She observed social norms such as drawing water from the village well only when there was no upper caste person doing the same. Without the permission of the village elders, there was no question of living on her own in the village.

I asked Manju a number of questions about her past and finally inquired about her future. At 20 years of age, Manju felt there was nothing to look forward to, and no hope for her in life. She had no support or cooperation from anyone, but she would be content if her relatives treated her properly. She was afraid to talk about her neighbors or the village elders.

"What is your biggest need?" I asked.

"Shelter," she said. "I am afraid no one will look after my son if something happened to me."

At this young age, she was already thinking about her death.

Chinnamma, a little over 30 years old, had been a laborer from age seven. Her parents married her off early. Her husband died of "liver problems" – he was an alcoholic. Her parents did not permit the young widow to live with them, so she stayed in her brother's house. Her two daughters were 13 and 11 years of age, while her son was nine years old. The children attended the local government school and she paid for their books from her earnings as a laborer. The government gave her a widow's pension of Rs.200 ($4.50) per month. She found it very difficult to live on her income and had pinned her hopes for the future on her children.

Roopa lost her husband after nine years of marriage. Her son was 12 years old, but he was not going to school because she couldn't buy books for him. The boy started working as a servant in a rich man's house two years back. The employer had promised that he would build a hut for her on government land in return for her son's labor. There was no written agreement, and he had done nothing yet to keep his end of the bargain. Roopa didn't mind her son staying at the landlord's home as he would get some food to eat. Her greatest difficulty was the rejection by her own parents and her husband's family, and there was not enough food or permanent shelter. She could not afford to buy vegetables or fruit. She said she wanted her son to be a good person and worried about who would take care of him when she died. She said she kept a little savings in a safe place.

Finally it was Lakshmamma's turn to speak. She was 40 years old. Married at the age of 15, she became a widow by 21. She did not like the idea of marrying again as her children would then have a stepfather. Her two daughters never went to school because she could not afford the books or uniforms.

The elder daughter lived with her grandparents in a nearby town to help them out. Her second daughter had started to work on a farm at the age of nine and now earned Rs.25 a day picking fruit but only once or twice a week. Lakshmamma wanted me to help her get a piece of government land to build a hut. Like the other women before her, she had been rejected by her family members and had to struggle for food and shelter. She wanted to marry off her daughters soon and was afraid of her neighbors.

All four women said that the poor people who worked in the homes and farms of the Panchayat people did not apply for housing. They were told by Panchayat officials to save money to build their own shelters, but it was not possible to save. They were unaware of savings schemes or plans, and they wanted Shanti Bhavan to run a bank where they could put away some money. They went to a government-run primary health center when they fell sick. They all said that they had accepted their fates and believed they would have to suffer. It was clear that, while these women lived uncomplicated lives, they had endured similar pasts, and their present problems were the result of perennial poverty, ignorance and social deprivation.

I could not leave these women without assuring them that we were trying to do things that would help people like them. We talked about potential employment on the farm soon to be run by the foundation and the hospital that was being built. I could not promise any individual help as that would have only invited others to seek the same; there were only so many we could assist. Still, I hoped the information they had given me could be used for the good of the community in the long run. We thanked them for sharing their personal stories with us and left for the next meeting.

We were led to a relatively attractive 50-year-old house in another part of the village. Its brick and plaster walls contrasted with the mud huts in the poorer section of the village. Inside a large room, stone bases supported wooden pillars that held up the roof. The room appeared to be a multi-purpose space for entertaining visitors, watching TV, storing grain and worldly goods, eating and sleeping. A motorcycle was parked next to a metal bed enclosed by mosquito netting. The TV sat beside a built-in wooden cabinet with glass shelves holding trophies, plastic flowers, a torch and a clay chariot. There were three school bags on the floor and several large sacks of *ragi* (the local staple food) and rice stacked neatly against the wall. A swarm of artificial butterflies were arranged in flying formation toward the wall clock. A calendar and poster completed the wall decoration.

The matriarch of the house, Subbamma, mother of Gowda the local land-lord, was introduced to me. Subbamma was 65 years old and a mother of six children – five men and one woman. According to local cultural beliefs, this meant she was singularly blessed. She also had six grandchildren. Subbamma had built a temple to intercede for her children. She served us biscuits and warm milk, freshly drawn from the family cow, in stainless-steel glasses.

Gowda and his brothers all worked on their 100 acre property. They cultivated ragi and rice on 40 acres. Eucalyptus was grown on the remaining 60 acres. Gowda also rented out his tractor. Their sister was married to an engineer who worked for the government electricity board and lived in a distant place. Gowda had three daughters who attended the Asian Christian Academy in the nearby town. Their family was one of four landowner families in the village and they were all related. The family claimed that 40 percent of the people in the village were rich and 60 percent were poor, a statistic that did not appear to be accurate. According to Gowda, 40 percent of the poor were landless laborers who would never be able to get government land as per Tamil Nadu rules. Labor for the landlords came from this population and from neighboring villages.

According to the Gowda family, government funds were not sufficient to meet the needs of the village people. The problems were numerous: health issues, infrequent public transportation, insufficient income for many families, no bank and no decent school or college for the local children. Commerce could not thrive as there were no amenities even for small things like bicycle repair. They wanted a good local market or a cooperative enterprise for buying and selling fruits and vegetables and other daily necessities. Government hospitals had no sanitation and offered poor patient care. Since the local people were all Kannada-speaking, the state language, Tamil, was of no help to them. Rich people saved their money in post offices or in banks, which both gave the same rates of interest. Boginna, Gowda's brother, was quick to add that "preference must be given to poor people." I was not impressed about his sincerity in helping the poor.

From the Gowda residence, we drove just a few minutes to the village of Opachjhalli, which is in the neighboring state of Karnataka. The jeep came to a halt outside the local preschool or *anganwadi* which doubled as a meeting place for women's groups. To the left of the one-room building was a makeshift shop selling local cigarettes, cold drinks and sweets.

To the right was a large mud and thatch house with several sheep in the front yard. We crossed a storm drain with filthy water that delighted the hens strutting in it. We were greeted by an elderly, good-looking, white-haired woman of fair complexion wearing a brown sari and a faded pink blouse. Her ear lobes were stretched with the weight of her earrings, and tattoos covered the backs of her hands. Her name was Chinnamaya and she introduced herself as a helper to the preschool teacher. The few children who had arrived were asked to sit silently against the wall while our interview took place.

The schoolroom was dingy, with stained walls, a table and chair for the teacher, a decrepit blackboard, and some educational charts – torn and stained – lining the wall. A trunk containing records was on the floor. A door in the far wall led to a dark, cluttered storeroom of firewood and government food rations for the children of the preschool. Near this storeroom was a mud stove for cooking the free midday meal. The cooking vessels were dirty. Firewood was bundled and stacked high. Chinnamaya said the children liked the taste of the nutrition powder prepared with *jaggeri* (unrefined sugar) and shaped into balls.

We asked why the children, who were obviously very poor, had not come for admission screening to Shanti Bhavan. The teacher, who had arrived by this time, stated that she would lose her government job if there were not enough children to teach in the village, and hence, she did not want them to go anywhere else. We said that we would admit perhaps only one out of ten children who applied. By now more children had trickled into the room.

The teacher explained that the children had to be fetched from their homes because the parents go to work leaving the children behind in their homes. She said the village was fairly well-off. Seventy percent of the people owned land, some as much as 20 to 30 acres, and only thirty percent were poor. Many poor people owned up to a half acre of land, but did not have the means to cultivate, and worked as laborers instead. They had access to health care about two kilometers away. Their water supply came from an overhead tank, but when the electricity supply failed, pumps could not work to fill the tanks. The teacher said the village needed two temples of worship – one for the upper castes and another for everyone else. The rosy picture she painted about her village did not match what I could see around me.

We went in to observe a primary school on the way back to the entrance of the village where our jeep was parked. There were several dozen children listed on the roster, but many were absent because they had chicken pox. The children were in the age group of six to ten, and from first to fourth grade. Girls were not sent to school after fifth grade so they languished all day, picking up a few household tasks if they were interested enough. There were two teachers for these four classes.

Our trek through the village revealed several fascinating sights. Girls and women sitting outside their houses stared curiously as we passed. Some were cleaning rice or grain, others were combing their hair, or just sitting there – probably resting after the morning's chores. We were ushered into the home of Karthika, a laborer in the construction work we had just begun. At 14 years of age she married a 32-year-old man. Her husband abandoned her six years ago after an affair with another woman, and she now lived with her three young children.

Karthika had studied up to the eighth grade in Tamil. She lived in her husband's home, but her father-in-law wanted her to vacate it. Neighbors and relatives harassed her, especially at night, by banging on her door. She had once gone to the police to complain, but they would not help. Her husband beat her if she went anywhere for assistance. She said that nobody would help her because she did not work for the Panchayat. She faced eviction from her home and had no money to educate her son or second daughter. If she or her children fell sick, no one assisted. We advised her to go to the nearby government-run health center to get medical care.

The next day, a government official escorted us in our jeep through a rocky, ragged landscape to the outskirts of the nearby town of Hosur. A few mud huts with decaying thatched roofs dotted the slope of the hill. There was no road or track to go to those huts; one had to simply climb the hill. As we alighted from the jeep, a motley group of women, children and a man came down the hill to greet us. They were curious about our presence in their area. Untouchables lived there, and the rare visitors were people like us, aid workers or government officials.

We crossed parts of the barren rocky outcrop as we walked toward their dwellings. We saw a narrow ditch with a little dirty water in it. We were informed that it was the water supply for the ragpickers' colony. The people got this name from their chosen occupation that entailed scrounging from the dustbins and garbage heaps in the nearby city of Hosur. They sold whatever could be recycled and lived off the proceeds. Since they belonged to the lowest caste of society, not many know nor care about how they live. There are several million ragpickers all over India.

We were led to a small, natural rocky platform that served as the meeting ground for the colony. The local elders, a couple, and a young man inquired about us. We informed them that we had come on a visit, that we were not from the government and that we wanted to interview some of them. In a few minutes, the entire population – young and old – had converged upon the spot. They were dressed in torn, dirty clothes. Their hair was matted, and many children were scratching their heads. Almost all the adults were chewing *paan* (a local version of tobacco). Right from the start, the women began telling us that they needed Rs.4 a day to buy *paan*. Their addiction to *paan* was even greater than their hunger. We began interviewing the people who had received us on the platform.

Mallappa, 35 years old, was a snake catcher and used to sell the skins. He now collected waste paper and occasionally worked as a snake charmer. He emphasized that he had "only one wife." He had curly hair, a matted beard, and wore a stained *lungi*, or piece of cloth wound around the waist reaching to his calves. His wife, Saki, was 25 years old. Her teeth were stained red from chewing *paan*. Mallappa and Saki had three children – one girl and two boys. They did not know the ages of their own children. I asked Saki how she worked with a six-month-old baby. She said she carried the baby with her and left her close to her on the garbage heap while she worked. Horrified, I asked what would happen if the baby picked something from the garbage and put it into his mouth.

"I always keep an eye on my child," she replied.

These people belonged to the Irular tribe, classified by the government as one of the lowest, both socially and economically. They said they did not get any benefits from the government except for small loans or ration certificates. We learned that the sub-collector had ordered a water tank to supply water once a week to this colony. Each household could fill six pots of water at a time, but no one had more than one or two pots. They used a pond about half a kilometer away for baths. They used the water that collected in the crevices of the rocks during the rainy season. No one except social service workers ever visited them.

Out of all the children in the colony, only four girls and three boys attended the government municipality elementary school. Most children discontinued their education to take up the trade of their parents. Several boys under the age of 15 worked with their parents. Each family averaged four to five children.

When they were sick they went to the government hospital because treatment was free. A man with a swollen face told us his lips were stitched without anesthesia at the hospital so he now preferred country medicine. Unless they gave tips, no one looked after them at the hospital. They had bigger problems like permanent unemployment and lack of water. Their homes flooded when it rained.

They said they were willing to be hired into better jobs than their present occupations. They believed their children would lead "luxurious lives" if they were educated. They believed that, if their sons were educated and employed, they would look after them in their old age. We told them to send their children for screening to Shanti Bhavan. They needed shelter, employment and education for their children.

This community of ragpickers badly needed our help. I told them that I would think of how we could help. I thanked them for giving me the opportunity to talk to them in their colony. I told them that they could become involved in the women's empowerment program we planned to start and that their children could study in Shanti Bhavan if they met the requirements for selection. I noticed that there were few elderly community members. An old man said he worked as a beggar to earn a living. He was proud of the fact that he had once sat near the collector at a government function.

As we walked back towards our waiting jeep, the people of the ragpickers' colony gathered to say goodbye. They formed a ragged band of derelicts, standing against the backdrop of low rocks. I was deeply moved and felt terrible about our inability to help them all.

From there, we continued on to Devarapalli High School where two single old women were waiting to tell their stories in the school library that had been built by The George Foundation. It is a one-room library lined with metal shelves on which sit some paperback volumes, children's books, and the like. The women sat on the floor, but chairs were provided for us. We preferred to sit on the floor with the women, but halfway through the interviews, we opted for the comfort of the chairs.

Gowramma, 80 years old, had been a widow for 12 years. She had no children, no house, and no land. Narayanappa, a landlord, provided a room for her to stay in free of charge. When her husband was alive, they had their own house. He sold the house before his death to meet some debt. She had no relatives. She got Rs.200 and two kilograms of rice per month plus two saris a year from the government. Otherwise, neighbors took care of her. She belonged to the Nayanvelu or hunters' caste.

"Do you agree with the caste system?" I asked.

"Yes, it is right," she replied. "We must respect the traditions of our ancestors."

I told her through my translator that I thought the caste system had many problems and was wrong. She kept silent. She had pain in her legs and back. She saw "darkness." She hadn't consulted a doctor until recently, when at the social worker's urging, she went to a local healer. She said she was happy with her life because her neighbors looked after her.

The stories I heard were not unique, but rather the rule of life in villages. All the poor people I met seemed resigned to their predicament, with no real hope or expectation for a better life in the future. Most of them thought their present conditions a matter of fate or destiny, and they were simply afraid that, if they failed to carry out their religious duties, such as frequent worship at the temple, some harm would come to them or their family. Their priorities were shelter, food and health, in that order. Education for their children and security were also mentioned, but not as their primary concerns. Social or gender equality as a right was never brought up, probably because most illiterate people have come to believe that their present status in society was predestined by fate or God's will.

My interviews continued for a period of time, and I compared notes with other social workers such as K. J. Yesupadam of the R.A.I.D. nonprofit group that focuses on health and education. There was much to consider and so much to work on. I returned to the United States with a lot of information in hand that I hoped would provide the key for us to assist the poor in those villages.

Most of us urbanites or so-called "outsiders," have a nostalgic view of rural India. We think of villages as peaceful havens where people live simple lives, where the air is pure, and the land is green as far as the eye can see. Some of those images are indeed true, but the realities of day-to-day life for a majority of the rural people are nothing short of cruel. It is a living story of economic deprivation, social injustice, and hopelessness that outsiders cannot comprehend.

The real story of rural India must be told with more than 350 million characters who live in poverty with less than a dollar a day in income for a family of four, and whose social status in their communities is relegated to below the holy cow, the venomous snake and the impish monkey. It is a land where the elite of the villages – the upper class and the landlords – prey on the helpless, often in collusion with government officials who are supposed to help and protect them. It is a life where hope for a better future is as distant as the burning sun, and nothing that happens around them, including the so-called "IT revolution," brings solace or improvement in their circumstances.

I do not consider myself to be an expert on rural India, nor will I ever be in this land of diverse peoples and problems. However, my work for the past eight years in the poverty-stricken Dharamapuri District of Tamil Nadu has made me more conscious of the predicament of the poor, whose lives depend on the benevolence of the politicians, the wisdom of the bureaucrats, and the generosity of the rich. I find a different world from the one portrayed in national statistics, but then, I may be seeing only the half-empty glass. Still, that half-empty glass is what we must focus on, for it is what we must strive to change.

Consider the following realities. Primary health care is delivered to the rural population through a network of government-run health centers and subcenters, but the entire rural health system is badly broken. Doctors do not turn up as required and important medicines are usually not available in the clinic. While grain production has been growing at an average annual rate of around 1 percent nationally in recent years, only a handful of farmers have the means to cultivate or own cultivable land in most villages.

Rural infrastructure is barely visible beyond those villages that are close to rural towns; interior villages still wait for electricity, and their muddy roads get washed away with each heavy rain.

There are claims that great strides have been made in the economic empowerment of women through entrepreneurial activities with micro-credit, but the poor illiterate women I have come to know can hardly hope to succeed from such programs. Discrimination based on caste has been prohibited from the early days of the nation's birth, but the Dalits (among the lowest castes) of India still huddle in broken huts within the secluded sections of villages. To deal with all these situations, central and state governments are allocating considerable funds. Bilateral and multilateral agencies are also making their contributions, and yet the intended beneficiaries have realized only marginal gains in the past 50 or so years. Even to a layman it is obvious that something is awfully wrong, and something very different must be done if we are to expect the situation to improve in the next 50 years.

To the rural poor, deprivation is both economic and social – the direct result of exploitation and lack of opportunities. Their condition of life is characterized by malnutrition, illiteracy, sufferings from diseases and long-term health problems, inadequate shelter and unhygienic conditions, high infant mortality, oppression of women, and social treatment devoid of human dignity.

Much of it is concealed from view, as outsider interaction is usually limited to village heads and other "authorities," unless one chooses to study the Harijan colonies and interior villages that are not easily accessible. That is not to say that government programs do not target these people or that non-governmental organizations (NGOs) do not work in these areas. What is missing is adequate emphasis in dealing with the root causes of these closely interrelated problems.

The barriers faced by the poor are not limited to the lack of opportunity to gain a good education and earn a steady source of income. These people are the victims of what appears to be a permanent social and economic arrangement wherein the local elite – landowners, merchants, moneylenders, officials – maintain a stranglehold over the poor. They accomplish this by consolidating more wealth and power through appropriation of additional land (either by purchase or through government lease allocations), and by employing the poor at low wages, while enforcing discipline and silence through punitive measures. Urban interests also gain from market-based exploitation, wherein rural products and services are kept at such low prices that without government subsidies, there is no profit to be gained.

Similarly, urbanization of villages for cheap labor may generate employment for some of the poor, but it also perpetuates their exploitation and misery. Excess labor, limited access to markets and market information, and the financial weakness of rural farmers all contribute to this inequity. They become indebted to landlords and moneylenders, a condition they can hardly expect to overcome in their lifetime. This powerlessness is clearly evident in their inability to obtain even those benefits intended for them from the government, without the local elite and administrators siphoning out most of the financial resources for themselves. Many of the programs currently in place benefit their administrators far more than their intended beneficiaries.

The poor people in the villages, especially women, are my window into India. They reveal what life is like for most people on this planet, far out of sight of modern day prosperity. The disconnect is too profound for me – one day I am under the bright neon lights of New York City, and just a day or two later I am among people who cannot afford to buy candles. In the simplicity of these rural folks I have found order, in their beliefs I have found faith, and in their misery I have found compassion. The richness of ordinary day-to-day life comes from their hard work and the caring they show for other members of their families even in the face of adversity and suffering. Still the joy that I derive from my work among these people cannot offset the burning anger within me for all the social injustice, hypocrisy and avoidable suffering.

My love for these people probably comes from my knowledge of their predicament and the admiration I have for them. I cannot say that I love India for what it is today, but I can say without hesitation that I love the people I have come to know and who have let me into their lives a little way. I consider myself very fortunate and humbled by my experience.

THE VIEW FROM THE OTHER SIDE

In contrast, my initial urban experience in India was quite different. My interactions were mostly with middle and upper class educated people. I was hoping to hear what they thought of rural poverty. After all, it is the urban intellectuals, bureaucrats and politicians who make all the major decisions that impact the rural poor. But most people I talked to did not have much to say about what could be done to address the problems faced by the rural people. They were more interested in the opportunities offered by foreign investment in India. Business was on everyone's mind.

Consequently, I had expected to see a changed attitude toward America from the earlier pro-Soviet days. The country had gradually discarded the socialistic economic approach in favor of free markets, and the information technology sector was betting on business contracts from U.S. companies. Many well-to-do families had at least one member of their family studying or working in America, and every young person I knew wanted to go to America. Yet, within a few days of my arrival, it surprised me to see that most people I had met had some degree of dislike for America. The media had a strong anti-American bias in their daily reporting.

Some people tried to make a distinction between their feelings toward the American people and the policies of the government, but as each discussion progressed, it was clear that their negative opinions were based on something more. They believed that Americans were money-minded, their moral values were poor, that white Americans discriminated and treated all other races badly, and that many were arrogant. Non-resident Indians (NRIs) were also included in this category, as they were accused of flaunting their wealth while in India, complaining about all the inconveniences they faced during their vacations in the country, while showing no willingness to help out. Even well-educated people shared similar opinions and blame the American media for supporting the so-called "imperialistic" policies of their government.

Even at recent dinner parties, I have to listen to long-winded, convoluted conspiracy theories about the CIA and the alleged mischief it is doing in India. A retired senior naval officer once told me at great length and with national pride how he confiscated an Instamatic camera and film from a young American college student who came to Vishakapatnam and shot pictures of the naval dockyard – a spying incident, in his opinion, orchestrated by the CIA. When I inquired why no one is allowed to take photographs when seeing off relatives at any of the airport lounges, he whispered, "national security." For decades, Indians have been told by their politicians and the media that America is an imperialist country trying to destabilize India in support of Pakistan. Bureaucrats and ill-informed intellectuals present theories shrouded in intrigue, with absolute conviction that Washington is trying to destroy India's great ancient culture. It is clear that America's tilt in favor of Pakistan over the past half a century has caused a great deal of mistrust and resentment in most Indians.

Despite all the frustrations of having to deal with government bureaucracy, corruption and inefficiencies, I was delighted to see in most people great vibrancy and resilience as they went about their daily lives. People were engaging in active social life, festivals were being celebrated with considerable fanfare, and weddings were as extravagant as one could imagine. Despite the tight financial conditions, Indians seemed good at adapting to practically any situation, improvising with what they had to meet many of their major needs. Almost every Indian I met appeared fatalistic about everything that had happened in his or her life, and their religious beliefs and spirituality seemed to carry them forward even in the face of major adversity. It was this blend of pragmatism and faith that intrigued me most.

I sensed a spirit of entrepreneurship and optimism among businessmen. People were talking mostly about opportunities to start new companies and export products to foreign markets. Trade, technology and investment were the new mantra. Within a short period of three years, following the initiation of economic liberalization measures, foreign companies were beginning to explore Indian markets. Five-star hotels in Bangalore were filled with Western businessmen, while their Indian counterparts were kept busy convincing them about the value of doing business in India. With this sudden burst of activity, the demand for housing and land within and close to the city had gone up, driving real estate prices sharply higher. I wondered when anyone would begin to think about opportunities in rural India.

Back in America, I occasionally get to interact with others of Indian origin in the country. Unlike the Indians who went as laborers to British colonies or territories during the 19th and early 20th centuries, those who came to Britain, Canada and the United States during the second half of the 20th century were mostly of a technical and professional background. There was also a large outflow of temporary, professional, and other workers to the Persian Gulf countries to fill the demand for engineers, doctors, teachers, nurses, accountants and tradesmen.

This latter category of NRIs in Gulf countries is not given permanent residence by their host countries, and hence, they migrate only for a few years to earn a much higher income. The technological surge of the 1990s in the United States offered great professional opportunities to many NRIs who possessed high technical skills. Some of them started their own entrepreneurial ventures in Silicon Valley in California and in a short period made their companies and themselves very wealthy by any standard.

NRI investment in India has become a major source of foreign exchange for the country, and the government actively seeks their money through a number of tax concessions. A key component of India's developmental strategy is the monetary and technical contribution of NRIs to the country. Unfortunately, NRIs do not have much interest in making direct investments in rural India, especially in the agricultural sector. Rural India is viewed as a potential future market for industrial and consumer products, but no one seems to have figured out a way to sell most products profitably to this huge population.

It is often claimed that NRIs are passionately interested in their country of origin and wish to see India prosper. But it is not clear whether this concern translates into concerted action on their part for any humanitarian issues such as poverty eradication, better health care for the poor, or social equality. To be sure, most NRIs have close relatives back in India, and are concerned about their welfare. By some estimates, there are more than 22 million people of Indian origin living in over 120 countries, of which 2.2 million are in the United States.[2] Most of them return to India on frequent visits and send money to their families. Except for a few entrepreneurs who are looking to make business investments in India, others are busy trying to settle down in their adopted countries and raise children. For most, India is what it is – a nostalgic place to return to occasionally and enjoy the company of old friends and relatives.

The new generation of Americans of Indian origin has assimilated fairly well with the rest of the society. It is their parents, the first immigrants, who still cling to their old ways, constantly comparing the values they grew up with in India against American values. Some have chosen to separate themselves from the rest of the society, as they establish communities of their own, such as the little "Indian town" of Edison in New Jersey and parts of Queens in New York. The compelling reason for such clustering could very well be business considerations, but they continue to project their distinct lifestyles reminiscent of the good old days back home.

Those NRIs who do remain "Indian" in America are looked upon as foreigners. This does not help to be accepted and treated as any other American. Equally important is what Americans see as the level of support NRIs show for their adopted country. Most Americans do not resent others following their traditions, but they do expect some degree of objective loyalty to the country from those living within its borders, especially during times of national tragedy. In America, for the most part, what gives identity is not one's memory of the good life gone by or the reputation of one's grandparents, but what one does to create opportunity for one's grandchildren. People want the benefits of modernity, but that requires a willingness to identify with one's new surroundings. The increasing contact between cultures must allow for finding the commonality between them, permitting the assimilation into "American culture" without necessarily giving up one's values and traditions.

Most NRIs in America and Canada did not actively participate in their host country's politics until the early 1980s. With increased economic prosperity among a larger number of immigrants from India, they began to feel recognized by politicians, especially in communities with a significant NRI population. These NRIs maintain close social ties with their families in India and wish to see changes that would bring about economic and social progress in the country of their origin. As their economic clout becomes visible from the funds they remit and from the investments they make in businesses in India, they also feel the need to be involved in its political processes. They want their voices to be heard by the government of India in determining economic policies, and consequently, they seek involvement in many bilateral issues concerning India and their host countries. Topics such as rural development rarely come up, and most of them have yet to involve themselves in any social work in India.

In recent years, the term "South Asian" has been coined to denote mostly Indians, Pakistanis, Bangladeshis, Nepalis and Sri Lankans. The label "Desi" is interchangeably used to denote South Asian, and this all-encompassing description has provided a regional perspective rather than a national one. The assumption is that the cultural backgrounds and the problems faced by immigrants from these countries are similar, and their united front could offer greater political strength than their national standing. So far, however, there is no such unity amongst the different nationalities, whether it is in political, social or cultural manifestations.

MY DUAL IDENTITY

As I sat by the large porch window in my parents' condominium, overlooking the Hudson river and the grandeur of the New York City skyline and watching the ships go by on the Fourth of July, I could not help but trace my own life spanning over 30 years in America. This was a time of exuberance, prosperity was everywhere, with the American economy surging ahead and financial markets at an all-time high. Americans had a lot to celebrate. I remembered the day I first set foot in America as a young man with just eight dollars in my pocket – the maximum permitted by the Reserve Bank of India in 1969 – with the dream of building a new life. Luckily, my mother was already in America to provide me financial assistance to get started.

Looking back, I realized what this country had given to me and how it had shaped my life. I was among the early immigrants to America from India, and though I stood out among both whites and blacks in the country, I did not allow myself to feel like an alien. Racism and discrimination were certainly obstacles to overcome, yet the hurdles I faced as a consequence of my racial origin were not insurmountable. I was able to transcend my origins and was free to make of myself whatever my talents permitted. My experience is no different from that of most immigrants; each has succeeded because of his or her self-reliance, independence, resourcefulness and pragmatism.

That is why, in America, one is not asked who one's family is, but what one does. I have often wondered what it would take for Indian society to accept its members for their accomplishments, rather than for their social backgrounds.

I do not worry whether I am seen as an American or an Indian. I live in both countries several months each year, but my home is not a place. Home is an ideal, a state of mind, an attitude. I think of the country I live in as an idea, constantly changing and open to newer ideas, cultures and possibilities. Hence, I do not attach much importance to patriotism as it is usually understood – "right or wrong, I stand by my country." Just like India, America, too, has made many historical mistakes.

I subscribe to the notion of loyalty that comes from experience. My sense of loyalty to America arises from my gratitude for all the opportunities I have had over my entire adult life, the comfort and security that I have enjoyed, and the friendships I have cherished. While I have spent a majority of my life in America, I am awakened to a deep appreciation of the many ideals pursued by India's fragile democracy. These ideals were what its founding fathers had offered the country.

Through the noble example set by Mahatma Gandhi in the nation's struggle for independence and human rights, the world is offered an alternative to wars by pursuing non-violent resistance – a principle that has had no other practical parallel in the history of humankind. Unlike the West, where people generally feel they have the right to do what they want as individuals, I have often hoped that such ideals would lead Indians to choose what is right. It is this spirit of India, its gentle people, and the friendships I have developed over recent years that attract me to India. But more than anything else, it is a sense of purpose in my work for the poor that makes me want to do whatever I can for the country of my birth.

I take pride in being of Indian origin. As I share this common bond with others like me who have been living abroad for long, I feel our strength derives from our diversity in backgrounds and even cultures. As NRIs, we must return to India because we care passionately about her and want to make a difference in the lives of the poor people. I hope most of us return to India not just because we want to benefit from India, but also because we want to give something back.

As President Kennedy once said, "Ask not what your country can do for you, but what you can do for your country." I believe that is what we must ask of ourselves today after being abroad for years. While we should consider investments in India only if the rewards are commensurate with the risks, we also owe something greater than our self-interest to our country of origin. We need to talk about what can improve the lives of our people.

AN UNCERTAIN WORLD

In the last decade, the world has undergone several dramatic changes. The interrelationships between nations have become interdependencies. In one sense, NRIs are the link between India and other countries, and they help to bridge the gap that might exist between cultures, political philosophies, and national interests. In my own work in India, I see a close link between what I do, and how I live in both countries.

There has to be a real common purpose in our existence. For me, it is this search for a true purpose in living that has brought me back to India. David Gergen, a frequent advisor to U.S. presidents and editor of several well-known journals, recently wrote a piece for *U.S. News & World Report* questioning whether the current decade would be seen as the veritable triumph of the human spirit. The world events of the past four years do not offer any such hope. Today, in the midst of plenty, people in the West are hungry for greater nourishment of the soul. People are adept at satisfying their hunger for material things in life, but they fail to appreciate beauty, spiritual growth, and human connection across religions, races and boundaries.

Charles Handy, an English writer, explained in *The Age of Unreason* (Harvard Business School Press, 1998), "In Africa, they say there are two hungers …. The lesser hunger is for things that sustain life, the goods and services, and the money to pay for them, which we all need. The greater hunger is for an answer to the question 'why,' for some understanding of what life is for." It was barely 800 years ago when Western Europe experienced an extraordinary burst of energy, art and technology that overcame the Dark Ages. Today, we are again experiencing a technological revolution, contrasted with terrorism, ethnic conflicts, and threats of mass destruction. The unanswered question now is whether we shall once again overcome destructive forces and keep the flame of human spirit alive for the common good. And if we do, in the process we might find our own answers to the question 'why.' India has just as much chance as any other nation, if not more, to satisfy this human hunger.

There is hope. Michael Mandelbaum argues in his book *The Ideas That Conquered the World* (Public Affairs, 2002) that the recent terrorist attacks by Al Qaeda are only a passing phenomena. According to him, three ideas dominate the world since the dawn of the 21st century: peace as the preferred basis for relations between countries, democracy as the optimal way to organize political life, and free markets as the indispensable vehicle for the creation of wealth. While these ideas are not practiced everywhere today, he believes that the world would soon find progress through the concepts of peace, democracy and open markets.

However, a lot appears to hinge on the American role in bringing about peace in many long-standing conflicts around the globe, and on whether it can successfully persuade the international community to work in concert on a new security order. America must continue to play its leadership role in the world and come to the aid of democracies such as India. However, it must also let countries solve their problems their own way. Not everybody wants to be like Americans. Not everybody should.

America will not find security within its borders simply by building barricades and inspecting everyone and everything. There are enough people in the world who have legitimate or misguided grievances against others to want to cause harm. Peace and security will come when America consistently stands with ordinary people in countries where their ruthless rulers, dictators and kingdoms oppress them.

Hatred toward America will turn into gratitude when Americans show their willingness to share a reasonable portion of their wealth and prosperity with those in other countries who are not as fortunate. After all, poor people in impoverished countries did not choose to be born in hostile climatic zones and on barren land. The expense of benevolence that America should demonstrate is far less than the cost of protecting the country from those who seek to cause destruction. The choice is for the American people to make, and I only pray that wisdom and compassion will ultimately prevail.

For India, the choices are very different. The preconditions for success are also clear. To start with, the most essential requirement for the country is the proper exercise of democracy. Democracy means that all people, regardless of their religion, caste and gender, have the freedom and equal opportunity to make the best of their lives.

Good governance in public and private sectors, based on performance as opposed to special privileges, corruption, bribes and favors, will make it possible to achieve desired results. Through vigorous competition, consumers benefit from superior products at lower costs. Enforcement of just laws, contracts, property rights and social justice permits fair economic activity to take place. The focus on sustainable development, wealth creation and rightful distribution of assets and income offers prosperity for all. Transparency in public activity and a free press ensure the necessary accountability. When one or more of the above conditions are absent to any degree, real solutions will be harder to achieve.

Perfection is only for the gods, as they say, and India cannot wait for all the pre-requisites for success to fall in place. Lasting solutions can be found only when the nation is prepared to face and tackle the root causes of its social injustice and economic failures. It is not enough to focus on aggregate economic growth generated through industrial expansion, which impacts mostly the urban population.

Rural development is what improves the lives of a great majority of Indians. The poor do not prefer handouts over permanent and sustainable solutions. Altruism, idealism and a spirit of service motivate many to do good, but compassion is not enough. What the poor want is financial and material help, and the guidance and support to create opportunities for themselves. The focus of assistance must shift from offering free services to employment creation and income generation so that everyone can afford to pay for basic needs. It is opportunity that the poor ultimately want. Some big steps in new directions need to be taken, combined with many small leaps forward; diversity in approach is fine as long as the ultimate goals are noble and consistent.

My social work with the poor people in rural South India has taught me valuable lessons, especially about what does not work today. It has also given me insight into potential new approaches to solving many of the perennial problems faced in several interrelated issues: education; health care; empowerment of women and socially deprived people; community development; income generation and asset creation; land, water and energy management; access to markets and competitive pricing ability; and rural partnerships within a redefined role for the government.

In all these issues, the real solutions lie in establishing good public governance, building strong human foundations through education and health care, creating economic opportunity, and ensuring social justice for all.

Chapter 3

THE *LITERATE* CHILDREN
OF RURAL INDIA

A PLACE TO START

Over the years, I have read many success stories on poverty eradication in developing countries. Education was described by every developmental expert as the long-term solution to hunger and social problems. I, however, was not convinced that it was the best way to go, but it was where I could start my work when I was ready. The idea of excellence among the poor through good education was something I thought would make a big impact for a few initially.

Most public and private initiatives targeting children and young people from poor homes talked about providing basic education or training so people could find jobs to support themselves. There was rarely any mention about children from poor families one day becoming leaders of the society or professionals in the global marketplace. I was convinced that professional success was necessary for the lower castes to break out of their social deprivation.

It was July 1995. This was my second visit to India following my earlier trip in January to start a charitable foundation. During the previous six months, some of our board members had tried to locate and purchase the land required to build a school for poor children. Their efforts had produced no tangible results, in fact, the foundation lost a good sum of money that was paid as advances to close on two land transactions that had looked promising.

Learning from this initial experience, I directed my staff not to make any monetary advances for any transaction. There are plenty of crafty brokers in Bangalore purportedly representing buyers and sellers and assuring everyone quite convincingly that they can easily get all the necessary government paperwork done to complete land transactions.

In Karnataka state, almost all the land outside the city premises is classified as "agricultural," and an official conversion is necessary to use it for any other purpose. Moreover, only those who are classified as "farmers" can purchase agricultural land. This implies that the seller has to obtain the conversion permit before he can sell it to a non-farmer. This process allows politicians and government officials to collect fees and bribes from both buyers and sellers of land. In the end, there is no guarantee that the seller will complete the transaction at the previously agreed-upon price.

I had approached the Karnataka government to permit us to buy some land for the school without having to pay large "fees" for conversion. Land prices had already risen considerably from all the industrial development that was taking place in the area, and with a conversion charge, the final cost exceeded even the United States' price for farmland. We were looking for some 30 acres in a poor district 25 or so kilometers away from the city, but the prices were around Rs.200,000 ($4,250) per acre. Conversion "costs" were also an equal amount, making the whole transaction prohibitively expensive for a charitable organization. After trying for three months to get an exemption from the government, I decided it was time to give up and move on.

I arranged with a couple of brokers to take me to potential properties outside Karnataka. The state of Tamil Nadu, barely 25 kilometers from Bangalore city, did not have any conversion requirements and one could buy any land for both farm and non-farm use. I was not familiar with the area, but I decided to find the land we needed on my own. Each morning, I hired a taxi and drove in whatever direction the broker suggested across the border into Tamil Nadu.

As luck would have it, one rainy morning, my broker brought me to a lake in the village of Baliganapalli in Dharmapuri district. Pointing across it he said, "There are some 35 acres on the other side of the lake for sale, but we will have to walk along the cart track to see them."

I soon realized that the lake had overflowed and covered the track with water up to my ankles, and the only way to get across was to walk with my trousers pulled up. The lake was beautiful and from a distance, I could see the raised ground with rocky formations. There was something majestic about the setting, and no matter how difficult the access would be, it was worth investigating. I was told that the villages nearby were very poor, and the district as a whole was also one of the poorest in South India. Female infanticide was reportedly prevalent in the area. I thought it would be a good place to start our humanitarian work.

After walking a kilometer or so and crossing a couple of *nallas* or ravines, I set foot on a raised piece of land that looked untouched ever since its creation. I ran up to a huge rock at the highest point of the property, climbed on it, and looked in all directions. The lake looked magnificently beautiful, and I could see the eucalyptus trees on all sides for miles at a stretch.

"Be careful about snakes," shouted the broker.

I looked around a little scared and asked, "Why are there no trees on our land?"

He replied that it was dry and rocky, and the landowner couldn't grow anything on it. I wondered to myself why he couldn't pump water from the lake or drill a well. Only after some years did I come to understand that most landowners found it too expensive to drill wells and develop hilly property. Everyone preferred low-lying, level land. Moreover, after the rains stopped, farmers in low-lying areas would use the lake water, causing the lake to be dry for a good part of the year.

I insisted on meeting with the landowner the same day. We left immediately and met with Gowda and his sons at one of the largest houses in the Baliganapalli village. None of them spoke English, and I couldn't speak Kannada or Telegu, the languages with which they were familiar. I sat on a mat they laid out for me on the porch and began to ask them about their family and the village, with all the translations made by the broker. I told them why I was there and what I wanted to do for the poor people in the village.

The senior Gowda expressed his appreciation and replied that he would be blessed for selling his land for a worthy cause and that he would offer it at the lowest price he could. His price was by no means any lower than other land I had seen before, but after some negotiations, we settled on a final price. Now, the challenge was to bring the transaction to a successful conclusion, with clear title and no encumbrances.

After the initial papers were signed by both parties, I thought it would be wise to meet with all the officials and heads of villages around the area and explain to them that I was planning to start a school exclusively for poor children. Gowda helped arrange the meeting the very next week, and with everyone present, I told them that I planned to buy the land only if they all agreed that I should set up the school there.

It was made clear that the school would be entirely private, there would be no quotas, and all employment would be at the discretion of the school management. There would be no government involvement and no government money. All these concepts appeared new to them, and I wondered whether they believed anything I said. After a few questions and answers, everyone expressed their consent and welcomed me to their village. We distributed some sweets and held a small *puja* (religious ceremony) on the open land. Within a month, Jude worked through all the formalities, and the land was ours to start the work.

MY INTRODUCTION TO RURAL EDUCATION

Devarapalli is a relatively prosperous village near Baliganapalli, where Shanti Bhavan was to be built. In preparation for opening our own school, I had interviewed the spectacled village school headmaster of the Upper Primary School in Devarapalli that imparts instruction in Telegu, the language of the surrounding villages. It had some 250 students in classes one through eight, and four teachers. These teachers alternate in two shifts, from 9:30 a.m. to 12:30 p.m., and from 2 p.m. to 4 p.m. daily. The district education officer appoints the teachers on the basis of seniority of applicants, with special consideration given to lower castes — ST (Scheduled Tribes), SC (Scheduled Caste), BC (Backward Caste), and MBC (Most Backward Caste). Once employed, teachers are not terminated from employment even for poor performance as long as they turn up at school frequently.

The government lays down the curriculum, and the headmaster and teachers control the testing process. Teachers' salaries start at Rs.4,500 basic pay plus "Dearness Allowance," which compensates for the cost of living, giving a total compensation of about Rs.7,000 per month. When teachers are on leave, the children do nothing.

The school was already short two teachers, and students from a couple of grades were combined into a single room for some of the classes. The headmaster said that the teachers needed good exposure and training, and hiring two additional teachers would not solve the problem.

"Teachers come when they please and go when they please," he said. "It is not easy to fire any state employee. The government has everything on paper, but very little is implemented."

Parents in rural communities are usually not involved in the education of their children. Most are illiterate. Well-off parents send their children to better schools in the vicinity, such as the Asian Christian Academy. Very poor children are kept as bonded laborers from an early age by landlords and moneylenders. Girls usually stop going to school after the age of twelve, and take care of smaller children or work for the landlord. If a bonded parent refuses to send his child for work, the Panchayat officials will ask them to pay sums of money toward *pujas*, or for constructing temples or for other community services as punishment.

If they can't pay up, they are harassed by injunctions such as "Don't cross my land," or "Don't take water from this well." The Panchayat members are often under the control of high caste individuals and landlords. In Baliganapalli, more than 30 percent of the people are from higher castes, and the remaining 70 percent are from lower castes. The high castes have land, money and other assets. The law of the land is set by the village elders and Panchayat officials.

The headmaster said that he could report to the police about children who were not attending school, and their parents could be fined. But when asked, he said he had never reported any such cases. Teachers said that they did not discriminate between children of different castes. They all sat together in school when usually lower caste children sit at the back. The government pays for the salaries of the staff and for electricity and water; the Block Development Office pays half the amount, and the Education Office pays the remaining amount.

Each child is entitled to 100 grams of rice, ten grams of dal, and five grams of oil per day. A cook and helper make the midday meal. At the very least, children were getting one meal.

Many parents said that they were not sending their daughters to school because they were afraid that girls would face problems on the bus or on the streets. This argument didn't sound very convincing, especially given the fact that everyone knew everyone else in the village. Some parents thought their girls should not go to school in case they fell in love. Their "dignity" would be impacted, and they would not find husbands.

Most girls study until the eighth standard and then find work. Many poor people send their sons to the tile factories and to the farms nearby. The tile factories give Rs.20 per day, and the farms give Rs.30 per day. The headmaster spoke about the few students who went on to high school and to college for their bachelor's degrees in commerce.

Devarapalli School is no exception. My subsequent visits to other rural schools have convinced me that literacy as a goal is a meaningless concept if these people are destined to live and die in abject poverty.

Major reforms are needed in primary, middle and secondary education in rural schools if the children are to benefit from the education they receive. It is disturbing to observe that poor people are coerced to accept learning in local languages while their politicians and the senior bureaucrats who make all these decisions send their children to expensive English-medium schools. The responsibility to "preserve our culture" is left to the poor while those with financial means educate their children in English and subsequently seek entry into elite Indian colleges and foreign countries, especially in America.

For today's global marketplace, every child needs to learn English as a means to succeed in professional careers. Nationalism and regional pride alone will not bring bread to the table. From Russia and China to Poland and Lithuania, every country is in a hurry to bring competency in English to the new generation; parents are placing more importance in learning English than to even music and arts to prepare their children to avail of opportunities in an open market.

It seems that India's disingenuous politicians are once again moving in the opposite direction. Insistence on education only in the local language is a means of oppression of the poor. It is a form of playing up to their ignorance with convenient and popular sentiment. Despite all the political and cultural rhetoric, more and more poor people are beginning to recognize that the English language is essential for upward mobility, and good education can break caste and class barriers.

The returns from pursuing the goal of good basic education for all citizens can be seen in the examples of Japan, China, South Korea and Taiwan. Japan's implementation of its Fundamental Code of Education in 1872 led to literacy among practically its entire younger generation within less than half a century later, and today, most Japanese have completed high school. China, South Korea and Taiwan are each able to keep up with technological developments elsewhere and turn out products that conform to world standards, thanks to a skilled labor force that is able to follow precise instructions and specifications.

These countries not only enjoy a far higher standard of living, but they also have greater economic participation by their women and lower birth rates. On the other hand, India has neglected basic education, spending only about

1.7 percent of the country's gross domestic product on primary education (3.8 percent for education overall), compared to over 5 percent for an emerging country like Brazil.[3] Up to 40 million children are now estimated to be out of school in India.

According to Amartya Sen, the Nobel laureate in economics, "The contribution of basic education is not, however, confined to economic progress. Education has intrinsic importance; the capability to read and write can deeply influence one's quality of life."

If India is to realize its economic promise and deal effectively with its social ills, it must embark on the goal of ensuring at least basic education for all its children of school-going age. More than two-thirds of the children in the country are in the villages, and with good rural education, India can realize the mostly untapped potential of its vast human resource. There is some hope as an increasing number of private schools offering somewhat better education and charging small fees are now opening up in rural areas.

Since September 11, 2001, the United States and other developed nations have become pre-occupied with fighting terrorism. Consequently, the agenda for economic and social development in third world nations has received far less focused attention in recent years. Many policy makers in developed countries do not see a direct link between poverty and terrorism, and blame religious fanaticism for the violence that has threatened them. Significant financial resources are being expended in eliminating the "evil doers," while no increased effort is being made on the positive goals of universal basic education, quality health care for all people, and better care of the environment.

The United Nations identified universal primary education by 2015 as one of the goals that the world should attempt to achieve, but it appears that the diversion caused by terrorism makes it far less likely even by year 2025.[4]

There is an overwhelming and urgent need to reform government-run schools throughout India. The problem of low educational standards in public schools is prevalent in the United States also. In an effort to revamp the school system, American states have begun to set higher standards for their students. The students would then be tested against the standards on a regular basis, and students, teachers and school administrators would be held accountable for outcomes.

"Standards, testing, accountability" – that is the new mantra. Underlying these reforms is the effort to professionalize America's teachers through increased training and better salary. Studies have shown that three good teachers in a row over a three-year period produce dramatically better results in children.

Another recommendation is remedial classes and support for those children who are on the borderline. The idea is to carry forward as many students as possible, but they must meet the standard. While some of these innovations in education may be controversial, the goal of improving the standard for as many students as possible is something that India should earnestly embrace in its educational program.

Adult literacy in India is approximately sixty-five percent. Rural literacy is slightly lower. Does this statistic have any practical meaning? Most of those "literate" village folks have hardly benefited from the schools they have attended, wherein poorly trained teachers irregularly hold overcrowded classes that often combine several grades or standards. Without knowledge, information, and the ability to comprehend, literacy offers very little. Literacy as the national goal for the poor is a disservice to their future prospects. Instead, the goal should be universal high school graduation under acceptable standards for reading, mathematics, and general knowledge. Today, very few children from poor families who attend rural schools go on to colleges, while those who are in high schools benefit little from the deplorable education they receive.

For quality education, the investment priority should be in trained teachers, not in today's high-tech tools that are thrust upon many rural institutions, at considerable expense, in the name of bridging the "digital divide" when the budgets are limited. All the gadgetry in the world cannot equal the impact that a skilled and dedicated teacher has on a child, even in the most rural of settings.

Every rural school can perform well if it has at least the minimum facilities – ventilated classrooms, basic teaching materials, toilets, a reference library, and of course, competent and committed teachers. Computers are good to have, but not at the expense of any of the basic necessities. Almost all rural schools lack good teachers. More qualified college graduates should be attracted to the teaching profession, and that calls for higher salaries for working at schools, especially those run by the government.

Teacher training institutions should be given public assistance to develop good teachers. Further, teacher incentive programs in the form of additional training in new teaching methods and financial incentives based on student evaluations conducted by independent private organizations are the key to developing and encouraging good teachers.

There is no question that education is the key to professional success. But not all children have the opportunity to attend good schools. Government-run schools in India, especially in rural areas, offer substandard education, while good private schools are beyond the reach of most people, even in the middle class.

The government has so far not seriously attempted to privatize government schools or to provide parents the necessary financial support for their children to study in private schools. It is generally accepted that quality education is only for the rich, and the poor are simply not entitled to it.

This stark reality has haunted me from my childhood days when I used to hear the names of exclusive schools like Lovedale and Doon School where the prime minister's grandchildren were studying. This contrasted with my experience in America where, with practically no money in my pocket, I was able to work my way through and study in one of the best universities. It is the collective responsibility of society to ensure that every child receives quality education, and all children with exceptional talent should be offered excellent education. To deny this is a social injustice and a waste of national human resources.

Excellence in education is hardly ever associated with the poor; it is only for the rich, for those who can afford it. For instance, can even one graduate of a rural school anywhere in India expect to pass the entrance examination to the prestigious Indian Institute of Technology (IIT)? That is not to say there are no children among the poor who have the capability to reach great heights. Bright, motivated children are lost by their early years of schooling in an unchallenging environment. If somehow these impoverished but talented children could be given the opportunity, they would one day become the role models for other children in their communities, role models for a better future. This noble goal is something that the wealthy non-resident Indians should consider embracing; after all, their own lives have benefited by adhering to the concept of excellence in their work.

India has profited from the technology revolution currently taking place in the West, and yet, there is also a considerable "digital divide" among the country's differing populations. The benefits of the Internet are confined to a few among the middle and upper classes – those who can afford telephone and personal computer access. In 2000, less than 30 million people had phone lines in use, while the Internet was accessed by some 5 million. Very few educational institutions offer Internet access to their students; less than five percent of India's 100,000 secondary schools use computers in education, and only a small fraction of them have Internet access.[5] The problem is further compounded in a rural setting where communication lines are unreliable or non-existent.

Numerous state governments, corporations, and non-governmental organizations have embarked on projects to make computers available to lower income individuals, schools and public institutions, but these subsidized initiatives can benefit only very few. What is needed instead is free competition among telephone and Internet Service Providers (ISPs) that would improve reliability and quality in service and lower the cost of access. After years of monopoly and unreliable service by a single ISP, VSNL, the Government has recently somewhat opened up the sector.

There are still too many restrictions and controls to prevent easy entry by newcomers, and consequently, both telephone and Internet services remain a distant aspiration for most consumers. The policymakers seem constantly to make major mistakes, some deliberately to benefit a few, and the nation suffers for decades before real changes are slowly implemented.

EXCELLENCE IN EDUCATION

Since the late 1960s, I experienced firsthand and also observed that every person in America, regardless of his or her race or background, has a fair chance to succeed. At that time, Americans began to take very seriously the idea of equal opportunity for all, white or black. My years of study and struggle in America were motivated by my desire to carve out a successful career and by the secure knowledge that, if I could prove myself to be capable, I would reap my just rewards.

The American system, while not totally free of defects, has the hard-won resilience to incorporate self-correction, self-criticism and evolution based on tried and tested concepts to move toward a just society. India, on the other hand, cannot expect to build a nation offering equal opportunity without first accepting equality and tolerance among all religions and castes.

After I had earned enough money and acumen to crystallize my ideas on how to make a positive difference in the lives of the poor, the concept of providing a world-class educational opportunity to children from socially and economically deprived backgrounds began to take concrete shape.

I wanted Shanti Bhavan to be an excellent school for the poorest in India. It would be no different from the many good schools for the rich in India or anywhere in the world. Enrollment would include a limited number of children with the potential to excel in school and later go on for higher education. It would be restricted to 24 children per grade so that they could receive the best care and individual attention. Shanti Bhavan children would one day achieve great professional success and break out of the vicious cycle of social and economic deprivation that has prevailed in their families for generations.

Since all eligible children could not be accommodated in Shanti Bhavan, we decided to assist the local village schools in improving their standard of education. For a start, middle school education should be the goal rather than primary education alone. Children should be stimulated to study, parents should be motivated to send their children to schools, and teachers should be given the incentive to teach well. Consequently, parents would find it worth-while to send their children to good schools, while children would enjoy studying in a stimulating environment.

An incentive program based on children meeting required educational standards would motivate teachers. The idea of special compensation for teachers based on the results of independent testing of children was well received by both headmasters and teachers. A good educational model could help bring about at least a few successes in every village and in every slum.

Those successful young women and men graduates would have a positive impact on their deprived communities. Nevertheless, it must be recognized that a good number of children might not be able to pursue higher studies, but those who stay through high school should be encouraged to pursue vocational training. Investment in the education of children and vocational training of young adults who are not prepared to go on for higher studies would undoubtedly contribute more to the long-term prosperity of the nation than what any other policy measure could bring about.

Once the concept of Shanti Bhavan was clearly formulated, the next challenge was to determine what it would take to implement the project. My sister, Lekha Keister, and I set out beginning in early 1995 to research the subject of childcare and education for children of deprived backgrounds. Lekha was well suited for this task having received a doctorate in education administration.

We met with experienced psychologists, psychiatrists, pediatricians, teachers, caregivers, community service workers, directors of programs such as Head Start, Boys Town, and others that cater specifically to the needs of marginalized inner city and ghetto children in the United States and in Central and South America. Our findings were tempered by our own experiences growing up in India and by my own observations of educational projects in India. We took about 18 months to put together a 200-page policy and procedures manual that clarified our ideas for Shanti Bhavan. The action plan was formulated even before I had acquired the land for the project in India. My longtime family friend, Angeline Nair, had suggested that I establish Bangalore as the base for our humanitarian activities. Bangalore, hailed as the Silicon Valley of India, promised opportunities for keeping up with the developed world.

While building plans were drawn up and approved, Lekha helped me identify two American couples with the special skills needed for a six-month training program for the staff – caregivers and teachers, including the principal and vice principal. We leased part of a farm homestead on the outskirts of Bangalore as the training center. With thick vegetation and farm animals, the surroundings were an ideal setting for the trainers and participants.

Meanwhile, on site, the building contractors came up with any number of excuses for their inevitable delays. The construction site featured mounds of bulldozed earth, gaping trenches and hillocks of concrete blocks. Cement mixers and earthmovers were parked between partially completed buildings. Undeterred, we decided to move in. We had already waited long enough and were in no mood to wait any longer. Moreover, it would be fun to see things change every day around us.

OPENING THE DOORS

We celebrated the 1997 Indian Independence Day with our inaugural dinner meal under the stars in an open field on metal tables and folding chairs and rented plates and spoons. An excellent meal was prepared by a gifted cook in a makeshift kitchen shack with minimal equipment. It was a special moment when we toasted our future students and staff of Shanti Bhavan. Around us were the ghostly silhouettes of construction activities. A couple of naked bulbs powered by a generator illuminated the scene. When the power supply failed, we turned on the jeep headlights. There were no telephones and no electricity but we did have water supplied from one of the bore-wells we had drilled earlier. None of this bothered us. In fact, it was a heady evening ripe with the promise of what was to come. We were all fired up and nothing could deter us. Ironically, a couple of weeks later, our foreign volunteers described the setting as "concentration camp conditions."

We had enlisted the services of Maya Mascarenhas, a pediatrician with an additional degree in public health, and an expressed desire for community service and an interest in children. She brought with her the experience of running community service programs and her own special training in community health from St. John's Medical College in Bangalore.

Assisting her in his spare time was Christopher, a social scientist with many years of field experience. We had also enlisted S.R. Venkatesh, a freelance clinical psychologist with a special background in child development, through the National Institute of Mental Health and Neurological Sciences in Bangalore. Venkatesh's wife, Bharathy, was pursuing her doctorate in an area of cognitive development of children at the same institute, and she too assisted her husband in our work whenever she could. Over the years, Venkatesh has amply demonstrated his genuine commitment to the emotional development of Shanti Bhavan children.

Lalita Law, the newly hired principal of Shanti Bhavan, had meticulously planned everything for staff training and the opening of the school. I had met Lalita at a friend's party, and she subsequently told me at her job interview that the motivation for applying for the job was something I had said to her then, "I want to give the children a sense of self esteem and confidence to learn."

As the daughter of an air-marshal, and the wife of an army brigadier, Lalita had traveled all over India and had taught at many excellent schools for over 16 years. She was teaching then at the elite International School in Bangalore, but with her strong belief in serving the poor, she was motivated to consider the responsibility of heading the institution. She knew that the job would be highly demanding, and she would be required to stay in Shanti Bhavan away from her husband and two daughters and her comfortable home in Bangalore. Moreover, there were the uncertainties of living in a remote village.

During the course of the interview, she asked me, "Will I be permitted to take time off for my daughters' baby deliveries, and for my occasional dental care needs?" It was very obvious to me that I was dealing with someone who was not only competent, but also committed and dedicated to the cause.

This team comprising of Maya, Christopher, Venkatesh, Bharathy and Lalita scoured villages, slums and orphanages in and around Bangalore and Baliganapalli for suitable children. Communicating our goals to impoverished rural and urban communities proved a big challenge to this team. They experienced failure and success in equal measure. Communities were naturally wary of people they perceived as "Christian missionaries" – Christian, because of the name "George" – and suspected them of religious conversion activities.

The fact that free care and education were being offered to their children provoked community suspicions about trafficking in organ transplants, slave traffic, foreign (meaning Western) adoption of children, kidnapping and related criminal offenses. Local social workers and community service personnel including enlightened Catholic nuns and priests helped dispel fear in the communities they served. They provided our team with free meals and space to work in, and they passed around the word to appropriate families.

Typically, families targeted by our selection team lived in conditions well below the poverty line. They had very little food, scraps of clothing, makeshift shelters of thatch or discarded and tattered plastic sheets, no water supply nearby, no electricity, and almost no hope. Other poor families had some semblance of these daily necessities of life, but the common thread among the communities with whom we interacted was abject despair and passive acceptance of their fate. Criminal activities were accepted as a means of survival. Shame, guilt and embarrassment appeared to be absent. Those emotions are, after all, the indulgences of privileged people.

Some parents decided to take a chance with us only because they felt that nothing worse could happen to them. Others needed someone to feed their children. Some expressed their desire to offer their children a better life than they had. A few went by the recommendation of the community leaders or workers they trusted. There were others who felt there was no harm in grasping at a free handout. Several decided to stay far from us and stated that they would rather suffer and have their children die with them than be handed over to strangers with dubious intentions.

Rationality as most people understand it does not apply to the rural poor. Their decisions are governed by their immediate needs for survival, fear of what could happen to them in the future, misplaced loyalty and threats of reprisal from the village leaders, fatalism, and religious beliefs. Irrational arguments based on emotion, tradition or the possibility of extracting money are likely to prevail.

You can explain anything you want about the good that could happen if their children were to get a proper education, but all it takes is a rumor about conversion to Christianity or foreign adoption for them to reject your offer of help. To make matters worse, Panchayat officials and other village leaders capitalize on the ignorance of the poor people and set them against us from time to time to extract money. The villagers seem to follow blindly the directions of their village leaders, probably because they are afraid of these leaders and need their permission for doing anything other than their routine activities. It is readily apparent that those at the bottom of the social ladder fear authority and often mistake consideration and kindness as signs of weakness.

Each time a senior influential employee of our foundation is let go from a rural project, he generally joins with the local leaders to cause labor unrest or make physical threats, as reprisal or an attempt to extort large sums of money. Recently, our farming initiative had to be put on hold from further expansion for several months following threats from some elements within the nearby villages. It might sound astonishing that the direct beneficiaries of our charitable work, such as those who are employed in our farms, have participated in disruptive activities on behalf of those who have never made any personal sacrifice.

The general belief among those who work with the rural poor is that the only way to handle rural laborers successfully is to discipline them constantly, and keep them financially dependent on the continuity of their employment. Hundreds of years of oppression have probably made the rural poor somewhat less appreciative of even honest efforts to help them, as they remain skeptical about the genuine character of any assistance. There are reports of serious labor unrest and violence against the management of the tea plantations of Assam in North India, and I often wonder whether we will also face the same fate at the hands of the poor people we are trying to help. All this can be very disheartening, but one must go on with the hope that some day the poor will begin to see that they can be trusting of those who are making an effort to improve their lives.

RECRUITMENT OF CHILDREN

Parents who partly understood our plan for educating their children came forward with conditions attached. They were used to demanding from officials what they were entitled to under government assistance programs. Prompted by troublemakers, they felt they could lay down terms and demand money that was theirs for the taking. We repeatedly communicated our vision and plans, all translated into the three languages of Tamil, Kannada and Telegu spoken by parents from different places.

We made it clear that we had not taken any money from the government and that this was entirely a private initiative. Parents were reassured when they understood they could visit their children and take them home for vacations. It was obvious that the first and the most important task was to establish credibility by winning the trust and confidence of the parents. Only then could the selection team begin its work.

As outlined in the policy and procedures manual, the selection of children is a three-way process that requires the combined skills of a social worker, clinical psychologist and pediatrician. The social worker screens the family through interviews and home visits to determine its socioeconomic status. The clinical psychologist administers tests to get an indication of the child's IQ and cognitive ability, while observing the child's behavior and temperament. The medical doctor examines the child for serious physical defects that are beyond the resources of Shanti Bhavan, as it is not a school for those with serious disabilities.

We have also had to determine the ages of children from physical and other characteristics, as many did not have birth certificates. On several occasions, our team clocked as many as 300 kilometers on terrible rural roads only to face utter disappointment in the form of non-cooperation by everyone in the village. We were confronted with closed doors in frightened communities that had changed their minds in a day or two after their initial agreement to allow their children to be screened. It was apparent that someone with influence in the village had spread terrible rumors about us and our intentions. Sometimes the response was heartening, but always it was thin. We were trying to sell a concept that appeared preposterous to most, rich and poor alike. There was very little to show on the ground, thanks to construction delays.

In the rural areas, we faced other obstacles as well. Landlords began putting pressure on us in indirect ways to take their children. Rumors that we let children die and hushed up these deaths began to fly and served to scare away poor, rural folk. With village officials and local rural bigwigs, the criticisms were self-serving – to keep the poor away and somehow get their children in.

They spread stories that we had buried dead children on our grounds after removing their kidneys or that we were converting them to Christianity. These rumors served as an effective deterrent to prospective school admission seekers. Initially, considerable time was spent quelling these unreasonable fears.

Panchayat officials asked us to lower our standards of initial screening and selection and to set quotas for each village regardless of whether the applicants met our criteria for selection. To achieve their goal of forcing us to set aside some admissions to those recommended by them, these officials try to threaten us with accusations of religious conversion activities.

It was purported that the question of our converting children to Christianity had been brought up during a recent meeting of the BJP party at Hosur, a nearby town. Government officials arrived on campus without any warning to check our "conversion efforts." Their real goal was to extort money from us, and we tried to appeal to their good senses. Do they go to schools run by Hindu organizations to see if Muslims and Christians are being converted to Hinduism?

Slowly, children whom we had cleared for admission in various deprived communities started trickling into Shanti Bhavan. If there were a few children from the same community or village, it helped boost the confidence of parents. At first, the children were bewildered, frightened, homesick and yet, fascinated, all at the same time. Most had never used toilets, slept on beds, sat on chairs, worn footwear, eaten a square meal in a day, or played with toys – the kind of things most of us take for granted. The caregivers expended tremendous effort to make the children feel accepted, secure and loved.

While children and staff were settling in, construction work was still in progress. The dining hall, kitchen, school building and teachers' quarters were not completed yet. Classes were conducted in dormitories and outdoors. Meals were also served in dormitories. None of this bothered the children; they began to enjoy themselves and feel at home. On Christmas Eve, we welcomed our 48th and last child for pre-school and kindergarten for the startup academic year that commenced in August 1997.

While the staff was prepared to follow guidelines and duty rosters, professional conduct was markedly absent. It was clear that they needed a different kind of orientation and education themselves. Their professed beliefs, ideas and values were at variance with what needed to be inculcated in the children. The vice-principal, who was from an internationally reputed institution in India, thought nothing of making personal arrangements with school-hired contractors for his own home. He felt he was entitled to such privileges and indulged in other self-serving activities and theft. Within a few months, his services had to be terminated.

Shortly thereafter, the facilities manager was found to be in cahoots with the building engineers. They had daily drinking bouts, got the kitchen staff to cook special non-vegetarian meals after everyone had retired for the night, sold building supplies, and, unknown to us, even provided safe harbor for an eloping couple on campus, complete with post-nuptial celebrations and a few days honeymoon at our expense!

The housemothers were led by confusing signals from the troublemakers; policy and procedures notwithstanding, the campus life was transformed into a hate campaign directed against the management. Western volunteers were carried away by sympathy for the lower staff who were also from poor homes, and they were encouraged to demand salaries that were somewhat comparable to those in America. By then I was back in America, and Lalita and her management team found themselves defending our decisions. If anyone was fired for misconduct, the principal would be depicted as one of those heartless upper-crust folks with no sensitivity to the plight of the poor.

I had met with the president of India, K.R. Narayanan, in Delhi to present the concept of Shanti Bhavan and to invite him for the formal inauguration in the summer of 1998. He was known to our family and expressed genuine interest, agreeing to attend the inauguration a year later. I had subsequently met with the then Tamil Nadu state governor, Fathima Beevi, to request her to preside over the function. A fortnight before the inauguration, the president's office communicated his inability to attend. Hearing of the last-minute dropout by the president, the governor also expressed her reluctance to attend, but with some persuasion, she consented. She had, after all, been my father's student at the Law College in Trivandrum some 40 years back and had spent half a day at my home in New Jersey during one of her visits to the United States, just before she was appointed governor.

The inaugural function was meticulously arranged, with a brief official ceremony followed by dinner and an entertainment program by the children and some well-known performers. The governor arrived with her entourage of government officials in some 20 cars, and a pre-positioned police force of about 250 officers and constables. From the moment she stepped from her car, it was obvious that she was not pleased to serve as a substitute for anyone, and there was no expression of familiarity or friendliness in her face. She kept more or less silent throughout the ceremony, and as she left, she inquired as to whether we had fed her policemen and support staff. Since we had had no prior intimation about feeding an additional 200 people, food ran short for our children, their parents and invited guests.

The sub-collector of the district asked that she be seated at the podium. Separately, a similar demand came from the deputy director general of police. There was not enough space for so many people on the podium, as we already had the collector and three other special guests. I told the sub-collector and the police officer that they could sit next to my 90-year-old father in the front row. The sub-collector was not satisfied with my response, and from then on, she became our bitter enemy.

Government officials in positions of authority are used to expecting everyone to be subservient to them. NGOs usually rely on government financial assistance for their humanitarian projects, and since we do not accept public funds, it became an even greater cause for her anger and vendetta.

The inaugural function served very little purpose other than to raise the morale of our staff temporarily. In fact, we created enemies of some key officials who were used to being made much of by everyone around. Subsequently, we found little or no cooperation or assistance from any of these officials on our requests for improvements in public services like electricity, telephone and road repair.

Claiming that Shanti Bhavan property had encroached on public land by a few feet, the sub-collector soon dispatched some officials to tear down our border fence. She also instructed her staff to break up the access road along the lake that we had improved at considerable cost. With the threat of harassment from government, I decided to file a petition in the state High Court, requiring the sub-collector and other officials to show cause. Fearing that we would take her on in the courts, she decided to back off and asked us to withdraw the case.

Chapter 4

A PROMISE OF HOPE

THE SHANTI BHAVAN APPROACH

Shanti Bhavan began its program as planned, but with the usual start-up difficulties. In a short period of two years, the daily routines and schedules were occurring as smoothly as could be expected. Children responded to their new stimulating environment with great excitement, and learning became part of their fun. In just over six years of starting Shanti Bhavan, our 10-year old children are using Word and Excel and learning art and dance, and many are playing piano. They are eating both Indian and international foods, such as spaghetti, tuna and turkey. We have introduced them to formal dinner nights as part of their developing social graces. They enjoy simple play and also activities such as soccer, swimming and roller-skating.

The gardens and clean dormitories provide healthy living and learning space. They see the use of solar energy and water conservation, and they learn to respect all animal life and the environment. We promote no philosophy of our own and always try to follow globally shared values in all our actions.

Daily morning assemblies incorporate world events that are presented to the children by the teachers. Most important, the children are developing positive attitudes. Older children are beginning to understand that the perspective of their parents is different for reasons beyond their control. We take a lot of trouble to explain to the children that poverty is nothing to be ashamed of, and that they should respect their parents regardless of their status in society.

The children have come to realize there is an honest way to live, work and prosper. Their sense of values and goals are being formed appropriately. One child, whose proud family has been insisting she become a doctor or engineer, replied in her own simple language that it is not necessary for her to become a doctor or engineer because she will be what she wants to be, according to her inborn talents and interests.

Children are being educated in their rights as human persons. While children are exposed to all great religions, no organized prayers and rituals of any religion are permitted within the campus. We focus our curriculum on doing away with discrimination based on caste and religion by promoting secularism and social equality, and we emphasize gender equality from early childhood. We explain to our children that the caste system is a creation of man, and not of God, and all children are born equal.

We also deal with health issues on sensitive subjects, such as sex and high-risk behaviors. Children have become aware of sexual abuse through their lessons in self-science (emotional intelligence), as most of them have admitted to being sexually abused even by their own family members. We see self-esteem in children as the key to success in adult life. This will enable our children to achieve more than academic success.

Recently, we chose the Council of Indian School Certificate Examination and the International Baccalaureate as the standards with which we wanted to subscribe. International baccalaureate affiliation was expensive, and while we intended to strive for that standard, we knew we might not be able to afford its formal accreditation.

Our commitment to our children is life-long, and we must save enough money for their college education also. Our student population is expected to increase each year by 24 new children until the maximum planned capacity of 336 is reached. We realize that the expenses will climb steadily each year, and we need to find other sources of funds to assure the growth and success of the many initiatives of The George Foundation. The major investment we have recently made in vegetable and fruit cultivation will hopefully help the situation in the future. In one way or the other, I pray that we have the ability to see to the needs of these and other future children.

Visitors are struck by our children's level of self-confidence and their joy. The children are not shy with anyone, Indians or foreigners. They ask many questions, starting with "What is your name?" followed by "Where are you from?" and "What do you do?" One visitor was told, "You look like the captain of the Titanic!" because of his beard. Children are asked to think for themselves, to inquire and to keep an open mind.

A fourth grader asked a journalism student whether he wrote the truth or just any rubbish, much to the amusement of the student. An experienced journalist was asked, "Have you ever been in jail?" and, "Has your life ever been in danger?" A visitor who said he played the piano was asked, "Do you have a Steinway?" because the children know that the Steinway on their auditorium stage is valuable. Visitors appreciate the kind of questions the children ask and their relaxed, confident manner. Shanti Bhavan children do not feel they are different from any other children, and they are not ashamed of their poor family backgrounds.

During my twice-yearly visits to India for the foundation work, I make it a point to talk to the children of the third grade and higher as often as I can. I speak on different subjects, such as self-confidence, leadership, keeping one's word, dealing with adversity, honesty, proper conduct, jealousy, spousal abuse, and so on. I encourage the children to ask questions and to tell me what they do not like about Shanti Bhavan.

Children have asked why their brothers and sisters cannot be admitted as students of Shanti Bhavan and why girls are not permitted to grow their hair long. They accepted my explanation that we would like to help as many families as possible, and therefore, have restricted admission to one child per family. They agreed that it would be unfair if some families got more help than others. The girls were told they could grow their hair when they were old enough to groom it themselves. I believe that young children are hungry for learning and that my words will have an impact on them, as they see me as someone they can look to for moral support and affection.

Schools are judged for the education they impart and the academic performance of the students. There is seldom any mention of whether school prepares the child to lead a correct life – to be truthful, gentle, caring, and the many other humane values that are equally or more important. I guess that responsibility is left to the family. In a boarding institution like Shanti Bhavan, which is both a traditional school and a home, we have the responsibility to contribute to the all-round development of the child. The problem is that we do not really know how to develop the character of a person properly.

In my opinion, no amount of talk will do the job; only personal examples can have lasting impact. Those who interact with the children every day must set the right example reflecting the values we want in our children. But when society itself does not practice many of these noble values, how can we expect the staff to set the example? This has been a difficult task for all of us at Shanti Bhavan, requiring the senior management, especially Lalita, to spend considerable time with the adults who teach and care for the children, to ensure their own good conduct. At the end of it all, it is the love and attention we give our children that matters, as they do not want to disappoint those who truly care for them.

Lalita holds regular sessions for the staff and children of middle and upper primary classes on human values, ethics, sex education, and emotional intelligence. Moral development is given special importance. Each morning, at the assembly, teachers take turns to present news to the children, and the moral and ethical issues that arise from daily world events are briefly explained further so that children can grasp their significance.

An example is the tragedy of the space shuttle Columbia. The children understood that each of the seven astronauts had dedicated and sacrificed their lives for all of humanity. Similarly, they know the implications of terrorism, war, drought, scientific research and breakthroughs in medicine, as these are daily topics that are thrown out for children to respond to and share their ideas and thoughts. Teachers prepare children from the preschool up to present projects at school assemblies. Our efforts are aimed at developing the children's confidence and openness to ideas. Needless to say, assemblies at Shanti Bhavan are fun learning events.

Debates among children are introduced on simple topics on which they could have differing views. Recitation is learned for enjoyment of speech rhythms and development of clear speech. Dramatics is another medium for self-expression and exploration of emotions. Reading for enjoyment and library research are also encouraged. Nature walks are opportunities for children and teachers to explore the outdoors. Self-science teaches children to recognize and accept their emotions and learn how to handle them.

Classes are conducted in corridors, dormitories, the library, the kitchen or the garden according to the topics to be taught. The campus infrastructure provides several learning opportunities. Visitors give presentations to the children about their professions, travels or other experiences that are of academic value. M.K. Srinath, formerly from the World Wildlife Fund, teaches the children every week about wildlife. He brings snakes and other animals with him for his classes, and the children have become aware that animals need to be respected.

Indoor and outdoor games and entertainment facilities have been provided for the staff as well. They look forward to staff training sessions and faculty meetings as they get welcome breaks from the children. We also emphasize the contribution of caregiving staff who play the role of parents. They utilize the same facilities as the teachers, though the salaries of teachers are higher because of their educational qualifications. However, we take great pains to ensure that caregivers are given respect and attention, and seek their input on children's behavior, psychological health, and personal relationships.

The consultants, too, play important roles. Medical doctors including pediatricians attend to health-related needs such as nutrition, immunization and hygiene. Clinical psychologists monitor emotional development, learning, behavior, and similar significant indicators of psychological development. Social workers assess the impact on the children and their families. Volunteers from different countries provide rich interaction for children and staff. Records are maintained.

In short, we leave no stone unturned to ensure the appropriate development of our children. We feel confident that the children will be successful because the school's teamwork composed of different professional skills will have a positive outcome on their growth.

Every night, teachers of the lower grades tell bedtime stories, while the others spend a few minutes of informal time with the older children in their dorms. The staff winds up their day when the children have gone to sleep at night. Caregiving staff sleep in the same residences as their children, while teachers return to their separate quarters. Staff is encouraged to avail periodic leave so that their emotional batteries are recharged for round-the-clock childcare.

Staff turnover has been moderate to high because of our insistence on performance and proper moral and ethical conduct. We expect our staff to adhere to universal values, such as honesty, integrity and transparency, and set good examples for our children by their own conduct. Of these and other important values, transparency and forthrightness are generally alien to much of modern Indian culture. Convoluted explanations are accepted, while polite inanities are socially demanded. If an unpleasant truth has to be told, or a fault pointed out, it has to be done in a roundabout way that cannot be described as impolite or uncompassionate. Genuine outrage is better unexpressed.

Deliberate negligence is passed off as a "mistake." It is all right to trick a person into compliance, while saving face is more important than pointing out the mistake. Lying is acceptable as long as no one is hurt. All these peculiar characteristics seem to be more widespread than I had assumed at the beginning of my work in India. For one brought up with universally accepted values, I find the management of our staff ripe with challenges. Those who are not used to a government system of low accountability and high benefits find the Indian system bewildering. We have no choice but to insist on globally accepted standards for staff conduct. Some staff stay happily, and some leave when they feel the heat.

The burden of good parenting is shared by many for most of the year, except when the children go home on brief vacations. All adults jointly responsible for the child make decisions; records are maintained and parents apprised of their child's progress or concerns. Each team member participates in the nurturing of the child. The danger of children becoming "institutionalized" is mitigated by the excellent staff-child ratio and the vigilance of the management at each level. The litmus test is the spontaneity and self-confidence of the children – evident even to a stranger.

Shanti Bhavan has abundant but not extravagant resources. The human resource is primary to the overall effort, and trained staff members who are willing to undergo on-going value formation ensure achievement of targets. We think of our resources in terms of physical, material and spiritual.

Physical resources ensure an acceptable level of comfort, clean surroundings, adequate water and electricity, zero pollution and nutritious food for a universally acceptable standard of living. The physical infrastructure presently consists of the school building, separate residences for each grade, gymnasium, kitchen and dining hall, administrative buildings, roller skating and tennis arena, and other structures exceeding 60,000 square feet.

Special attention is given to living in an environmentally friendly manner. The vegetable and fruit gardens are fed with specially treated sewage water. Our gardens grow all the produce needed for the entire campus. At night, the campus glows under solar battery-powered lights.

Material resources available include audiovisual educational equipment in the form of computers, DVDs, videos, books, child-friendly classroom furniture, and good writing materials.

Spiritual resources are what we offer by way of training in the code of universal ethics, social graces, community service, and religious tolerance that make up the spirit of Shanti Bhavan. Our common prayer hall displays the great holy books of all major religions of the world, and both staff and children are encouraged to pray silently on their own during convenient times. The environs and atmosphere of the place are deeply spiritual. All visitors, without exception, are visibly touched when they come to this abode of peace.

CHALLENGES TO OVERCOME

Despite all our best efforts, there are still significant problems. After four years of intensive work with children of low IQ combined with severe learning disabilities, we decided to rehabilitate, at our expense, 10 to 13 percent of our children in other schools that have less demanding standards. This was a severe emotional wrench for us, a traumatic experience for the children and a hard reality for the parents to accept.

This situation occurred probably due to genuine mistakes in selection. It is very difficult to evaluate a four-year-old at the time of admission for potential academic success, when learning disabilities manifest only by age seven or eight. All children do not show progress in spite of the nutrition, stimulation, high-quality care and monitoring in our program. Serious attention and learning problems begin to show up only when the child moves into a formal classroom environment after kindergarten. A few deteriorate in their development over time.

Intensive teamwork by all professionals, such as psychologists, doctors, social workers, teachers, and primary caregivers involved in looking after these children, failed to bring about desired outcomes. Staff were getting worn out by these children, as all efforts were focused on them while the other children were neglected. The peer group failed to move forward because they were slowed down by the constant behavioral- and academic-related problems of a few children.

Critics of our dismissal policy fail to recognize that quality institutions must not lower their standards to accommodate a few, regardless of the very low family income levels of the student population. I have come to realize that compassion alone cannot be the decisive factor in our efforts to help others, and with finite resources, difficult and unpopular choices have to be made for the greater good.

Our decision to let go of children who are unable to cope with the academic standards initially affected parents' confidence in our willingness to give them a helping hand. Over time, everyone began to realize that we try hard to avoid dismissing any child. Moreover, our efforts to place dismissed children in other schools and pay for their tuition fees for a transition period of three years assured parents of our genuine concern for all children.

A great majority of parents now have a positive attitude because they enjoy firsthand their children's attitudes, behavior, and educational progress during the two annual vacations and on three monthly visits. They have not found anything detrimental to their family life in what their children are exposed to at Shanti Bhavan. Parents express their appreciation and gratitude whenever their feedback is solicited by our social workers during home visits or on the occasion of parent-staff meetings. Sometimes one or two express fears, such as conversion to Christianity, fueled by rumors and sour grapes from those whose children have not been selected or those with vested interests. Now, when the season comes for recruitment of new children in February, the applicant lines are long at the Foundation House in Shanti Bhavan. With experience, we are now able to make better initial selection, and dismissals are now less than ten percent.

After losing more than half our staff in the start-up year, regular weekly training sessions for childcare workers, to bring about awareness and change their culture of skepticism and suspicion, became a priority. Issues such as caste and spirituality in its ritualistic manifestation require discussion and follow-up. Other training sessions deal with ordinary practical life tasks such as how to wear socks and buckle or lace shoes, or table manners.

Expectations are tailored to our staff profile, but universal ethical standards are not compromised. The challenge for the management is to empower the staff to deliver the vision and goals of the foundation. Getting teachers to buy into the mission of Shanti Bhavan means dealing with their cherished beliefs about the social fabric of Indian society, fatalism and karma. Changing their mind-set from seeing our children as lucky beneficiaries to seeing themselves as fortunate to serve our children is our main thrust, accompanied, of course, by financial and professional motivation.

Working with the local labor who maintain our facilities is another matter. Our female assistant facilities manager has learned how to handle male laborers and workers who refuse to take instructions from a woman. She has to manage laundry, kitchen, horticultural, cleaning and security staff who are a mix of men and women.

It has been our experience that changing staff attitudes or ways of doing things, such as teaching approaches and methods or childcare practices, is a big challenge. On the one hand, staff is eager to learn. They want to better themselves and hone their professional skills. On the other, they feel comfortable with the old ways. As with all good institutions, there is a need for continuing training programs, constant managerial vigilance for keeping up a certain amount of pressure, evaluation meetings and maintenance of records. It takes very little to slide backward. At the same time, staff need to be comfortable and secure, to have fun, and to feel that their personal needs are being met. Lalita has experienced that private sessions during which a staff member gets her undivided individual attention go a long way in boosting individual morale even if she cannot solve the perceived "problem." This is very time-consuming because there are several people vying for attention and recognition, and by the time the exercise has gone full circle for everyone, it is time to begin again with the first one.

Lalita feels the investment in terms of personal time with the staff is worth the effort because it ensures, for a while at least, the quality care of the children. On a residential campus, personal problems assume proportions that interfere with harmony among the campus community. This, in turn, directly affects staff approach to children. Children become victims of adult moods or emotional exhaustion. This exhaustion stems from the nature of the job.

Caregivers and teachers are constantly meeting children's demands for attention, love and affection. They are constantly giving but not receiving that degree of attention, love and affection themselves. Children innocently assume that adults have boundless wellsprings of energy and emotion exclusively for them. As is common to caregivers the world over, our staff is emotionally needy. The burden of meeting the emotional needs of the staff on a daily basis falls on the shoulders of the principal. Friends help to a certain extent. Some personality types feel gratified by the love of the children, but they still need adult emotional interaction.

The greatest challenge for Lalita and her senior staff is to create the right culture within the institution that would carry children and staff, in the right direction. It is not enough for the children to be academically strong. It is my hope that Shanti Bhavan will teach them to be good human beings, sensitive about the predicament of others in difficulty. The humane values of kindness and caring are just as important.

Even in their gentleness, they must acquire the ability to motivate and convince others to follow them – to be the leaders of tomorrow, regardless of the professions they choose. I want our children to go out into the world feeling good about themselves, no matter that some may not be brilliant successes in the global marketplace. If they do the best they can, and be honest and decent human beings, we will have done our job right.

Closed communities present their own share of problems. The divide between the workplace and the home scarcely exist, or the two merge. Social intercourse becomes a necessary part of professional interaction and vice versa. It is not a straightforward separation of office and home. It is like being on call 24 hours a day.

A change of scene is expensive and inconvenient. Shanti Bhavan is not a place for those who hanker after the distractions of city life or for those who are in constant need of entertainment. It is for those who find their entertainment and excitement within. Generally, it is the mature age group that finds peace in Shanti Bhavan.

For young people, it is a comfortable place to wait until marriage or better job prospects beckon. They understand that they have a workplace that is the envy of most, not only in India, but anywhere in the world. They are treated with respect, consideration and fairness. Yet all this does not take away from the relative isolation of our location. In a few years, commerce will open up close to Shanti Bhavan, and then perhaps our staff will yearn for days of peace and quiet.

A venture of this magnitude is rife with loneliness and heartache. It is not for the fainthearted. There is incisive criticism from every quarter, ruthless interrogation from those who fancy themselves as guardians of the poor, and dissent among our own rank and file when higher ethical and professional standards are enforced.

Key persons decide to walk out when they cannot keep up with the pressures of the job, leaving a dislocated program in their wake. Tough decisions are perceived as heartlessness or harshness though everyone agrees in principle about the need to resolve problems. NGOs are not expected to operate in a business-like manner, and those who have worked earlier with other NGOs in India may find our way of operating somewhat authoritative and business-like. Children are often bewildered by the fickleness of grownups. Countering their feelings of insecurity, transient it may be, demands a double effort from the remaining staff.

However tough the going for the adults, they must at all times be cheerful and loving toward the children. When someone leaves unexpectedly, we spend the time to explain to all, including the children, and try to move forward. In a closed community such as Shanti Bhavan, it is taxing for Lalita to enforce high standards of conduct on her staff while presenting a sense of security and confidence to the children.

People want to know how or why we have taken the responsibility of so many children as our own. Our response is that whatever we want for our own children, we want for the children of Shanti Bhavan. How will we manage when they are adolescents? What will happen when they grow up? Will they help their parents? What if they turn against us and criticize us for what we might fail to do for them?

To these and all other questions our response is the same. Responsibility entails risk, and as we do so willingly for our natural children, we take heart and go forward with hope for these children. We will face whatever problems we must and address our best efforts to their solutions, as we do for our own. In life, there are no guarantees, and Shanti Bhavan is no exception. We can only do our level best for our children. By now, their parents are appreciative of our work as is evinced by their championing of our institution.

One could argue that an environment like Shanti Bhavan could be too protective and sheltered for children. They are not exposed to the realities of urban life in their early school years. But our children have exposure to the reality of their family life twice a year, when they go home for the holidays three weeks in the summer and two weeks in the winter. Their parents visit every three months. Their family life and concerns form the central theme for lessons in emotional intelligence, sex education, human rights, ethics and values.

We are not training them to return to their homes but to change the world around them. The greatest aspiration or motivation that our children have is in saving their families from their present circumstances. Children often talk of the big houses they would build one day, where they would have their parents, brothers and sisters live together happily ever after.

Themes such as sexual intercourse or sexual abuse that may appear premature to some are no strangers to our children. The majority live in one small room at home, witnessing everything that constitutes family life, including sexual relations between parents. Our children are only too familiar with drunken brawls, spousal abuse, theft, rape and even murder – if not in their immediate family then in the neighbor's house or the community.

Some parents talk of getting their girls married by the age of 12. We have come to learn about a situation where the parents have already decided on whom their daughter should marry and permitted that boy to fondle her sexually by the age of 11. What privileged people consider the stuff of movies is real life for our children. They thirst to discuss their observations, experiences, anxieties, fears and insecurities.

During a self-science class, all our fourth and fifth graders reported sexual abuse, some by family members, some by friends, some by neighbors. One child even reported a doctor who had molested her twice and her cousin separately. Apparently the man was known for this, but no one confronted him because he was a doctor. Our subsequent investigation revealed he had left the locality and moved elsewhere – no one knew where or would not tell for fear of reprisal.

A month before each vacation, we encourage our children to think and discuss ways in which they can protect themselves and their siblings from possible sexual offenders, even within the family. What worries us is that the children who have described their sexual experiences with immediate family members still want to go home on vacations.

Apart from sexual-related problems, children often return from vacations with diseases and behavioral problems. Children come back with skin diseases such as scabies, infestations such as head lice and intestinal parasites, and respiratory infections. It is not unusual to have one child return from home with chicken pox and spread it to ten others.

We usually spend a month to six weeks getting the children back to proper health because infection spreads from one child to another. Class schedules are altered to accommodate absent children who stay back in the dorms or in isolated rooms. In such instances, the residential staff's burden is increased with so many sick children, and teachers are unable to progress with their lessons. Each time, the staff complains that the "cost" of sending children home for vacation is too high in terms of health and their ability to cope with so many sick children. But by the time the next vacation comes round, the staff is only too relieved to relinquish the burden of care. Some of this anxiety has dissipated since the opening of our own rural hospital next door that attends to problems at the earliest signs.

Our most compelling reason for sending the children home is to allow the child and the family to maintain their emotional bonds. We sometimes wonder whether it is worth all the trouble and expense we have to undergo upon their return. Perhaps as the children get older, they themselves may opt for vacationing at school. Whether they do or don't, we are committed to sending them home twice a year, if their parents are in a position to look after them.

Sometimes parents request us to keep their children with us during the vacation period, which we do. This might happen if a new baby is expected or if they are moving. Sometimes we advise parents not to take the child home if there is a serious problem, such as tuberculosis, in the immediate family or if the child reports sexual abuse by a father or brother or any close relative. Our clinical psychologists are usually present during such delicate interactions. While we cannot accuse parents, we need to protect the children as well. We allow supervised visits if children are not sent home for compelling reasons.

The few children, as few as half a dozen, who remain behind during vacation, have a whale of a time. Special food is prepared, outings are arranged, entertainment movies are shown, and swimming and picnics are in order. The children who do go home ask us to wait for their return so that they too can do these fun things. Most children tell us they don't want to go home, but when they see their parents, they run to them. Parents tell us that, after a couple of days at home, their children ask to be taken back to Shanti Bhavan.

We face criticism from some quarters for "taking away the children from their families" at an early age. They argue that "displacement" of children from their families is a serious act of injustice. In normal family situations, this concern would be justified as boarding schools have many downsides. But here we are dealing with a population that is unable to feed their children and where most mothers are single or living with a man other than the real father of the child.

Drunkenness, domestic violence and sexual abuse are common occurrences, while their daily life is characterized by the indignity of caste discrimination. These families are not tribal people living in remote communities far from civilization; every day they watch their landlords enjoying many of the luxuries of modern life.

Like all other parents, they, too, want to enjoy at least one square meal a day, watch television at home, travel by bus to a health clinic when sick, and educate their children in a good school. Their hopes for the future are pinned on their children taking care of them in their old age.

As a reputed journalist from the Times of India commented, "Those who criticize you for taking these children out of their home environment have not seen their dwellings or lack of them, or heard the sounds or smelled the smells or touched or tasted abject poverty. They do not know what they are talking about."

We constantly remind our children to respect their parents always, no matter how ignorant and poor they are. As they grow older, the children themselves will realize that their parents are simply victims of ignorance, traditions and superstitions. They know that we are not training them at Shanti Bhavan to go back to their huts; the children dream of the day when they will take their parents, brothers and sisters out of those huts into beautiful homes they plan to build for them, with their own money. Without exception, every parent has expressed the hope that his/her son or daughter at Shanti Bhavan will one day lift the family out of misery. Shanti Bhavan is all about opportunities we can give our children and the choices they will make when they become adults. If our children aspire to become doctors, engineers and government officials and work far from home, that will be their decision. If this is displacement of the poor, so be it.

Some Indian critics feel our children are living in luxury. On the contrary, Westerners see our facilities as adequate and clean. They see what we offer as the basic needs for living – space to sleep, work, play and eat. If ours were a school for rich or otherwise privileged children, this criticism would not come up. In fact, demands for additional facilities would probably arise as they would be paying fees.

Even some middle class and upper class Indians opine that they are the underprivileged because they have not been to a school like Shanti Bhavan. They say that our children will be spoilt by the care we give and will not be able to return to their original homes. They probably think that poor children do not deserve an excellent school. Obviously, they do not accept or understand our mission. We want our children to aspire to a better life, enjoy clean, harmonious surroundings and be comfortable in such surroundings. We want them to work hard to achieve success in all things for a better tomorrow.

Another serious challenge we constantly face is finding and keeping good staff, especially teachers. Very few people are prepared to leave home and work in a rural area for children from lower castes and poor homes. Since we deliberately do not offer any assurances of permanency, there is a certain amount of job-related insecurity. For those who do not have confidence in their own ability to do a good job, the prospect of bi-annual evaluation is scary at first. By the time they relax and understand that no one is under the gun, we lose a few panicky types.

Restructuring teaching assignments and schedules to accommodate sudden departures of staff has become routine. These are not unusual for any school, but our rural location and the section of the society we serve compound our difficulties.

The four to six months I spend in India each year in two installments do not give me sufficient time for all of the seven projects on which the foundation has embarked. Shanti Bhavan has it special needs, especially when it comes to children, and the biggest asset one must have is endless patience – something I am lacking.

I consider it my main responsibility to support and encourage my senior staff and keep everyone's spirits high. This is not a one-time thing each year. Instead, I must be in constant touch with all project directors at least once a week. When I am not in India, I keep up the communication through daily international calls that last from early morning to mid-day and numerous emails to each one.

By now, I have learned to appreciate with immense gratitude the dedication that each of the project directors has shown for the cause on which we have embarked and for their personal loyalty toward me. Jude and Lalita have been the founding senior members of our staff, and their tireless efforts and friendship have made everything possible. One day, I hope they will tell their own stories.

Lalita's footprints are everywhere in Shanti Bhavan. The very culture of Shanti Bhavan has been shaped by her personality and character. Her background was ideally suited for an institution such as this. She was schooled in convents for girls run mostly by British and Irish missionaries, and subsequently she received her teacher's training in a Catholic institution. Courses on personal character formation were a significant part of her student life, which she amply used with children. She had traveled with her father in her early days to many places, including two foreign countries where he was posted as a senior air force officer. Her background as a military wife, combined with stubborn determination, prepared her well for the difficult task of building up Shanti Bhavan.

Right from the outset, Lalita was excited about the idea of giving poor children the same facilities as privileged children, about the challenge of setting up a brand new institution from scratch, and about being a founding principal. On numerous occasions she has told me that she was always conscious of having led a privileged life, and the plight of the poor had haunted her from her childhood years. In her letters to her parents from boarding school, she would liberally pepper them with references to "our brothers and sisters" (meaning the poor), so she earned the nickname "the preacher" from her mother.

But preaching alone did not satisfy her, and when the opportunity to serve children from poor families came her way with Shanti Bhavan, she reached out without hesitation. The principalship of Shanti Bhavan did not scare her, and she dove straight into her job without hesitation or complaints. I once heard her answer a friend on how she got involved with Shanti Bhavan. She said, "I have been preparing for it all my life."

To be a principal, one has to be a teacher first. Not everyone has the psychological makeup of a schoolteacher. I have seen how high Lalita stays emotionally when she is with the children. When she is with children, she is her natural self – straight, open, loving and supportive. She is motivated by her personal hopes, aspirations and dreams for the children of Shanti Bhavan.

One needs a special gift to see through the eyes of a child, to play like a child, to understand like a child – all this is necessary for anyone in childcare professions. Abundant energy is needed, too. At the end of the day, Lalita is totally drained, both emotionally and physically, but she never complains.

I cannot think of a better person in the world for her job, be it for competence or commitment. But more than anything else, she is the best role model for all our children, boys and girls.

IMPRESSIONS OF VISITORS

Visitors remark that the children of Shanti Bhavan are very well behaved. I know they are lively or mischievous or downright pains-in-the-neck at times, just like any other children. I know that, if we leave visitors alone with a bunch of kids, they would soon feel helpless and overwhelmed and yell for help. Many of them have done so already. Not a single volunteer to date, irrespective of age or experience, has been able to handle our children without the help of our staff members.

They complain that the children "go wild." Well, what do they expect? Angels? Or do they think they have come to some magic place where the children behave differently from children anywhere else on earth? Not that these children misbehave when left free with strangers, but they are inquisitive and ask questions nonstop. It is difficult to control their enthusiasm and eagerness to interact with outsiders. They feel free and confident, and think of Shanti Bhavan as their home away from home.

We insist that volunteers must be mature enough, say 21 or so, to stay for an extended period at Shanti Bhavan and work with children. We have enough of a burden of childcare without having to extend ourselves for enthusiastic teenagers as well. Our experience with several high school volunteers, except for a few unusual young people, has revealed that they are unable to sustain their interest and keep up the momentum once they realize they have to fulfill children's demands for attention constantly. Lalita makes several departures and adjustments in the schedule and classroom arrangements to accommodate volunteers. Our observation is that volunteers have to be screened before they come to us. They are a mixed blessing, and we have learned to avoid bringing volunteers to Shanti Bhavan unless we are reasonably sure they have something of value to contribute to our children.

Visitors are welcome on Sundays, but some are very disruptive. As one sensitive visitor remarked, "Don't turn Shanti Bhavan into a zoo." Children should never be on display for visitors and should never be asked to behave any differently from how they always do. Discerning visitors will see for themselves that the children are progressing if they are happy and relaxed.

There is no need to ask children to dance, sing, or otherwise perform for visitors, as is the practice in many institutions, unless it is an occasion or a spontaneous gesture. Further, we do not allow class time to be interrupted by visitors, as it would be difficult for the teacher to regain the attention of students when the momentum of the lesson is lost.

Occasionally, we have visitors come unannounced on weekdays, and in some instances, the security is asked to turn them back. However, on Sundays we permit visitors to go around the campus escorted and interact with the children in one dorm or the other, without intruding into the privacy of everyone else, especially the caregiving staff. The arrival of all visitors is always without prior announcement to the children, even when the former Prime Minister I.K. Gujral chose to drop in one morning at short notice.

After seeing Shanti Bhavan and learning about the background of the children, many visitors have commented on how lucky the children are and that they should be grateful. While I believe we can ask the children to be appreciative of what they receive, I do not want them to feel obliged to anyone for what they readily deserve. They are born poor only by the accident of birth for which they need not feel any less deserving than those from rich homes.

The rich have gotten where they are not entirely by their hard work and talents, but to a great extent by the circumstances under which they were raised. The children of Shanti Bhavan are just as wonderful as any other, bright and loving, and I think of them as my own. They deserve the very best that every child should have, and it is for those of us who are lucky to be financially well off to do our share to make that opportunity possible.

What do I want our Shanti Bhavan children to retain in adulthood? An ever-renewed interest in what happens around them, a spirit of inquiry, courage to take risks, a thirst for adventure, service to fellow human beings, and pride of honor. I want them to retain a certain grace and willingness to acknowledge success in others. I want them to be innocent without being stupid and simple without being foolish.

I want them to develop a sense of style and form. I want them to appreciate ceremony and tradition if both are good and noble. Yet, the children must be prepared to face and suffer the heartaches of adult life; they must understand that no human being is spared pain. Suffering is perhaps what makes us human and fully alive. In falling, we must have the strength to get up, and start all over again with faith and hope. This is an education of another kind, more valuable than academic degrees.

HELPING HANDS

Though Shanti Bhavan is in India, many well-wishers in America are rooting for our children. They make endless telephone calls and car trips in their private vehicles to chase up promising donation leads. Then they collect, sort and pack all these items and keep them ready for shipment months in advance. After all their efforts, including aching backs and sore muscles, they would be pained to know how the government officials view their donations and the treatment meted out at the port customs in India.

We have paid substantial customs charges to clear used computers, school furniture, and other valuable items. One of my visits to get a permit from the central ministry in Delhi was met with a sharp question from a joint secretary as to why poor children need computers. It appears that anything of quality is the prerogative of the privileged alone. Few care to recognize that the shipped goods are for poor children. Instead of appreciation and support for the effort, we are always put through expressions of suspicion, interrogation, endless documentation, and inordinate delays.

Some wonderful people have helped us with their personal or their institutional contributions. My longtime friend, who recently passed away, Angeline Nair, financially supported the annual expense for one child each year. I had met N. Vaghul, chairman of ICICI Bank, some years ago when he spontaneously volunteered to sanction a substantial low-interest loan funded by KFW, a German development bank. He himself has embarked on programs to prepare slum children for schooling through preschool programs.

The Latter-Day Saints (LDS) Charities in Utah has been our greatest supporter with tons of milk powder, clothing and many supplies. Their generosity and willingness to help the poor children of India has been nothing short of admirable. The children of Shanti Bhavan and all the other beneficiaries should always be thankful to them for their help.

We have not been fortunate to receive much assistance from anyone else, particularly from individuals or institutions in India. International donors do not find our projects meet their models for development. On the other hand, the Indian concept of charity and philanthropy is limited, especially when it comes to communities other than their own.

There is a sea of difference between the reactions of Indian and foreign visitors to Shanti Bhavan. Foreign visitors usually want to know how they can help, and follow-up with action. While most Indian visitors wish us well and express their appreciation of our work, some react with skepticism and suspicion. The skeptics scoff at "some rich NRI's money thrown around – there must be more where that came from. These people definitely don't need any help." After visiting Shanti Bhavan and showering praises on our children and staff, no Indian visitor to date has parted with any money for the children.

In vain, we appealed to some of the corporate giants in Bangalore for help. After our initial application for used computers to one of the largest technology firms in the country, and several follow-ups for six months, we were granted an interview. We were told by their foundation that purports to have a "global vision" that computers would be given to Kannada-medium schools only.

A major health care company claims to offer revolutionary remote heart monitoring of poor rural people. I wonder whether this is what the poor really need by way of health care. Another organization has set up computer touch screens on their boundary walls for slum children to view international news and events. At the press of a button a whole new world is opened up for poor children. Amazing?

The people who have come forward to our aid are of a different mind-set. My relationship with the Church of Jesus Christ of the Latter-Day Saints started with my five-year tenure as an international financial advisor to the church during my professional career. After several years, when my social work began in India, they wholeheartedly agreed to help The George Foundation's charitable projects in whatever way they could.

LDS Charity in Salt Lake City regularly sends foodstuffs, clothing, school furniture, educational kits, hygiene requirements, bed linen and toys for the school. In addition, they assign volunteers who are prepared to do any kind of work from clearing garbage and sorting supplies to assisting or conducting educational programs for the children. They have worked tirelessly for our children, set up our school art room, and supported several projects. With LDS funding, their volunteers built a multipurpose sports arena and a laundry-drying shed for the school. One day, an LDS volunteer arrived with a pony to teach our children riding, but we found it difficult to look after the animal. We didn't want to offend them by rejecting the offer, and as luck would have it, a few days later the pony broke the rope and ran away never to be found again.

Back home in New Jersey, my friends Jack Barno and Kay Robinson, who moves around on crutches, both spend the better part of their day campaigning for used or new items of sports equipment, musical instruments, foodstuffs, footwear, clothing, library books, toys, and even dog food for use in the school. They personally collect, package and transport goods for shipment to India and deposit them in my garage at home in New Jersey.

We are constantly networking with individuals and groups of people to solicit their help, and several hours of phone time and human energy are expended to pursue a lead or appeal to donors. Jack and I often get excited calls from Kay, which go something like this: "Abraham! Guess what I found!" "Can't wait to get the stuff to you!" or "Can Jack give me a hand to pick it up?"

At times I get to see the cartons being unpacked in Shanti Bhavan. I wonder if our staff will ever know what has gone on behind the scenes to procure what they generally take for granted. I sometimes express my feelings about this to Lalita and Jude. Besides his functions as the chief operating officer, Jude runs around from pillar to post negotiating with all kinds of suppliers, and he does his best to protect the interests of the organization and its beneficiaries. He is tremendously good at improvising and solving problems, no matter how difficult they may be.

Lalita communicates her insights about all these matters to the Shanti Bhavan staff and the children at her regular training, orientation and formation sessions so that everyone is aware of what goes on and values the effort. Jude and I use Lalita as a sounding board for every major decision we make, as she has a clear sense of what we are trying to accomplish and our daily struggles to keep the projects afloat and our finances from crumbling. When I am in India, it is part of our daily routine for the three of us to meet after dinner to discuss the immediate tasks at hand and make decisions on all difficult matters. These meetings seldom break off before midnight or later, when we are all exhausted.

While those of us who are part of the venture can be proud of our achievements so far, we must not forget that the road ahead is even tougher to navigate. We need to be open to suggestions and learn from the experience of others, and we must correct our course when needed. The moment we start thinking that we have all the answers to bringing up children the right way, we are likely to make major mistakes. Yet, we must go by our convictions that are formed over time from experience, and we should never be afraid to try something new if it would make good sense under the particular circumstance.

Ours is a unique project, never before attempted anywhere in India or possibly elsewhere, and given its ambitious vision, we have to create a new model. Mistakes will be made along the way, but we must be brave enough to experiment and find our own solutions. Only then will the Shanti Bhavan model become a universal reality in practical terms.

Initially, when the idea of Shanti Bhavan was born, I thought I would start several similar institutions, but with experience I have come to realize that it would be beyond my means. I hope that Shanti Bhavan would serve as a model for others who believe in excellence among the poor.

There are hundreds of thousands of Indians or those of Indian origin, both at home and abroad, who are in a financial position to afford investing in institutions like ours, and Shanti Bhavan could help with their efforts. I dreamt of a thousand such institutions throughout the Indian rural landscape, offering the next generation of poor children that special opportunity. In the next 50 years, I thought, such an endeavor would turn out one million students who would one day be some of the most productive members of society.

They would break the cycle of poverty for their families, carry their communities with them and make major contributions to the country. It would positively impact no less than 100 million others, or many more, uplifting the economic and social status of the deprived members of our society. This is still my hope, but I am no longer confident that the world will embrace this concept. Maybe, in a few years, when the children of Shanti Bhavan begin to demonstrate the validity of this idea, others will join in.

Shanti Bhavan is a humble beginning but a major departure from the traditional ways of dealing with rural poverty and social injustice. It is just one of many steps to be taken, but it is an important one in offering good opportunities for some of the talented among the poor. This program and others like it need to coexist with a generally improved rural educational system that offers a lot more than literacy.

An educated people will be more productive, and they will demand of their institutions the kind of reforms necessary for a better life. In a developing economy like India, an educated workforce is just as important as capital. Our rural children are the future of the nation.

Chapter 5

BEYOND PROSPERITY FOR THE FEW

INDIA IN ECONOMIC TRANSITION

In 1995, I made my return to a new India that had finally decided to free itself from the constraints of the socialistic economic system it had embraced in the first 44 years of independence from British rule. During those years, successive governments had promised that a centrally managed economy would bring prosperity to all, and a vast government bureaucracy was best suited to deal with the many problems facing the country. What developed was a "mixed economy" consisting mostly of government-run industries, mixed with a few private monopolies.

People had come to expect that public enterprises would deliver the goods, employ most of the urban population, and be responsible for meeting the societal needs of everyone. The poor would be looked after with subsidies and concessions. But the results to follow were something else.

By 1991, India was drifting rapidly into economic chaos. The country's foreign exchange reserves had dwindled to dangerously low levels, foreign debt was no longer manageable, and most public industries were losing money. The government was forced to turn to the International Monetary Fund (IMF) for a financial bailout. What followed, at the urging of the IMF, was the devaluation of the rupee, elimination of several government licenses, and the unveiling of a new industrial policy that opened the economy to the private sector.

In less than two years, the government fiscal deficit fell from 8.4 percent of gross domestic product (GDP) in 1990-91 to 5.7 percent in 1992-93, and foreign exchange reserves rose to $20 billion from barely $1 billion.[6] The country was finally on the right economic path. Indians quickly learned the many lessons of capitalism that had eluded them for decades.

In the early 1900s, A.P. Giannini worked as a senior banker with a San Francisco bank. At one bank meeting, he tried but failed to get his colleagues to approve lending to small businessmen– something that banks did not do in those days– instead they lent only to wealthy people and large corporations. He got frustrated and quit and started a small bank which he called The Bank of Italy.

Shortly thereafter, the great earthquake of San Francisco leveled everything, including his bank building. Bank owners in the city closed down all banks for six months to wait and see if the city would rebuild. Giannini vehemently protested but without success. The next day he came down to the central square, placed a wooden plank over two drums and put up the sign of his bank announcing he was doing business. He made the point that a bank does not require a big building to serve the needs of the people.

Over the years, Giannini lent to small and big businesses, and when it became quite successful, he renamed it Bank of America (BoA). BoA went on to become the largest bank in America. During the Great Depression, BoA financed the building of the Golden Gate Bridge and the production of many great films, including Disney favorites Snow White and the Seven Dwarfs, Peter Pan, Cinderella, and Bambi, as well as It's a Wonderful Life and Gone with the Wind. BoA also pioneered the world's first successful use of computers in business operations and created BankAmericard – now known as Visa.

At age 75, Giannini delivered a speech at a major university in which he said, "How many of you understand the real meaning of capitalism? Capitalism comes from capital. Capital comes from savings – savings that people put in the bank. These savings are lent to businesses and individuals who are willing to take risks. Part of the returns from those loans is the profit of the bank and its investors. It is a partnership between the people, investors and the bank, democracy at its best."

Capital is like frozen energy. When you mix it with the live energy and ideas of individuals, you create new wealth and prosperity. When capital is made accessible to anyone with ideas, initiative and determination, both human and financial resources are best utilized. Ideas are turned into products and services to meet the needs of the consumer. Superior products offered at competitive prices win markets. This fact is the secret of every prosperous nation.

Giannini's story exemplifies the spirit of entrepreneurship, the importance of meeting the needs of customers and the efficient use of capital to create wealth and income. With the new reforms, India had finally begun to embrace these business values.

The first task of the Indian government in the immediate post-independence period was to improve the material and human conditions of life by stimulating rapid industrial development and to set the country upon a path for higher growth, redistribution of income and social justice. The conditions that prevailed in 1947 were simply miserable; famines adding to the interminable misery in a barren wasteland.

The country was chronically short of clean water; most people lived in villages in hunger and despair. Bullock carts, wooden ploughs, spinning wheels and thatched huts were the face of rural India. Agricultural growth was around 0.3 percent per annum, unable to keep up with the population growth rate of over 5 percent per annum. Large factories, few in number, produced mainly consumer goods like textiles and sugar, intermediates like steel and cement, and exports like jute and cotton. Illiteracy was as high as 84 percent; public health services were inadequate to handle epidemics such as influenza, typhoid, malaria and cholera; the mortality rate for children below one year of age was among the highest in the world.

National leaders promised the nation that industrial development would occur without the need to rely on foreign investment in India, poverty would be eliminated with agrarian reforms and government-supported initiatives, universal health care and education would be offered free by state run institutions, and social justice and secularism would be the very foundations of the society. These objectives were to be achieved within a democratic political framework using the mechanism of a mixed economy, where both public and private sectors co-exist, with the state guiding all social and economic aspects of life. The results that followed these policy measures were mixed at best.

Despite gains in the agricultural sector and a few others, the first 45 years following India's independence did not spur much improvement in the socioeconomic status of a great majority of its people. India's national leaders, present and past, do not like to be reminded about those years of costly mistakes or to be compared against the current performance of China or any of the successful "Asian Tigers. "

They argue that democracies cannot push through economic programs without considerable debate and deliberation, and unlike authoritarian regimes, they have to wait for consensus. These architects of India's slow growth fail to admit that it was not really democracy that delayed India's progress. Instead, India's belief in the wisdom of a centralized economy along the lines of the Soviet Union translated into everything controlled by the bureaucrats.

India adopted an economic system that discouraged the private sector through controls and licenses. Competition and predictable business conditions were absent, while intrusive labor laws handcuffed employers. Inefficiencies and incompetence were covered up by subsidies, and money-losing public enterprises continued to turn out outdated and defective products.

The bureaucracy became arrogant in its absolute power and failed to provide even minimal services without bribes and favoritism. Imports were curtailed by quotas and high tariffs, while foreign investment in the country was restricted for fear of competition and to safeguard the self-interests of politically connected Indian companies. Together, these policies punished success and rewarded failure, while politicians and bureaucrats found it comfortable to live off the people and from foreign borrowings. Citizens could not and did not use their talents and energies fully to seek progress. The result was a more-or-less stagnant economy.

It was only when the country almost went bankrupt in 1991 that its leaders were forced to listen to the IMF and make some radical changes. Since the initiation of a number of liberalization measures, the economy has witnessed rapid growth in several sectors. Annual GDP growth has averaged more than five percent, industrial growth around 6 percent and services growth nearly seven percent, while export growth has been in excess of twenty percent annually in recent years.[7]

According to some estimates, India is expected to be the next trillion dollar economy in the world. Some claim that India is poised to become the third largest economy in the world by 2050. Much hope is pinned on a steady rapid expansion of the market for global information technology services, especially in business process outsourcing, on which India expects to capitalize.

India was not the only country to embrace free market economic principles in recent years. Following the breakup of the Soviet Union in 1989 with the fall of the Berlin Wall, and before India's initiation of economic reforms, Russian President Boris Yeltsin applied his economic shock therapy of radical change at the behest of Western thinkers. A sudden lifting of price controls and tight money fired up an inflationary spiral, forcing many businesses into bankruptcy from lack of enough credit.

Russia was not a suitable patient for shock therapy. The only people who initially profited from radical economic measures in the new Russia were criminals and the old-comrade networks of bureaucrats and politicians. These new operators used illegal exports in oil and other natural resources to shift billions of dollars into private accounts in Western banks. Mafia thugs controlled many of the distribution channels. Education and health services have both deteriorated. With President Vladimir Putin's arrival, Russia is attempting to stabilize the situation with a more moderate policy leading to a free private economy, but its leaders have not yet abandoned the past militarism, as seen in Chechnya and Georgia and in the government control of the media.

Joseph Stiglitz, winner of the Nobel Prize for Economics in 2001, argues in his recent book, *Globalization and Its Discontents* (W.W. Norton & Company, 2002), that a quick implementation of market-based policies such as open capital markets, free trade, and privatization are not the right solutions for a developing country facing financial crisis. He blames the IMF for making this mistake in several Asian countries in 1997, in Russia in 1998, and Argentina in 2002, which contributed only to economic turmoil in these countries.

Stiglitz recommends that developing countries facing serious financial crises keep interest rates low and make credit available, rather than tightening the belt through fiscal austerity and monetary restraints. Instead, the time to implement the ideas of open markets and control of fiscal deficit is when the economy is doing fairly well, as is the situation in India currently.

India's change of direction that started more or less at the same time in 1991, did not involve political and social reform, as was the case in Russia, in addition to economic adjustments. The corrections needed in the Indian economy were privatization of public enterprises, relaxation of restrictions on domestic commerce and trade, removal of unnecessary licenses, fiscal and monetary restraints, reduction of bureaucracy, and introduction of competition in an economy dominated by monopolies.

At the urging of the IMF, some of these measures were implemented in a limited way, which ignited the fuel for vigorous business activity. Unlike Russia, which has been mostly an urban economy for several decades now, much of India was and still remains rural, and hence, the country could afford to apply the reforms gradually without creating major dislocations. The impact of economic liberalization on urban India was significant. The rural sector, however, was totally left out of the new policy design.

The emergence of a somewhat vibrant urban economy in India is not the result of any positive policy initiatives by the government. There was no "Marshall Plan" implemented by the government. On the contrary, the economic success of recent reforms in India is from less government involvement and from the transfer of many public companies into private hands.

Government policies, both fiscal and monetary, still remain detrimental as they channel public resources into many inefficient and undeserving sections of the economy, while fiscal deficits have crowded private enterprise out of the credit markets. However, the newfound economic freedom was enough to kindle entrepreneurship in Indians, and major consumer benefits began to be realized. The pace of reforms – more of less government – slowed down considerably following the initial three years of rapid change, as though the economy needed time to assimilate the initial dosage, and consequently, improvements in the economy were also far below the potential.

Following the early successes from economic liberalization, subsequent changes have been slow, and the country is still lacking the leadership needed to bring about steady and bold reforms. Many of the burdensome practices that held the economy back in earlier years still exist today. Equally important, India's economic liberalization was not accompanied by the development of social opportunities for all people. Consequently, the benefits have been confined to only a small segment of the population.

Even today, it is politics and not smart economics that drives economic policy in India. Instead of promoting deliberate and determined policy changes in the right direction, the present architects and "gurus" of India's economic system are simply looking for ways to find politically expedient minor corrections.

India continues to struggle with its past – centralized planning, state-run bureaucracies, and monopolistic practices that are largely responsible for the burgeoning corruption, curtailed entrepreneurship and low investment. Despite the accelerated industrial growth experienced recently, much of the nation remains poor by any standard.

While the country boasts of self-sufficiency in food, nearly half of its population does not have the purchasing power to buy enough grain, vegetables or fruit for a square meal a day. I suppose, if more people go hungry, there will be surplus food aplenty! Further, the rising expectations of the middle-class, widening income and wealth inequalities between the haves and have-nots, and lack of opportunities for a great majority of its citizens trouble the country immensely.

Today, almost every quality of life indicator shows that India is among the worst countries in the world. Hundreds of millions of Indians live their lives under deplorable conditions. There are some 350 million people (or 35 percent of the population) living below the poverty line of $1 a day, as defined by the United Nations. Under a broader definition of $2 per day, more than 50 percent of the nation is poor[15].

Many of these people have no proper shelter, no clean drinking water, no adequate sanitation, no education, and no access to basic health care. This statistic is worse than the 40 percent for all of South Asia and compares dismally with the newly formed nation of Bangladesh whose poverty rate is 29 percent. China has an even larger population than India, but only 19 percent of its people live below the poverty level.

India can no longer blame the British for the current misery facing the country; after all, even the countries of sub-Saharan Africa that became independent after India have a combined poverty rate of 43 percent, lower than India.

RELATIONSHIP WITH INTERNATIONAL ORGANIZATIONS

The World Bank and the IMF offer few apologies for their many failed attempts to increase prosperity in the world's poorest countries. Over the past 50 years, considerable developmental funds have been made available to countries like India, but severe poverty still prevails among a large section of the population. India's cumulative borrowings from the World Bank alone were nearly $50 billion, comprising over 15 percent of the bank's total lending in the past 50 years.[8]

Both the World Bank and the IMF have played major roles in the formulation of India's economic policies, and have exerted pressure at critical junctures to alter the course. Examples include the financial crisis in 1991 and the devaluation of the rupee in 1994.

Both the World Bank and the IMF want poor nations to privatize industry, improve fiscal management and embrace free trade as the way to develop their economies. The hypocrisy behind some of these recommendations is the fact that wealthy nations continue to impose barriers to imports, particularly of agricultural products and textiles.

The Doha Agreement worked out in Qatar in late 2001 by developed nations to help the world's poorest by lifting trade barriers on import of farm products has not been followed up with action. James D. Wolfenson, president of the World Bank, recently accused wealthy nations of squandering $1 billion a day on farm subsidies that often have a devastating effect on the ability of poor nations to export to rich countries. For example, the average subsidy toward maintaining a cow ranges anywhere from $3 a day in Europe to $7 in Japan, while a great majority of the people in most developing countries live on less than $2 a day[10].

The collective $50 billion in foreign aid worldwide barely offsets twenty percent of the damage from this protectionism. Subsidies have kept commodity prices low, and consequently it remains difficult for poor farmers in developing countries to compete in the export markets. Furthermore, with free trade practiced selectively, cheap imports of agricultural commodities into developing countries have increased. These products are produced on a large scale in wealthy countries using modern technologies and with the help of huge subsidies. Their import drives poor farmers in developing countries out of their livelihood.

Farmers in developing countries must first receive assistance by way of technology and capital before they can be asked to compete with imports from developed countries whose farmers are heavily subsidized.

There is no doubt that trade has helped poor countries deal with poverty at home. No longer is prosperity determined by domestic conditions alone. The technological revolution that started in the early 1990s in the West has been a boon for many Indian companies. The IT sector in India earns considerable foreign revenue from the export of technology services, and that has helped fuel the 6 percent or so annual growth experienced during the past decade. Similarly, China is in the midst of an export boom that has dramatically impacted its economic fortune.

According to the former president of Mexico, Ernesto Zedillo, "Every case where a poor nation has significantly overcome poverty has been achieved while engaging in production for export and opening itself to the influx of foreign goods, investment and technology; that is by participating in globalization."

The real question is not so much whether globalization is good or not, but how to bring about free trade and investment in a fair and reciprocal manner so that domestic industries can make the necessary orderly adjustments.

Arguing about the perceived inequities in free trade as practiced today, India continues to demonize the World Trade Organization (WTO), instead of figuring out ways to accommodate the new relationships. Its tariffs are, on average, 32 percent – more than three times higher than most Asian countries, and other hidden barriers also block trade. India has to learn from the trade and investment policies that China and Japan have adopted in the relationships with their Southeast Asian neighbors to benefit from globalization. Needless to say, the country needs political leaders who have the background and capacity to comprehend the true dimensions of globalization.

Frequent protests in front of the World Bank and the IMF headquarters in Washington, D.C., and at international economic conferences bring to focus the lack of sufficient progress in dealing with poverty in most developing countries. It is true that after half a century of assistance by these and other international institutions in areas of agricultural output, job creation, education, health, and infrastructure development, more people are in poverty now than at any time before.

Most of the aid-recipient countries have shown little or no economic progress. For decades, aid was used by wealthier nations as a reward for political allegiance, and economic results were only secondary. Protesters point out the increasing concentration of wealth and power in a few nations, widening disparity in living standards, and the mindless destruction of the environment. The countries that are recipients of aid have not used those funds for the intended purposes.

Despite all the aid, the gap between rich and poor nations has only widened. Today, this ratio is 72 to one. About half the people on this planet today live on less than $2 a day, and a third on less than $1 a day.

Is it that the people at the bottom of the ladder do not have the same opportunity for upward social mobility, and hence, the inequity between the haves and the have-nots is simply destined to increase? All available statistics point to that unacceptable conclusion. United Nations Secretary General Kofi Annan thinks that $50 billion in additional annual aid could solve the problem, but that is only if the funds are put to productive use.

Admittedly, the protestors are generally correct in their assertions about the condition of poor nations, but the questions that need to be asked are: who is to be blamed for this failure, and what fundamental changes are needed? There is no doubt that both corporations and governments need to break out of their patterns of indifference and acceptance of the status quo. It is also no secret that billions of dollars have been wasted by many governments on projects that have yielded little or no benefit to the intended segment of society, the poor.

Even in countries that have experienced rapid industrial development in the past decade, the living conditions in rural areas have improved very little. The World Bank's own internal documents reveal that the bank had for years focused on promoting foreign investment in developing countries without considering how the governments were likely to spend the money they received. In India alone, despite considerable sums of money lent for rural development to benefit more than 650 million people, or nearly two-thirds of the total population, their social and economic status has changed little. The way programs are currently managed by the government, the present condition is not likely to change significantly in the foreseeable future. The situation is not much different in most other developing countries.

Corrupt governments and inefficient bureaucracies are to blame for the failure to surmount poverty. The reason for most failed projects is not lack of funding. When governments use the funds for political patronage rather than development, they support incompetent but politically connected administrators and employees, create institutions that are not properly conceived or operated and hire crooked contractors who build substandard roads.

Yet, corruption has long been the forbidden "C-word" inside the World Bank. Although that climate started to change by the mid-1990s, it is still difficult for the institution — whose board consists of countries that finance and borrow from it — to criticize its members openly, let alone do something about it. International institutions, generally working through governments, are in no position to bring about the much needed internal reforms and fundamental changes in governance in any developing country.

So, how should international development and lending agencies reform themselves? Perhaps, the protestors ought to be telling the World Bank not to fund projects through corrupt governments and inefficient bureaucracies. Alternately, new ways need to be found to directly involve the private sector and NGOs, without the crippling governmental intervention. Also, as it would be expected in the private sector, projects that fail to meet their milestones should not receive continued funding. Officials at these developmental agencies cannot simply complain among themselves that they have to work with corrupt officials who are not likely to put the funds they receive to any good use, and then go on to finance projects that later turn out to be failures.

The time has come to demand strict accountability and performance on the part of recipients of funds in developing countries. Unless the provider

of funds is able to conduct independent audits, free of governmental interference and claims of sovereignty, developmental assistance should not be
made available. By the same token, international funding agencies must be
made accountable for demonstrating the value added by the funds they have
dispersed previously.

ADEQUACY OF ECONOMIC RESOURCES

Wasted foreign assistance is one thing, but are the limited resources of the
country also to blame for the extreme poverty in which many Indians live
today? Since the government considers it a duty to care for the poor, let us
first examine the resources available to the central government through taxation. The central government expenditure on defense (twenty percent), debt
service (fifty percent), and payments to central government employees (7.5
percent) is in excess of seventy-eight percent of the total government expenditure, leaving barely twenty-two percent of the budget for all other items,
including programs for poverty eradication.[11]

Obviously, the country has piled up a huge debt over the years, one that
has to be paid back periodically, drawing away the much-needed capital for
infrastructure, maintenance and social spending by central and state governments. In addition to the interest burden, the main culprits for the budget
deficits are low tax revenues from a narrow tax base and the high costs of
subsidies.

A significant portion of individual and corporate income is either exempt
or hidden from taxation (less than 20 million tax payers), while the growing
service sector is inadequately taxed, and the agriculture sector is exempt from
taxes. Implicit and explicit subsidies at the central and state levels consume
nearly sixteen percent of the GDP. One has to wonder how the nation got
itself into this mess in the first place and why it has not come out of it after
55 years of independence.

India does have its share of the world's natural resources and sufficient
cultivable land and water resources. Then why is it that the country has not
accumulated sufficient wealth to repay its debt? The ability to create wealth is
fundamental to a successful economy.

Lack of natural resources do not make countries poor, just the same way
as natural riches do not make countries wealthy. South Korea, Taiwan and
Japan are clear examples of countries with limited natural resources that have
prospered through policies designed to create new wealth. Wealth creation
depends on a country's human and natural resources being open for competi-

tion and innovation and whether businesses can rely on secure and fair rules of the game before taking prudent risks. It is not clear whether the absence of a homogeneous population in India is a contributing factor for the inability to mobilize the country's human resources effectively.

OVERCOMING HURDLES

Until recently, the West had overlooked India's potential as an economic partner. It took the global demise of socialistic economic policies and the general acceptance of free enterprise to bring the West and India into a closer economic relationship. The economic reforms of 1991 and the liberalization measures subsequently introduced show that the country's leaders finally understand the importance of an open economy.

The West has now recognized India's vast pool of technically qualified engineers and computer programmers, and with low wages and salaries, the country offers significant cost advantages to foreign companies in outsourcing and setting up manufacturing facilities for both domestic and export sales.

There is no doubt that India cannot surge forward without major investment in both the public and private sector. The government cannot afford to increase its already high fiscal deficit (2001-2002) of nearly 6 percent of the GDP for the federal and over 4 percent of the GDP for the states to finance its much-needed investments in physical and social infrastructure.

With financial institutions forced to buy up government debt instruments, such as treasury bills and bonds, private companies do not have access to sufficient domestic funds at reasonable interest costs to make major improvements in technology and for modernization of factories. India cannot rely on knowledge-based companies alone for growth or to finance its external capital needs; the manufacturing sector must be improved to broaden India's offerings.

What's needed is considerable inflow of external capital in the form of foreign direct investment in India. Substantial foreign investment will not arrive until India projects a welcome attitude, as opposed to the present barrage of criticism about multinational companies and their profit motives. Investor concerns about poor infrastructure, rigid labor laws, communication difficulties, red tape, lack of confidence in the sanctity of contracts, uncertain property rights and corruption have to be addressed seriously before India is seen as a real investment alternative to China.

As Amartya Sen points out in *Development as Freedom* (Anchor Books, 1999), it is expanding human freedoms that we want to strive for, rather than the narrower views of development as measured by GNP or the rise in personal incomes. This broader goal of freedom encompasses several other determinants such as education, health care, justice and individual freedom. Sen defines five types of freedoms: political freedoms, economic facilities, social opportunities, transparency guarantees, and protective security.

Political freedom is more than the ability to elect those who should govern; it is also the possibility to scrutinize and criticize authorities and to express the citizens' views through uncensored press. Economic facilities refer to the opportunities that individuals must have to avail themselves of the economic resources, especially access to finance and credit, for consumption and production. Social opportunities are those that the society makes available for education, health, and so on. Transparency deals with the openness that people can expect in government and private transactions to prevent corruption, financial irresponsibility and underhanded dealings. Finally, protective security ensures that people who fail do not fall into abject misery and that they are supported while trying to get back on their feet.

All these freedoms complement and strengthen each other. When any one of these freedoms is denied, society fails to achieve its broader goals measured in terms of quality of life. India needs to find its right balance in economic policy between Western forms of corporate capitalism and the active involvement of the state in meeting the pressing needs of its large underclass.

India ranked 119th in the "2003 Index of Economic Freedom" published by The Heritage Foundation and the *Wall Street Journal.* The index ratings reflect an analysis of 50 different economic variables, grouped into 10 categories: banking and finance, capital flows and foreign investment, monetary policy, fiscal burden of the government, trade policy, wages and prices, government intervention in the economy, property rights, regulation, and black market activity.

Hong Kong retains the top spot as the world's freest economy followed by Singapore. Luxembourg and New Zealand tied for third place, while the United States was ranked 6th. Economies that are in the top ratings have relatively low levels of corruption and have cracked down on the black market. The report finds that countries enjoying the highest economic freedom also have higher long-term growth rates and prosper more than those with little economic freedom.

Countries like India that have lower ratings suffer from extensive corruption in politics and governance. The latest data available from the World Bank shows that per capita income for "mostly unfree" or repressed economies averaged only about $3,400 in 2000, about a third of the average of $12,569 for "mostly free" economies. "Highly free" economies on an average had a per capita income of $26,855. According to some estimates, India's per capita income on a purchasing power parity basis was around $2,000 to $2,500 in 2000, and in nominal terms less than $500 per annum.

When we compare the success of some of the leading economies of the world to India's present conditions, what lessons can we draw about the country's economic system and policies? During the last 50 years, we witnessed the strong re-emergence of Western Europe and Japan from the destruction caused by World War II, bringing about great prosperity to their peoples. Even China has made considerable economic progress during the past 25 years following several years of international isolation.

The very foundation of those notable achievements is nothing other than the economic freedom and opportunity enjoyed by their citizens. The socialistic path followed by India until recently failed to meet the needs of a rapidly growing population, but have the reforms of the past decade or so produced an exemplary economic outcome?

Every country is unique in its own way, but there are also many similarities with other nations that permit one nation to learn from the lessons of another. With that thought in mind, let us take a look at the post-reform economic progress of India, compared to China. A decade ago, both India and China had close to the same per capita income, but today China's per capita is around $920, double that of India.

In 1991, China produced 670 billion kilowatt hours of electricity compared to 290 billion in India. Today, China's electricity production exceeds 1.25 trillion kilowatt hours while India is about 500 billion. In 1991, China received $2.8 billion from tourism, and in 2001 it was more than $15 billion, while India's tourism income rose from $1.4 billion in 1991 to around $3 billion in 2001. In 1991, both India and China had less than one computer for every 1,000 individuals. Today, China uses 15 computers per 1,000 individuals, as compared to around four per 1,000 in India.

The manufacturing sector of the Chinese economy grew from 37 percent of the GDP in 1990 to 45 percent by 2001, while India experienced a decline from 30 percent to 24 percent during the same period. China's trade as a percentage of the GDP grew from 35 percent in 1991 to over 50 percent by 2001, while India's trade grew from 18 percent to 30 percent. China's exports are nearly six times India's current exports.

Finally, foreign direct investment in China was $47 billion during 2001, nearly 21 percent of worldwide investments, while India attracted only $4 billion, or 2 percent of the total. What is truly notable is that China's transformation is trickling even into the poor interior, pulling all 1.3 billion people into the world economy. Human and financial resources are growing and being deployed more sensibly, and a ferocious drive and work ethic are galvanizing the entire country.

When historians look back on our time, I think they'll focus on the resurgence of China after 500 years of weakness – and the way India drags along without clear focus and bold policies. These disparities illustrate an underlying trend: Yes, India is making progress but far below its potential.

How does India remedy the present situation quickly? Obviously, the strategy for national development has to be based on clear and proven principles and priorities to be successful. The aim is to have long-term sustained economic growth that would steadily raise the real standard of living of all India's citizens. Uplifting the lives of the poor should be a major priority. To accomplish this goal, the nation must address many of the root problems that have prevented it from surging forward.

Prior to the reforms that started in 1991, the country did not encourage private ownership of businesses. Even today, there is some reluctance to make the much-needed transfer of business ownership from public to private hands. India's privatization program has been stalled now for several years mainly because of the political rift between those who still want to maintain stiff government control over the economy and those who are prepared to allow gradual transformation. Also, privatization must not lead to the creation of monopolies within the private sector. The oil and gas industry is an example where sale of public companies to major private companies who dominate the energy markets is being considered.

The key to faster economic growth in India is to replicate the productive processes evident in some of its best companies in other businesses and government establishments. Productivity is the result of implementing new ideas and methods freely and investing in people to be creative. To unleash the potential for higher living standards and job creation, the nation's leaders must make an unwavering commitment to good governance, economic freedom, and investment in people through education and health.

Higher capital and labor productivity translate into greater wealth creation. Higher productivity comes from smart tradeoffs companies make between giving customers what they want and operating efficiently. For example, reliable and low-cost telephone and high-speed communication capability encourage consumers to use more Internet services in America than anywhere else.

Efficient use of capital is essential to avoid waste; low entry barriers, intense competition on price and value, and frequent business failures and start-ups make American managers conscious of the productive use of capital. Publicly run companies in India fail to understand the true importance of productivity as the driving force for wealth creation. As in the case of the Soviet Union and now Russia, whose economic model India followed for 45 years, the people of both countries are still paying for the mistakes of the past and deliberate mismanagement by present day governments.

NEWFOUND ECONOMIC OPPORTUNITIES

Much of India's hope for rapid economic growth seems to hinge on the gains to be made by its IT sector, which in turn is impacted by foreign economic forces. As India embarked on its economic liberalization program in 1991, America also began to realize a sort of industrial revolution fueled by technology. Innovations that brought about faster computer chips led to explosive growth in the use of computers in industry and in personal computing.

Fiber optics networks, cable, faster modems and routers, satellites and other communication devices made the transfer of large volumes of information possible in milliseconds. The distribution of goods, services and knowledge is now carried out through the Internet, bringing down the cost of products, services and research. The result: increased productivity.

After two decades of annual productivity growth in the United States of around 1 percent, the 1990s experienced two percent annual increases, and the current decade is expected to show no less than a two and a half percent increase per annum. This environment drew investors into new and existing companies, and capital spending nearly doubled during the 10 years ending 2000. According to a McKinsey study, data-gathering efficiencies could further increase by a factor of three over the next decade, written and oral communications by around two times and group problem solving by 1.5 times. Despite the economic slowdown experienced since early 2000, technological innovations and productivity growth are expected to continue at a fast pace in America.

All these did not come to pass without any impact on India. From the mid-1990s, a shortage of technically qualified personnel to support the expansion in America, and to a lesser degree in Europe, prompted Western companies to turn their search for computer software programmers to India. Companies like Infosys, Tata Consultancy and Wipro recognized this huge demand for technical personnel and promptly set up their organizations to meet the needs of foreign companies.

Bangalore, Mumbai, Chennai and Hyderabad soon became the recruitment grounds for software specialists. Also, many Western companies set up small shops in India to conduct and supervise their software work using relatively low-salaried Indian software engineers. The result was an explosive growth in IT services provided by Indian companies and by Indian personnel working for foreign-owned companies in India.

Technology parks sprung up in many places, and export revenue from software development brought in much-needed foreign exchange. Salaries of computer-trained workers shot up several-fold, while their employers substantially increased their revenues and profits. Indians joyfully called this the "IT Revolution."

On the eve of the new millennium, I asked one young software engineer in Bangalore what he thought of the IT boom taking place in his city.

He replied, "We have just completed removing all the zeros. After all, Indians invented the zero."

He was referring to the year 2000 programming bug that existed in millions of lines of software code that could have caused havoc with computer systems. Thousands of Indian software programmers were working on fairly low-level and repetitive jobs but generating hundreds of millions of dollars for their employers. These engagements opened doors to many Indian companies for future contracts from Western companies, mainly for what is called "contract programming."

Sitting in Bangalore and other Indian cities, Indian software teams would work on specifications provided by foreign companies, and those newly written programs would be tested and altered until they met the necessary requirements. Indian companies also sent young programmers to America and Europe to work at lower than the normal host country salaries, offering significant cost savings and filling many open jobs in the software industry.

There was nothing to be ashamed of in this humble beginning. After all, technically qualified Indians filled the great demand for software programmers during the technology boom that was taking place all around the world during the late 1990s. Today, there are more than 250,000 IT-related Indian workers in the United States on temporary visas and work permits. Realizing the cost savings, Western companies looked for many other IT-related services that could be handled remotely from India.

Indians were soon hired to enter volumes of information such as medical records into databases, operate back-office activities such as generating reports and confirming transactions, monitor the execution of routine computer tasks, and provide online and telephone customer support through what are termed "call centers." For foreign companies dealing with their Indian IT service providers, the emphasis has now shifted from development of new applications to maintenance and product enhancements that would add value much quicker and demonstrate a higher return on investment.

Many of these activities do not require highly qualified software personnel, but the number of staff needed is fairly high, opening job opportunities for many. Familiarity with the English language is another favorable factor. Quality, low cost and reliability are the *mantras* that attract foreign companies. With proper training in the operation of relevant applications, Indians quickly began to service Western companies in a range of routine back-office tasks at considerably lower costs than management could find in their own countries. With this new thrust, the IT industry in India now expects to contribute as much as five percent of the GDP by 2007 from the 2001 level of 1.7 percent.

India has an estimated half-million individual software developers, and more are in the making. They are ready to write programs for some of the world's largest corporations. Further, India and China potentially offer two of the largest software markets of the future for multinational companies. Companies like Microsoft would like to see several applications developed in India that would use its Windows operating system and other software tools, instead of alternative platforms like Linux.

Watching Indians harvest the opportunity in technology-related services, many other countries began to enter the field. China, Russia and several eastern European countries also have qualified programmers, and they have begun to gear up to compete with the Indians. At least for now, Indians have a major competitive advantage in their familiarity with the English language, something that these other countries are now trying to gain. All have begun major initiatives to teach their software engineers the English language, and in a few years, they could be formidable competitors for many of the tasks required by Western companies.

Unless the Indian IT industry is able to move up the technology ladder in terms of the services offered to foreign companies, global competition for low-paying activities will soon cut into both market share and profit margin. Foreign companies can be persuaded to shift some of the higher-end services to India, if they are offered quality and value, as opposed to simply cost savings.

Indian companies must offer a professional workforce with high technical skills, personal integrity and cultural sophistication to deal with senior managers in foreign multinational organizations to win and keep major contracts. Political and social stability and adequate infrastructure are also factors that play a major part in the decision by foreign companies on where to locate their offshore operations.

Realizing the impending threat from foreign competitors, major Indian companies have already started to move up the value chain and expand the kind of services they offer. They are approaching Western companies with proposals to run part of a company's IT department or shift many of the IT activities to India. Their sales pitch – high quality services at highly competitive prices – is music to the ears of cost-conscious business executives in the United States and Europe. Now, in addition to business processing and "call centers" that provide customer support and telemarketing, Indian IT companies are trying to find customers in recession-proof industries such as pharmaceuticals and utilities.

Western companies are most interested in shifting IT operations to India where salaries are only a fraction of what is paid in their home countries. Some have even opened new research laboratories in India. By 2003, Indian companies began to win larger outsourcing contracts in excess of $1 million annually, compared to the average contract award of $250,000 previously.

With a large arsenal of qualified engineers, India is well poised to attract continuing foreign outsourcing contracts and production facilities for export of manufactured goods as well. The domestic market created from the rising income levels of some 250 million middle-class Indians is in itself a major attraction to foreign investors.

The two to five million rich people (by Indian standards) and another 50 million or so who have attained the upper middle class status are an attractive market for higher priced foreign goods. They have shown great appetite for the many comforts of life, which are being met by a wide array of products and services, both domestic and foreign, with designer labels, reputed brand names, and convenience packaging. Most business observers are excited by this new lucrative market and predict even further prosperity for both consumers and producers.

The increased economic activity will certainly benefit even those who are not directly involved. The unanswered question is whether there will be sufficiently large foreign investment in India and exports to major markets abroad to create enough new jobs and higher income for a great majority of the population. Despite all the predictions of a boom in offshoring by foreign companies, the best bet is that only three million or so jobs will move out of the United States in the next decade.[9] There is also mounting pressure placed on foreign companies, especially in America, by state governments, labor unions and some political groups to limit or possibly curb outsourcing.

The main concerns of foreign companies are about social and political instability, bureaucracy, and the infrastructure constraints they face in India. Until recently, India was rated among the worst countries for business climate due to its prevailing bureaucratic red tape, unpredictability of regulations, corruption, and poor enforcement of contracts and patents by the legal system.

While the experience of the past decade in the IT sector has eased some of those worries, the recent military confrontation with Pakistan that led to the recall of foreign nationals from India and the Gujarat communal violence in 2002 have not been helpful. Further, India needs to be seen as more open to foreign goods, services, and investments, with lower tariffs and less constraints on foreign ownership. Better professionalism among Indian managers with good work ethics and broad understanding of foreign cultures would also help an economy led by service exports.

The advent of the Internet age has opened up many opportunities for India, especially given its large technological human resource. It should be noted that war-torn countries like Japan, Germany and France slowly gained ground during most of the post-World War II era by adopting United States technology and adding their own innovations. In 1970, United States per capita income was thirty-one percent higher than that of other major industrialized countries. By 1991, the difference had narrowed to only ten percent. But with the dawn of the Internet age, the gap started to widen to over twenty-two percent by 2000.[12]

This phenomenon is historically unique and shows the power of technological improvements. Unless India finds a way to embrace the technological advances currently taking place, other industrialized countries will gain the advantage. It is not enough to focus on the export of business processing services. Concerted initiatives must be made to extend quickly the benefits of information technology internally to all sectors of the domestic economy.

This requires a change in mind-set from India's policy makers to abandon worthless old practices for bold changes that would stimulate an innovative business environment. For example, what good has it done to limit the number of Internet Service Providers (ISPs) to just one for a long time and charge for local telephone call. The goal should be to make it easier and cheaper for as many people as possible to use and benefit from the Internet?

Even today, consistently making clean telephone connections on calls within Bangalore, the IT capital of India, is not possible, and international calls into Bangalore offer nothing better than third-rate service even at one of the highest tariff rates in the world. These types of problems cut productivity significantly, make commerce difficult and project an unfavorable image to foreign businesses, when in fact the solutions can be easily implemented.

Without improvement in productivity to compete in the global marketplace, the relative cost of production will remain high unless labor wages and salaries are kept low, which is what Indian companies have been doing. The benefits of an expanding economy are not sufficiently felt by ordinary workers.

The wrenching revelation of an increasingly open market is forcing a fundamental rethinking of what a company does. More and more savvy companies avoid building expensive, time-consuming in-house capabilities. Instead they form partnerships with their suppliers and outsource much of the manufacturing, assembling and even distribution. Consumers are given direct access to manufacturers to customize exactly what they want, bypassing the traditional channels of order taking.

These innovations in business have offered opportunities to Indian companies and NRIs to start new businesses utilizing new technology and processes to cater to Western companies. So far, several new Indian enterprises have been immensely successful, while many have failed. Business has never been about avoiding tough choices and risks. What is different this time is that past experience may be the worst teacher of all. Indian companies that have incorporated new technologies and world-class management methods are able to win foreign contracts and export orders.

The Internet will soon begin to shape the future of India's democracy and its economic system. It has already opened up dialogue among citizens and with the outside world, forcing increased transparency in public affairs. Governments are not always aware of the fire that is smoldering; the invisible revolution created by information, ideas and discontent cannot be stopped.

When a large segment of the population starts accessing the Web, governments will not be able to manipulate public opinion with false or partial information through the conventional media. Secret practices that are in self-interest instead of public interest will be uncovered. Through real democratic processes, people will gain the upper hand and governments will be forced to assume their legitimate role as the servant of the people.

India has little choice about international trade and foreign investment in the domestic economy. The country must export $5-$6 billion worth of goods additionally each year to service the $20-$25 billion of foreign investment it must have to improve infrastructure and introduce modern technologies.

India's cultural reaction to imperialism and Nehru's socialistic philosophy that spilled over into economic policy has caused a misguided mistrust of global economic forces. Economic self-reliance, as opposed to economic interdependence, had become the defining character of national independence from foreign powers. The current thinking has changed somewhat, thanks partly to the influence of NRIs seeking new investment opportunities in India. With their business experience abroad, it is for the NRIs to illustrate the virtue of assimilating new ideas, innovation, and change.

Unfortunately, the image among many foreign investors is that India is only partially open to foreign investment and the opportunity to make money there is limited and could be restricted further in the future. Rule-based treatment of foreign direct investments consistent with international norms, as opposed to licenses permitted by negotiation with corrupt government officials, would be a step in the right direction.

Foreign companies are always looking at several alternative investment opportunities, and they still don't see India's present and likely future business environment to be conducive enough to attract them. The principle of economic self-reliance that is rooted in a profound mistrust of global economic forces is misguided and will greatly reduce India's economic opportunities in the Information Age.

Participating in globalization is essential for India's economic success in the next century, and this must happen all across the board – manufacturing, service industries, finance, and even defense. Just as China has done in the past decade, India must also broaden its offerings to the world marketplace in sectors other than information technology and textiles. That would require, to start with, a better business environment to attract foreign investors into India.

The economic system must permit and encourage new ventures to compete and thrive among established firms, and that includes foreign companies in partnership with Indian businesses in practically every sector. This openness alone will assure continuous inflow of technology, efficient production processes, improvement of quality, economies of scale, responsiveness to consumer needs, and fair pricing practices. When companies operate with increased productive efficiency, they create more wealth for their shareholders and offer better value to consumers.

ENTRENCHED PROBLEMS

Inefficient domestic companies in many sectors are still protected from foreign competition through high tariffs on imports and restrictions on foreign investment. Also, there has to be a real acceptance of the fact that entrepreneurship is the key to economic development; the entrepreneur is willing to undertake investment activity in a competitive economy, take financial risks, innovate, and introduce new products, all of which create wealth, employment and new capital for further economic activity.

It is the opportunity offered every individual that creates economic wealth. Until politicians and policymakers truly embrace this fact, economic reforms will be slow in coming.

Even after a dozen years of liberalization, restrictive labor laws and monopolistic practices are still widespread in India, and they have led to inefficiencies, poor quality and higher cost to consumers. Sheltered from internal and external competition, monopolies and publicly run companies feel less compelled to improve quality, offer superior services, or reduce costs through improvements in production processes. The problem is best overcome by operating as far as possible on an international rather than a national scale in a competitive environment.

For example, when the government opened the door to foreign investment in automotive manufacturing and relaxed licensing requirements for carmakers, overall productivity increased by over two-hundred fifty percent during an eight-year period from 1992 and increased employment in the industry by twelve percent.[13] This successful model has not been copied in most other industrial sectors.

International attention on India, especially among those who deal with foreign and economic issues, has lately shifted to the implications of foreign investment and export on aggregate growth and balance of trade. For a country like India, with wide disparity in income among its population, standard measures of national economic performance, such as the GDP, can be misleading.

Information derived from market-based numbers is probably a more reliable measure of the country's performance than government statistics on the health of the economy. The total value of a country's marketable securities, such as stocks and bonds issued by government and private industry, adjusted for inflation, might represent a superior indicator of national wealth creation.

But this presupposes efficient capital and money markets that are adequately regulated and grounded in internationally accepted accounting and audit standards. However, most measures of economic performance, whether market-based or government-published gross national statistics, fail to highlight the disparity between rich and poor, between urban and rural.

Much of the focus is on measures of overall performance such as GDP and inflation rate, but this does not tell the story of nearly the majority of Indians who are below the poverty level. Wealth creation for a few might mask stagnation and even deterioration in living standards for citizens. What is more important to know in a country like India is the economic status of rural population and whether income distribution is indeed taking place.

What is really holding India back? While the Indian economy has been among the fastest growing in the world on an aggregate basis for the past decade, its social indicators are still poor by most measures of human development. The transition from a state-dominated economy to a market-oriented system that offers equal opportunity for all has been uneven. Economic progress is mostly confined to the urban sector, but even there, it is much below its full potential. The explanations given for the failures range from the country's culture, religious beliefs and caste system, to the climate. But it is also evident that Indians are sufficiently entrepreneurial to adapt to changing situations, discarding old ways when they are permitted to do so.

The real reason for India's troubles may lie in the fundamental fact that the country has been poorly governed for decades. For all these years, individual rights have been subordinated to the "interests of the society," the latter being defined in each instance to suit the wishes of those in power. The result has been and continues to be that laws are not uniformly enforced, individual rights are not sufficiently protected against the excesses of the government, entrepreneurship is not adequately encouraged and economic opportunities are not fairly available to all.

To compound all these difficulties, the heavy hand of the government is still a burden that its citizens must continue to bear. As Prime Minister Atal Behari Vajpayee pointed out in his address to the National Development Council in 1999, "People often perceive the bureaucracy as an agent of exploitation rather than a provider of service. Corruption has become a low risk and high reward activity." It is now apparent to most people both in and outside the government establishment that the government is often the problem, not the solution.

Most people will argue, and rightly so, that heavy regulation, choking bureaucracy and poor governance are the three major reasons for the nation's failure to realize its potential. Public service in India has become synonymous with inefficiency, arrogance and corruption. According to a 2003 World Bank report, India is among those countries in the world that have heavy regulations. Further, the regulations are enforced unevenly in its various states.

Compounding the problem is the long delays in resolving commercial disputes within the court system. It takes 10 years on average in India to finalize a bankruptcy settlement. The report concludes that heavier regulation is usually associated with more inefficiency in public institutions, causing longer delays and higher costs. The consequence often is higher unemployment, more corruption, and less productivity and investment.

Since such government policies as price controls, licensing restrictions, permits, subsidies, duties and other interventions place burdens on transactions, they present clear opportunities for corrupt authorities and businesspeople to seek special favors. Corruption usually results in closing competitive doors and reducing efficiency. Only through a reduction in the government's role in the economy will corruption also decline.

That is not to say that regulations are not necessary. In fact, free markets and regulations go hand in hand. What is needed is strict enforcement of regulations to prevent many of the excesses – anti-competitive practices like price fixing, deceitful manipulation of markets, untruthful advertising, and so on – without being intrusive in the free working of markets and their self-corrective mechanisms.

In addition to getting rid of unwanted regulations and red tape, there is a need to place checks on government agencies' ability to institute new regulations. A broad set of regulatory reforms must encompass upgrading regulatory norms to international standards. Paperwork reduction, elimination of unwanted regulations and cost-benefit justification must be addressed before implementing new regulations.

If a regulation is likely to result in a major increase in consumer costs or a significant adverse impact on competition, it should not be implemented. These measurers alone could contribute another four percent to the nation's annual growth. According to a recent McKinsey Global Institute study, India could achieve ten percent growth rate if it would remove barriers to free markets and relinquish control over government-owned businesses.

There is a high degree of cynicism over the transparency and accountability of the Indian government at practically all levels. The misuse of public funds for personal and party purposes hardly gets any scrutiny. India is one of the few democracies where ministers and senior officials are immune to prosecution for most crimes unless special permission can be obtained from the governor and the cabinet.

The uncertainty resulting from the discretionary authority of government officials and the arrogance often associated with it, as opposed to the clarity provided by purpose-independent laws, necessitate the diversion of effort from the economic function of production to the political function of influencing the decision-making process. Corruption in government is so widespread and entrenched that it has terribly lowered the respect for constituted authority. There is very little redress possible as corrupt officials occupy positions at practically all levels.

With erosion of belief in the evenhandedness of public officials comes the need to cultivate special contacts, to develop enough "pull" to offset the claims of others. The amount of time and energy devoted to making these contacts is immense. The opportunities for bureaucrat bribing are directly related to the scope of the government's intervention in transactions between private parties. To those in the private sector who have dealt with India's bureaucracy on any major project, it is clear that the government is a drag on progress. The public sector drifts along with inefficiency, while the private sector is constrained by a government bureaucracy with a finger in every pie.

To get a sense of the bureaucratic hurdles and corruption that businesses face in India, one need only examine the customs process. Our foundation's humanitarian operations in India periodically receive donations from abroad that arrive in containers at one of the ports. The difficulty in clearing customs starts from the moment the container is brought from the ship, and we have to obtain an order to open it for inspection.

The customs department says that the collector's certificate of our status as a trust doing humanitarian work is not an original. The original certificate had already been submitted once before for an earlier shipment. The fact that we had previously established our charitable status does not count; each time, we have to get our status re-established. In a couple of days, we usually manage to obtain another letter from a senior government official and satisfy the customs officer.

Invariably, the value of goods shown is not accepted. Used items also have to be valued. Since we seldom know the variety of used items contained until the last moment, it could take up to three days to find their values in the local market.

For each shipment, Jude Devdas, our operating executive, has to attend to the matter personally to convince the customs officials on the genuine nature of our charitable work. Copies of trust deed and official letters stating our humanitarian work do not satisfy the customs officials. The stated value of imported items is always in question regardless of their non-commercial purpose. In the mean time, demurrage charges mount.

With some luck, we manage to satisfy the officials and wait for the customs officer to turn up to give the "open lock" order. Orders are now issued to "de-stuff" or take out the goods from the container. This manual operation requires the hiring of local labor. Three-fourths of the items in the container are usually removed. The customs officer can inspect all the cartons or a few samples of items depending on how much trouble they would like to give us. This procedure starts in the afternoon and often continues until late in the evening. If the process is not completed by that first evening, there is a serious risk that the items left outside for inspection will be stolen. We usually have at least two of our own staff at the docks to keep an eye on the items when the container is opened.

We usually have some donated items, such as used desks, chairs and computers, that fall into the category of customs duty. Sometimes, even food items such as tuna fish and cheese are "suspected" of being sold to hotels, as poor children are not expected to eat them. Female customs officers like books, clothes and dolls. Male customs officers like items such as VCRs and electronic equipment. We have to agree to give them a few choice things to escape high duty on such items.

The customs agent carries his report to the deputy commissioner in the Customs House on the docks. The deputy commissioner might or might not create problems. Either way, the shipping agent gives a standard premium or "personal fee." If there are any "tricky" items, additional special fees must be paid. This process could take up to three days. If any official is not satisfied, the process could take up to ten days.

The appraisal officer goes through the papers to check their authenticity. We are asked to sign a bond saying the items are for charitable purposes. Some food items, such as milk powder and wheat flour, may have to be certified by the health department. The appraisal and the health inspection reports could take up to a week. If the appraisal officer has a problem, the papers go to the deputy commissioner or commissioner for a resolution. If the health report turns negative for some reason, we have the option of sending samples to another laboratory several hundred kilometers away, which takes several days, if not weeks.

In the past, we have had to discard large quantities of wheat flour, milk powder, canned tomato sauce and even spaghetti donated by their manufacturers in the United States as they were declared "unfit for human consumption" by the customs laboratory. Even those products canned in vacuum-sealed containers by the world's best brand names, such as Chicken of the Sea tuna and Heinz ketchup, have been rejected by the customs laboratory. Whether these laboratories are technically incompetent, or whether they serve as well-organized mechanisms for siphoning out good food products for their own benefit, is not fully clear. No one questions the validity of these inspections; after all, they are protecting the poor people of India from the unhygienic processed food from America!

If any of these problems aren't easily solved, the container could sit at the warehouse for a long time. A request to keep the container in our own warehouse is never accepted. The papers move from the appraisal officer to the deputy commissioner to the commissioner and then back to the appraisal officer, who approves and sends them to the audit department. Unless you watch each step, documents could just remain with one official or the other. Officers disappear for hours on end with no explanation. We must wait. We cannot show our irritation or the duty will go up, or they might find loopholes to fine us.

Finally, the audit department checks whether customs rules have been complied with. Audit officials can reject the approval, but that has not happened to us so far. The audit department sends the papers to the duty payment department that issues an out-pass that must be cleared by 5:30 p.m. Friday; otherwise we must wait until Monday. The subsequent steps of paying customs duty, obtaining an out-pass, and clearing of warehouse rental and container demurrage charges, all involve considerable effort and time.

The entire ordeal usually takes from two to three weeks, and along each step, bribes are extracted in some form or an other. The customs clearing process is designed under the basic assumption that everyone in the chain of inspections is dishonest, and hence, someone else must verify each step. I wonder when India will invent a way to complete a normal customs clearance activity in one or two days.

Each time we try to get a duty exemption from the central customs department in Delhi, the process takes several months. The customs department wants us to get the permit first and then bring in the donation, as if the donor is just waiting around for our convenience. Charitable institutions usually do not know in advance what they might receive from potential donors, and when they receive donations they must ship them immediately as storage is expensive. With each duty exemption request, officials ask for the same documents: the trust deed, original history and structure of the organization, and supporting documents showing the need for medical supplies, equipment, educational tools, computers, school furniture, filing cabinets and other donated items. The government's usual response is, "Why can't you buy it in India?" At which time, I explain patiently to these officials that the idea of seeking donations is to avoid spending money on purchases.

Officials in Delhi say computers are not needed for poor children. By the time the duty exemption request gains partial or full approval, the container has already arrived and the duty has been paid. Any attempt to get a refund ends up in nothing but paperwork. It is better to pay nominal duty than to try to get exemptions. I guess that is what the government wants you to do in the first place, regardless of the purpose of the import. Charity and social service seem to receive only lip service from the government.

We have been pleading with officials but have not been able to convince anyone that donated goods for charity should not be subject to duty. Senior government officials tell us that there are just too may crooks, and hence, they assume that you are also one. It is ironic that these corrupt officials are quite comfortable in labeling everyone else a cheat. The result is that nonprofit organizations waste money on a lengthy process, and many of the imported charitable goods lie at the docks as the recipient is unable to come up with the duty. Bureaucracy, corruption, inefficiency and assumption of guilt turn the simple act of compassion into a frustrating and wasteful experience.

Each time I meet with a senior government official to seek his/her assistance in carrying out our humanitarian work, such as leasing public land (that has been left unused) for farming, the initial response has generally been one of support. We are encouraged to submit proposals with no-objection certificates and recommendations from Panchayat officials and numerous other officials, each one seeking some "compensation" for his seal of approval. The paperwork goes through several levels of bureaucracy before it finally ends up at the desk of the district collector. If he/she chooses to send the proposal to higher authorities at the state level, he/she then seeks more inspections and recommendations at additional lower levels. That opens up another opportunity for the lower level staff to demand bribes. Regardless of the merit of the application and its potential to benefit the poor, very few bureaucrats want to take any initiative without some personal gain.

The chances of getting a sanction from a state official is practically nil, unless one is prepared to pay monetary rewards at different levels for pushing the papers up the ladder. Practically every bureaucrat we have dealt with at the district level or below for legitimate official sanctions has asked for money or a personal favor before completing the approval process. At every level, the personal assistant to the official and even the clerk are very important because they are the ones who decide which papers would be presented to the officer. If you are not prepared to reward them for moving your proposal, it could easily remain at the bottom of the pile forever or simply vanish without a trace. There is always an explanation for these unhappy occurrences, and the official in charge is usually not prepared to take any action.

Only politicians and those with influence can accomplish the task of obtaining approvals, regardless of the merit of the proposal, but it is dangerous to approach local politicians because they are certain to come back to you later with their own demands. The chances are that ideas that do not conform to routine activities hardly ever get approved in the normal course, but with influence and money, anything can get done. The fact that someone is prepared to invest his money for social good does not seem to bear any significance on the official decision-making process. The net result of all this is that many innovative ideas and honest efforts to improve the condition of the poor are not likely to receive fair hearings, while precious limited resources of the government are wasted on projects that serve the personal interests of those with influence. Undoubtedly, this state of affairs is one of the main reasons for the nation's inability to solve widespread perennial poverty.

It is not just inefficiency and corruption that one has to face when dealing with government officials, but the arrogance of their authority. Official misuse of power is displayed in so many different ways, often blatantly and in public, and people just seem to accept it. It is hilarious to watch official vehicles traveling along village roads, flashing lights and sounding sirens, carrying middle-to-high-level government officers. Unlike overcrowded city streets, there is hardly any traffic on rural roads, and the lights serve no purpose other than to show the importance of these officials and attract the attention of the poor villagers who stop their work in the nearby fields to watch the vehicles go by.

The collector of the district is the most senior official for the area, and his/her presence at any event is always orchestrated to be as important as the presence of a maharaja during and before the British rule. The general practice of these officials is to arrive late by an hour or two for any rural function. Of course they never apologize for the delay or for keeping the audience waiting under the burning sun or in unventilated meeting halls, because the presumption is that these officials are just too overworked with their official duties.

Speaker after speaker profusely thank the collector for sparing the few minutes to attend the meeting, and he/she in return expresses his/her concern for the welfare of the poor. His/her demeanor is invariably one that oscillates between arrogance and humility, and everyone around accepts all these pretentions as though they are to be expected. Villagers have never seen anything better, and they view these officials as their masters and not as their servants in a democratic system.

ROLE OF THE GOVERNMENT

Despite all these inefficiencies, there is no arguing that the government must retain the responsibility to be directly involved in, and in some cases be the sole agent for, the delivery of certain services, such as the administration of the legal system, the protection of consumer welfare from fraudulent and unfair practices, the enforcement of social justice, the promotion of rural education, the improvement of infrastructure such as roads and bridges, internal and external security and similar activities for which the private sector may not be adequately suited. The government can also play an indirect role in industrialization through fiscal and monetary measures, such as tax incentives for small businesses and investments in economically backward areas, stability of money and exchange rates, and the forging of global economic relationships.

But the lesson of central planning is that risk-averse bureaucracies are unsatisfactory sources of economic dynamism. The government is a blunt instrument, not a precision tool – a hammer, not a scalpel – that is inept at intervening in the organic processes of a complex society. The government must be humble enough not to try to solve all its citizens' problems but strong enough to give them the tools to solve their problems for themselves.

Government's role does not include directing the daily lives of its citizens. The pre-eminent mission of the government is to create the right environment for strong and fair social and economic activity that gives all Indians a real opportunity, but not a guarantee, to build better lives for themselves.

Efficient economic activity presupposes clear laws, their effective enforcement, and smooth and swift resolution of disputes. Respect for the rule of law, property rights and protection against public or private theft are essential requirements for the orderly conduct of business. Sound legal and regulatory frameworks that protect property rights and enforce contracts are prerequisites for investor confidence. Government must create an environment of fair and prompt legal remedies within which individuals and enterprises can seek resolution of conflicts. Unfortunately, many of India's laws on the books are simply outdated, but the government can revive any of them after decades of dormant status to suit its interests.

In addition to some 1,200 Central Acts in the statute books, there are thousands of statutes at the state level, for a combined total of some 30,000 laws among all states. It might be interesting to note that of the 395 articles in the Indian Constitution, nearly 250 were taken from the Government of India Act of 1935, created under the authoritarian rule of the British. There is a great deal of confusion about the relevant laws applicable to most cases, and the courts are simply clogged with pending disputes. As of 2001, there were an estimated 22,000 cases pending with the Supreme Court of India, while state courts had some 30 million outstanding.[14]

The inability to attain justice within a reasonable time has eroded the usefulness of courts; justice delayed is often justice denied. The delays are caused by a host of factors, but the net result is that commercial transactions cannot rely on legal enforcement through contracts and agreements.

Corruption, favoritism, and political alliances have settled in throughout the court system in India, especially in lower courts. Equal justice under the law is a concept that is far from reality in India, at least as perceived by most people. It is common practice to seek a lawyer who has a "special relationship" with the judge to argue one's case or to find someone who has access to the judge to discuss the case privately. It is also alleged that some states' highest court judges extract money from claimants in civil disputes before rendering verdicts. Even the Supreme Court of India is alleged to have succumbed to pressures from the government in some cases.

Recently, a claim was made by a local village leader on a piece of land owned by our foundation, stating that his ancestors once had certain rights and ownership to it. He demanded money for settling the dispute. We brought the matter before the local judge and asked that the claimant produce appropriate documents to prove his rights.

Even after several court appearances, he failed to bring a single official document, but the judge kept postponing a ruling on the case. Finally, after several months of delay, the word was sent out to us through an intermediary, a middle level police officer, that a substantial sum of money would be required from us to finalize the judgment. We refused to make the payment, and the hearing was postponed several more times, usually as a result of the last-minute absence of the judge for the session. At the time of writing this episode, no final judgment has been rendered.

The system does not protect ordinary citizens from corrupt judges or allow them to seek redress when unfairly dealt with by the judiciary. Many fear that the present legal system in India is no longer capable of enforcing the laws and delivering equal justice. Despite the fact that corruption within the system is well known to the public and the government, no one has taken any serious steps to fix it. Obviously, justice often goes to the highest bidder, and there is no compelling reason for the powerful in the society to do anything about the present state of affairs.

There are also issues of the actual independence of the Indian legal system from the legislative branch, especially at state levels. Until such time as the general public sees justice as fair, and everyone else has an effective sense of justice, no one is likely to comply with even just laws and just institutions. The legal system in India is used by people more as an obstacle to be placed upon the other party, rather than a means of seeking just remedies. Also, the failure of the justice system to meet the commercial needs of the society is a serious impediment to economic growth.

The only solution now is to completely revamp much of the justice system, getting rid of outdated laws, reformulating many to suit present day needs, and instituting procedures to speed up the processing of cases. Independence of the judiciary from political influence and pressures, and safeguards against bribes have to be further assured.

INADEQUATE INFRASTRUCTURE

No nation can build a sustainable and prosperous economy without good infrastructure in its transport facilities, electric power, telecommunications and irrigational water. Infrastructure represents, if not the engine, the wheels of economic activity. India's industrial progress is hindered by fragmented and uncoordinated urban development that is a result of poor or nonexistent long-term planning.

Consider the results of a survey conducted by the consulting firm, Feedback Consulting. Only two percent of the companies in Bangalore said that they never faced power disruptions, as compared to four percent in Chennai and twenty-two percent in Hyderabad. According to this study, India could be having productivity loss of over Rs.20,000 crores (Rs.200 billion) annually due to interrupted power supply. This is around two percent of the gross output of the entire industrial and service sectors in the country.

Another example is the telephone service that is plagued by service disruptions, connection to wrong numbers, and erroneous busy signals. The problem is even more acute for calls made from abroad to a city like Bangalore; no less than a dozen different messages and signals can be heard when international calls fail to make connections. When one succeeds in getting through, the call sometimes ends up with an echo that permits only one directional voice transmission.

All these problems with basic services do not ever seem to go away permanently, but the claim is made that dramatic improvements have occurred from the fiber optics lines and new exchange equipment recently installed. There does not seem to be a commitment to zero tolerance of technical faults, and consequently, the service remains mediocre to poor, resulting in tremendous loss in productivity and a weak business environment.

Reliable energy and water supplies, transport and communications are essential to the development of an efficient industrial base. Agriculture, on the other hand, employs more than seventy percent of the nation's population, but is still at the mercy of a good monsoon. Resources allocated to both urban and rural infrastructure have not been properly used in the past. Facilities are not maintained properly; unreliable and outdated systems burden users with extra costs and time; infrastructure has often been built in the wrong places or using the wrong techniques; and cities expand without proper long-term planning to accommodate the increased demands placed on transportation, housing and sanitation.

Furthermore, infrastructure services are often run with terrible inefficiency. Innovations in delivering infrastructure services, along with new technologies available through the private sector and foreign participation, point to solutions that can deliver the required services and improve performance. Without serious competition and transparency in the contract bidding process, penalties for non-performance and independent audit by reputed private institutions, there is going to be ample scope for corruption and wasted use of resources.

Economic liberalization affecting mostly urban enterprises is not sufficient for assuring prosperity for all. According to a Mumbai-based think tank, the Strategic Foresight Group, the Indian economy now has three classes: a "business economy," a "bike economy" and a "bullock cart economy." The business class economy with access to cars, computers, the Internet and many of the modern amenities consists of less than 20 million people, or two percent of the population. The bike economy consisting of middle-class people is around 150 million, mostly those employed in government and private companies in urban areas. The balance of 830 million or so people belonging to the bullock cart economy enjoy few comforts of modern living, have far less education, and are under- or unemployed.

Some 350 million people live in poverty as measured by less than one dollar a day in earnings. By the government's measure, a family of five is considered poor if their total monthly income is less than Rs.1,500 a month or around $30. That works out to Rs.300 or $6 per individual per month.

Much of the economic progress that India has made over the past decade is confined to the business class economy, and the trickle-down effect has been marginal. The government seems to implement policy changes in small increments, mostly concentrating on urban industrial and technology sectors that contribute significantly to foreign exchange and GDP growth. Growth does not necessarily lead to development in all sectors, especially those that are traditionally poor. If this pattern of policy implementation continues for another decade, the rural sector will definitely fall behind, driving more people into poverty. Sooner or later, the country as a whole could face a seriously uneven economy, with civil disorder and internal conflicts among and between classes.

Chapter 6

FOREVER LEFT BEHIND

ADDRESSING RURAL DEVELOPMENT

Spurring development in rural areas is the key to alleviating poverty in India. It is where two-thirds of India's population lives. This calls for the creation of opportunities for more people in the villages to engage in farming and small businesses and to find new markets for their produce so that they may realize adequate profits. The market economy of today cannot ignore the needs of the rural sector. It is there that the old socialistic practices have to be replaced to permit easier access to credit and markets.

A broader section of the rural population should be able to participate in the prosperity that a market economy brings about. That would require access to better education, job training, basic health care delivery, credit and markets, and an opportunity to own income-generating assets. Real income of the rural people must improve significantly, and this will happen when agricultural commodities find broader markets in India and abroad, and labor is trained in new job skills. It is through the creation of economic opportunity for the poor and good governance that India can hope to significantly reduce rural poverty within any reasonable timeframe.

Unfortunately, governments are focused more on countering their loud critics who seem to concentrate mostly on aggregate economic growth, national debt, foreign investments and balance of payments. The so-called intellectuals of the country are just too busy analyzing the impact of globalization and technology on the urban industries. There is no coherent policy or determined effort on the part of governments to accomplish the task of meeting the basic needs of the poor. The feeble voices of the nation's silent majority, farmers and other rural people, do not seem to cause any urgency or threat, as long as their minimal expectations are met through minor subsidies that are dished out in each national and state budget.

The notion that urban prosperity will somehow trickle down to the rural poor in the foreseeable future is simply misguided. The newfound wealth for some 25 million and the improvements in the standard of living for another 100 million or so of the urban population in the past decade are not being distributed to the rest of the population. The main relationship that the urban society has to rural people comes from the farm products they buy and the cheap migrant labor they use for their industries and other services.

Urban companies would like to sell some of their products to the large rural population, but they have not yet found it profitable due to the low purchasing power of the rural people. Yet, many companies, especially those in the technology sector, manage to unload their computers and other accessories, paid for by the government, at rural schools and primary health centers in the name of bridging the digital divide. Politicians are only happy to oblige, and bureaucrats go along with such decisions as long as there is money to be made on the side. The computers serve more as decorative pieces than anything else, with no useful software applications in local languages made available. All these occur in the name of benefiting the poor, when their basic needs such as safe drinking water, health care and education are ignored.

Much of the agricultural produce from the rural farms ends up in local urban markets that determine prices. There are not enough refrigeration, processing and packaging facilities available for most of the farm produce to be shipped to distant markets. Moreover, the farmer is usually not aware of prices at other markets, and even if he is, he cannot displease his local buyer and attempt to transport his produce to non-local markets.

The farmer is caught between two unhappy situations – if he grows little, he does not earn enough; if he grows too much, prices in the local market fall significantly. Baldev Farms, operated by The George Foundation, has on several occasions been forced to sell vegetables far below costs – as little as one kilogram of tomatoes at Rs.1, or $0.02, and one kilogram of bananas at Rs.4, or $0.08. The urban society wants to buy food cheap, and the gradually increasing demand that comes from their rising purchasing power is met by small increases in farm production without affecting prices. The farmer gains very little.

Agricultural development initiatives are, at present, designed around projects, patronage and subsidies. There is very little attempt to reform the complex agricultural policy that cuts across several departments within the state and central governments. There is talk about reducing or eliminating subsidies toward agriculture, particularly for electricity and fertilizers, in order to reduce the fiscal deficit. Subsidies to the agricultural sector are around twelve percent of the total subsidies provided to all sectors; given the thirty-two percent contribution to the GDP by the agriculture sector, its subsidy share is far less than that of other sectors.

Without finding ways to gain higher prices for crops, it is hard to see how farmers can be expected to generate any profit if subsidies are cut. If the farmer is lucky, his profits barely cover the value of his personal labor. Larger farms employing workers who have to be paid wages do not have any assurance of making sufficient profit. Consequently, most farms are run by small landlords who continue to practice outdated technologies, and the produce from their farms often does not meet export standards demanded by other countries.

The Indian government has pursued agricultural policies that cater to political allies and farm lobbies in key farming states. Despite huge surpluses in wheat, the farm belts continue to grow even more grain, and the government is prepared to buy it at higher and higher prices. At the same time, to protect higher prices, the government is reluctant to offer the grain widely at lower prices through its half million "ration shops."

Very poor people are offered basic commodities, such as grains, sugar and kerosene at heavily subsidized rates, while others entitled to rations are offered at slightly lower than open market prices. Still, most poor people cannot afford to buy what they need, and over 350 million go to bed each night hungry, and forty-seven percent of the country's children are malnourished.

As a result, in 2002 the government was sitting on 55 million metric tons of wheat, an incredibly large quantity by any standard. The government has filled all its warehouses, and with poor quality storage bags, a significant part of the surplus has already rotted and been infected with worms and rats. According to some estimates, the government now spends more money on storage-related efforts than on agriculture, rural development, irrigation and flood control combined.

Despite this national scandal, not a single government official has been held accountable. With this kind of terrible mismanagement motivated by political patronage, it is hard to see how the nation can effectively deal with many of its serious human problems.

As former Prime Minister Rajiv Gandhi once pointed out, only fifteen percent of the money the government allocated for rural development reached its target. Now, the Planning Commission of India admits that this figure might be an overestimate; only 10 to 15 rupees out of every 100 spent by government reaches the poor.

The present deplorable state of rural poverty in India is the result of over 55 years of failed policies that continue to rely on subsidies that go to undeserving individuals and activities, and ineffective allocation of land to scheduled castes and other poor people without providing them the necessary support for productive use. The other reasons are ill-conceived and badly managed rural infrastructure development, and wasted resources on poorly run basic services in education, job training and health care.

The reasons for rural poverty are many: skewed distribution of cultivable land, shortage of water for irrigation, non-availability of electricity, lack of access to credit market, low level of education and training to pursue non-farming jobs, poor health care, caste-based oppressive practices, and several other economic and social factors. The government has set up numerous institutions to deal with all these issues including the Integrated Rural Development Programme (IRDP) to fund self-employment ventures, the Training Youth for Self-Employment Programme for providing technical skills to the rural youth, the National Rural Employment Programme, and others. The underlying philosophy behind all these programs is the generation of new employment or self-employment opportunities through policy interventions in the form of financial assistance to farmers and small businesses and job training.

Unfortunately, none of these programs have made any significant impact on poverty. Corruption, political influence on credit, land allocations and other related decisions, diffused focus and priority, poor execution, shortage of rural infrastructure, social inequality, and a host of other factors have led to their poor outcome. Inequities in land ownership are also a major hurdle for most of the rural population. Increases in population have overtaken productivity gains, while the number of beneficiaries who are able to move out of poverty has been minimal.

According to the distinguished economist and former finance minister Manmohan Singh, India can not have an industrial policy because its standards of governance are poor, especially when it comes to infrastructure, education and health. These problems are particularly acute in India's rural sector. A recent report by the United Nations Development Program (UNDP) shows that India's rural economy is characterized by a heavy dependence on agriculture, inadequate infrastructure, rudimentary industrialization, narrow economic base, highly skewed distribution of income and wealth, and limited capacity to generate employment.

Given the potential for major contribution from rural infrastructure development, it is essential to build the required capacity for economic development. This includes rural road development, linking of rivers and canals to supply irrigation water to larger areas, clean water supply, electricity, and sanitation.

Access to adequate sources of water for irrigation is a basic requirement for rural development; today, underground water is pumped out at twice the rate at which it is replenished by rain, and soon many farm belts will run out of water unless conservation, water harvesting, and efficient practices are used. Without basic infrastructure, the ability to generate sustainable self-employment and employment will be weak.

Public projects in infrastructure development must be designed to support the rapid progress that can be gained from private schemes in farming and related activities. At the same time, government-initiated and -managed rural projects to improve infrastructure succeed only when they are driven by clearly identified needs and executed with community awareness and participation. Transparency on the part of those who manage these projects and social auditing of their performance are essential for ensuring that funds are used only for the intended purpose and the outcome is as planned.

Unfortunately, most rural infrastructure development projects are motivated by political considerations, with little importance given to the actual need. Even when NGOs are prepared to undertake major humanitarian and developmental work, such as schools and hospitals, for the poor in rural and remote areas, the government seldom responds with assistance to make their efforts easier.

Officials are interested only when a private individual or organization is prepared to fund one of the government projects, and not when private initiatives are undertaken independent of government participation. All the talk about the need for private participation in helping the poor really means being part of a government-controlled program. Even those subsidies and other incentives that are officially set aside to encourage private participation are seldom made available for such efforts. The greater the investment you make as a private individual for social projects, the lesser the chances for getting any assistance from the government.

As we have often heard from several government officials, "If he can spend all this money, why can't he spend a little more to fix up the road next to his project?"

Participating with the government on projects is no easy task. As we were preparing to start the Shanti Bhavan project, our foundation submitted a request to the chief secretary of Tamil Nadu for the improvement of basic infrastructure in the area. We asked that the roads leading up to Baliganapalli from the nearby town of Bagalur be improved.

Even after numerous follow-ups over several years, nothing was done. By then, we had already built Shanti Bhavan and the Baldev , and we were running several programs to serve over 100,000 poor people in nearby villages, all without any assistance or support from the government. By the year 2000, a seven kilometer stretch of rural road leading up to Baliganapalli had become so bad that it was taking over one hour by jeep to navigate. Realizing that the government was not going to improve the road any time soon, we decided to take a different approach.

We learned that the government had a "People's Contribution Scheme" whereby it would be obliged to fund and undertake the road repair work if twenty-five percent of the cost was borne by those who live along the road or in the nearby area. The block development officer estimated the cost of the repair work to be around Rs.6 million, and we quickly submitted our application with an initial deposit of Rs.1.5 million.

Within a week, the local Panchayat chairman and a member of the legislative assembly approached us asking for Rs.100,000 in advance to undertake the repair with funds from some other scheme under his jurisdiction or authority, but we soon realized that the requested amount was nothing more than a bribe, and there was no assurance that the work would be done. We turned him down and waited for the government to approve our application under the Contribution Scheme. We also laid down the condition that we would supervise the construction of the road.

The next year was spent moving the papers from one office to another and obtaining the required "recommendation letters" from several village officials, all calling for bribes of varying amounts. We met with the district collector, state rural development officer, and lastly, the state finance secretary. Finally, the project was sanctioned, and the district project officer agreed to disburse the money. Work on the road commenced, but we were then told that our financial contribution had to be higher now, as the proposed width of the road and the thickness of gravel were more than what were usually approved for rural roads. We agreed to pay another Rs.1 million provided we could supervise the entire project.

Just as the work was about to begin, we found out how the approved funds would be used. The estimated costs included thirty percent of the money "hidden" for the block development officers, and from the balance of seventy percent, another thirty percent needed to be set aside for payments to inspectors and other government officials.

An engineer from the block development office provided poor-quality gravel that kept disappearing soon after it was delivered to the roadside. The contractor expressed his inability to fulfill our requirements as specified and threw in the towel. We brought in another contractor, and asked the project officer to advise the engineer to stop interfering. The engineer retaliated by getting some villagers to write letters to the collector stating that the road was being poorly constructed. The collector sent the project officer to inspect the road, who then concluded that the work was proceeding as best as possible under the circumstances.

We spent additional money from our own resources to purchase more gravel and to provide proper drainage, and in two months we completed the construction. None of the local residents or the few companies located along the road were now willing to contribute their share to the costs incurred by us. We were not done yet. A final payment needed to be made to the engineer soon thereafter for her "non-interference;" she was the collecting agent representing the local officials for all bribes.

Despite all this, our road is of a better quality than most other rural roads. It has already lasted two years without any problems – unusual for roads built by the government. One can imagine how public funds are usually expended when there is no one to oversee the government work.

Rural governance is dictated by the interaction between several constituencies and forces, each one trying to exert influence over the allocation of funds by the state and how those funds are used. At the bottom of the ladder is the village Panchayat consisting of officials elected by people from a group of nearby villages. However, true power and influence of the local Panchayat rests mostly with village leaders and landlords who have a hold over the poor and lower caste people.

Several local Panchayats come within the taluk Panchayat, and several taluk Panchayats under a district Panchayat, with each higher level exerting greater influence with government officials. There are also leaders of the Scheduled Castes, or low castes, who have considerable weight as a result of their large constituency.

Separate from these so-called local bodies are the elected political leaders, mainly members of the legislative assembly (MLAs) who represent the people at the state governing body. The next group is the government officials of which the tahsildar, taluk collector, district project officer, district revenue officer and district collector hold considerable authority. These and other district level officials report to numerous state government bureaucrats headed by the chief secretary.

In addition, there are the police and the courts at different levels and numerous other officials who can exert influence and authority. Very few initiatives requiring government approval can reach the top without passing through most of these bodies and officials. No official is prepared to overrule a negative recommendation by his or her subordinates for fear of accusations of corruption or favoritism. As a consequence, there is ample opportunity for corruption at every level.

Of all the corrupt practices, the biggest obstacle our foundation faces in its daily work with the rural communities is having to deal with Panchayat officials and village thugs. They work in unison, with Panchayat governance offering cover for their attempts to extract money from us on some pretext or the other. In the name of self governance and delegation of power to local officials, the government has created a monstrous bureaucracy of unimaginable proportions throughout rural India – layers of officials with powers to do little other than carry out extortion, take bribes, misuse funds, and dish out favors.

From the very first month following the start of our work in Baliganapalli, we have faced constant demands for money and for assignment of contracts for construction and other work in our projects. From time to time, we have been falsely accused of carrying out improper activities and disrespecting the temples or religious beliefs. These accusations on religious grounds are particularly effective in stirring up emotions and anger among the local population. The fact that our foundation has built two small temples in nearby villages that did not have places of worship, and repaired an old traditional chariot that had been lying idle for over 20 years, has not stopped them from making these accusations.

When we refuse to accede to the threats made by these local leaders, they organize our farm labor to strike on some pretext or the other and make unreasonable wage and benefits demands. Written petitions of complaint signed anonymously are presented to the collector, who then initiates investigations. Though these are usual occurrences known to senior government officials, there is no effort to improve the bureaucracy or eliminate such disruptive practices. No one wants to reform a system that offers the opportunity to extort funds even from institutions that are doing charitable work. Even well-meaning government officials are unwilling to stop the activities of trouble-makers for fear that they might write false petitions to politicians.

For NGOs like us, courts may be our only protection, but there is no assurance of a prompt remedy. The system is so badly broken that only a good government with some courage can fix it. In the meantime, the way to help the poor is to "help" the rich first.

ASSET OWNERSHIP BY THE POOR

Ownership of land is one of the biggest aspirations for people in the rural economy. The economic success of Australia following the arrival of convicts from England more than 100 years ago can be attributed to the fact that they were able to own property and make it productive. State governments in India still own large areas of land, and if ordinary citizens, especially the poor, can be offered ways to purchase and make them productive, the nation will quickly witness a major economic miracle. But today, the process of allocating government-owned *parampoke* or waste land requires bribes to the officials involved.

The recipients of cultivable government land, as opposed to dry land, are usually landlords, power brokers in villages, and commercial enterprises that can exert influence with officials. Poor people have no means of obtaining any useful land on their own. The George Foundation has been trying to get government land in Dharmapuri district on lease so that it can employ poor people and grow high value crops. The nonprofit scheme we presented to the government required no financial commitment by the government. In addition to the wages paid by the foundation, a portion of the profits from the crops would be set aside and used for the future purchase of new parcels of land for each of the workers.

Despite the social motivation, and the fact that all financial risk was being borne by a private NGO, the officials had no interest in awarding us the lease without our paying large bribes.

We submitted repeated applications to develop at our cost the government-owned land in front of Shanti Bhavan into a park for the children and people of the two neighboring villages. A Panchayat resolution was obtained in support of the application. The revenue officer and village officer came to inspect the land, to check whether anyone lived there. They then submitted the proposal to the tahsildar, who inspected the site, talked to the villagers and submitted the proposal to the sub collector. The sub collector visited the site with an inspection team and then endorsed the papers. The application then went to the collector who forwarded it to state officials.

After obtaining the required approval from the district revenue officer, we took our proposal to state authorities in Chennai. As expected, serious objections were raised by the land acquisition department. Jude met with the rural development secretary who had rejected the application, and he agreed to revisit it after we made some revisions. After six months of renewed efforts, the proposal was moved again from the lowest levels to the state officials.

Unfortunately, during one of Jude's visits to the state offices, he met with the superintendent in charge of the approval process in the corridor of the offices and asked where he was seated in the office hall. The superintendent was offended at the inquiry. Once again, the under secretary received our request with a new set of objections. No senior government official wants to question or overrule his subordinates. It was time for us to abandon our proposal.

Over the years, we have submitted a couple of other proposals to lease government parampoke land and to develop it at our expense for farming and employment of poor women in the area. None have materialized to date. Without waiting for the government to allocate cultivable parampoke land, our foundation bought from landlords over 150 acres of barren land surrounding Shanti Bhavan. Since the area is generally dry, and no surface water sources are available, the first and urgent task was to drill deep wells. Applying "fracturing" technology, and with wells at depths over 500 feet, we were able to tap reliable water sources to meet the needs of vegetable crops like beans and capsicum, and even bananas which require at least 10 liters of water each day per plant.

With water conservation, and major recharging measures to replenish wells during rainy season, we have been able to transform a somewhat drought-stricken area into fruit and vegetable farms. Today, the foundation runs the second largest banana farm in South India, covering some 100 acres, entirely for the benefit of the local population. Profit from the farm is ploughed back into other humanitarian projects. Plans are in place to double the area cultivated in a couple of years, employing poor people from lower castes. Fruit and vegetable processing and packing facilities are under construction, and we hope to firm up export agreements with foreign buyers.

Farming is what villagers have a natural affinity for and an industry where large numbers of people can be employed. Rural development hinges on agriculture. Agriculture and its related products and services contribute twenty-four percent of the GDP and employ about two-thirds of the country's labor force.[16]

Farming offers poor women, especially from backward communities and lower castes, who are mostly illiterate, untrained, and with very little social and economic status, an opportunity to better their lives. In India, there are more than 400 million such people. The unemployed are 150 million to 200 million, a great majority of them belonging to these deprived sections of society. Without meaningful skills, social status and economic power, they are unable to do any business on their own, even with financial assistance. These people can be readily employed as labor in the field and also in processing and packing of farm produce.

With increased purchasing power of the rural population, urban industries will be able to open up a huge new market. There is much written about companies like Unilever selling soap to the villagers and Bajaj marketing two-wheelers to farmers, but the reality is that such sales are limited to a minute fraction of the rural population, mainly landlords and officials. A great majority of the rural poor cannot afford to buy even the basic necessities, such as toothpaste or body soap.

Modern farming using precision agricultural tools is the key to increased output and profitability. Reliance on traditional methods by the small farmer is necessitated by a lack of adequate funds; hence the goal should be to teach new techniques and offer financial credits to implement them. As a step in that process, and to empower poor and socially deprived women, we set up the Baldev Farms as a "learn while you earn" program for vegetable and banana cultivation.

The land we had purchased from landlords was converted into arable land with proper grading, drainage and soil preparation. An Israeli company, Netafin, was contracted to introduce us to superior technology in drip irrigation and water-soluble fertilizers. With deep ploughing, precision application of fertilizers and careful use of preventive pesticides, our farms started growing a variety of high-value vegetables and banana crops.

Apart from paying daily wages to each farm worker who takes care of quarter of an acre of land, we set aside a portion of the profits generated from the produce as savings to be used by the end of 4 to 5 years for the purchase of half an acre of land for each family. In rural India, the ownership of physical assets, such as land and cattle, offers higher status, continuing income and financial stability. We believe this ownership is the key to eradicating poverty for a great majority of the poor. Subsequently, the newly purchased land would share resources, such as wells and tractors, among several farmers.

The foundation would remain as a support organization, addressing concerns and difficulties faced by farmers, while offering know-how and access to information and markets, such as what high-value crops to grow and when, which markets offer higher prices on a given day and how to tie up long-term purchase and export contracts. Within less than two years of starting Baldev Farms, more than 150 poor villagers, mostly women, have found labor and supervisory employment in the field, and many have already come out of poverty and their bonded-labor status with landlords. As the foundation expands its farming activity in high-value fruits and vegetables, it will soon generate sufficient positive cash flow to finance some of its other humanitarian initiatives.

Though the final chapter on this program is not yet written, the concept of getting each poor family a piece of land to cultivate high-value crops is unquestionably sound. It is becoming increasingly clear to us that good management and dedicated work by the labor force can assure a profitable commercial venture to empower the poor.

If all the parampoke or waste government land can be transformed into fertile cultivable land, the poor as well as the nation as a whole will benefit. Further, the government must find ways to purchase and distribute un-utilized land owned by major landlords for cultivation by poor farmers. Ownership of cultivable land and the ability to successfully grow high-value crops year after year will ensure a permanent change in the economic and social condition of the poor.

The concept of permanent asset creation as opposed to temporary income generation is the key to sustainable financial progress by the poor. When income-generating assets are owned by many, the purchasing power of the community is increased. That purchasing power would set the stage for starting small businesses catering to the daily needs of the community. Larger companies, such as those involved in food processing and packaging of farm produce, are a natural progression in the development of the area.

It is the partnership between poor farmers, NGOs, and private companies, with the government offering financial assistance in the form of subsidies for electricity, fertilizer and so on, that offers effective solutions to the problems of rural poverty. These and other models that focus on creating the opportunity for physical asset creation by the poor, in return for their dedicated work, represent bold new concepts that need to be pursued for reducing rural poverty.

Though our farming project is entirely a private initiative, there can be effective models of public-private partnership along similar lines. Private institutions can be appointed by the government and rewarded on the basis of crop output from those farms they oversee. It is important to ensure that the farmer receives all the subsidies and other incentives to which he is entitled, instead of these benefits going to the officials who administer them. Special incentives should be provided for dry-land cultivation and water management using drip irrigation, fracturing of wells, and water collection and storage. Use of solar and wind energy is a good alternative to conventional power, as there is usually plenty of sun and wind during most of the year in large parts of India.

Once again, lowering the cost of such technologies and providing long-term financial credit can pave the way for reducing the cost of farming. Vigorous competition among private companies in these product areas will assure the introduction of superior technologies and cost-effective solutions.

Most small farmers lack access to non-local markets for their produce, mainly as a result of inadequate market information and transport costs. Most countries, including the United States, have not found a way to make agriculture profitable for farmers without some sort of government price support mechanisms. The government can assist small farmers by helping them form cooperative marketing arrangements and by offering daily price information.

Farmers are at the mercy of middlemen to sell their produce at whatever price offered. Farmers may need to circumvent the middlemen who, through their exploitative market conventions and practices, set not only lower than market prices but also lesser weights or quantities than what are actually sold. The strike organized in November 2003 by several trade groups in Bangalore to prevent a major German retailer, Metro Cash & Carry, from opening a large retail market for selling produce and several other consumer products is an example of the effort by special interest groups in curtailing competition.

Unless the government is committed to the concept of competitive open markets, farmers are unlikely to find fair prices.

Electronic auction markets linking local and distant buyers can assure competitive prices as determined by supply and demand. The auction market, Safal, opened in 2003 in Bangalore by the National Dairy Development Board (NDDB), with major financial assistance from the Central Ministry of Agriculture, is an excellent step forward in creating a well-organized facility for producers of vegetables and fruits to sell to buyers in a competitive environment. With similar auction markets in other parts of India, farmers are likely to obtain better prices and avoid transactions that are inefficient, lack transparency, standardization and quality differentiation.

Despite India's huge grain surplus and the potential to grow large quantities of vegetables and fruits, exports in these commodities are minimal in comparison to even smaller countries. For example, India is the world's largest producer of bananas, but its exports are negligible. Countries like the Philippines and Malaysia dominate the Asian and Middle East markets for bananas.

The government needs to assist farmers in penetrating foreign markets by making contacts and establishing relationships. Processing and packaging of many produce items could also add value to the importer, and this could be done domestically. Further, seasonal fixed-price purchase arrangements may be negotiated by the cooperatives with buyers and processing companies.

The goal should be to find ways to improve the collective bargaining power of small farmers, help find new markets and introduce competition between buyers. This should be done without the direct involvement of government officials in determining market prices, except for setting floor prices at which the government always stands ready to buy directly from the farmer.

The nation must make a real commitment to rural development and eradication of poverty within the next decade or two. If it is serious about improving the lives of the rural population, government policies must encourage the transfer of wealth through increased production and higher prices received by the farmer, instead of simply benefiting the middlemen and urban consumers.

Governments always want the prices for food commodities to remain low to keep consumers happy, but it should not happen at the expense of farmers. Without government support in one form or the other, most farmers cannot make a return commensurate with the risks they face; individual farmers can hardly make enough profits to justify their own labor. The government must offer farmers sufficient subsidies to offset their ever-increasing costs for fertilizers and electricity, and always assure reasonable floor prices for produce through price support guarantees.

With India's large rural workforce, the country has the potential to become a world leader in agricultural produce for both domestic and foreign consumption, offering not only raw commodities but also processed items for different market segments. That will be possible only when rural resources are effectively utilized and private urban participation in agriculture-related activities becomes attractive.

The government must facilitate the transfer of cultivable land from the few landlords who own most of it in every village. Unfortunately, poor people are being offered parampoke land held by the government, but much of what is made available is not suitable for cultivation. Major landowners almost always manage to obtain cultivable government land with water sources, while poor people are left landless or with unusable land for cultivation.

The government must actively embark on a program to purchase idle land from owners at fair market prices and sell it to both corporations and individuals who are prepared to put it to good use. Poor people should be able to buy land from the government for cultivation, with attractive mortgages spread over 20 years. Water resources such as canals and rivers must be made accessible to farmers, even if it requires laying pipelines and setting up pumping stations to transport water to distant areas.

Following three continuous years of drought, we ourselves had to bring water through pipes laid over five miles from deep wells we drilled near dry lakes. NGOs that have the expertise in managing such efforts should be given the incentive to work with farmers, instead of the government trying to implement such projects directly.

Small farmers should be encouraged to form cooperatives to share tractors, wells, and water sources, and the government should provide financial and technical assistance to support the initial development of the land. Financial assistance in the form of free electric power to run wells may be necessary to support the small farmer, but no one should be allowed to waste ground water by excessive pumping for flood irrigation.

Food packaging and processing companies should be given financial incentives to establish factories in rural areas, thereby assuring a steady demand for the produce as well as generating additional employment. Export markets should be explored with government assistance by establishing international trade arrangements. With increased farming activity in high-value farm produce, both income and wealth of rural farmers would steadily rise, enabling them to buy many industrial and household products. Foreign exchange earnings from exports would contribute to the nation's balance of trade, further enabling the development of other sectors of the economy.

This chain of economic activity is possible with a substantially higher initial investment on the part of the government, the returns from which are likely to be very attractive. It goes without saying that good governance of a time-bound program is essential for the success of the program.

Access to credit is essential for most business enterprises. Small businesses rely on bank loans to get started, and with adequate capital, they have some chance of success. Unless credit is made available on the basis of merit, as opposed to favors and kickbacks, capital is wasted on less deserving projects. Financial institutions must operate in a competitive environment, bound by regulations that safeguard the interests of consumers.

Instead of trying to protect badly managed banks from failing, the focus ought to be on introducing stiff competition among banks and ensuring fairness in the distribution of credit so that financing costs are lowered and access to credit is improved. Contrary to the interest of the consumer, the Reserve Bank of India frequently directs all banks to charge interest rates on loans no lower than a set minimum or spread over deposit rates, and to compound interest on loans as frequently as every month, while allowing rates on deposits to be compounded only once every six months. It is not unusual for banks to charge interest on loans at twice the rate of interest earned on fixed deposits, even when those deposits serve as full guarantees for the loans.

Banks frequently engage in the practice of holding as collateral practically all the physical and monetary assets of a borrower, disproportionate to the amount being loaned. Interest rates charged on loans to small businesses and ordinary customers are frequently exorbitant and may not reflect current market conditions. Transparency on the part of banks is practically absent, and consumers seldom get to know the real cost of their borrowings when finance charges, fees, and monthly compounding are all added up. Any ordinary citizen who has ever approached a bank for a loan would confirm how insulting and humiliating his or her experience has been in concluding a borrowing transaction, in addition to the delays and troubles to which one is subjected.

If one has made a fixed deposit in bank some years ago and now wants to borrow money against it without breaking the deposit, the bank is likely to charge a significant spread over the interest rate being earned on the deposit. Today's market interest rates do not seem to matter, and banks are free to follow any rule of their making. The captive customer base does not truly have other choices as every financial institution behaves similarly.

These inconsistent and exploitative practices by financial institutions are either ignored or sanctioned by regulatory institutions in India. Failure to enforce proper banking laws and fair practices, and undesirable intervention in the free working of markets to the advantage of banks, go against the interests of consumers who end up paying for the losses incurred by badly managed institutions. It should not come as a surprise to ordinary citizens to find out that even the venerable government institutions in India function to safeguard first the interests of the powerful before that of the consumer.

Credit to rural people is a cruel arrangement and many poor people fall victims to moneylenders in the villages. Interest rates charged on loans and credits are usually above ten percent per month, or over one-hundred percent per annum. Some moneylenders advance "interest free" loans to small farmers against the purchase of the future crop at fixed low prices. Often these farmers end up in losses as the cost of farming exceeds the value given by the moneylender for the crop. Consequently, many have lost their land to moneylenders or have been forced to "lease" the land for free. There are also many poor families that become "bonded labor" to landlords as a result of their inability to repay money they have borrowed for their special needs, such as for dowry and marriage ceremonies.

People in bonded labor cannot work elsewhere and are virtual slaves to the landlord. They are paid lower wages than usual, and in some cases compensated only with leftover daily meals and excess grains. The landlord might give a small living space for one member of the bonded family, usually a woman, to stay in return for taking care of household duties. Without the ability to repay the loan and the mounting interest, the borrower remains totally under the dictates of the landlord throughout his/her entire life. The government claims that there are few such cases, but our survey of the villages around Shanti Bhavan has revealed several. There is no organized effort to free these people from their predicament.

Most poor people, especially from lower castes, do not have the ability to demonstrate their potential for making business ideas succeed. Only with the backing of NGOs and other support groups can they ever hope to get loans from banks.

The success story of Grameen Bank, started in 1976 in Bangladesh, is often cited in developmental circles as an example of how even small loans as seed money to the poor can help them start businesses to work their way out of poverty. Some 60 million borrowers have availed microcredit in several developing countries, and even with twenty percent or so in annual interest charges, it is reported that more than ninety-five percent of the beneficiaries have been able to generate sufficient income to repay the loans. It is hard to believe such statistics about business entrepreneurship among uneducated and socially deprived poor when well-trained and educated people venturing into business have less than a one in 10 chance of success. There is no doubt that microcredit can serve as an additional financial source for those who have other support mechanisms, but it is far from certain that small loans alone can help very poor people on a scale that would make even a dent in poverty eradication.

TECHNOLOGY IN RURAL DEVELOPMENT

Is introducing modern technologies the real answer to the problems of poverty, especially in rural India? In recent years there has been considerable talk among many constituencies, both nationally and internationally, about the need to bridge the "digital divide" between developed and developing nations. The term "digital divide" is used to highlight the gap that currently exists between the developed and developing world in information and communications technology (ICT). The assumption is that, without a major effort to close the digital gap, development of poor countries will lag behind rich nations.

Telephone and wireless communications, personal computers, and the Internet are seen as the essential ingredients of the digital world for all countries. Many proponents of ICT claim that, through these capabilities, even those in poor communities are expected to benefit from "sharing new ideas, opportunities and horizons" in their effort to improve productivity and quality of life. Some have labeled ICT the panacea for development in the future. Consistent with this thinking, leaders of the G-8 nations embraced the idea of closing the divide and pledged to help the process. Under the auspices of the United Nations Development Program (UNDP), the Digital Opportunity Initiative was formed as a collaboration with Accenture, a private consulting firm, and Markle Foundation, an organization that makes grants as well as investments in private companies. These and other multilateral organizations, governments, and members from private and nonprofit sectors have formed a G-8 Digital Opportunity Task Force (Dot Force) to accomplish the task.

There is no question that better communication and access to technology and information are valuable to development. However, the questions that arise are fundamental and several-fold: who are the intended beneficiaries in the near to intermediate term, what types of services would add value to whom, and are these the appropriate priorities for communities that are presently struggling for want of food and health care? No less an authority than Microsoft Chairman Bill Gates has expressed grave doubts about the power of technology to close the global development gap. Some of the top investment managers of the International Finance Corporation, the World Bank's private investment arm, say that many officials who have worked with developing countries have a difficult time seeing the value of investing in information and technology projects when their budgets for more traditional work are shrinking.

Other critics label the effort as a ploy for the private sector to get big government contracts and subsidies to set up large IT projects. The skeptics should take comfort in the fact that none of the developed countries have so far come through with any major donor funds to back up all their talk.

Practically every city in India has privately run telephone booths that permit customers to make even international calls. Hundreds of thousands of Internet Cafes have also sprung up in cities allowing ordinary citizens to walk in and use the Web and email for a fee. There is no shortage of computer training schools in the country that enroll those who wish to pursue a career in information technology. Educational institutions that can afford personal computers have included them as part of the facilities that are offered. Public and private institutions have begun to use computers for many of their routine tasks. All these changes have come about as a result of the demand for such services and are mostly paid for by customers. With lower charges for these services, more people will use them in the future. But this is a naturally evolving urban phenomenon.

The goal of Dot Force and other similar projects is to introduce ICT in rural and other poor communities. The assumption is that poor people do not use these services because they do not have access to them. But the fact is that these services have not yet come into rural areas because people have not yet found much use for them and are unable to pay for the related costs.

In my conversations with several village leaders, I did not find a single person who wanted computers or the information that they could obtain from the Web, certainly not for a fee. Sure, they would like their children to learn the use of computers, but the teachers could not see how they could use any of the English language educational tools when they teach in local languages.

After considerable prodding, I could get people to agree that it might be useful to know in advance the weather for the next day, so they could decide on whether to sow the seeds, or to learn about the prices of commodities in the nearby markets. If this information were available through the radio, they said they would be very happy. The need to make telephone calls was no more frequent than once a month and that was just for a few in the entire village.

"Whom do we call on the telephone?" asked one woman. "We need steady jobs to support our families, and when we fall sick, we should be able to get help."

For a great majority of the village folks, their needs are very basic, but even those are not being met. Rural people are not worried about making "informed choices" when they have no choice in most matters. ICT is far from what they have in mind for survival.

While the individual needs of rural people may not include telephones and computers at the present time, these are essential tools for running the institutions that support the community. The rural hospital run by our foundation has set up a personal computer to gather the medical history and hospital visit records of the entire 15,000 or so population in the nearby 18 villages. Each time a patient visits the hospital, health complaints are immediately recorded, and treatment recommendations are produced for further action by the doctor or, during his absence, by the nurse.

Up-to-date medical records allow the medical staff to monitor the health status of everyone in the community and to take preventive action. The computer system alerts social workers to visit pregnant women who have not been showing sufficient weight gain in their early months of pregnancy, so they can be provided with protein-rich preparations. Well-trained staff at the hospital are able to make use of software applications that are designed for their specific needs. But without serious commitment and constant follow-up, the computers would only serve as decorative pieces in the offices.

Technology is also put to good use by one of the leading Indian companies, ITC Ltd., which has set up computers connected to the Internet at central locations in several villages. Through this service, farmers are offered usually three to six percent higher prices for the produce they grow than what they could otherwise get by selling in the nearest open market.

By cutting out middlemen, ITC is able to bid at a higher price directly from the farmer and then turn around and sell in the wholesale and retail markets at good profits. While this has offered farmers one more outlet to sell their crops, it does not represent a competitive market where multiple companies bid for the same commodity through the Internet. When many buyers bid in open auctions through the Internet, farmers are likely to get the best prices based on supply and demand. The introduction of technology in rural areas for creating new markets is a step in the right direction for improving the profitability of farmers.

IMPROVING HEALTH, EDUCATION AND ENVIRONMENT

The government certainly has an important part to play in channeling adequate resources toward health and education. A majority of Indians still live below the real poverty level, with little or no access to proper health care. Preventive and primary health care, including adequate nutrition, is an essential service for all regardless of their income levels. India has the largest stock of food grains in the world, but it also has one of the highest rates of malnutrition; forty to sixty percent of the children in India are undernourished.[17] Similarly, basic education has been neglected to the point that, even with higher literacy levels, a majority of the nation has not benefited.

An educated and trained population significantly adds to the productivity of the nation. The literacy rate in India is presently around sixty percent[18] but this points out only part of the problem; the labor force does not have the skill base to be productive in today's industries. Moreover, rural India is entirely dependent on agriculture, but its real incomes have not kept pace with those in the cities. As a result, more and more unskilled people are moving to cities from villages in search of job opportunities.

The available labor force must be sufficiently educated and trained in those fields that are demanded by the private sector so that progress and employment are not constrained for want of skilled labor. It is not enough to rely on the schools of higher learning; basic quality education must be made accessible to all. An educational system that is flawed by sub-standard quality, poorly defined objectives and insufficient commitment cannot generate the necessary human resources to equip a world-class industrial base.

While the current policies attempt to generate employment mostly through the private sector, they must also address the essential needs of the disadvantaged who cannot find jobs. The concept of a "safety net" is still a social necessity, but it should not become a permanent feature in anyone's life, depriving people of the incentive to work and earn.

There is much written about Kerala state as a success story in India. High literacy is cited as the main reason for its higher income levels. But the reality is that literacy has helped people in the state to understand their rights more than their responsibilities. Labor unions are stronger in Kerala than in any other place in India, and they have managed to drive away industries ever since the country's independence. Lack of opportunities within the state has caused an exodus of its literate population to elsewhere. Yet, any visitor will find shops in Kerala overflowing with consumer goods of all kinds, both foreign and domestic. There are enough people with sufficient purchasing power to avail of them.

Kerala is a consumer state with few major industries. Foreign money has been flowing into the state from expatriates working abroad, especially in the Middle East. Despite the lack of major industries, this state prospers more than the rest of India. It is the wealth earned by these non-resident Indians that is fueling the state economy, not positive government policies. Literacy and quality education have both helped, but the state's successive governments cannot take much credit.

Last but not least, population growth and modernization in India have taken their toll on the environment. Shortages of clean water, insufficient public utilities, industrial and vehicular air pollution and open dumping of toxic waste are some of the major environmental health challenges the country is facing. In addition to air and water, there is growing pressure on other natural resources like forests, where indiscriminate deforestation has led to numerous environmental problems, such as fragmented natural habitats, unchecked erosion, water pollution, loss of livelihood and man-animal conflict.

Typically, environmental issues have social and economic dimensions. These challenges must be approached in a holistic manner because blame-seeking will only yield poor results. There is also the need to encourage the development of an environmentally friendly culture within corporations. The country must give priority to the preservation of its environment and remedy the damage that has already been caused. This approach will ensure the sustainability of the environment and that of the economy as well. If we don't pay attention to these problems there will not be many livable cities, and the country will be forced to put the brakes on economic progress.

ESSENTIAL PARTNERSHIPS

In accomplishing the many tasks that India faces, it must bring in many partners – government, private companies, NGOs, and individuals. NGOs have played a major role in poverty eradication, health care, education and social services, especially in rural areas and urban slums. The government has also found that it is easier to get its work done by NGOs and is willing to fund projects through them. There is no doubt that government-run projects with NGO involvement have done better than those managed entirely by bureaucrats and government officials.

However, many NGOs display a herd mentality, following what other NGOs have previously done, and they find out later that they could have been more effective with imagination and originality. The trouble is that most funding agencies prefer NGOs to follow existing practices and tend to reject new ideas that do not fit known models.

Most NGOs in India prefer to stay away from government assistance due to the bureaucratic hassles involved. Unfortunately, bilateral and international agencies channel their funds through state and central governments. Therefore, NGOs do not have any choice in this matter unless they want to rely only on private individuals and foundations. In villages, one can find NGOs doing work in a village on health, on education, and the watershed – all funded by different agencies. NGOs often act as coordinating bodies, with the implementation of tasks usually given to local officials. Looking at the evaluation reports of projects carried out by some of the NGOs, I find there is definite positive impact in their intervention areas.

Sustainable projects supported by the government which give the poor the capability to own income-generating assets are one effective way to deal with poverty. Policymakers need to realize that rural India offers more than the production of food for the nation; it has the potential to generate significant foreign exchange that could be used in other sectors. When this underutilized rural sector is given sufficient support, the nation will realize the goal of reducing poverty and hunger. It will also contribute to national prosperity. The time has come for the country to create new rural partnerships among and between the poor, and all the outsiders – government, bilateral and international agencies, donors, private institutions and NGOs – to solve poverty and all its related human rights issues.

India is often compared to an elephant, as opposed to a tiger, that moves forward slowly but deliberately. Elephant it might be but for sure chained by its master, the mammoth bureaucracy. The "Indian elephant" carries only the privileged on its back, leaving others behind, frustrated and disillusioned. If India continues with a business-as-usual attitude, it will lose a great opportunity at a crucial moment in history when countries around the world are making major strides. Beyond achieving rapid aggregate growth and higher per capita income – measures of which are skewed by the income generated by a small section of the urban population engaged in technology and other successful industries – the country must address the paramount need to eradicate poverty and elevate the standard of living of the rural people who comprise a great majority of the nation's population.

Great riches lie untapped in this neglected group. Effective solutions demand creating opportunities through ownership of income-generating assets, opening up access to credit and competitive markets for successfully running small local businesses, offering financial incentives for larger companies to set up agriculture-related factories in rural areas, and providing education and skills needed for wider employment.

It is no longer acceptable to offer excuses and explanations for not meeting aggressive and realistic national goals within set time periods. Only through good governance and transparency can the authorities earn the necessary trust to implement effectively the required steps. All well-meaning citizens must ask themselves who they are today as a people and how fairly do they want the country's economic progress to evolve.

India can learn from both the good and the bad of Western economies; discard those practices that are simply excesses of capitalism and embrace the sound principles of individual freedom, fairness, and entrepreneurship. Through a free press and the electoral process, people must persuade their governments to act fairly and with courage in the national interest, and alter the country's course of history to realize a brighter future.

Chapter 7

HOLY COWS, UNTOUCHABLES, AND NON-BELIEVERS

TERRORISM AND OTHER FORMS OF VIOLENCE

After September 11, 2001, many tried hard to explain that the terrorist attacks had nothing to do with religion and that it was about America's policies in the Middle East and elsewhere. There have been numerous efforts in many circles to legitimize terrorism and the indiscriminate murder of civilians. The fact of the matter is that people don't commit such horrendous crimes against innocent people without some belief in the supreme correctness of their actions.

Salman Rushdie, the author of *The Satanic Verses* (Viking Press, 1989) which caused the Iranian government to condemn him to death some years ago, says "… it was about an unpleasant and fanatical reading of Islam. Look what's being done in the name of God right now. Whether it's planes flying into buildings or children being burned alive in Gujarat, India, the fact that it's done in God's name is a serious part of the problem, because it appears to give people moral validation for immoral acts. Religion is the poison of the blood."

The terrorist attack on the Indian parliament in December 2001 and other incidences of violence in many parts of the country, particularly in Kashmir, are a reflection of the social and religious conflict between communities, with political and economic undertones. Discrimination based on religion, caste and gender has prevailed in India for centuries, and while the resentment and anger among many sections of the society have been fairly contained for all these years, there is no guarantee that peace and tranquility can be maintained in the future. With terrorism as a new tool for those who have grievances, there is greater danger than ever before to India's stability and economic progress.

Many United States leaders, including President George Bush, tried to separate terrorism from Islam as a whole, but there are others who do not accept such distinctions, explaining that Islamic culture is hostile to the West and to democratic values. The political context of America's support of Israel's security cannot be sufficient justification, they argue, for the consistent public display of Arab hatred for the United States and the religious backing in many circles for their terrorist acts. There is some reluctance in America to examine the complex historical dimensions of this hatred in the Arab world; in the same way the Hindu fanatics fail to recognize the origins of Islamic terrorism in Kashmir.

The argument that Islam supports terrorism is a dangerous one, as it could lead to a confrontation between cultures and between religions. By ignoring the underlying reasons for terrorist acts and by placing the blame on religion, no constructive solutions can be found. The war against terrorism can be won only with disapproval expressed in both the West and in the Arab world, and a universal determination to confront it.

Most of the killings taking place around the world in recent years have been the result of religious conflict or supported by religious beliefs, and India is no exception. From the time of India's independence from Britain, conflicts between Hindus and Muslims have taken innumerable lives. Today, terrorism with religious undertones fuels killings. Terrorists place bombs in crowded areas to cause maximum deaths and injuries. In the Middle East, suicide bombings have become common occurrence. Many of these bombers believe they are doing God's work even when innocent people are murdered. Like Joan of Arc, some perpetrators say they heard voices from God.

The human race is presumed to turn to religion for peace, to have a calming influence. Instead, religion often brings violence, conflict and war.

Maureen Dowd in her op-ed column for *The New York Times* wrote recently, "As the need for spirituality is growing, the credibility of various faiths is waning. Instead of addressing itself to the angels of our nature, religion seems to be inspiring the demons in our nature."

Scripture is used as a warrant for political aggression and outright militancy. Islamic extremists are supposedly fighting a holy war to drive infidels out of their holy land of Saudi Arabia (where some American troops are stationed). On the other hand, Palestinian gunmen hid for days in the Church of the Nativity in Bethlehem, the very spot where Jesus is believed to have been born, to escape from an Israeli siege.

President Abraham Lincoln, like Mahatma Gandhi after him, was one who derived his sense of purpose and moral courage from his religious convictions. In his second inaugural address, commenting on demands from some of his supporters who wanted him to punish his former enemies in the Civil War, he said, "The Almighty has His own purposes." This thought offended many "true believers" who knew what God intended. Lincoln further observed, "Men are not flattered by being shown that there has been a difference of purpose between the Almighty and them."

This very thought is embodied in the American Constitution, which makes a clear separation of "Church and State." It is not an inadvertent omission by the framers of the American Constitution in failing to insert the word "God" anywhere in the document.

Reinhold Niebuhr, the preeminent American theologian of the past century, wrote, "Religion is so frequently a source of confusion in political life, and so frequently dangerous to democracy, precisely because it introduces absolutes into the realm of relative values." The time has certainly come for our religious leaders to exemplify true religion by intervening to halt all acts of hatred and violence. Not to do so would be to corrupt religion. "The worst corruption," wrote Niebuhr, "is a corrupt religion."

Wars, another form of violence legitimized by governments, have taken innumerable lives over the centuries. Chris Hedges, a foreign correspondent for *The New York Times* for more than 15 years, knows about the horrors of war firsthand, as well as anyone possibly could. He was imprisoned in Sudan, expelled from Libya, ambushed in Central America, and shot at in Kosovo; he has witnessed atrocities and uncovered mass graves. His haunting eyewitness accounts have been documented in his recent book *War Is a Force That Gives Us Meaning* (Public Affairs, 2002), which makes the central point that wars are made, not born.

Hedges finds that "war exposes the capacity for evil that lurks not far below the surface within all of us."

National leaders try to demonize the enemy, while projecting themselves as the embodiment of absolute goodness, with morality and God on their side. Most reporters assigned to cover wars do not go near the fighting, and their stories rise out of what the military and the government put out for public consumption. Nationalism warms the heart, he says, and people want to believe in the nobility and the heroic self-sacrifice demanded by the war, without adequately questioning their leaders who get the nation into avoidable conflicts in the first place.

The dispute over Kashmir and the ensuing armed conflict between India and Pakistan have resulted in the loss of thousands of lives in the three wars fought over the past few decades. The conflict with China in the 1960s also caused major casualties and required large expenditure in defending the borders. The question to be asked is whether India could have avoided these conflicts with its neighbors or whether they were unavoidable through no fault of India's.

RELIGIOUS FUNDAMENTALISM

The Hindu fanatics in India, supported by certain elements within the ruling Bharatiya Janata Party (BJP), are blaming Islam and Muslims for the violence within India and for the conflict with Pakistan. These accusations and efforts to oppress minorities in general have already caused a backlash, as communal disturbances are now on the increase. According to a report released in late 2002 by the Intelligence Bureau, the central agency for detecting internal security problems in India, the country faces grave internal threat in almost all states from terrorism, left-wing extremism, and communal disturbances. Attacks and reprisals are now a daily occurrence.

Minorities do not have the same level of confidence as they had some years ago in the police and the government in general to offer them the necessary protection. Many have begun to organize their communities to counter the perceived threat on their own. Without genuine confidence-building efforts by state and central government authorities, and community leaders, the alienation and fear felt by minorities will only increase. Consequently, the danger of confrontations breaking out between Hindu fanatics and minority groups, especially Muslims, will undoubtedly escalate and could lead to serious civil unrest in many parts of the country.

The apparent contradictions seen in the practice of modern day Islam baffle many people. The word Islam means surrender or submission to the will of God, to Allah. Prophet Mohammed had demanded that his followers be just, compassionate and tolerant. How could the self-proclaimed "true faithfuls" of Islam destroy the 2,000-year-old Bamiyan statues of Afghanistan, fly airplanes into buildings, and commit other acts of terrorism across the world in the name of God? To understand this, one has to examine the evolution of modern-day Islam.

The armed struggle between Christianity and Islam had its origins in Mecca in the year 612 AD. Within a few years, Muslims had conquered much of the Christian world and propagated the belief that there is only one God, and he is Allah. According to Islamic scholar Bernard Lewis, there has never been a distinction between politics and religion for Muslims.

The Islamic culture made extraordinary gains for centuries, only to begin its slow decline after the 17th century, culminating in the collapse of the Ottoman Empire after World War I. Since then, many Muslims have been debating how to regain their past glory. Some Muslims believe that the only way to move forward is to embrace the good aspects of modern civilization practiced in the West. Then there are others who believe that what went wrong was the result of abandoning Islam's true heritage.

Osama bin Laden and his followers want to start a crusade to bring back past greatness and erase "present humiliation." This humiliation turned into hatred toward the United States, because American troops dared to set foot in Saudi Arabia, Islam's holiest land.

What is behind the Arab anger toward the West? Happy people do not kill themselves for abstract causes. The answer to this question lies partly in the fact that most Arab regimes have created an environment of political repression and no freedom. Oppressive leaders and "noble" families rule most Arab countries, and their lifestyles are grossly different from those radical fundamentalists of Islam.

In some of the Islamic countries, especially in Pakistan, Egypt, Sudan, Syria and Yemen, economic conditions are also deplorable. In the absence of domestic political freedom and economic opportunity, it has become convenient for these governments and their citizens to blame outsiders for all their troubles, and the anger toward their rulers is deflected toward the West.

The conflict between Arabs and Israelis has now expanded into one between Islam and the West. Similarly, the dispute over Kashmir between India and Pakistan has now turned into a conflict between Islam and Hinduism. According to government statistics, more than 250 communal riots on an average take place in India each year, with a majority of casualties being Muslims.

Muslims complain that the press reports such events in vague terms, usually not disclosing the true casualty statistics. In recent years, the rise of Hindu fundamentalism has threatened the uneasy peace that had existed in the past, and Muslims have turned inward to seek protection. In the communal riots and killings that took place in Gujarat in 2002, India's National Human Rights Commission has "found substantial evidence of premeditation by members of Hindu extremist groups; complicity by Gujarat state government officials; and police inaction in the face of these violent attacks on Muslims in which many persons were shot, stabbed, raped, mutilated, and/or burned to death."[19]

What is equally disturbing, according to the United States Commission on International Religious Freedom, is that the government of India "has tolerated severe violence against religious minorities." When national leaders repeatedly dismiss incidents of violence and killings of even a few minorities as isolated events, it suggests an implied official tolerance of such deeds.

The violence that took place in Gujarat was not simply a conflict between two religious communities. Instead, it was an attack by certain members of the Hindu community on Muslims with the prior knowledge of several high government officials of the state. There is evidence of participation by some officials who might have provided specific information about where Muslims lived and worked, so that targeted attacks could be made against them.

During the initial stages of the riot, the absence of state intervention by way of applying legitimate force by the police to prevent an escalation of the violence was also evident. Even after hundreds were brutally murdered and women were raped and mutilated, the state failed to apply any credible force to put an immediate end to the massacre.

Until Gujarat, there was never a riot in India where the sexual subjugation of women was so widely used as an instrument of violence. There were reports of the gang rape of young girls and even pregnant women, often in the presence of family members, followed by their murder by fire or with knives and hammers. Eyewitnesses were exterminated. India, which has stood in defense of the victims of racism and violence in South Africa and the Middle East, finds itself accused of some of the cruelest crimes against innocent and helpless minorities, committed by its majority community with the complicity of the state.

The strong pro-Hindu ideological wing of the BJP is blamed for the killings that took place in Gujarat. The central government, also ruled by the

BJP, refused to see this incident as anything out of the ordinary within the context of many previous communal riots. Defense Minister George Fernandes expressed his personal opinion that these things have happened before in India, and Prime Minister Vajpayee showed his unwillingness to take the chief minister of the state to task by asking for his resignation or dismissal.

What was lacking was any resemblance of moral courage on the part of political leaders of the country to do what was right, or any willingness to exhibit the moral authority by guiding the nation accordingly. Initially, many newspapers and intellectuals were trying to analyze and rationalize the incident, instead of expressing their outrage and revulsion. Only when world opinion began to question India's commitment to secularism and the government's failure to intervene forcefully, did the central government begin to take meaningful steps to prevent continuation of the carnage.

It now appears that Hindu nationalism is gradually becoming mainstream in India. One now finds many liberals and intellectuals, businesspeople and slum dwellers, higher castes and untouchables, all expressing Hindu pride. Some people want to write a new chapter in India's history, which they think would make them feel proud of their religion and heritage.

If the election victory of the BJP party and its allies in Gujarat following the communal riots is any indication, a silent majority in India now favors the creation of a Hindu nation. The ruling government has found a common thread running across all castes that can possibly win political affiliation, and we can expect a similar winning strategy in future elections in most other states also.

The difference between Arab and Indian Muslim resentment is profound. The Muslim minority in India is a powerful group of over 150 million people who tend to be more urban than rural. In some towns in Northern India, Muslims make up one-third or more of the population. The Muslims of India are not preoccupied with what the Arabs consider Western injustice toward them. Instead, what is still fresh in their minds are the atrocities committed against their fathers and mothers at the time of partition of India in 1947, and the subsequent religious riots that have taken place in several northern states.

They are more concerned about everyday prejudices and threats faced in their localities. Even small incidents trigger violent reactions among both Hindus and Muslims, with no display of trust between them. Most newspapers and television stations run by non-Muslims avoid reporting stories that reflect negatively on the Muslim community for fear of reprisals. The police do not wish to get involved even when criminal incidents take place within the Muslim community.

The uneasy relationship between Muslims and non-Muslims in India, and the reluctance to speak openly about each other's misdeeds, reminds me of my first serious encounter with African-American parents of young children who were part of a school soccer team in New Jersey that I once coached some 20 years ago. I had noticed that my white assistant coach would not discipline the three black kids on the team despite their being consistently late for practices. After several warnings and discussions with parents, I decided to deal with the situation by not allowing any kid who was frequently tardy to partake in Sunday matches against outside teams.

I found myself confronted by the parents of the three black children, accused of racial discrimination and threatened with "consequences." My assistant coach kept himself out of this matter, and later told me that, given the serious mistrust between races, it was ill-advised on my part to punish black children. In the name of racial difference, a wrong could not be set right.

Muslims in India also see the need to safeguard their religious beliefs and values from the influence of the overwhelming Hindu majority, and they bring up their children strictly in accordance with what they have learned as the teachings of Islam. Consequently, they have formed their own small communities in every place they exist, joining together for physical security and comradeship, while following the directives of their religious leaders.

They generally feel free to practice their religion and follow its traditions and customs without any serious outside threats. However, they are conscious of the mistrust that exists between the two communities, and they feel uneasy about the potential for major communal violence that could be sparked by minor misunderstandings or events.

The common thread of Islam has resulted in shared national loyalties, among a majority of Indian Muslims. On the one hand, many Muslims feel that they can prosper in India and have found their true home in the land of Hindu majority. Many Muslims serve in the armed forces of India and have fought in conflicts with Pakistan. Even the current president of India, Abdul Kalam, is a Muslim. Yet most Muslims feel a sense of close brotherhood with Muslims elsewhere, including those of India's neighbor, Pakistan.

Some accuse Indian Muslims of supporting Pakistan on the Kashmir dispute and cite as an example of disloyalty the cheering that Pakistani cricket teams receive from Muslim spectators when they play on Indian soil. Indeed, mutual hatred and suspicion linger between Hindus and Muslims everywhere in India. Despite the efforts of many who wish to see a secular country with all its citizens living in religious harmony, there is continuing tension in the air. Nothing much has changed since Tagore translated Kabir's poem "Kabir: One Hundred Poems of Kabir" when he saw the failed promise of unity between Islam and Hinduism.[20]

Thomas Friedman, the distinguished columnist of *The New York Times*, wrote an opinion piece after his visit to India in 2002 saying essentially that democracy is the prescription for tranquility. He cited the Indian democracy and its "free press" as the reasons for containing the violence that took place against Muslims in Gujarat from spreading to other states.

"Even when Gujarat was burning, practically the whole of India was at peace – that is the normal pattern here," he quoted an editor of a Muslim newspaper.

True, democracy and freedom might help soothe the frustrations and anger of the masses, but it is not an assurance for peace. What Friedman might have failed to recognize was that religious hatred still exists in large measure everywhere in India, and democracy has not contributed to its decline. The reasons for the government's ability to contain violence lie elsewhere. Namely, there is no strong cultural or personal bond between people from different states, for one group to take up violence in support of another.

"I wouldn't marry a Gujarati, so then why should I kill myself or someone else for him?" says a South Indian when asked why there was hardly any disturbance elsewhere. The secular national press and a disciplined military are probably the other reasons the carnage was confined to Gujarat.

Religious hatred is not confined to Hindus and Muslims. In recent years, Christians have faced threats and violence at the hands of Hindu fundamentalists, once again supported by the overt actions of some state officials and the passive response of the central government. Christian missionaries are accused of carrying out "forced conversion" of low caste and tribal people. The word "forced" gives the erroneous impression of gun-toting nuns and priests; in fact, it is about the use of financial and personal help to persuade people to convert to Christianity.

For decades, Christian missionaries had sought conversions, and some still continue to do so, driven by their conviction and faith in the "salvation" of those who believe in the teachings of Jesus. Many carry out their social work motivated by the desire to serve the poor, often in places where no one else wishes to go. Initially it was the Jesuits, an order within the Catholics, who embarked on a wide range of services and activities to help the poor, but subsequently other Christian congregations joined the effort.

Today, most groups are far less involved in direct conversion activities, and they concentrate instead on changing existing conditions that the poor face in the villages. This work has drawn the resentment of upper castes, and they in turn use the "conversion slogan" to oppose the efforts to improve the social and economic status of the poor. Many Christian missionaries continue to make immense personal sacrifices living among the poor for years at a stretch, helping them cope with hunger and disease and resisting the oppression by landlords and upper caste people in the villages.

Since India's independence from British rule, there have not been any reported instances of conversion to Christianity attempted by threats of violence. The few thousand conversions of tribals and *Dalits* that have taken place each year have been motivated by their desire to escape the social underclass status and to find a way out of poverty. In fact, the opposite has been the reality; recently converted individuals have been compelled by Hindu extremists to reconvert to Hinduism, and consequently they return to their original social status.

In all such instances, people who had previously converted to Christianity were threatened with reprisals and were required to convert back into Hinduism in group ceremonies. Despite all this, many educated people loosely use the term "forced conversions" to describe conversions that take place with consent, while those that occur under threats of physical violence are condoned, though they are intended to maintain the oppressive statusquo of the religious caste structure.

During the past decade, and especially since the BJP government came into power, there have been numerous incidents of atrocities against Christians. Many churches were bombed, nuns raped, priests beaten and killed, and missionary workers threatened with physical violence in several states. State governments with a BJP majority or affiliation have been reluctant to protect these powerless and peaceful believers of their faith, and only in rare instances have the perpetrators of violence been apprehended and punished. The central government's response has also been meek; the prime minister dismissed many incidents of violence and murder as isolated events. To date, no national leader has seriously sought to impress upon its citizens the immorality of such hate crimes. It appears that India's political leaders have not yet fully grasped the fundamental lesson that history has taught us over and over again: social justice and communal harmony are prerequisites to long-term national prosperity and peace.

Leaving aside issues of constitutionality concerning religious freedom and free speech, the fundamental question is this: is an individual free to choose the religion he or she wishes to follow? A low caste person is doomed to remain in his low status, and even those helping him deal with his miserable life are not permitted to persuade him to change his humiliating status or faith.

The government is preventing private financial contributions from reaching the socially and economically disadvantaged people if those contributions encourage them to change their religious faith. In all other walks of life, financial rewards are the main motivation for people's actions, and they include bribes that are accepted by government officials.

The freedom to choose a religion different from what a person has been born into is deprived of him, and all such rights are vested with his oppressors and the state. Such is the moral and legal argument made by those who oppose conversion and who feel justified in committing violence against those who persuade another to convert – all this in a country where just a few thousand people convert each year to Christianity and where the entire Christian population is less than the number of newborns in Hindu families each year.

Yet, except for a small minority of Hindu and Muslim fundamentalists, most Indians are sufficiently tolerant of other religions. The problem lies in the fact that the number of fanatics is steadily increasing and so are their passive supporters and sympathizers.

Democracy does not assure freedom from fanaticism and religious hatred, just as a free press does not guarantee secularism. But that is not to say that true democratic values and free press do not contribute to peace and stability. In the case of Gujarat violence, however, it is probably cultural diversity and long-standing values of peaceful coexistence within a generally secular society that kept India from burning itself. Unfortunately, when the state shows deliberate ignorance or indifference to the communal hatred displayed by religious fanatics, it becomes a license to commit crime on powerless people.

BJP's landslide victory in the December 2002 re-election in Gujarat came about after a campaign based on hate. Britain's *Guardian* newspaper observed that many officials from the government hinted that the state's Muslim minority should consider leaving India for Pakistan.

Financial Times of London said, "... the campaign exploited the communal antagonism that disfigured the state earlier this year." *The Hindu* concluded that the BJP's strategy of "retaining political power through deliberate and aggressive communal polarization has indeed paid off ..."

Religious fanaticism has blinded people of their ability to acknowledge facts, and distinguish right from wrong. When governments and national leaders engage in political activities such as supporting the alienation of minorities, both democracy and peace are threatened.

In his book *The Germans* (Policy Press, 1996), which was finally translated into English in 1996, the great Jewish-German scholar Norbert Elias makes the observation that many people initially perceived the Nazis as "a cancerous growth on the body of civilized societies, whose deeds were those of people who were more or less mentally ill, rooted in the irrational hatred of Jews by people who were particularly wicked and immoral or perhaps set in specific German traditions and character straits." On the contrary, he asserted, "Explanations such as these shield people from the painful thought that such things could happen again anywhere."

After all, Adolf Hitler furiously denied the widely held dream of regaining the greatness of the old German empire. It was subsequently obvious that the pursuit of that goal justified anything, including the elimination of minorities as potential enemies. Like the Jews in pre-Hitler Germany, minorities in India had until recently assumed that the secular traditions of the country would guarantee their permanent security, but the divisive events of the past five or more years have cast a major shadow on that belief.

Racial and religious hatred are practiced with such blind fervor that rationality has very little ability to assert itself. J.M. Coetzee, the 2003 winner of the Nobel Prize for Literature, makes the fundamental point in his novels that the inhuman values and conduct resulting from South Africa's apartheid system could arise anywhere. The current Indian experience is not unique and should not be casually dismissed. History has repeatedly taught us that bigotry and hatred are human passions, and the capacity to commit mass atrocities is without bounds. With the cover of nationalism and false spirituality, some people feel free to pursue evil that ultimately offers nothing but suffering. Invariably, religious fanaticism is absolute, devoid of reason and tolerance, and absorbed by blind faith and abhorrence.

Some argue that the threat to secularism in India does not come from any excessive religiosity of its peoples. People nurture their passion for violence from religious fervor, ethnic identity and nationalistic pride, but these emotions do not come into play when their actions are motivated by rationality. Individuals act in their economic self-interest when they have equal opportunity within a vibrant economic system. Socialistic practices of the past had crushed entrepreneurial creativity. Even today, the bureaucratic and corrupt nature of public administration places structural impediments to innovation and risk taking. Politicians can do all the talking about secularism, but until people see the opportunity to make personal gains through hard work, they will resort to seeking scapegoats.

CASTE DISCRIMINATION

Religious hatred is not the only major social evil in India; caste has been the source of India's "hidden apartheid." Of the one billion people in the country, some 200 million to 250 million are Dalits (meaning "broken people," formerly called "untouchables"), and another 300 million or so are among the lower castes. Brahmins who are approximately 35 million in number have claimed the status of uppermost caste, and everyone else is in between.[21]

Untouchables are barred from the prominent sections of villages, and they may not draw water from higher caste wells, touch food vessels used by upper castes or pray in higher caste temples. They are expected to perform society's most menial and degrading tasks, such as cleaning waste of all sorts and collecting items from garbage heaps that could be recycled. Mobility on the part of lower caste members attracts stiff resistance from upper castes.

Caste was not always present in India's very ancient history and culture, though there is evidence of it in since the 7th century AD. At some point, conflicts within the society resulted in the creation of groups that subjected each other to different tasks, and castes came into existence. With the advent of Buddhism, the caste system was rejected, only to be revived later in a more repressive fashion.

The theological justification of caste can be found in the Rig Veda around 1200 BC. According to it Brahmins came from the mouth, Kshatriyas from the arms, Vaishyas from the thighs and Sudras from the feet of Brahma, the creator. The Brahmins were considered the intellectual and priestly class, Kshatriyas were the soldier class, Vaishyas were traders, and Sudras performed menial jobs. Subsequently, a fifth category of untouchables or Dalits was added.

Over time, caste became entrenched theologically and jurisprudentially, thereby remaining a part of daily life. Notions of "purity" and "pollution" govern the separation between castes. Unlike race, wherein the physical difference between people is available to perpetuate injustice, imaginary differences and elaborate social rules were created to separate people on the basis of caste. Caste status is maintained by symbolic religious observances; rituals and prayers known only to those in each of the upper castes. All real and imaginary differences between castes are assumed to be naturally ordained.

Today, the caste system flourishes more in rural areas than in cities. Socioeconomic changes sweeping urban areas have opened up opportunities for lower caste persons. Those upper caste individuals who would normally discriminate against lower caste people are now prepared to approach them if there is some material benefit to be gained. Urban Dalits resist any oppression and exert their rights and special privileges, but individual prejudices and discrimination continue.

Many people do not socially associate with those of other castes, and marriages between them are uncommon. Higher caste persons avoid eating meals with lower caste individuals, even when they have known each other for a long time. Some doctors will not even touch the skin of a lower caste patient; they place a cloth in between when taking the pulse. This indignity is still not viewed by most Indians as offensive behavior. People who are otherwise good and gentle practice bigotry and deny what is rightful to others, especially to the depressed class in the society. It is the same India that is proud of its record in opposing racial discrimination of both Indians and blacks in South Africa by the whites.

In rural India, the caste system is a well-engrained aspect of the society. Members of the dominant and higher castes own more fertile land, where they have easy access to water. Lower caste men, on the other hand, are often exploited by upper castes who appropriate their land (usually when they fail to repay high-interest loans), give them low wages, use them as bonded labor and otherwise deny them basic human rights. Lower caste families are asked to live in that section of the village from where the wind will not blow toward the upper caste dwellings and "contaminate" them. They are forbidden the right to bury their dead anywhere near the village for fear that the "ghost" would harm the high caste people. Dalit children must sit in a separate section of the classroom; lower caste people may only take seats that are not near upper caste persons while traveling in public transport.

The recent report of the National Commission on Scheduled Castes and Scheduled Tribes reveals the brutal fact that many women belonging to this segment of the population are victims of rape by upper caste men. There are numerous incidents of violence against lower caste people, especially if they violate any of the unwritten oppressive rules of social conduct. A recent example is the beating to death of five Dalit youths in a village in Haryana state for skinning a dead cow they had bought for hide. The police watched the mob attack but did nothing to rescue the victims; the next day several Hindu organizations had a protest march for what was done to the dead cow! One has to wonder how a civilized society allows such atrocities and why governments fail to act forcefully to avoid future repeat occurrences.

Mahatma Gandhi struggled against the caste system and tried to bring human dignity to the deprived people until his death soon after independence. Gandhi set the moral tone within which the founding fathers of the nation created its constitution. The preamble to the Indian Constitution proclaim the goal of accomplishing social justice and equality, while Article 14 lays out the principle of equality. Further Articles prohibit discrimination in employment and in educational institutions. Articles 16(4), 330 and 332 make provisions for reservations or quotas in services and political positions. However, the establishment of a casteless society as a national goal is not mentioned anywhere in the Constitution.

According to Prof. Marc Galanter, a constitutional expert from the University of Wisconsin, the "Constitution sets forth a general program for the reconstruction of Indian society. In spite of its length, it is surprisingly undetailed in its treatment of the institution of caste and existing group structure in Indian society."

To eradicate untouchability the Legislature passed two enactments, the Civil Rights Acts of 1955 and the Scheduled Castes and Scheduled Tribes Act of 1989. A National Commission for Scheduled Castes and Scheduled Tribes was formed in 1992 to protect the interests of the Dalits and integrate them into the mainstream of society. The laws make the practice of untouchability a punishable offense but do not directly abolish untouchability. It is not absolutely clear how untouchability can be punished without first abolishing it. Despite these steps, untouchability is still widely practiced in many parts of India. Indians who use lofty claims of a country "united in diversity" and cite the anti-discrimination laws as proof choose to ignore the reality of social injustice perpetuated with impunity on a large segment of the population.

Caste discrimination violates all human rights norms accepted by civilized societies. Stories of punishment by death of one's own children who cross over and marry from a lower caste can be read in Indian newspapers. Classified matrimonial advertisements invariably specify the caste requirement, even by those of Indian origin who seek spouses in America and elsewhere. To date, the nation has not made a real attempt to abolish the caste structure. Punishment for discriminatory actions is not severe, and compensation for victims of religious- and caste-related violence is not adequate.

According to the Human Rights Watch report, "The Indian government has been successful at manufacturing an image as the world's largest democracy, with none of its discrimination laws effectively implemented." It is not surprising that India tried to prevent its caste system from being included in the conference agenda at the U.N. Conference on Racism in Durban, South Africa, in August 2001. The Indian delegation managed to get the conference to exclude the word caste in its final document advocating the elimination of racism and other forms of discrimination. There was no cry of outrage within the country at this hypocrisy. The silence has been deafening for too long.

The hope for a casteless society may lie with the judiciary. The judiciary was thought to be an institution of the government during the early stages of post-independent India, but now it is being looked at as an institution of governance in its own right. Courts have begun to enforce laws when the rest of the government machinery has been reluctant.

Public interest litigation over the past 20 years reflects the transition of the judiciary toward an autonomous institution of governance. The bold, though controversial, decision on the closing of the polluting industries in the capital city of Delhi is an example of this new role of the judiciary. Yet, without government cooperation, it is unlikely that even judicial rulings will be properly executed in a timely manner.

The desire to use the Constitution for ensuring socioeconomic justice is evident in the institution of public interest litigation as an instrument of governance in India. In public interest litigations, a group of citizens or organizations can bring to the notice of the courts issues that need immediate attention on behalf of the affected parties. It is intended to address violations of constitutional and legal rights of people who are poor, ignorant or in a socially or economically backward position.

Courts have used commissioners to do fact finding and experts to recommend courses of action before directives are issued; implementation is monitored by report-back procedures. The Supreme Court has approved efforts to provide constitutional guarantees to the 1990 governmental notification implementing the Mandal Commission's recommendations for job reservation for economically and socially backward classes. Setting quota or reservation in education and employment was earlier confined to the most downtrodden castes and tribes, known as the Scheduled Castes and the Scheduled Tribes. But the new government legislation extended reservation to other economically and socially backward castes.

In America too, preferential programs of education, training and employment were put into effect in the 1960s, as just and necessary compensation for the deprivations African-Americans had suffered from generations of slavery. President Lyndon Johnson, endorsing affirmative action, stated that the victims of past injustice should be given a helping hand beyond a level playing field. Simultaneously, laws concerning discrimination on the basis of race, gender and national origin were put into effective enforcement.

Affirmative action was originally intended for African-Americans and Native American Indians, and there was no thought of expanding it. Moreover, it was not designed to help those who no longer needed help. Somehow this common sense interpretation of the law got lost in the political shuffle. Over the years, the criteria for affirmative action were widened to include Hispanics, Asians and certain other nationalities, and finally, women. The absurdity of this new definition of the deserving is evident in the fact that over two-thirds of the U.S. population is now a minority. I suppose the balance of the population should also be a minority for the simple fact that they comprise only one-third of the total.

The country got into this mess because of the confusion over race. What began as a measure of justice and fairness became itself a source of injustice and envy. Is the wealthiest African-American or Hispanic American today more deserving of the preference than the poorest white person?

Today, in India there is a wide range of people of all classes, religions and castes who fall into preferred groups that are guaranteed quotas in employment and other privileges. Unlike the United States, where quotas are resisted and minorities are given preferences on an individual basis, India relies on set allocations for various groups of people. While the original intent was fair and just, the program as administered now has no real sensitivity or relevance to the underlying reasons for its creation.

If a certain group of people has been deliberately harmed in the past, the goal should be to ensure that injustice does not continue. It is not sufficient to offer preferences to victims while allowing the victimization to continue unchecked. The social injustice perpetuated on lower castes and certain other minorities cannot be an acceptable proposition within the sphere of legal enforcement just because the victims are offered concessions. The state must use all its powers to promote social justice through the enforcement of laws concerning discrimination.

It is not clear whether the Dalits of India can rest all their hopes on the judiciary when politicians and bureaucrats are not prepared to change the system. After all, the judiciary consists mostly of upper caste judges who may not wish to change the status quo entirely or who do not fully appreciate the indignity.

The thought of a united Dalit movement is the greatest fear in the minds of the upper classes and castes. The chief minister of Uttar Pradesh, Mayawati, who is a Dalit, has launched a popular movement of the lower castes in her state against the upper castes, asking her 40 million followers to beat their oppressors with shoes. But the reality of Dalit power in India today is that their leaders also join the corrupt government machinery for personal gain, exploiting the benefits of caste politics.

Religious convictions, traditions and cultural habits can no longer be treated with respect when they have been used for too long to oppress people. They have endured their winter of discontent, and something drastic must be done to alleviate the situation quickly.

This may be an opportune time for aggressive efforts to effectively counter discrimination based on caste and religion. After all, social transformation is much easier when accompanied by overall economic revival and expectations of continued improvement in the lifestyles of the privileged. The unanswered question is whether there will soon be a national leader with the moral courage to persuade the nation to bring about a casteless society before violence sets in. President Abraham Lincoln's struggle in abolishing slavery during the Civil War nearly two centuries ago should be an example to emulate.

THE SAFFRON AGENDA

The basic needs of the masses whose lives remain sub-human are relegated to a contrived communal philosophy to serve the political aspirations of the party in power. This new divisive and destructive force has become fairly well entrenched within the country, raising the threat of future events that could tear the country apart along communal lines.

The retired Karnataka High Court judge H.G. Balakrishna states in his recent book *Secularism in India* (2002), "Never before in the history of post-independence India has there been such grave urgency and concern for the restoration of public confidence and communal harmony instead of sowing the seeds of discord among various faiths and religions. Time has arrived to protect India's secular fabric against the forces of division, disintegration and subversion."

It is the union of political power and fundamentalist extremism that produces discrimination and violence.

What is most troubling about the atrocious incident in Gujarat is not just that the state might have been a participant, but the possibility that communal hatred was being nourished by certain elements in the government and the ruling party to further their ideological and political goals. Following September 11, and with tension prevailing along the border with Pakistan in Kashmir, it has become convenient to label the entire Muslim community as terrorists or supporters of terrorism and play to the fears of many people in India.

For the BJP (and, by implication, the central government), the hope is that a majority of Hindus will buy into the ideological goal of turning India into a Hindu Nation and consequently, boost the party's popularity at the next general elections. Such efforts have served to institutionalize communalism by influencing the philosophical and ethical underpinnings of civil society institutions.

What is happening in India today is a shift of political power from moderates to religious fundamentalists. Politicians with a religious agenda have joined forces with Hindu fundamentalists willing to carry out their political and social agenda remotely through mercenaries and fanatics, often with protection from some state governments and the central government. Religion, history and education are being politicized and interpreted to suit the new fundamentalist ideology, while the central government fails to show any genuine concern.

Since the BJP-led National Democratic Alliance government came into power in India, there has been concerted effort to rewrite the history and culture of India, as taught in schools and colleges, to conform to their view of Hindutva or Hindu traditions. This task was delegated to the union education minister, M.M. Joshi, who has been working closely with members of the Rashtriya Swayamsevak Sangh (RSS), the religious fanatical wing of the BJP party.

Prime Minister Vajpayee maintains a silent and distant posture as though he is not a party to this effort, while many of his cabinet members are allowed to coordinate their activities to accomplish the "Hindu agenda."

The government has appointed a Hindu fundamentalist group, Bharatiya Shikshan Mandal, to make policy recommendations in education. The aim of this group, in its own words, is "Indianization, nationalization and spiritualization of education in India."[22]

The campaign to transform the educational system to suit this goal is taking place all across India with great vigor. At the same time, this nationalistic fervor is whipped up by a generally patriotic media and a film industry that has taken a belligerent posture against Pakistan. It appears that the government is attempting to convert a culture into a religion by merging religion into politics. When politics and religion become indistinguishable, we have fully corrupted both religion and politics.

Minister Joshi wants the agenda of "Indianization, Nationalization, and Spiritualization" to be accomplished through educational and cultural organizations. The BJP sees intellectuals as antinational leftists and liberals under Western influence. According to Joshi and others, what is needed, instead, are lessons in patriotism and a revival of their version of India's history and culture. Their concept of government seems to be founded on divine authority rather than human reason.

As Nalini Teneja explains in her well-researched essay *The Saffron Agenda in Education* (Sahmat Publication, 2001), the BJP considers secularists and leftists as Western-educated rootless people who have little to do with the nation because their gaze is turned westward, and they know little about India and appreciate it even less.

Consistent with this view, and accusing the intellectuals of distorting India's history and culture, the government has already made several changes to the curriculum offered at schools and colleges, altered textbooks, appointed biased people to key positions and suppressed the opinions of those who oppose them. The National Council of Educational Research and Training (NCERT), the pivotal central institution responsible for nationally accredited educational programs, has now become an extension of the RSS and is fully engaged in promoting this ideology in classrooms.

In late 2002, the council introduced a new set of textbooks that feature the "Indus Saraswati Civilization" (Saraswati is an ancient river central to Hindu myth) in place of the well-known Indus Valley Civilization, and other chapters on "Hindu Culture" and "Hindu Pride." The assassination of Mahatma Gandhi by a Hindu fanatic in 1948 has been removed from all texts so as not to offend Hindu nationalism. The council has promised to test "Spiritual Quotient," or SQ, as a measure of student sensibility to Hindu values.

The New York Times in a recent op-ed article observed, "While some of us lament the repetition of history, the men who run India are busy rewriting it."

The BJP government is in a hurry to bring about a Cultural Revolution.

To accomplish its religious and cultural aims, the RSS has opened some 20,000 Vidya Bharati schools and colleges in many parts of India. More than 100 seminars have been held to date to promote the controversial changes to the curriculum offered by NCERT. The BJP-led state government of Goa has literally handed over its educational system to the RSS. Children are taught to be "patriotic" and "believers," as opposed to being thinkers, and to value the accomplishments of the ancient Hindu society.

In addition, the invention of "zero" by India is credited for spurring all the developments in science and mathematics and the rise of the West. Vedic mathematics and Vedic astrology are given prominence, and medical colleges are asked to include alternate traditional medicine into their curriculum. Girls and boys may go through the same educational program up to primary school, but subsequently girls must get training in "home keeping."

While these changes are taking place, there is silence among the educated or at best a muted cry from a few intellectuals. The illiterate masses are likely to welcome this Hindu revival. One has to wonder whether the docile response of the media and the indifference among the general public are a reflection of a secret desire on the part of the silent majority to support Hindutva.

Consider some of the changes that have already taken place to promote Hindutva. Lucknow University, a state-run college in the ancient heart of northern India, known for its rigorous engineering and science programs, now offers a degree in astrology and provides on-the-job training in conducting religious rituals and ceremonies. The government has succeeded in placing party people in top jobs at many colleges that now offer diploma programs in subjects, such as Hindu birth, death and wedding rituals, and Vedic math named after the ancient Rig Veda; it is presumed that calculus problems can be solved with the help of ancient scriptures. The government has even named several of its nuclear missiles after weapons and animals taken from Hindu mythology.

While the BJP government is promoting its religious agenda for the nation, it has virtually shut down the flow of funds from foreign sources into educational institutions run by other religious groups. Christian missionaries and churches established many privately run educational institutions of excellence over several years in India, and these institutions continue to offer quality education to millions of Indians of all religious affiliations. Yet, these unaided minority institutions run by Christian organizations face continued harassment from state governments.

Christian Medical College, Vellore, in Tamil Nadu, and St. John's Medical College, Bangalore, in Karnataka were directed by their respective states to admit more than forty percent of the student body from those selected by the state without consultation or regard for the national merit requirements set by these institutions. Both colleges were forced to seek rulings from the Supreme Court of India several times over the years, and despite earlier favorable judgments, they still face interference by the state on new grounds each year.

I wonder what the government stands to gain from forcing these institutions of international repute to abandon the historic traditions that have ensured quality education for students from their own and other communities.

Through a number of approval processes, including those established by the Home Ministry, the government has blocked virtually all foreign sources of funding for these institutions. Even visa applications from foreigners affiliated with non-Hindu religious institutions abroad who wish to do social work in India are routinely rejected or subject to considerable delay. Indian consulates abroad are directed to forward such visa applications to the Home Ministry in Delhi. The applicant is usually kept unaware of this scrutiny aimed at shutting out foreign volunteers and funds even for worthwhile causes.

Volunteers from Christian charitable organizations are constantly denied visas even when they are known to carry out social work all around the world. Visa applicants are deliberately not provided any guidance, and visa rules are changed frequently so that proper requests can be legitimately rejected after several months of waiting without adequate explanation.

In the name of preserving a Hindu nation, the government denies the poor much needed help from outsiders. All these underhanded efforts by the government take place while large amounts of money are freely allowed into Hindu organizations from abroad. According to the Campaign to Stop Funding Hate, a U.S.-based organization that monitors contributions by institutions and individuals abroad, the India Development and Relief Fund (IDRF) alone has contributed more than $5 million in the past seven years, of which nearly $4 million went to RSS-affiliated organizations in India. The BJP government has overlooked these contributions and has thus far taken no steps to stop the inflow of such funds.

I recall my own efforts some years back to mobilize blankets, tents and food for the victims of the Orissa cyclone and floods that killed thousands of people. The Latter Day Saints Charities, run by the Mormon Church, came forward to help, and several large containers of material were arranged for shipment, along with a volunteer from the charity group to supervise the distribution. The visa for the volunteer was held up at an Indian consulate in California, and after almost two months, it was rejected without any explanation. I wonder whether there would have been any such difficulty if the foreign donor had been a Hindu organization.

It is indeed sad that even the suffering victims of a natural disaster could not persuade the bureaucrat in Delhi to permit external help to come into the country, as the assistance was from a perceived ideological enemy. Such decisions are not made without the clear dictates of senior officials who follow or interpret government policy or regulations to suit their goals. A culture of discriminatory practices based on religion has been created in many government institutions to further the political and social aims of the ruling party.

In a recent incident, a group of "officials" from the criminal investigation department came to Shanti Bhavan to "inspect" whether the institution was carrying out Christian activities. This was followed by a visit by a Central Labor Ministry official. These officials did not bring any paperwork authorizing them to make an inspection, and they claimed they had the right to disrupt our routine activities to question our staff and children. These visits have now become frequent. Each time they demand the list of all students and staff, including addresses, religion and caste.

Though more than eighty percent of our children and staff are Hindus, mostly from lower castes, we refuse to provide such information without a proper official request in writing. The fact that Shanti Bhavan is a charitable private school that does not receive any government funds means nothing to the inspectors. After meeting with the school staff and children, and questioning some of them, the inspectors caution us from engaging in any "conversion."

One of our senior members responded, "We convert the children from ignorance to knowledge."

We asked if the officials inspected schools run by Hindu organizations, and whether those institutions were permitted to teach Hinduism. One of the officials responded, "This applies only to Christian organizations and your name 'George' is Christian."

It appears that the government's complacency in this matter has created a public perception that harassment of "Christian institutions" in the name of "conversion" is legitimate.

The harassment and threat are not confined to "conversion" activities. All institutions that carry any sort of association to Christian organizations or individuals face similar incrimination. Sometimes these inspections are carried out at the urging of local village leaders who have been trying to extract money from us for their personal needs. It appears that government officials are let loose to harass anyone for whatever reason they deem fit, and private citizens and institutions have very little recourse.

During a recent visit to India, I was approached by the local Panchayat officials who demanded money for their having supported our foundation against accusations by the BJP. These officials told me that at a BJP group meeting at Hosur in January 2003, our foundation was listed among "targets for action." These Panchayat officials claimed to have protected us and felt we should now reward them.

I replied that The George Foundation did not need anyone else to speak for its secular orientation and sarcastically added, "No one in this foundation is permitted to utter the word Jesus, and everyone is urged to say Rama and Krishna." The absurdity of this comment brought laughter even from the corrupt local officials.

What is now taking place in India has many similarities to the Cultural Revolution that occurred under Chairman Mao Tse-tung in China during the 1960s. Unlike China, where the revolution was brought about with military force, in India we are witnessing the misuse of political and official power in promoting a religious ideology through democratic institutions. Mao wanted to arrest the so-called capitalist trend, while the RSS wants to eliminate Western influence on India's culture. Mao launched the Socialist Education Movement (1962-65) for the purposes of restoring ideological purity, reinfusing revolutionary fervor into the party and government bureaucracies, and intensifying class struggle.[23]

In India, the RSS wants people to view other religions and cultures as detrimental to the interests of the country. The Socialist Education Movement in China echoed another Mao campaign, the theme of which was "to learn from the People's Liberation Army (PLA)."

Minister of National Defense Lin Biao's rise to the center of power was increasingly conspicuous. It was accompanied by his call on the PLA and the Central Communist Party (CCP) to accentuate Maoist thought as the guiding principle for the Socialist Education Movement and for all revolutionary undertakings in China. In India, we see a similar pattern in which major institutions, such as NCERT and the Indian Council for Social Science Research (ICSSR), are called upon to execute the required changes in support of the government's religious ideology.

The Socialist Education Movement in China was aimed at a thorough reform of the school system, which had been planned earlier to coincide with the "Great Leap Forward." It had the dual purpose of providing mass education and of re-educating intellectuals and scholars to accept the need for their own participation in manual labor. The drafting of intellectuals for manual labor was part of the party's rectification campaign, publicized through the media as an effort to remove "bourgeois" influences from professional workers. Intellectuals were criticized for their greater regard for their own specialized fields than for the goals of the party.

In India, the focus of RSS is on Hindu traditions, and the group's members seek to discredit all those who oppose their viewpoint. All non-Hindus must adopt the Hindu culture and language, and they must hold in reverence the Hindu religion. Patriotism is defined in terms of hatred against external enemies, mainly Pakistan and America, and internal enemies, mainly Muslims and Christians.

Is secularism in India in danger? Secularism, as it was understood in the Indian context, emulated the ideals of the liberal West and was admired in America and Europe. It was generally accepted that India would remain a multi-religious state, with no group enjoying any advantage or disadvantage by virtue of religion. Religion was acknowledged to be an integral part of everyone's identity, but the state was to be free of religious affiliations. Today, this dual but separate character of the nation is under attack.

It is unlikely that any long-term dominance by one religious community (represented through its affiliated political party) over other communities is possible without serious repercussions and harm to all communities. The strength of a nation lies in its diversity and tolerance of differences, not in the ability of the majority to oppress the minority. One way to make pluralism work in practice, as a force for progress rather than confrontation, is to harness its diversity for common endeavors.

It is this diversity in past experiences, ideas and approaches that brings out workable and sustaining solutions. One sure way to build confidence among all groups of people is for the government to dismantle official and informal policies and practices that interfere with religious freedom, and strictly adhere to the doctrine of separation of state and religion. If history has taught us anything, it is that no nation has achieved peace and tranquility through oppression and dominance. India's political, religious and community leaders are well advised to remember this lesson, if they are indeed the patriots they claim to be.

In our modern age and throughout history, when a state has taken an exclusive and intolerant view of religion or ethnicity as its foundation in the pursuit of nationalism, it results in a mainspring for violence and destruction. A truly democratic government cannot be nationalist because it must pursue the good of all its citizens. One of the reasons that philosophical liberals leave religion and morality out of politics and law is the possibility of the majority imposing its convictions through the organs of governance.

By embracing a richer form of democracy, where people with different viewpoints and beliefs debate what is in the social good, we can bring in pluralistic values that are acceptable to the entire society. Through such a process and with tolerance, all citizens are able to transcend the accidents of their backgrounds and participate in the essence of universal humanity.

When individual rights are subordinated to collective rights, or when a political entity tries to create a "distinct society," the social fabric begins to break, pulling people apart and tearing the soul of humanity. A state that is incompetent to expel the rightful fears of any section of its society condemns itself and harms all. Without security and human rights for minorities, democracy has no future.

Following the World Trade Center incident in 2001, the United States government instituted several restrictive and invasive measures that many feel unnecessarily curtail individual freedom. India's response to the concern about worldwide terrorism threats was to enact the Prevention of Terrorism Act (POTA) in 2002. Like its much misused predecessor Act, POTO or Prevention of Terrorism Ordinance, POTA has already been applied to target minorities and political opponents. The new Act has expanded the state's investigative and procedural powers, allowing the detention of suspects for up to three months without charge and a further three months with the permission of a special judge.

In a short period of less than two years following the enactment of POTA, there has been systematic curtailment of civil liberties and alleged improper application of the law against political opponents, religious minorities and Dalits. It is yet to be seen whether current and future governments will use the enhanced powers for the intended purpose of dealing with terrorism or for oppressing dissent.

Partial view of Shanti Bhavan from the water tower.

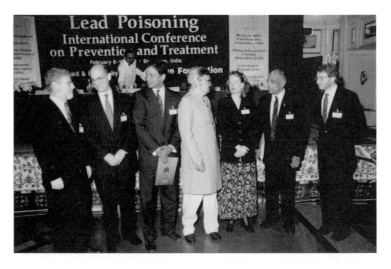

International lead poisoning conference, Bangalore, Feb. 1999.
Left to Right: Henry Falk (CDC); W.A. Nitze (USEPA); Author; K.A. Khan (Governor, Karnataka);
Yasmin von Schirnding (WHO); O.S. Dawson (TGF); Richard Ackermann (World Bank)

Villagers gathering at Baldev Medial Center for health camp

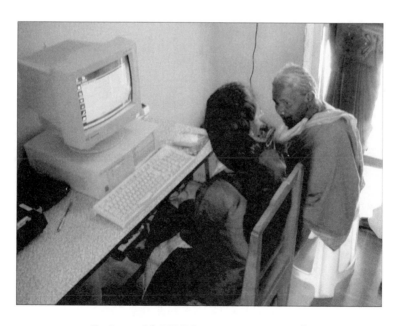

Patient with EDPS operator entering data

Women workers at Baldev Farms Empowerment Program

Chariot festival at Deveerapalli village revived by
The George Foundation after 20 years

Tillany fine Arts museum and Gallery brightens up
the rural landscape at night

Indian Institute of Journalism & New Media
— a front runner in South Asia

Chapter 8

UNEQUAL AND POWERLESS

GENDER DISCRIMINATION

Domestic violence has long been one of the major causes of death, especially among women.[25] In India, there are numerous daily occurrences in which a woman is set on fire after kerosene has been poured over her, followed by claims that she died in a kitchen fire. The incidence of crime against women in India has risen substantially in recent years. Reports published by the World Health Organization (WHO) and other international agencies probably understate the number of violent deaths, as many people even in developed countries do not make a report to police when the assailant is a family member or someone they fear.[24]

Many violent crimes involve alcohol use, and drunkenness is often cited as an excuse for the commitment of crime. In India, people are not usually arrested for disorderly behavior from excessive drinking, driving under the influence of alcohol or wife beating when drunk. The society seems to tolerate family violence and bad behavior if attributed to excessive drinking, as though the offender cannot be held responsible for drunken actions.

Gender discrimination is just as evil as discrimination based on religion and caste. Despite the fact that, in most aspects of life and development, women have been playing an equal role, they are subordinated by men. Rural women are expected to look after the home, work in the field, take care of the animals and do handicrafts at home. Many women are also part of the formal labor force, working in offices and doing manual labor to bring in some income though the family income is usually managed by the husband, who decides what is available to her and the family for the day-to-day needs.

When it comes to making decisions that impact personal and family matters, women are usually excluded. With eighty-eight percent of the women listed as dependents and only twelve percent as heads of households, women in general are not likely to improve their status without financial independence. The lower status of women, especially in rural life, has made their lives unnecessarily difficult in many ways. Rural women in India do not ask for gender equality. What they really want is equal human rights – right to education, health care, employment and safety. The concept of human rights is gender neutral.

The "typical" Indian woman lives in a village, can neither read nor write, and has rarely traveled beyond the nearest town a few miles away. She works on the landlord's farm when he needs her and takes care of her children and her home with little or no physical help from her husband. Her husband controls all the money and gives her whatever he thinks is sufficient for the family's needs; the rest he uses for his drinks and other pleasures.

Most women do not find companionship in their men, and feel they exist only to meet the sexual needs of their husbands and to produce babies. Everyday life is a chain of drudgery, starting with collecting water from a distant well, walking a considerable distance to work in the field, collecting firewood for cooking, and cutting grass for domestic animals, if any. The children have to be fed, the clothes washed in dirty pond water, and the house and surroundings swept. The man of the house returns late at night, usually drunk. He has to be fed in the morning before she leaves for her own work in the field. The small children are left behind with her mother-in-law. Her human rights are dictated by her husband; her future is at his mercy.

Bhimram Ambedkar, one of India's greatest humanitarians who fought for the rights of lower castes and women in the early years of India's independence, noted that the Hindu Dharma-shastras are responsible for much of the thinking behind the subjugation of women. These ancient teachings define the role of a woman as the bond slave of her father when she is young, of her husband when she is middle-aged, and of her son when she is a mother.

Most uneducated Indian women, especially in rural areas, are raised with such pre-defined roles, and they carry those beliefs until death. The most compelling explanation for crimes against women is the prevalence of a patriarchical society where women are considered both the weaker sex and the property of men. Despite Ambedkar's efforts to introduce a bill on the rights of women, especially on matters relating to property, marriage, divorce and maintenance, the Indian parliament chose not to take any effective measures.

According to many studies, the key obstacles to empowering women are the caste system, unequal legal standing of women in matters of inheritance and divorce, economic dependence and illiteracy among many women. Even when laws grant them the right to inherit land, women find resistance from their own brothers in exercising it. The dowry set aside by the family for daughters erodes their sense of ownership in anything else. Early marriages for most women also contribute to their great dependency on men.

For thousands of years, women have been victims of traditions, customs and superstitions that define a lower status for them in society. Consequently, the basic human rights of women are constantly violated, even on matters of reproduction, and many face violence at the hands of those who control them. The police are generally not sensitive to women's complaints, and at times, even they try to exploit the weak situation that female victims face. Some states have set up *Mahila Courts*, or courts for women, and all-female police stations, but these institutions will be successful only when there is greater sensitivity on everyone's part toward women's issues.

In 1999, a National Policy for Empowerment of Women was formulated by the Indian government, which seeks to make reservation of seats for women in the parliament and state assemblies.[26] It also proposes a quota for representation of women in the public sector and in the Civil Services. The National Commission for Women (NCW) was created earlier in 1990 to intervene when rights are violated or when violence is committed against them. There are a number of initiatives and goals for improving health care and education for women and for funding female entrepreneurs. Women are to be given greater assistance in the agricultural sector and in rural development employment schemes – as much as thirty percent of the funds are to be allocated to women for development programs. As an overwhelming percentage of women are employed in the agriculture sector, the government has taken some measures to protect their interests.

Also, women are now being trained in skills beyond farming, opening up opportunities for other types of employment. While the government plan appears forward thinking and bold, it has yet to become a reality. If and when it does, one has to wait and see how its various components are actually executed.

At the 1994 International Conference on Population and Development held in Cairo, governments agreed to undertake a series of steps for the advancement of women, especially in areas of reproductive health.[27] The focus was on ensuring healthy and safe childbearing, preventing sexually transmitted diseases, and other factors such as sexual trafficking and violence against women.

The Cairo conference defined reproductive health broadly as " … a state of complete physical, mental, and social well-being and not merely the absence of disease or infirmity, in all matters relating to the reproductive system."

It takes into account notions of rights, equity, dignity and responsibility in relationships. Women must have the right to make decisions on sex free of coercion. Improving reproductive health involves providing care during a woman's reproductive years, but also caring for her health needs during childhood and adolescence. Signatories of the conference report, including India, agreed to implement a number of measures, such as contraceptive information and services, prenatal care, safe childbirth and abortion.

The lack of sufficient progress in successfully implementing many of these recommendations reflects the failure on the part of governments to give women's issues the priority they deserve.

Past experience has taught us that attempts to control the number of children through behavioral changes in men have failed because families do not see the benefit of fewer children. Children, especially boys, are viewed as extra hands that can provide income and help with family chores. The poorer the family, the more children they seek. Hence, it is evident that the economic status of the family plays the major role in family planning.

Birth control and reproductive health of women are behavioral issues affected mostly by economics, access to health care, and education. Until this reality is adequately dealt with by putting in place effective strategies, the desired changes may not be attainable in the foreseeable future.

In addition to the disadvantages that women in India face, the nation is now confronted with a dangerous disparity in the female-male sex ratio, which is estimated to be 927 females to 1,000 males, as compared to the worldwide ratio of 1,050 females for every 1,000 males. Several states are below the 900 level, while the national ratio has been steadily worsening over the past half a century.[28]

India has the lowest ratio of females to males among the 10 most populous countries in the world. The burden of unaffordable dowry is forcing families to avoid having girls. Families that already have a daughter are more likely to terminate pregnancies when expecting a female child. Neglect of the health and nutrition needs of girls and women and high rates of maternal death in childbirth are other contributing factors.

The declining sex ratio should be of serious concern to everyone, as it would undoubtedly impact the socioeconomic fabric of the society. In communities where there is a shortage of marriageable young women, there have been reported increases in rape and other violence against women. There is no doubt that the birthrate discrepancy is caused by before-birth sex determination and abortion of female fetuses, and outright killing of newborn female babies. Today, even villagers check out the sex of the unborn using an ultrasound machine, instead of using it to detect abnormalities in the fetus or danger to the mother's life.

The government is attempting to curb the use of ultrasound machines by licensing the clinics that make these machines available, and by restricting their use to women 35 years of age or older, or in those situations where there is a potential danger to the life of the mother or the baby. This approach is doomed to fail because those who want to get rid of the female baby will find ways to achieve just that. Female infanticide and mistreatment of the female child are the more likely outcomes of this restrictive approach. It appears that the Pre-Natal Diagnostic Techniques Act of 1994, which places restrictions on the use of ultrasound machines, and its subsequent consent by the Supreme Court were hastily made without sufficient thought and study.

The crux of the problem lies in the belief that woman is somehow inferior to the man and that she is a burden to the family for reasons of dowry and being another mouth to feed.

"Bringing up a daughter is like watering a plant in your neighbor's garden," says a social worker describing how many families think. "Ultimately she is going to be married and go to somebody else, so what is the worth of all that?"

Many patriarchal families expect their children to care for parents in their old age. The daughter's responsibility ends at marriage, while the son's lasts for life. This sort of belief is an outgrowth of ignorance, lack of education and the brutal realities of poverty.

The much-needed cultural change to respect women and their human rights cannot be realized without sensitizing children to these issues from an early age. Further, it is not enough to create laws giving women rights as men in all matters. Women's groups should also be encouraged and financed with public funds to offset present and past disadvantages.

Though the practice of dowry is illegal, it takes place in almost every class of the Indian society, leading to instances of extortion and murder of women for money in marriages. The media, especially television, can play a powerful role in creating awareness on issues such as reproductive rights, human rights and equality between sexes. Only then can laws be effectively enforced to prevent the killing of female babies, unnecessary abortions solely to avoid birth of a female child, violence against women and dowry as a practice.

Efforts to empower women economically through job opportunities will help women to be seen as an equally productive segment of the society deserving of equal rights. Study after study has shown that there is no effective developmental strategy in which women do not have a central role to play. When women are fully involved as equal partners, the benefits can be seen immediately: Families are healthier, they are better fed, and their income, savings and reinvestment rise.

And what is true of families is true of communities and eventually, the whole country. Successful use of a country's human resources is the key to development and creation of wealth. Women represent half those resources and are crucial to the betterment of the whole society.

In a society where men control the destiny of women, how is it possible to empower women? Gender equality could be achieved through a variety of sustaining actions that include enactment and enforcement of proper laws, support of women's groups, meeting the health and educational needs of women, equal opportunity in employment, economic empowerment of women, and awareness creation through the media on the role and rights of women.

However, the situation currently faced by rural uneducated women is somewhat different, and it requires efforts that are specific to their backgrounds and conditions. Gender equality as a concept is not likely to be perceived as a realistic or even correct objective today by a great number of women or men in the rural setting. Simply encouraging women to resist the wishes of men will not only fail but will also create mistrust of any goodwill attempts from "the outside" to help rural communities. Women will gain power only when both men and women begin to respect and accept the contribution of women.

Developing women's capacity for income generation without threatening men is key. Women's empowerment depends on their ability to be economically self-dependent and contribute financially to the needs of the family. Only when women are confident of financially supporting themselves can we expect them to demand human rights. That is why it is so important to focus on education, job training and financial assistance for women small business owners.

Opportunities in modern farming, processing of farm produce, handicrafts, and small scale rural businesses can lead to meaningful employment for rural women. When combined with proper counseling on subjects such as the need to save money, care for the health of all family members, practice of birth control, and education of girls, women will be able to make better decisions for themselves. In turn, mothers will ensure that both sons and daughters are educated, opening up many more opportunities for them when they grow up.

In promoting the advancement of women in Dharmapuri District, The George Foundation has embarked on a multidisciplinary program that involves education and awareness creation, health care, employment and savings. The program is managed by Baldev Medical & Community Center and is staffed by health and social workers. It also draws on the resources of Shanti Bhavan and Baldev Farms for educational and employment support. Training and awareness creation classes are held at the center every week for women and young girls on a variety of topics dealing with nutrition, personal hygiene, prenatal and postnatal care, childbirth, contraception, abortion and other women's issues.

Women's rights are presented in a non-threatening manner for men, but the emphasis is on what women can do for themselves even without the cooperation of men. These discussions also take place in the villages where women's groups are organized to meet periodically, and the message is further taken to classrooms in the nearby government schools.

Women's self-help groups, or *Sanghas* as they are called, are formed in each village. Under the overall supervision of Baldev, these groups are encouraged and taught to save money, which is deposited in interest-bearing accounts in a nearby bank, and the bank makes small loans among the members for worthwhile projects. Amazingly, many women began saving a significant portion of their daily wages, keeping the money away from their husbands and other dependents, for future needs, such as improvement of their homes, dowry, and purchase of household essentials.

With the withdrawal of funds restricted to purposes approved by a majority of *Sangha* members, men do not interfere much with the savings plan.

Women feel more confident about themselves and their financial status as their deposits keep increasing. Landlords and Panchayat officials, on the other hand, feel threatened and have been trying to shut down Sanghas, claiming that they have been formed without official approval.

In all our efforts to enhance the rights of rural women, we subscribe to the central view that ultimately their financial independence will make the real difference. In most rural areas, the primary symbol of wealth and respect is in owning cultivable land and/or cattle. When a woman earns and saves enough to buy either on her own, she automatically gains immense respect and voice in her family and within the community. With her ownership of physical assets, many of the traditional barriers that have kept her silent begin to break down. Her husband and other elder members of the larger family are now prepared to listen to her and accede to her personal needs. She then has a bigger voice in how she brings up her children and in how the family is run.

The foundation's own efforts to enable poor women to learn modern farming methods, earn competitive wages and share profits over a period of few years to purchase cultivable land have just begun. It takes a concerted effort to break age-old traditions that men perceive to be in their own self-interest.

Education plays an important role in bringing about awareness of women's rights and worth. When boys and girls grow up with mutual respect and understanding of their capabilities and roles in society, women are more likely to find their rightful place within the family and the community. But, sadly enough, rural education perpetuates the myth that boys are inherently superior to girls. This myth is reinforced even by mothers who tend to give more attention and opportunities to their boys.

These ingrained attitudes toward women can be changed by a persistent nationwide effort using classrooms and mass media, especially television, to impact people's prejudices and social behavior. It may be necessary to force the display of visual messages on gender equality and women's rights in every school and public place. It is not new laws that we need but effective ways of changing many of the gender-based cultural practices.

There is no easy or quick fix to issues related to women's empowerment and reproductive health in rural India. The real solution may lie in a holistic approach that deals with all the major interrelated issues of economic welfare, social justice, education, health, traditions and spirituality. We have found that the three key ingredients for programs initiated from the outside are trust, infrastructure for delivery and financial incentives. Women need to be part of the planning, implementation and evaluation processes on programs that target social and economic upliftment.

When people see genuine commitment on the part of others to help them, the entire community slowly begins to join the effort. With increasing economic prosperity for both men and women, and visible financial contribution by women, many of the age-old discriminatory practices based on gender begin to break down.

CHILD LABOR AND DISPLACEMENT OF TRIBALS

Protecting the interests and welfare of children and others like the tribal people who cannot speak for themselves is very important to a civil society. Of the total population of more than one billion people in India, some 320 million are children below the age of 14 years. Millions of children from poor families are forced to join the labor force even as early as eight years of age. According to some estimates, at least 40 million children work as child laborers. Of this, over 15 million – most of them Dalits – are bonded child laborers.

Hundreds of thousands of young children and women from poor families are sold into prostitution. There are "flesh markets" in major cities like Mumbai where young girls and women are routinely sold in auctions to highest bidders. Sexual bondage and exploitation are such common occurrences that newspapers no longer bother to cover those stories, and readers do not seem surprised or enraged. Many government officials are not only aware of these practices, but are also beneficiaries of the sex trade.

More than sixty percent of the child labor in India is employed in the agricultural sector.[29] Parents are forced to send their children as labor to pay off debts, and landowners like to employ them as they can get away with paying one-quarter to one-third the normal wages of adults. Children miss schooling and end up working under the hot sun all day, with little time for play. Several industries, such as match and firework factories, local "beedi" or cigarette plants, and carpet manufacturing facilities are usual employers of child labor.

The working conditions for children are frequently inhuman. Child laborers are beaten, physically confined to deplorable living quarters, uncared for when sick and given very little to eat. The employment of child labor is common knowledge to local authorities, but very little is done to curb the practice. Employers are hardly ever brought to court and convicted, and punishment is usually limited to a fraction of the revenues from a day's production.

Take the case of the silk industry in India, which is the second largest in the world. According to Human Rights Watch (HRW), a New York-based international watchdog group, over 350,000 children are currently working in the Indian silk industry. Despite this, the World Bank has been heavily financing the industry, and the United States alone imports more than $175 million in silk products from India annually.

The HRW study has found that children work 12 hours or more a day, for six and a half days a week, throughout the year. They assist weavers who work at cramped looms in damp, dim rooms. They breathe smoke from the machinery and guide twisting threads that cut their fingers. By the time they reach adulthood, they are impoverished and illiterate, and their hands are crippled by the work. The state of Karnataka, known for achieving global standards and success in information technology, is the largest producer of silk in India.

Despite worldwide condemnation of child labor, India has yet to ratify the International Labor Organization 182 Convention of 1999 that prohibits the practice and calls for immediate action to eliminate the worst forms of child labor.

Many children are also victims of abuse – physical, sexual and emotional – and are robbed of the innocence of childhood. In our own investigations of the children at Shanti Bhavan, we have found that no less than fifty percent of the children have been sexually molested by someone within the family or the community. Remarried mothers were found to be reluctant about protesting sexual abuses by their husbands against stepchildren. Financial dependency is another reason parents overlook such acts by others against their children.

Regardless of the laws governing child labor, only through poverty eradication and financial independence of mothers can there be effective protection for children against abuses by adults.

Another serious act of injustice is the displacement of poor people, mostly tribals, from their ancestral homes in the name of development. Hydroelectric and mining projects have caused people in rural and remote areas to move out in large numbers; one out of every 10 Indian tribals is a displaced person. Compensation is minimal, and no serious effort is taken to settle these people elsewhere. The result is landlessness, homelessness, unemployment and poverty.

Acquisitions of land are made in the "national interest," and the laws governing them are arbitrary and leave displaced people without recourse. The government's National Policy for Rehabilitation admits that almost seventy-five percent of those displaced since 1951 are still waiting for rehabilitation. While the government has set up institutions to develop the skills and provide financial assistance for Scheduled Castes and Tribes (SC and ST), the overall callousness toward the plight of these voiceless people is unpardonable.

SOCIAL OBLIGATIONS OF BUSINESSES AND THE GENERAL PUBLIC

The importance of the role that business plays in bringing about social harmony and justice cannot be overstated. The great drama being played out in urban India today is not about good and evil, but about success and failure. The country is preoccupied with economic liberalization and technological progress, and the talk is about businesses that have grown tremendously with foreign investment and exports.

The problem is that rural poverty and social injustice are insulated from the rest of the country, and the victims do not seem to pose any immediate threat to the winners. Further, moral and social developments lag far behind technical and scientific achievements. As long as the distance between winners and losers exists, there will be an underlying current of instability in the nation.

The enormous distance between these two cultures cannot last long. The prevailing social and economic injustice in India would have, by now, under similar circumstances, spawned a revolt anywhere else in the world, but Hindu spirituality and emphasis on the afterlife have kept it submerged.

The task of bridging the gap cannot be left to government alone. Businesses need to display much greater social consciousness. All entrepreneurial organizations, as part of society, possess certain obligations to those who are left behind. Businesses have a moral and social responsibility to help the poor in whatever way they can. That includes finding ways to offer their products to poor communities at affordable prices.

The real question for the future is how we will delineate the appropriate responsibilities of business and government in taking responsibility for meeting the needs of the society.

Modernity is a worthwhile goal, but it often results in a simultaneous disregard for many of the old ways of living, traditions and values. The winners in the struggle for financial success tend to look down on those who have failed to join the race – the lower classes of society. Resentment begins to breed, and soon there is a hostile environment. Civilization and culture do not matter as much as how we live today, and when great prosperity for a few is not matched by better life for the remaining, there will soon be a conflict between classes. It is for businesses and governments to realize the aspirations of all people and find a happy compromise between self-interest and public interest, between prosperity and equity.

The act of helping those who are in need is a social obligation that all well-to-do persons must fulfill. The habits that everyone must develop ought to include the concept of charitable giving consistent with one's means. Only then will there be social harmony and less resentment. Philanthropy seems to be an American invention, though many other prosperous countries have taken it up more on an institutional, rather than an individual, basis. Very few rich Indians, both at home and abroad, offer humanitarian contributions proportionate to their incomes. While people are prepared to make significant donations to their temples and churches, the concept of giving to those in need outside their own communities or place of birth is somewhat alien to most Indians.

Visitors come to see Shanti Bhavan every Sunday, and almost everyone tells us how happy the children look. These guests are genuinely moved by what they see in the children and contrast their backgrounds and lives to the villages and urban slums. They say that they are saddened by the poverty all around them, and feel sorry for those who don't have the opportunity to be in a school like Shanti Bhavan. These sentiments reflect momentary emotions of kindness, but unless one is prepared to do his or her share to change the deplorable conditions faced by the poor, words mean very little.

Most people are poor by an "accident of birth;" they did not choose to be poor. Others who are fortunate enough to be well-off financially have an obligation to help create the opportunity for the poor to succeed. Instead, the poor are exploited by everyone: government officials, landlords, and city folks who buy labor and agricultural produce at the lowest possible price. People have generally become apathetic to the misfortunes of others, while at the same time expressing words of sympathy.

We might reflect on the point in Leon Wieseltier's touchingly written book *Kaddish* (Alfred A. Knopf, 1998), in which a man who has been mourning the loss of his father takes up the teachings of Rabbi Menahem ben Zerakh: "There is nothing for an intelligent man to mourn over and to grieve over except his sin."

The essence of sorrow is remorse, and those who do not act to help those in need live in sin.

Charity is a noble concept, but that is not sufficient. Many charitable institutions have failed in their missions because the beneficiaries are not able to sustain their efforts when donor funds stop flowing in. Administrators of donor funds must change the concept of "giving" to "partnering." People need to be given the responsibility to find ways to carry forward programs even in the absence of further external help. All long-term projects must become self-supportive within a reasonable period of time after they have been initiated. Otherwise, it will not be a sustainable situation.

Take the case of Habitat for Humanity International, the world's largest nonprofit house-building organization that has been constructing low-cost residences for poor people in India for some years now. As of 2002, 10,000 houses have been built in India with funds provided by the organization and with the participation of prospective residents and volunteers. The beneficiaries of the program are expected to repay the cost of the interest-free "loan" over a period of time. Initially, the concept worked well because sufficient attention was paid to helping these people find jobs. Subsequently, it became a "giving" effort, with very little partnership. The result is that many failed to repay the loan and faced eviction.

The good news is that the program has recently made several corrections to help the noble concept work. Most charitable giving organizations now insist on sustainability.

It is not handouts that poor people hope for from those who are well-off. What they want is an opportunity to make a decent living to care for their families. They want some stability in their lives, to be gainfully employed, to care for their health and to educate their children for a better future. They want their lives to be safe from violence and the indignity of social injustice. Poor people have the right to expect fair distribution of goods and privileges. They cannot be expected to accept an unjust social arrangement that maintains the status quo, just the same way as minorities cannot be forced to accept any subordinating proposal that the majority wishes to impose.

As John Rawls states in his major work *Justice as Fairness* (Harvard University Press, 2001), each person has an absolute right to an adequate set of basic liberties, and the prevailing social and economic inequities must be reduced to protect the needs of those worse off. The basic necessities that the poor want and are entitled to are fundamental, the very essence of human rights.

EQUALITY AND TOLERANCE

What will bring about increased tolerance of diversity within the society? It is unclear whether increased prosperity and education will result in a decline of religious hatred and intolerance. History has demonstrated that scientifically advanced and culturally sophisticated countries, as was the case with pre-World War II Germany, could embrace nationalistic ideals and carry out barbaric acts.

What really counts is political leadership with a moral conscience that can guide the people along civilized paths – something India has not had for quite some time. It is wonderful to have your country stand up for idealistic, moral and righteous principles, such as equal opportunity, individual freedom, human rights and liberty. But it is another matter when governments begin to tilt toward self righteous and spiritual positions that are usually hypocritical.

It becomes dangerous when leaders turn to propagating values based on religious beliefs, racial or ethnic superiority, and nationalistic propaganda on supposedly patriotic assumptions, while pretending to maintain moral high ground. Without good leadership, there is little hope for tolerance and justice.

India does have a long tradition of religious pluralism, long before the idea was conceived in Europe and elsewhere. The Indian Constitution gives great importance to religious tolerance, composite culture, minority rights and special rights for the weaker sections of the society. The framers of the Constitution expressed their dream of a pluralistic and just society that embodies communal harmony, peaceful coexistence and equal respect for all religions.

India's first prime minister, Jawaharlal Nehru, had hoped that his mode of secularism would keep religion out of politics. The concept of liberty encompasses the idea that all citizens are equal partners in building a modern India. Then how, in this land of Buddha and Gandhi, where the universal philosophy of Hinduism was born, has such a powerful and destructive force of religious intolerance and bigotry come into being?

The answer may lie in the simple truth that religion is the poor man's bread, and politicians find it more convenient to offer religion than bread to its disheartened masses. When politicians are short of ideas for bringing about prosperity, and self-interest takes over common interest, they turn their attention to the powerful forces of mystic spirituality to encourage an overreaching sense of pride in religion, culture and traditions. They urge their followers to accept faith without doubt, and form convictions without facts.

Attention is diverted to dealing with nonconformists who are labeled as enemies of their faith, and all struggles are now against them in the name of God and country.

History has repeated itself many times over, and millions of lives have been lost in religious conflicts and acts of hatred in the belief of superior faith. What good have these conflicts brought? As it is said of many past despotic kings, it appears that we have forgotten everything and learned nothing.

Our spiritual fulfillment can never be attained if we choose to ignore the misery of the helpless. No amount of worship and prayer can substitute for humane acts. Generosity and kindness toward fellow human beings in need symbolize true spirituality. Can we learn to treat with dignity the people with whom we share this earth? The value of service to others, the value of caring for others, the value of not ignoring social misery – these are not issues on which religion has a monopoly.

As Cornel West, the renowned cultural critic at Princeton University, points out, "The quest for truth, the quest for good, the quest for beautiful, all require us to examine how we live, and let suffering speak, let victims be visible, and let social misery be put on the agenda of those with power. The life of a thinking man, one with feelings and a soul, cannot be separated from the struggle of those who have been dehumanized on the margins of society."

No justifications, philosophical or religious, can excuse the conscience and the soul of the more fortunate if he fails to act in compassion. When we pursue our hopes and opportunities, we must also be conscious of the potential for indifference and callousness. We must not be blinded by our few successes. Yes, we are excelling in computer science, engineering and technology in general. But where is the heart?

When we demonize others and fail to see their humanity, we have allowed the forces of hatred to overtake our spirituality. Through our abhorrence we pass on the worst instincts in us, projecting our misery and suffering on to others, but never getting rid of our own. We fail to see the goodness in an other person. But if we allow our spirituality to take the chance, to trust the possibility of bringing about a positive alliance, then there is hope. The recent creation of a secular South Africa is a modern day example of the courage and strong spiritual beliefs of two different men, Nelson Mandela and F.W. de Klerk, that allowed them to risk all for a future free of intolerance and hatred.

What Martin Luther King Jr. said in his famous speech at the steps of the Lincoln Memorial in Washington, D.C., in 1963 was a reaffirmation of the

American Constitution, declaring that all people would be guaranteed the "inalienable rights of life, liberty and the pursuit of happiness." Modern India was founded on the great ideals of Mahatma Gandhi and a spirit of tolerance, and the nation cannot now allow the forces of divisiveness to take hold and destroy what is so precious to all as free and fair people.

India cannot build a just and prosperous society without seriously attempting to offer equal opportunity and protection for all regardless of differences of religion or gender. Caste is a social evil and should have no place in a civilized society. Opportunity denied to lower castes and women is a major detriment to India's progress. The special needs of poor people, especially those living in rural areas, is a national priority that calls for special attention. Poverty cannot be successfully addressed by appealing to the negative emotions of prejudice and hatred. When government practices are inclusive of everyone, as opposed to creating divisions, the country's human resources are fully and effectively utilized to achieve common goals.

Chapter 9

BEYOND REDEMPTION?

Disease and Health Care in Rural India

INADEQUATE COMMITMENT TO DEAL WITH HIV/AIDS

Kalavathi sits quietly in her one-room hut with her two-year-old son, not knowing what tomorrow will bring. Her dwelling is in a secluded corner of the village designated for low caste people. The word has spread in the village that her husband recently died of AIDS. She had married him just two years before his death, not knowing that he was already infected. Her mother had persuaded her to marry him as he had a steady packaging job in a nearby factory. He had looked ill even before marriage, but she is not sure whether he knew the reason. Now Kalavathi is also infected with HIV and experiences frequent colds and coughs.

No one in the village wants to employ her, and her in-laws blame her for her husband's illness and death. She somehow manages to survive with the help of neighbors and some free rations from the government. What worries her most is what will happen to her son when she dies.

There are thousands of women like Kalavathi in India – all unknowingly married to men infected with HIV/AIDS. Similar stories have just begun to surface. Until recently, India denied its AIDS problem, and no clear estimates of infections could be authenticated. The world attention focused on Africa, where proportionately large numbers of people are dying of the disease in countries with small populations. Botswana, the thinly populated land of 1.6 million in southern Africa, is often cited as the hardest hit by the AIDS epidemic for its infection rate of thirty-nine percent of the adult population. This once fast-developing nation is now in reverse gear both economically and socially, and in the words of its president, "threatened with extinction."[30]

Many reasons, such as a mobile labor force, proximity to major transport routes, and permissive sexual behavior, are given for the rapid spreading of the virus in Botswana, even though the country is considered more progressive than its neighbors. After years of neglect and denial in the early stages of this national calamity, the government has mounted a comprehensive and intensive effort during the past four years that includes testing, prevention, treatment and support for the affected families.

More than 16 million combatants lost their lives in World War II, but already 17 million people have died of AIDS in Africa alone. In Southern Africa, at least one in five adults is infected. In Zambia, Zimbabwe and Botswana, as many as seventy percent of teenagers are expected to die of AIDS. AIDS caused 2.5 million deaths in Africa in 2002 alone. It has left 12 million African children orphaned since the epidemic began. It is obvious that these desperate African nations cannot cope with the problem on their own. The struggle against AIDS and other infectious diseases in Africa presents one of the greatest moral tests of our time. Will the developed nations of the world come to the aid of these people who cannot win this fight on their own, or will they offer half-hearted solutions?

Beyond Africa, many countries have begun to experience large numbers of cases as the disease gains momentum. The story of Botswana should serve as a warning for all nations, especially China, Russia and India, whose combined number of HIV/AIDS victims is expected to reach 75 million people by the end of this decade (25 million in India alone), according to a recent report published by the United States government. China and India may be able to cope with the problem for the remainder of the decade but only because the infected people will be diffused in very large populations.[31]

Without an effective program to combat the spread, however, AIDS will consume a major share of India's resources and seriously affect its economic and social stability within a short period of time. AIDS has not yet been given the high priority needed to stem the epidemic, and the country is well advised to embark immediately on a concerted national effort focused on prevention.

Until recently, the Indian government did not want to acknowledge the growing problem of HIV/AIDS; statistics were released in 2000 indicating fewer than 100,000 cases throughout the country. But by 2002, several community leaders began to speak out, breaking the reluctance to discuss sex, drug use and the disease.[32] The government also updated its statistics to 3.97 million people with HIV, the virus that could lead to AIDS, more than any country other than South Africa.

HIV was first diagnosed in India in the mid-1980s. It first emerged in India's urban centers; Mumbai (Bombay), Chennai (Madras) and Bangalore were among the early high-risk cities. Studies suggest that the disease spread through two geographic pathways: first, along the main trunk roads that serve as the transport network for this enormous country, and second, along the border regions near Burma where drug use is widespread. According to some estimates, there are some 200,000 long-haul truckers, two million prostitutes, 300,000 brothels and tens of millions of seasonal workers who come into cities from villages each year.

Many fear that men, who might have contracted the virus from their extramarital affairs during business travels and temporary job engagements, are increasingly infecting thousands of monogamous women in India each day. Given the high levels of illiteracy among women in India and the taboos concerning sexually transmitted diseases, very little information is available to the country's adult female population about HIV risks. AIDS clinics report that ninety percent of all women who are found HIV positive have a single partner.

"It is more important to match your blood tests than your horoscopes," says a social worker to young women about marriage, but today such ideas are rejected outright in a society dominated by the male sex.

In 1995, India set up its first AIDS program under the National AIDS Control Organization (NACO) with an annual budget of $38 million. This amount represented just 0.03 percent of the country's health and family welfare budget, and it compares with $400 million allocated by Brazil. The World Bank lent India $191 million in 2001 for the AIDS program, but it is not clear how the government is using the funds.

Only when the international community began to focus its attention on the problem in India in late 2002 did the government show any real concern. Even today, the government has not used explicit messages on television or in any print media to create awareness of how one becomes infected and ways to protect oneself.

According to Microsoft's Bill Gates, India may be one of the developing nations best positioned to contain the AIDS epidemic by concentrating on prevention through awareness creation and the use of condoms, and by marshalling its impressive scientific research sector. By concentrating on truckers, soldiers and migrant laborers, whose HIV rates are 10 times greater than the national average, the spread of the disease could be contained. If there is a national will, India might be able to limit the spread of the disease with the help of wealthy nations, businesses and philanthropic institutions.

Gates announced a donation of $100 million, while the United States government set aside $63 million to combat HIV/AIDS in India. To elevate the issue, Gates personally visited India in November 2002 to launch the AIDS campaign. The United States Ambassador Robert Blackwell spoke openly about the dangers of not aggressively tackling the problem, only to the irritation of the central health minister.

"I don't think anyone should contribute to spreading panic among the general public. We are aware of the situation, and it does concern me personally," said Minister Shatrughan Sinha.

Despite the generous financial contribution that Gates had just made, the minister showed his displeasure at the vocal international concern over India's AIDS epidemic by initially refusing to meet with Gates and then demanding the entire donation in cash. This kind of governmental attitude does not bode well for the future.

India is currently in the second phase of a 10-year program for combating the spread of HIV. The program has given wide latitude to states, and they have shown varying levels of interest and competence in dealing with the problem. In April 2002, New Delhi announced a nationwide target of "zero new HIV infections by 2007." These unrealistic and somewhat absurd pronouncements only raise questions about the sincerity of the effort overall.

Instead of trying to raise awareness about serious health concerns faced by its citizens, the government is busy downplaying them so as not to "create any panic." Somehow, the authorities believe that it is better to have an uninformed public than one aware of the problems. The national policy on HIV/AIDS seems to be one of denial, concealment and incompetence.

In the United States, drug companies typically charge $10,000 to $15,000 per patient per year for HIV/AIDS cocktails, while they offer the same to developing countries at prices below $1,000 per year. Some years ago, Cipla, a generic drug manufacturer in India, offered to sell a combination of AIDS-retarding drugs as a cocktail for around $500 to poor countries outside India.

In India, however, the government levies a number of taxes to increase the cost by some forty percent; Cipla has offered the government the cocktail for $350 not inclusive of any taxes. This offer of low-price drugs and others are bogged down in controversies over patent violations, but efforts are being made to deliver them at affordable prices.

Shorter patent life for drugs may be a solution that needs exploring. Developed countries and private donors have pledged around $3 billion annually so far, but according to the United Nations, some $7 billion to $10 billion will be needed each year for the foreseeable future. Since The Gates Foundation and others have joined the battle, finally there is hope for alleviating some of the suffering and limiting the spread of the dreadful disease. The world is beginning to realize that national and international health issues are inseparable.

The rapid spread of HIV/AIDS in poor countries is just one example of how their dysfunctional health care systems fail to address adequately the health needs of the general population. While HIV/AIDS has received considerable attention in recent years, there are many other diseases and health problems that are taking lives in India each year. Infectious diseases, such as malaria, cholera, typhoid and hepatitis kill more than 12 million people a year in poor countries.

Clean water and good sanitation are two interrelated methods of preventing infectious diseases in rural areas. More than one billion people around the world lack access to clean water, and two billion do not have proper sanitation. Women bear the responsibility for fetching water from village wells, and they spend a considerable amount of time and effort each day on this task alone. In many parts of rural India water is a scarce commodity, and drought-ridden villages are periodically supplied with water by truck from distant places. Shortage of clean water forces people to make use of any water source that may be available.

Similarly, access to proper sanitation is either unavailable or considered unimportant, and many use nearby makeshift latrines that are usually kept in unhygienic conditions. Consequently, waterborne diseases and illnesses spread through human waste are a common aspect of rural life.

PREVENTABLE HEALTH RISKS

Infectious and parasitic diseases as well as chronic or degenerative diseases feature among the top 10 causes for both mortality and morbidity. Respiratory infections, communicable diseases, gastrointestinal problems, ailments caused by malnutrition and skin diseases are the most common causes for morbidity in rural India. Unhealthy lifestyles and behavioral problems contribute to many avoidable ailments. HIV/AIDS, other sexually transmitted diseases, and alcohol-related problems are outcomes of unhealthy behavior in adults. Healthy life expectancy can be increased by five to 10 years if governments and individuals make efforts against these top regional health risks.

The World Health Organization 2002 report on world health details the top 10 preventable health risks globally: childhood and maternal underweight; unsafe sex; high blood pressure; tobacco; alcohol; unsafe water, sanitation and hygiene; high cholesterol; indoor smoke from solid fuels; iron deficiency, and obesity.[33] These risks account for about forty percent of the 56 million preventable deaths that occur worldwide annually. According to the report, 170 million children in poor countries are underweight, while three million deaths occur each year from overweight and obesity. Unless action is taken, by 2020 there will be nine million deaths caused by tobacco, compared to almost five million a year now.

Unfortunately, the illnesses that make up ninety percent of the global diseases burden, such as malaria, tuberculosis and hookworm anemia, get only ten percent of the research money because these are primarily the diseases prevalent in poor countries. The high cost of developing and introducing drugs force pharmaceutical companies to charge prices that are unaffordable in poor countries.

Rich nations need to find ways to encourage drug companies to offer affordable treatment for neglected tropical diseases. With further assistance from developed countries, the spread of many major infectious diseases can be limited. According to WHO officials, $400 million a year in additional funds could bring tuberculosis under control around the world. Without such help, the suffering will continue for most of the world's population.

Beyond infectious diseases, the main cause of ill-health is malnutrition. Poverty, hunger and malnutrition are interrelated silent realities for a majority of Indians. More than half of all children under the age of four suffer from malnutrition, thirty percent of newborns are significantly underweight, and sixty percent of women are anemic. According to a recent report by the United Nations World Food Program, thirty-eight percent of children in India are below their normal weight and thirty-six percent are shorter than they should be due to malnutrition. A recent World Bank report shows that malnutrition costs India at least $10 billion annually in terms of lost productivity, illness, and death and is seriously retarding improvements in human development.[34]

While poverty largely explains the high level of malnutrition, other factors, such as the low status of women and poor eating habits also contribute to the problems faced by women and girls. A large proportion of women are at high risk of maternal mortality because of their low pre-pregnancy weight, which may cause obstetrical difficulties. Malnourishment and nutritional anemia significantly impede cognitive development and learning achievement in the early school years and the problems carry into the future. While the government has taken a number of measures to address the problem, and malnutrition has come down by twenty percent in the last 40 years, the number of cases has increased with population increases.[35]

Despite the high level of malnutrition in the country and the resulting loss of productivity, direct spending by the Indian government on nutritional and micronutrients programs amounts to less than 0.19 percent of the GNP. This figure compares with spending in Sri Lanka of one percent of the GNP on direct programs, and additional use of significant resources on health education, services and anti-poverty programs, with successful results beginning in the 1980s.

If India is to succeed in dealing with malnutrition, the most essential requirement is a higher level of sustained political commitment. Programs must be structured around models that assure quality and impact, targeting more vulnerable groups first. Decentralized programs that draw on private and non-governmental organizations are more likely to yield superior results.

Many of the health problems are caused by the absence of safe procedures and ignorance. Thirty-six million abortions take place each year in developing countries, of which 20 million are done under illegal and often unsafe conditions. Many women are forced by their families to undergo abortions, and most are willing to risk unsafe procedures. Further, inadequate care during pregnancy and especially during labor and delivery results in complications for one out of every four women. Life-threatening complications in pregnancy and delivery cause more than three-quarters of maternal deaths, and contribute substantially to infant deaths and poor health.

Around twenty percent of maternal deaths result from indirect causes, including iron deficiency anemia and infectious diseases, which can be addressed through antenatal care. More than one pregnancy in 350 is fatal. While these are global statistics for developing countries, they mirror what India is currently experiencing. For the period 1996-2001, life expectancy at birth in India was estimated to be around 63 years, and the infant mortality rate (IMR) was estimated to be 74 per 1,000 live births. For the rural population, these statistics are even worse.[36]

Given the child-bearing role of women, meeting their health needs must be a top priority. Attention must start from an early age; poor nutrition during childhood and adolescence leads to poor health during pregnancy and childbirth, which in turn is often transferred to babies. Other women's health issues include expanding the use of family planning, reduction of maternal deaths at delivery and lowering sexually transmitted diseases. In India, many women get pregnant at a very early age, and most do not use contraceptives before they have already had more children than they intended.

Women are frequently dissuaded from using contraceptives by their husband or by family pressures to have more children. Difficulties in obtaining contraceptives and inadequate counseling are two other major reasons that restrict family planning. While price discounts and donations have made it affordable for most people to buy contraceptives, the poorest segment of the population still do not have the luxury of spending money on them.

Women and female babies face many dangers. Before or at birth, parents who prefer boys may try to carry out sex-selective abortions or infanticide. Where food is scarce, girls are fed less than boys. These practices are common in many parts of India, including the district where our foundation carries out most of its work.

More often than not, women are unable to deny sexual advances or persuade partners to use condoms even when their partners are known to be promiscuous. Further, women are far more likely than men to experience domestic violence, especially when their men are alcoholics. According to some studies, no less than forty percent of all women in India have faced physical assault by male partners during their lives.

The mean age at which women marry in India has gone up from the age of 13.1 in 1901 to nearly 20 in 2000.[37] Despite this advance, many rural girls are married off by the time they are 16 years old. The health status of many women is poor during their optimal reproductive years as they are burdened at a young age by too many children. Nearly one-third of pregnancies take place to lactating mothers.

For women to benefit from health services, they have to be active recipients of health care throughout their life cycle. Many health workers fail to see women's health needs beyond what is involved at childbirth. Only a very small percentage of the female population ever goes for gynecologic checkups any time during their lives.

The connection between poverty and gender disadvantage in health is profound. Women from poor families have the highest fertility, poorest nutrition and limited access to health care, which in turn contribute to higher maternal and infant deaths. The fertility rate for the poorest twenty percent of the population in India is around 4.1, while for the richest twenty percent it is nearly half that at 2.1. Eighty-nine percent of the richest twenty percent get prenatal care, while only twenty-five percent of the poorest fifth get some degree of such care. The disparity between the two segments is similar for births attended by skilled staff: seventy-nine percent versus twelve percent.[38]

Much of the improvements that have occurred for the poor have come about as a result of the efforts by non-governmental organizations, particularly women's groups. Governments have begun to place more importance on the delivery of care for women and children, but where NGOs are not involved, such efforts have not been effective. It is also clear that until the poor can be lifted from the day-to-day struggle for survival, progress in all other areas of human rights may be elusive.

In the face of all these health-related problems, India has built up a vast infrastructure of public health services, managed by a huge bureaucracy with little oversight. Its effectiveness is limited, however, in part because overall investment in health services remains low. Today, public spending on health is about one percent of the GDP, which puts India among the bottom 20 percent of countries.[39] This proportionately low allocation of funds is spread throughout the large public network of health providers, mainly Primary Health Centers (PHC), government hospitals and other secondary care facilities. The bulk of public spending on primary health care is spread too thin to be effective, and a major portion of what is available is used for salary expenditures of government health care staff. This leaves very few financial resources for essential drugs, supplies, operations, maintenance and preventive efforts.

Health care is experiencing a transition wherein the private sector has grown considerably without much public scrutiny, while the public sector has become less attractive to those favoring careers in medicine. This fundamental shift has introduced a widening disparity in quality health care for the rich versus the poor, raising issues of equity. Further, the public remains inadequately informed about much of the health system; in rural areas, most people do not know the seriousness of many of their ailments and what they need to do beyond consulting their ill-trained local health practitioner.

The spread of many diseases is mainly the result of poor living conditions and undesirable lifestyles. This statement is true for both rural areas and urban slums. The poor who migrate from rural to urban areas seeking better jobs are illiterate and unskilled, and a vast majority of them have to settle in slums whether working or not. Open defecation, sewage and garbage, and contaminated drinking water are the normal conditions of extreme urban poverty. Many of these people are also participants in the use of illicit liquor and unsafe sex.

Bringing about behavioral change in adults is a desirable outcome when dealing with regular excessive drinking of alcohol, wife beating and multiple sex partners leading to the spread of sexually transmitted diseases. The traditional approach of persuading people, especially men, not to engage in these activities centers around health counseling and community services to create awareness on the dangers involved in such behavior.

My experience in dealing with these issues in rural communities has made me a skeptic of spending time and money to convert men who have engaged in such activities from their early adulthood. The question that needs to be studied carefully is whether any of the limited financial resources that are available for developmental projects should be used on efforts to convert these people into good citizens. To me, the answer is very clear – an emphatic "no."

Adults behave the way they do for a variety of reasons, some of which are psychological. Without the investment in long-term treatment and consistent monitoring, these well-set behavioral patterns are unlikely to change permanently. Culturally tolerated behaviors and practices within the community cannot be changed by education or awareness creation alone, especially when the people you are dealing with are mostly illiterate.

What can be attempted, however, are targeted measures that could lead to short-term positive results. These measures must be clear and direct, and must demonstrate immediate benefits to the individuals involved. An unemployed or underemployed alcoholic might be persuaded to reduce his drinking if he had the opportunity to work and save money through a monitored program. Wife-beaters might batter less frequently if warned of loss of employment, humiliation and threat of legal action, while encouraging good behavior through work-related financial rewards. The dangers of communicable diseases like HIV/AIDS may be sufficient to bring about safe practices, as long as health education and preventive measures are made available.

Behavioral change can be initiated and promoted only by those who have earned the trust of the people they claim to serve; government officials are amongst the least trusted, and hence, they are the most ill-suited for the task. People listen to those whom they trust, but they still may not act without financial incentives offered through economic opportunities, and without actually seeing the infrastructure for delivery of services. Hence, projects run exclusively by private and non-governmental institutions (assisted by government, international agencies and private donors), without unwanted governmental interference, have a better chance of success. Institutions that have been functioning within the community for some length of time are likely to know the problems at sufficient depth and would be able to find specific solutions.

Regardless of all such attempts, the chances are that adult behavior will not change without a great measure of one-on-one involvement to help the individual through his problems. In a vast country like India, that is an impossible proposition. The limited financial resources that might be available are better utilized on children to educate and set their behavior in the right direction from an early age.

Today's adults are a lost generation as far as changing their behavior without serious counseling, and the effort should be to contain rather than to solve their problems through a combination of incentives, threats and punishment. On the other hand, we can place much of our hope on the children, provided we make the required investment in offering health education.

DELIVERING BASIC HEALTH CARE

Where do we begin our attempt to tackle major health hazards and deliver basic health care, especially in rural areas where a great majority of Indians live? Primary health care is the backbone of the health system in the villages and where patients initially come for medical help. It is the first, and sometimes only, line of intervention against frequent health problems such as viral infections, gastrointestinal disorders, and contagious diseases. Combined with public health initiatives in sanitation, immunization, nutrition and health education, most of the health problems faced by the rural population can be addressed very effectively.

Every knowledgeable health professional emphasizes the importance of public health services focusing on prevention, and primary health care concentrating on early intervention, as part of a successful and cost-effective solution. Unfortunately, public and primary health care is viewed by most donor organizations as a complicated and "non-glamorous" area that does not offer visibility and measurable immediate results to make it worthwhile for their involvement. Consequently, NGOs are unable to attract even a small share of the overall funding from donors toward primary and public health initiatives.

Despite considerable financial investment in PHCs by the government, most of these centers are not meeting the basic needs of the population. Inadequate infrastructure, too few physicians and lack of accountability have turned these centers into ineffective institutions. Even with all these problems, it is very unlikely that central and state governments will surrender their control of the health care system, as it is one of the explicit expressions of benevolence by politicians to the poor.

To most politicians, the fact that the system fails to deliver even basic health care is not as important as the need to demonstrate that they are the "guardians of the poor." There is also the issue of "health equity" necessitating access to proper health care for all regardless of income, and this social goal is presumed to be the responsibility of the state alone. For now, if anything good is to be accomplished, somehow the solution must include a pivotal role for the government.

Recent World Bank reports emphasize the importance of public-private partnership in the delivery of quality health care. Opportunities exist for public-private collaboration in delivering products and services for public health protection, health care delivery to treat the ill and injured, and health insurance and financing. Private sector participation is based on the assumption that their products and services will be offered at affordable prices to meet the health care needs of the general public and still make profits. This assumption might be applicable in the case of a majority of the urban population who fall into middle-class income levels. Private sector companies might be prepared to offer their products at concession rates to the poor, but they are not likely to be participants where there is no profit to be made.

Private providers of health care services might be encouraged to offer their services at low charges while the government makes products available to them for free or at significantly subsidized costs. Such an operation should be viewed as a public-private partnership. Private sector participation in government-funded programs should not be confused with the free market activity of health care institutions.

The rural sector is not in a position to afford even half the cost of health services and products offered – and consequently the involvement of the private sector tends to be sub-standard and exploitative at this time – unless they are funded by the government or contracted out at reimbursable fees. There is no escaping from the reality that private participation in whatever form will occur only when costs are met either directly or indirectly and there is some possibility of a return on investment. By camouflaging the real costs of government or donor financing of health care to the poor, one cannot make honest claims that private participation is the solution to the poor state of rural health care in India.

It is pointed out by many that more than eighty percent of all health spending in India is by the private sector, and hence, the need is for more coordination between the public and private sectors. This statistic masks the fact that in rural India, where more than two-thirds of the country's population lives, practically the entire spending on public health programs such as immunizations, antenatal care, and detection and treatment of major infectious diseases is from public funding.

Yet, only ten to twenty percent of the patients are treated at rural PHCs. The remaining eighty percent or so go to so-called "private practitioners," most of whom are in fact nonqualified medical personnel, often unlicensed. There are also those offering herbal medicine working in rural areas, and they constitute a significant part of the rural primary health care system. NGOs operate health clinics and engage in related activities in some villages, and most of them are funded by the government and private donors. There are also mission hospitals in some rural areas that offer inpatient care, but in most cases, patients go to secondary and tertiary medical facilities in nearby urban areas when they need hospitalization.

A number of new initiatives involving the private sector have received significant attention recently. One of the leading hospital chains that caters mostly to patients with significant financial means has introduced a telemedicine facility in two of its hospitals in two cities to offer villagers a second opinion and diagnosis in complicated cases. Former United States President Bill Clinton was shown a video demonstration of the telemedicine consultation of a rural patient during his visit to Andhra Pradesh state in 2002, and he is said to have justifiably expressed his amazement and appreciation. But it is hard to understand the value of such expensive services at a time when most villagers go without even basic medical care.

It is also claimed that an insurance scheme that requires only one rupee per day in premium per family for full medical coverage has been successfully introduced in a few villages. The presumption is that these insurance schemes are fully paid for by patient contributions alone, and no public funds are involved. Once again, the long-term financial viability of such programs needs to be seen before one can get really excited about them.

Whatever the solutions, they must be sustainable, quality oriented, cost-effective and widely applicable to cover the needs of large populations. If we are looking to provide quality health care to rural communities throughout the country, prototypes of probable solutions must lend themselves to scaling-up for serving the medical needs of hundreds of millions of people within a few years.

The great majority of the rural population is not in a financial position to pay fully for quality basic care. At this time, PHCs offer their services free of charge. Involvement of the legitimate private sector for quality medial services is a desirable outcome, but realistically, it would happen only when there is profit to be made.

Any effort to bring about public-private partnership for the delivery of rural primary health care and disease prevention – the most important aspects of the entire health care system for a majority of the people – cannot ignore the reality that, at best, only twenty-five percent of the costs involved might be borne by the patient. Rural areas now attract from the private sector mostly providers who are really not qualified to offer services. The present situation does not resemble any reasonable level of basic "health care for all." At least for now, government subsidy is needed to make it financially viable for legitimate private health practitioners. Equity in health care delivery between urban and rural India is an issue that needs special attention.

The inequity in health care delivery is further evident from the fact that the poorest twenty percent of the nation's population receives only ten percent of the total net subsidy from publicly provided clinical services. The richest twenty percent receives more than three times the subsidy received by the poorest quintile. This disparity is a result of the fact that the rich utilize health services more than the poor, as they are prepared to pay the non-subsidized portion of the costs involved. Further, the secondary care public hospitals serving rural areas are under-utilized as they deliver poor quality care.

The pro-rich bias is more pronounced in both inpatient and outpatient hospital care; they are more expensive than outpatient primary health care.

Needless to say, health equity calls for shifting the subsidy currently enjoyed by the rich to those services the poor are unable to utilize for cost reasons.

Meeting the basic health needs of all, and assuring equity in its delivery are issues that require not merely policy pronouncements but long-term commitment and a willingness to make major changes in health and development strategies. Poverty alleviation and increases in personal income of the poor could lead to affordability of private care in the longer term, but for now, the strategy has to recognize the ground reality that most rural people in India cannot afford quality health care from private providers.

The gap between the haves and the have-nots for access to reasonable basic health care cannot be bridged without substantial government support. Private participation must be looked at as a solution for improving efficiency and effectiveness and not as an alternative to government funding.

The strategy for bridging the gap needs to concentrate more on those areas of health care that affect the poor disproportionately. Infant mortality among the bottom twenty percent of the population is nearly three times that among the top twenty percent in India. These differences can be narrowed by concentrating on preventive measures. For example, improvements in drainage and sanitation, availability of clean drinking water and timely inoculation of children could significantly bring down the number of cases of infectious diseases among the poor.

Simple measures to reduce malnutrition among pregnant women and children would assure lower infant and child mortality. These are not strategies that require significant increases in the financial resources allocated, or new innovative solutions, but they do call for proper assignment of priorities and a commitment to get the job done.

Having said the above, conversely, it should be pointed out that the success of any new ideas for improvement hinges on the recognition by the state of its inability to manage an extensive network of PHCs alone with any degree of acceptable accountability. It must leverage its limited capability by involving the business community, nonprofit organizations, and the civil society in general.

Credible non-governmental institutions that are already doing work in rural health must be encouraged with financial assistance and recognition, while incentives must be provided for others to join the effort. Basic health care needs of rural populations can be met only through the joint efforts of the different constituencies, with government and donor funds making a significant contribution until such time the income levels are raised through poverty eradication efforts.

TODAY'S REALITIES IN RURAL HEALTH CARE DELIVERY

What should be the nature of private participation in rural health delivery? The answer to this question must be derived from the many realities of doing business in the rural society, and from the present failed health care system. To start with, there is no hiding from the fact that rural populations in developing countries are very poor. Most people do not have the ability to pay for basic medical services and products. Until rural incomes rise considerably, a significant portion of this cost must be borne by the state from public funds.

Our foundation's experience at the Baldev Medical Center in Baliganapalli has shown that patients can at best cover twenty percent of the costs involved in delivering basic health care; this is to be expected of a population wherein a majority earns less than Rs.75 ($1.50) a day. Hence, no private institution can hope to make a reasonable return from direct patient charges without government subsidies or other compensation.

For the foreseeable future, privatization of rural primary health care will remain nothing more than government funding and outsourcing of services. The challenge then is to make government-funded programs run by public and private institutions more effective and efficient.

The second important reality is that not enough qualified doctors are available or willing to work in rural areas. Given the living conditions in the villages, they cannot be expected to stay there; the few doctors who do work in rural clinics commute from nearby cities. In India, there are nearly 500,000 doctors by some estimates, of which eighty percent are engaged in private practice or working for private medical institutions. The rest are mostly employed in government hospitals in urban areas.[40] Only a small number of doctors have been engaged by the government to serve rural communities in India. Further, most doctors are not competent to manage effectively the staff and activities of their respective PHCs.

Those government doctors assigned to rural PHCs turn up there infrequently, and when they do, most are in a hurry to return to the cities to conduct their private practice. Some doctors have set up their private practices adjacent to the PHCs where they are employed, and patients visiting the PHCs are directed to their private clinics for treatment. The government looks the other way, as it does not want to lose their services. The result is that rural patients do not receive quality care when they fall ill or need medical help. PHCs administered by such uncommitted doctors operate poorly, and there is little concern for the patients.

Another aspect of today's rural health care delivery system is the absence of sufficient accountability. The bureaucrats in government are most interested in receiving reports showing that targets have been met. Field nurses and others assigned to detect cases with medical problems and provide assistance by going into the villages spend a considerable part of their time filing numerous forms called for by the government. Summary reports are sent up the chain of command from the district level to the state and central agencies, and to funding organizations. There is no real attempt to verify and validate the accuracy of the data collected, and no one really knows what is done with all that information.

If you talk to any senior government health official, he/she will tell you about all the epidemiological studies being carried out and the new programs being introduced. Occasional government "camps" on specific health problems, such as skin ailments, malaria and tuberculosis are conducted, and they do add some value, but very little is done to improve the daily delivery of primary health care. Most outside organizations are interested in specific issues such as HIV/AIDS and polio eradication. Their volunteers come in for a day or two, and then move on to some other location, and there is no change in the ongoing delivery of basic health care.

At least on the surface, it appears that international organizations that provide much of the external funding, such as the World Bank, WHO, bilateral government agencies and many of the leading private donors, believe that a targeted approach to addressing some of the top health concerns can be successful without worrying much about the actual institutions that deliver primary health care. In my view, this is a grave mistake. PHCs are the backbone of the health care delivery system in rural areas, and if well run, they can identify serious medical cases at an early stage and intervene. Combined with aforementioned prevention measures, major outbreaks of many ailments can be prevented. Legitimate private sector participants may also be encouraged and brought in partly with public funds, but that should occur in a competitive environment and not as an alternative to PHCs.

Without sufficient financial incentives, legitimate private practitioners are unwilling to work in rural areas today. The majority of private practitioners who do work in rural areas are nothing more than quacks who exploit the ignorant people.

On a daily basis PHCs are best suited to take up these tasks, including health education, awareness creation and training. Armed with up-to-date medical records of patients, these centers can become more proactive. Without PHCs, targeted efforts will ultimately fail to solve the overall health care problems of the rural poor, as there is no institutional support to assure sustainability.

It appears that, for political reasons, substantial government funds are allocated to run an inefficient primary health system, while practically everyone has given up on fixing it. Governments are asked by donors and international agencies to encourage the creation and support of parallel private institutions to perform tasks that could otherwise be done by effective PHCs. The hidden agenda might be to support effective private institutions to offer real services while maintaining ineffective government-run PHCs for political comfort.

There is no need to embark deliberately on such a wasteful and unsuccessful strategy. No doubt, private institutions must be encouraged and supported to help improve what the government-run PHCs fail to do well. Many specialized tasks can be outsourced to private institutions. NGOs are better suited than government organizations in counseling and helping female sex workers, who do not trust government employees. Private institutions that have expertise in communication can carry out health education and training. Similarly, family planning services can be outsourced to organizations with good social work skills. These and other tasks complement the work of a well run PHC. None of these specific functions, however, substitute for the delivery of proper medical care at PHCs every day.

Most PHCs are overstaffed at lower levels and have excess capacity to provide better care for a lot more patients if run properly. Eighty percent of allocated funds are spent on salaries, and only the balance is available for medicine, equipment and other necessary supplies.[41] As long as PHCs exist and substantial public funds are spent on operating them, the goal should be to find ways to make them effective and avoid duplication. A desirable outcome would see the state retain the responsibility for planning and financing much of the rural health projects, while seeking the participation of private institutions to carry out many of the activities in a coordinated fashion.

Many newly proposed and implemented programs originate from ideas generated by the so-called experts working in the World Bank and WHO or from local NGOs who receive support from international donors. Many academicians are also involved directly or indirectly with these institutions, and they study specific problems faced by countries like India. The result is an array of recommendations to address individual problems and issues, but there is no coordinated effort to bring together interrelated aspects of the wider problem.

For example, to prevent HIV/AIDS from spreading, a number of individual but interrelated activities need to be undertaken, ranging from awareness creation, reproductive health education, and the promotion of condom use to targeting of mobile laborers, the counseling of sex workers, and the early detection of HIV cases. PHCs are likely to be where people suspected of HIV first turn up with some symptom or the other. The institutions that are best suited to handle them might already exist, but unfortunately, the solutions are often thought of as discrete and separate, requiring new organizations and structures.

Further, issues of health care delivery for the rural poor and middle-class are clubbed together with those of urban areas. The underlying methods for accomplishing all these differ not only by country, but also between urban and rural areas. There is no single body within most governments and international institutions to bring about the fusion of ideas, the coordination of activities and the effective use of existing institutions, while at the same time maintaining the distinctions between differing populations.

PARTICIPATION OF THE PRIVATE SECTOR

Let us examine the nature of private participation in rural health care delivery by looking at some of the existing models in other countries. Private institutions are brought in by governments under any number of arrangements, from simple service contracts to perform specific tasks within a limited period to total divesture of a publicly owned health care facility to a private entity. In between these two extremes of the public-private relationship are management contracts for taking care of certain facilities and offering specified services, and lease arrangements wherein the private entity takes over the entire operation of a facility by payment of a lease fee and is permitted to operate freely within set guidelines.

All these arrangements vary in the degree of risk shared. While the goal is to increase efficiency, improve services rendered and reduce costs, one must not lose sight of the fact that, to involve the participation of private institutions, their expected returns must be commensurate with the risks assumed and the opportunity costs involved.

In recent years, there has been considerable talk about the concept of "social franchising." Under this model, a private franchiser entity licenses other private institutions or businesses (franchisee) to operate under its brand name. The assumption is that the franchisee is prepared to bear financial risk, and hence, there is the possibility of making a return. While this model might be appropriate for a number of urban medical services and products, the low purchasing power of the customer does not make it a viable proposition in rural markets.

A more promising model along the same lines is the outsourcing of services to a number of private institutions either directly by the state or through a private intermediary institution that would be responsible for managing the entire network. Under this outsourcing model, the government pays predetermined outsourcing fees to private entities within the network, and they in turn are required to provide services and products either free of charge or at an affordable price. The service provider expects to make a profit by running an efficient business well within the outsourcing fee received and in some cases, by complementing such fees with minimal charges to the customer for services rendered or products sold.

The concept of output-based compensation to the provider for services may be desirable when the targets are easily quantifiable. The problem is one of measuring the quality of services rendered as opposed to the number of people who might have received care. In efforts such as administering immunizations or conducting health surveys, compensation based on meeting quantitative targets might be appropriate.

Regardless of how payments are made, the need to set standards and measure performance against quantitative and qualitative indicators is imperative. But what should be avoided are bureaucratic paperwork and performance measurement schemes based on unrealistic standards that are inappropriate for rural conditions. Accreditation of privately run health clinics in urban environments is usually necessary, but what rural clinics operating under government oversight need is a simple set of standards and protocols that lower-level health workers can be motivated to follow.

There are numerous examples of the outsourcing model in many countries of Africa, South and East Asia, and Latin America. In Kenya, a local NGO, Kisumu Medical Education Trust (KMET) outsources to rural health care providers, including midwives, nurses, and doctors, to provide better treatment for women who are suffering complications from poorly performed abortions. KMET offers post-abortion care training to service providers, who in turn collect some fees from their customers. It is not clear whether customers who are unable to pay the fees receive care, or whether KMET subsidizes such cases.

Janani, an NGO operating in Bihar, India, has established "social marketing" relationships with an extensive network of private shops and institutions to offer family planning counseling and birth control devices at low cost to urban populations and at no cost to rural populations. As of 2002, nearly one million couples have received condoms or oral contraceptives through its initiatives. As an affiliate of DKT International, a United States-based charitable organization involved in social franchising around the world, Janani offsets approximately twenty percent of its expenses with international donor funds, an equal amount mostly from urban customers, and the balance of sixty percent by Government of India grants.

In the delivery of primary health care in a rural area, the closest outsourcing model available is practiced in Cambodia where the Ministry of Health has contracted out a complete line of responsibility for service delivery to international and local NGOs selected through closed bidding. In some cases, NGOs work within the government structure to strengthen existing programs. Depending on the arrangement, the autonomy for the NGO on issues of hiring and firing of workers, salary setting, and purchase of supplies and medicine varies.

A subsequent study has revealed that, where the NGOs are given greater autonomy, the quality of service is superior, and the cost per capita is lower ($5.04 for government controlled versus $2.50 for NGO controlled in Cambodia). While it is difficult to confirm the accuracy of these figures, it is generally accepted that NGO-controlled institutions in Cambodia perform better than those managed by the government.

THE PRIMARY HEALTH CARE SYSTEM

India's current health policy is rooted in the thinking of the Bhore Commission Report of 1946 that has its origins in nation-building activities at the time of independence. The fundamental principle adopted by the nation with regard to health was that primary health care is a basic right to which people should not be denied due to inability to pay or socioeconomic reasons.

India embraced the Alma Ata Declaration of 1978 by committing itself to the goal of "Health for All" based on a primary health care approach.

While the specific tasks and policies to achieve this basic goal have evolved over time, the nation still maintains its stated objectives of improving the health status of the population. Until recently, health policy in India did not pay serious attention to the private sector, allowing it to develop on its own with little coordination with the public sector. Today, there is considerable talk about integration and cooperation, but this should not result in unwanted interference by the government in the private health system other than to assure quality and standards.

The government has created a number of public institutions to deliver curative care and to offer family welfare and disease control programs. These institutions include PHCs, subcenters, dispensaries, urban family welfare facilities, community health centers (30-bed hospitals) and secondary and tertiary hospitals. The main institutions serving rural areas are PHCs and subcenters, staffed by some 29,000 doctors, 18,000 nurse midwives, 135,000 auxiliary nurse midwives (ANMs) and thousands of other support staff.

The public sector provides most health services to those below the poverty line, accounting for ninety-three percent of the immunizations, seventy-four percent of prenatal care, sixty-nine percent of institutional deliveries, and sixty percent of hospitalizations. On the surface these large numbers look impressive, but it is also true that only twenty percent of the outpatient care is provided by the public sector. Shortages of doctors in the government-run rural PHCs are the main reason for the low attendance. There are only 0.04 physicians per 1,000 people, far below the 1.5 per thousand rate for the world population as a whole.

The greatest problem lies in the fact that there is very little commitment and motivation to offer dedicated service to the rural poor. PHCs have become a disgrace to themselves and their noble profession; in the words of a senior central government health secretary, these institutions are "beyond redemption."

According to a recent World Bank report, public health management in India is affected by structural problems, such as overly centralized planning and control of resources, high levels of political interference over staff postings, bureaucratic administrative processes that focus on paperwork, understaffing of key medical personnel at PHCs, inadequate monitoring of performance and absence of quality assurance systems. The public sector is chiefly constrained by staffing limitations, particularly in poor and remote areas that are not served by qualified private sector participants, and by poor maintenance of facilities and unavailability of drugs and supplies.

In the face of a non-functioning rural health care delivery system in India, what are the realistic solutions at hand? The answer probably lies in the three M's: mandate, management and mobilization. The involvement of the private sector may begin with each PHC managed by a small team of non-governmental staff, trained and appointed by a private health care company that should be responsible for daily work flow, patient record keeping and administration.

With adequate infrastructure, proper administration and staff incentive programs based on performance, a much smaller team of government health workers than are currently assigned at each PHC can be motivated to deliver far superior service. The work carried out by the PHC staff may be assisted by NGOs and other volunteers who can be mobilized from the community.

The above strategy does not require more spending on PHCs; in fact, streamlining of PHC work flow and automation of many functions could result in lower operating costs. Successful public-private partnerships at PHCs are possible only when governments give the necessary mandate and authority for private management teams to administer effectively the delivery of health care.

These centers must deliver quality primary care with the services of nurses and other paramedical personnel. It has been successfully demonstrated at the Bagalur PHC in Tamil Nadu that disease diagnosis and treatment recommendations can be made by an expert computer system for a great majority of cases, even in the absence of a doctor. The goal should be to leverage the limited number of physicians who are willing and available to serve in rural communities.

Only in those medical cases when a doctor's intervention is warranted should there be a need to contact a physician or refer to a hospital. Many studies have shown that a great majority of cases do not require the intervention of doctors, as long as trained nurses or paramedical personnel are available. Quality can be assured when these medical personnel are assisted with appropriate diagnostic tools and clearly defined treatment protocols.

The solution proposed by many for fixing government-run institutions is more oversight. I do not believe that a generally corrupt government bureaucracy can be entrusted to oversee a poorly run public system. Routine management and administrative activities can be better executed by private institutions whose compensation is based on meeting or exceeding set targets and performance standards. Periodic independent audit of all activities should be done by separate private organizations that have previously demonstrated high integrity.

There are many such models of private participation in other public activities in America as well as in Europe, e.g., education, health care, and prisons. There should be clear separation of responsibilities on who makes policy decisions and sets targets, who manages the activities, who delivers the services and finally who audits performance and results. As far as possible, the role of the government should be confined to setting policy and targets, while all other activities should be reserved for the private sector within a competitive environment. What we are striving for is to improve quality, increase accountability and promote equity in the rural sector where the population is generally not able to meet the full cost of quality health services and where the private sector would find it unattractive to invest without the government paying for the services when individuals cannot. This change can be made within the PHC system, by competitively contracting out to independent private practitioners and organizations that meet set standards.

No less than six national committees and panels have made recommendations since 1946 on improving primary health delivery in rural areas. The policy formulated thus far provides for one PHC per 40,000 to 50,000 people, one subcenter for every 5,000 people, and one hospital at taluka level (consisting of several villages within a district) to cover 100,000 people. There are specifications for the number of doctors, health supervisors, and workers and for budgets for drugs. As mentioned earlier, almost eighty percent of the funds allocated for primary health care are spent on salaries, and only the balance is available for medicines, new equipment and supplies.

National Population Policy 2000 calls for increasing the number of PHCs, subcenters, and Community Health Centers (hospitals). To deal with the shortage of doctors available to work at these centers, the proposal being considered is to make it mandatory for all graduates of medical schools to do rural service for at least two years before they can seek admission for postgraduation training. There are also suggestions about recruiting Ayurvedic doctors to be posted at PHCs after some administrative training.

The problem with these ideas is the emphasis on increasing the number of doctors available for rural service without adequately considering the effect on quality and commitment. It is fair to require medical graduates who have benefited from government-subsidized education to do a couple years of public service in rural areas, but the focus should still be on finding ways to motivate people to do committed work. Altruism might be a motivation for a few young people to serve, but that won't attract enough qualified doctors; similarly, drafting recently graduated MBBS students will not assure commitment. Sufficient financial incentives and acceptable working conditions alone will attract a greater number of physicians to serve full or part-time in rural areas within the framework of PHCs and private establishments.

Our own experience in Tamil Nadu, India, has convinced us that a good NGO working within a PHC setup along with government employees can make a significant improvement in the quality of health care provided. It all began for us when I first visited the Bagalur PHC in Dharmapuri District in 1998 and observed that the facility was in terrible shape; the assigned doctors were absent, the employees were indifferent about their responsibilities, and the patients were demoralized.

The doctor in charge of the PHC also had administrative responsibilities for the PHC, which he tried to fulfill during his occasional visits each week to see the patients. Patients would not know whether the doctor would be available during their visits, and if the doctor was absent, a nurse or attendant would offer some simple medications and ask the patients to come another day when the doctor was expected.

Each time the doctor's absence was detected by his superiors, the staff at the PHC covered up well by giving some excuse or another. In return, the doctor allowed the staff to take advantage of many unauthorized privileges such as extended vacations for family functions and the private use of the telephone. Patients' concerns always came last. They waited hours, and sometimes days, to see the doctor for a few minutes before he would leave in a hurry by noon.

Many prescribed medicines were simply not available at the PHC; painkillers substituted for antibiotics, no serious effort was being made to maintain a steady supply of necessary drugs, some equipment at the laboratory needed repairs, and supplies were not available to do even the most basic tests. Toilets were practically nonfunctional as there was no running water. The roof leaked badly, and some essential furniture was either missing or stolen. All in all, it was a terribly maintained and poorly managed PHC. To my surprise, I was told that it was one of the best in the state.

Chapter 10

UNCONVENTIONAL POSSIBILITIES

TECHNOLOGY IMPROVES RURAL HEALTH CARE

As a businessman running my own company, I could tell where the problem was with the Bagalur PHC: poor management. A doctor who had no commitment to the PHC was put in charge, and his superiors were tied up with bureaucratic paperwork. Since doctors were appointed as heads of PHCs, and since none of them likely wanted to work in rural areas, I surmised that all PHCs must be in the same condition. The solution lay in bringing in good management and also in leveraging the few doctors who might be available to put in a few hours each week at the PHCs.

Given my background in designing fairly complex computer systems for a wide variety of companies around the world, I thought I could figure out a way to substitute for the doctor during the initial visit of the patient with an expert software system. I had no doubt that the software engineers in my own company back in the United States would help me develop such a system as long as I could provide the application design for handling every possible medical condition we needed to cover.

As soon as I returned to the United States, I began discussing with several doctors the process they went through each time they met with a patient. It became clear to me that the most important design requirements for such a system were flexibility and the ability of my own team of doctors to enter the logic for the diagnostic process to be used in each disease, all specified in a simple language without having to rely on programmers. The result was an interactive application that prompted new questions based on each previous response from the patient to arrive at a diagnosis.

In many cases, the system would require that the patient undergo a lab test to confirm diseases, such malaria, typhoid or cholera, or be referred immediately to a doctor. After nearly a year and a half of program development under the direction of my good friends and systems experts, Richard Niedzwiecki and Chris Arndt, and the able leadership of our doctor, Maya Mascarenhas, we were ready to test it in a controlled environment.

It was the year 2000, and we called our "doctor-in-the-box" EDPS2000, which stood for "Early Detection and Prevention System." With the help of two eminent doctors in Bangalore, M.S. Mahadeviah and M.K. Sudharshan, we installed EDPS2000 at three hospitals. The idea was to run several thousand patients through the system, while attending doctors would independently evaluate the same patients. None of us, including my own team of doctors, knew what to expect.

I was told by many other doctors that the experiment was not likely to succeed, as the mental process that doctors go through while examining patients was too complicated to be programmed into software. Moreover, there are so many possibilities, and it would be almost impossible to cover them all. There are problems of "false negatives" and "false positives," but I had all along believed that at least in a good majority of cases the system could be programmed to arrive at probable diagnoses.

At the end of four months and after running over 10,000 patients through the system, the moment of truth had arrived. The system results were compared with each of the hospital records and tabulated. To our amazement, it was found that in more than ninety percent of the cases, our little doctor-in-the-box had generated the right diagnosis. EDPS2000 had a future. None of us could believe what had been accomplished, and we soon began to study the cases where the system had gone wrong.

Changes were made to the logic to improve its accuracy, and new tests were conducted to further evaluate the logic. Graduating medical students from St. Johns Medical College were asked to do their own tests with the system, and from further feedback, more improvements were made. We were lucky to receive a volunteer physician and epidemiologist, Faisca Ritter, from Canada, who worked to refine the logic and treatment protocols. In the meantime, the government of Tamil Nadu had allowed us to install EDPS2000 in Bagalur PHC as a pilot project. We began using the system on patients in a rural setting by the middle of 2001.

The practical use of EDPS2000 at the PHC began to generate requests for numerous enhancements beyond the diagnostic and treatment capabilities. Several new functions and capabilities, such as the recording of patient medical history and visit data, generation of follow-up actions, laboratory requisitions and reminders for field activity, for example vaccinations, were added. Subsequently, the system was enhanced for the capability to transmit patient visit information to another location (via wireless or telephone) for consultation, when required. At the end of the day, all new patient records and visit information could be readily transferred to a central computer designed to collect data from several PHCs for carrying out surveillance functions.

The system was now being conceived as the backbone of all work flow at the PHC. With data updated from each patient, we could easily produce management reports for the district level in a few hours, an activity that had previously consumed several days for the field staff.

By then, Jude Devdas, our foundation's director of operations, had organized nearly 100 student volunteers to go out in rented buses to 50 or so villages to interview the population, record their medical histories and issue EDPS registration cards. Maya taught them how to gather the right information, and these young people were excited to do social service for the villagers. Maya had been a public health physician for years, and her intimate understanding of village folks helped formulate an effective information-gathering process.

In less than two months, we were able to document the medical records for over 20,000 people based on the information they could provide, and each one was given a newly laminated identity card with a unique number. Villagers were surprised at the thorough nature of the process, and all the attention they were receiving. They were asked to visit the PHC and "talk" to the computer – an idea that excited practically everyone, as most had never seen a computer in real life before.

Changes began to occur at the PHC every day. Jude had the building repaired in less than one month: the roof was fixed, the well pump installed, the generator repaired and the toilets made functional. Tables and chairs were brought in, the grounds were cleaned up, a little garden was created with a few flowering plants and grass, and a waiting area was set up. The George

Foundation appointed its own staff of two EDPS operators, an interviewer, and a team leader named Gracie.

Soon, we added two high school graduates as field staff to cover a dozen or so villages, visit homes, gather all the necessary information and advise those who needed medical care to visit the PHC immediately. Children who were due for vaccinations were asked to come for shots, while pregnant mothers were told to get check ups. We had our own brand of "co-management" at the PHC, working in parallel with government staff.

Initially, the PHC doctor and many of the staff were nervous about our intrusion into their protected environment. The doctor was afraid we would report his absence, and other staff were afraid that they would now have to work hard. We assured them we were at the PHC as an independent party engaged in a pilot project, and we had no intention of getting anyone into trouble. We were not given the authority to instruct any government employees, and Gracie had to use her skills to solicit the cooperation of the doctor and the remaining staff. None of the government employees knew what connections we might have with their superiors, and hence, they were afraid of being visibly non-cooperative.

Fortunately, the director of health at the district level who oversaw Bagalur PHC, G. Prakash, was a dynamic physician who believed in our sincerity. Soon, the attitude of practically all the government workers began to change, and we were able to bring about a number of improvements slowly.

Every patient was required to go through an EDPS2000 interview that took approximately six to 10 minutes. Patients were surprised at the length of time our staff spent with them, taking their weight, blood pressure, temperature, and recording every complaint they had and then asking a number of questions as prompted by the system. At the end of the process, a diagnostic report was generated and handed over to the patient to be given to the doctor when he or she would get the chance to meet him.

If the doctor did not arrive that day, and if the medication required did not involve a prescription from a doctor, Gracie would ask the PHC nurse to give the medicine. The process was far from efficient, but we had no choice except to work within this arrangement without the real authority to instruct any government staff. It did not matter too much, as we simply wanted to prove that, even under such a difficult setup, a government PHC could be made to deliver improved health care.

By the end of 2001, the director of health for the district declared Bagalur PHC the best in his jurisdiction, and probably the best in the state, and started to invite other officials to visit his proud clinic. Within another year, more than 50,000 patients were registered in EDPS2000 and many of them were served more than once during their visits to the PHC. The system was also used extensively to assist field nurses and social workers in tracking those patients who needed follow-up services.

The news had spread to the state health secretary and director levels that the Bagalur PHC had become a model center. The director noticed that he was receiving monthly reports from our PHC on time, correctly prepared in a printed format. I called on both officials to brief them on the progress and suggested that the state conduct an independent review of the new process we had put in place at Bagalur. The secretary promised that he would ask the World Bank to do the independent study, and soon a letter was sent out to the bank by the state.

When I returned to the United States and met with Richard Skolnik, the sector director for South Asia at the World Bank, he was already preparing to respond to the state request. He suggested that we ask a major medical institution in India or in the United States to do the study, and the bank would provide guidance on what needed to be done. The ball was thrown back at us.

The state asked us to find a credible institution to do the study. I concluded that Johns Hopkins School of Public Health in Baltimore, Maryland, would be the ideal one to undertake the evaluation, as they were familiar with India and its health problems. My colleague Bill Schroth and I set out to meet with the panel of decision makers at the school, and after several meetings, it was clear that Johns Hopkins was interested in conducting the study, provided we could find the funds to cover expenses for a three-member team for six months and several trips to India.

At the time, I realized it would not be appropriate for our foundation to provide the funds, as that could negate the perception and reality of independence. David Peters, a physician and former India expert from the World Bank who recently joined Johns Hopkins, was assigned to head the team, and he promised to work with us to find a source for funding the study.

For the next few months, Bill Schroth and I called on several philanthropic institutions engaged in the health arena, but soon realized that practically all of them had no real interest in improving government-run PHCs. Their attention was turned to specific diseases such as HIV/AIDS, malaria and polio, and funding an NGO would only be in their area of interest as a limited project. Fortunately, we found a receptive audience in the Rockefeller Foundation, and their team headed by Tim Evans recognized the potential for our approach and its implications.

The Rockefeller Foundation said it would provide the grant directly to Johns Hopkins for the study that would begin in November 2002. We had found two of the best health partners in the world committed to evaluate the system and its impact, and to understand what it would take to scale up the implementation throughout the state and the country. We couldn't have been more excited.

A RURAL MEDICAL AND COMMUNITY CENTER

While all the effort to move forward with the PHC project was going on, the foundation had just completed the construction of its Baldev Medical & Community Center in Baliganapalli, thanks to a generous contribution from my brother Bijoy. The name Baldev, or "child god," was coined from the first three letters of the names of the two neighboring villages, Baliganapalli and Devarapalli.

This center was set up to cover a 15,000 plus population in Tamil Nadu and the neighboring state, Karnataka. It is staffed by a medical doctor who stays at the center and is available around the clock, a part-time doctor who goes into villages, a residential nurse, two social workers and others who assist the medical personnel and maintain the facilities.

Unlike the PHC at Bagalur some 20 kilometers away, Baldev not only provides outpatient care, but also does birth delivery, emergency care and overnight observation in its 10-bed facility. Our focus is on reproductive and child health interventions, nutrition, infectious diseases, sanitation and clean water, with special emphasis on prevention and early detection of diseases and on health education. A number of community services such as helping women save money, forming self-help groups, counseling and other related activities are also being undertaken.

Nutritional dry powder, high in protein and suiting the tastes of the local population, is prepared at the center and distributed to pregnant women who do not show sufficient weight gain. Sanghas, or self-help groups, are set up in every village and large numbers of poor women join to learn about income-generating activities and savings. They attend classes on reproductive health and contraception, pre- and post-natal care, nutrition, personal hygiene and a host of other topics.

The health status of the community can be improved significantly at a low cost by educating the people on the importance of these subjects. Baldev is a totally independent private institution, setting an example of how a rural health clinic and community center ought to be run with scarce but adequate funds.

Baldev charges patients a nominal fee for each visit (Rs.5 or $0.10 for each poor patient and higher fees for others) and additionally for medicines and supplies. A few destitute people are provided free services and medicine. For all others, a three-tier payment system has been established at Baldev using our own "health equity model" based on the income and assets/liabilities of each family. Wealthy landlords are required to pay five times the charges paid by the poorest patients. Patients are charged for medicine and supplies at prices ranging from sixty to one-hundred twenty percent of the prevailing retail prices at pharmacies in the nearby town.

We were told by many people familiar with rural health care that villagers are used to receiving free medical care from PHCs and are unlikely to pay for such services. I do not think that quality medical care should be provided totally free, and everyone, regardless of income levels, should be asked to pay for services commensurate with one's financial ability.

Baldev competes with medical doctors, field nurses, registered medical practitioners (RMP) and other practitioners in ayurveda and homeopathy. Most of them are not qualified and do not have the license to offer medical services, but no one seems to care. Low educational levels and traditional practices lead villagers to rely on local healers whose advice is taken at face value. Most people who offer medical services in rural areas outside the institutional framework of PHCs and qualified NGOs are not fit to treat patients.

Patients are usually not fully satisfied unless they receive shots; consequently, many rural physicians administer injections and drips when they are not needed. The use of steroids and sedative medicines is common practice to make the patient feel good. Our informal survey of patients indicates that practically all patients receive injections from allopathic practitioners each time they visit. Further, instead of giving the required full dose, the patient gets only a partial dose, and the quack medical practitioner makes money from as many as five to 10 people for the cost of one dose.

Some private practitioners and their assistants go on house visits and give injections. They carry their own syringes, but no disposable needles and no sterilization equipment. They do not test for allergic reactions before giving antibiotic injections. Children are often given steroid drops for illnesses, when there is increasing evidence showing that diabetes might be caused by steroid abuse. Medications not needed are often prescribed because of the commissions doctors receive from the nearby pharmacies on purchases by patients.

Shocking as they may sound, these practices do not face any controls from the government. World Bank's estimate of the private sector offering eighty percent of the health services in rural areas includes mostly such practitioners. It appears that anyone who claims to offer medical services in a rural area is counted as a private practitioner.

It soon became clear to us that patients were motivated to visit one health clinic over another for reasons of convenience, cost and quality, in that order. In rural areas, public transport is either unavailable or sporadic, and patients end up walking several miles to get to a health clinic. In any case, many poor people do not have the means to pay for their travel expenses. Private transport by van or bus is not usually economical as there may not be enough passengers willing to pay the necessary charges. The only immediate solution to the travel issue might be subsidized government transport also along routes that are somewhat less dense.

In addition to convenient transport, the cost of services is a major consideration. The rural population has come to expect health services free of cost, as the government-run PHCs do not charge for consultation by the doctor or for medicine. Moreover, poor, uneducated people are unable to distinguish quality easily. Only after a few visits can they begin to understand that a center like Baldev is truly different.

In their attempt to avoid charges or to save money, they might go to government-run PHCs. Still, health-related incidents are not planned for ahead of time; there is very little understanding of preventive check-ups among the rural people. They visit the clinic only when they are seriously ill or unwell for prolonged periods. Whatever savings they might have set aside are usually meant for wedding ceremonies, religious celebrations, dowry and the purchase of a few gold ornaments that symbolize status in the community. Spending money for health care is a far lower priority for most rural people.

Most hospitals and health centers concentrate on the curative aspects, while community outreach is generally left to a few major teaching hospitals. Baldev, on the other hand, is one of the few private rural centers in the area to offer curative care for the population and to work passionately within the community to bring about changes in outlook and awareness.

Health awareness programs are conducted by Baldev at individual and community levels, while public health work for proper sanitation, drainage and smokeless chimneys is also routinely carried out. Baldev has presently adopted 20 surrounding villages and is committed to improving the health conditions of their entire population. Our social workers plan several activities with the villagers to improve their living conditions and to help them carry out those priorities that are immediately affordable.

We survey an entire village to identify the sanitation and drainage requirements, map them out on paper and coordinate with all those who live there to work for a day or two on a "clean-up operation." We make our bulldozer and backhoe available to dig latrines and trenches, fill ditches that collect stagnant water and level play areas for children. Villagers and volunteer students from colleges join us with shovels, and by the end of the day, the face of the rural landscape is changed for the better. We carry out this program every other month for one village after another, but only after everyone has agreed to what needs to be done and is prepared to work together.

One doesn't need an economic expert to prescribe what it takes to improve the productivity of the rural work force. Practically everyone who lives in the unhygienic conditions of most Indian villages suffers from some type of gastrointestinal parasitism, such as stomach worms, roundworms, hookworms and tapeworms, while a substantial majority also have iron deficiency anemia and protein and calcium deficiency. Prevention and treatment of these ailments is both simple and inexpensive. Proper sanitary conditions and use of footwear can help avoid worm infestations. Given the poor living conditions prevailing in rural areas, it is necessary for the villagers to take de-worming tablets periodically to get rid of worms from their systems.

Baldev has undertaken de-worming of almost the entire population in several villages. Iron and calcium tablets and a specially prepared supplement in powder form with locally available grains rich in protein, groundnut and jaggery are distributed for use by women and children. The program has cost less than two dollars per person for an entire year. Within a few months following the initiation of the program, many people reported considerable improvement in their energy levels and sense of well-being. Our farm workers say their productivity has nearly doubled!

Baldev surveys and maintains in the EDPS2000 system records on morbidity, geriatric morbidity and disability profiles in all the adopted villages. Based on this information, the center executes community-level activities, often in conjunction with the government's community health initiatives. Women's empowerment is also one of the top priorities at Baldev as women are more likely to involve themselves in the welfare of their families leading to better health and socioeconomic conditions for the community. Our goal is to reach out to patients in the early stages of their illnesses and work earnestly to improve the health standards of the community so that people will fall ill less frequently.

The community now realizes that Baldev offers better curative care than other hospitals in the vicinity and wants to utilize its services, but due to transportation hurdles, a majority of the population that is keen to utilize Baldev is unable to do so. The long distance to walk discourages many from seeking medical help until the illness has worsened to a critical stage. Yet, a few patients from far away districts with bigger hospitals visit us occasionally on the word of others who have been previously treated at Baldev.

Suspected cases of typhoid, malaria, HIV/AIDS and several other diseases are tested in our laboratory, with results made available in a short time. The population served by Baldev is quite pleased with the fact that they now have a medical center closer to their villages than ever before, thus encouraging them to address their health problems much earlier than they would normally do.

I believe the local people are so engrossed in their struggle for existence that they do not have the time to spread misconceptions about Baldev. The exceptions are a few people from socially and economically higher classes who for whatever reason might disapprove of the assistance we are providing to the poor and socially deprived in their villages. One bad rumor spread in a village can set back our efforts for weeks and months. In one instance a previously arranged and organized event to distribute de-worming tablets in a village was met with no takers as someone at the last minute spread a false rumor that we were trying to make women infertile.

Our social workers try to anticipate and offset criticism and rumor leveled against us before they can take hold and derail our initiatives. We make a real effort to explain to the people that they should not fall victim to unfounded stories. People have come to realize that we are different from the government-run health centers. These activities provide a strong link between us and the community at large, and they also serve to enhance faith in our work.

People do understand and appreciate our holistic efforts to improve their general well-being. The cooperation we receive from the poor villagers in our community programs is a testimony to this very fact. In five to 10 years, we hope to have a very healthy community around us.

We have found that patients repeatedly visit Baldev because they find its doctor and health staff friendly and caring. Cost of services is a major consideration, but all patients are generally willing to pay whatever is asked of them. No real resistance is noticed on the part of patients in paying a small sum. Even poor people, especially women, have begun to understand the importance of good health, and many have changed their priorities.

Our goals for Baldev are to eradicate malnutrition, achieve one-hundred percent inoculation of children below the age of four, eliminate iron, calcium and vitamin A deficiency among most of the population, carry out de-worming of all children and a great majority of adults, and facilitate proper drainage and sanitation for the 20 or so villages covered. We hope to accomplish these goals within five years for a total population of more than 25,000 people. We believe that with rising income from our poverty eradication programs, Baldev will, in a few years, be able to recover most of the annual operating expenses toward curative care from direct payments by the population.

The primary health care needs of the people in the geographic area covered by the Bagalur PHC and in particular the Baldev are now vastly improved. These projects represent two different models: partnership with government in one case and nonprofit private initiative in the other. The former model can be further strengthened by the participation of village Panchayats in ascertaining whether the delivered services are meeting the needs of the people.

Caution is the watchword in such collaborations, as any excessive involvement of local officials, corrupt in many cases, will only introduce another layer of unnecessary government bureaucracy. The latter model representing the private sector should demonstrate the true costs involved in delivering quality primary health care and effective public health services. It should also provide some insight into the willingness and ability of the village population to pay for services.

In both the government and private clinics, it will be interesting to see how computerized patient records and management processes can improve the work flow, make the allocation of tasks effective for all health workers and help monitor the health status of individual patients. It is our hope that, with wider implementation of EDPS2000 in several PHCs and private clinics, epidemiological surveillance of an entire geographic area can be accomplished. Up-to-date statistical and analytical capabilities provided by the system have the potential for tracking disease epidemics, hence offering the ability to initiate early investigations and interventions. Last but not least, the use of such technology for assessment of population health profiles, including morbidity and mortality figures, as well as risk factors and measures of inequities in health status among the poor and other vulnerable groups, is of current interest to health care authorities.

There is no doubt that prevention is more cost-effective than curative care. Improved surveillance systems and pro-active steps such as inoculation and prenatal care can make major contributions in reducing both morbidity and mortality. Efficient and effective execution of these measures requires access to up-to-date patient health records and the socioeconomic status of every individual.

Patient records are all the more important when dealing with an uneducated rural population that does not have a good understanding of health risks. Armed with proper information, health workers can intervene effectively without wasting unnecessary time and effort. Governments are well advised to set their health care priorities and allocate sufficient funds to those activities that improve efficiency, reduce costs and yield maximum results. Combined with sound poverty eradication measures, major improvements in rural health can be achieved without substantial increases in public fund allocations.

The Johns Hopkins team just recently released the findings of its evaluation of our new approach using EDPS2000 at PHCs, and whether it can be scaled up for wider implementation. Their report concluded that "... there is large potential for the expansion of EDPS and similar decision-support technologies in low-income countries, particularly in areas where non-physicians provide health services." Even after four years of successful pilot projects and several studies to validate the application, it is far from certain that state governments can be motivated to allocate the required resources to improve efficiency and work flow at PHCs through the introduction of systems like EDPS.

The personnel at PHCs are always resistant to changes that bring in more accountability, and it is doubtful that the officials who make decisions on such matters can successfully counter them. It is also uncertain whether anyone in government will even recognize the value of maintaining proper and accessible patient records of the rural population.

To those of us who have been working with the community, however, it is abundantly clear that dramatic changes have already occurred in less than three years at Bagalur PHC and Baldev, and more improvements are in the making. Regardless of whether or not EDPS2000 is accepted for wider implementation by the government, it is essential that PHCs implement a different approach to the delivery of health care in the future. The new model must involve the participation of other entities in addition to the government. The government should rightfully retain overall control and responsibility for the effective delivery of rural primary health care, and it must ensure that the existing physical infrastructure and facilities are maintained properly.

Yet, the actual day-to-day running of PHCs needs to be assigned to private health care companies and NGOs. The government can then finance the operation of PHCs with assistance from international development institutions, such as the World Bank, bilateral agencies, and major international private donors. Pharmaceutical companies, computer software and hardware firms, and other suppliers need to offer their products and services at discounted prices to keep the costs low. Patients should be expected to contribute as much as twenty to twenty-five percent of the operating costs by way of fees for services rendered, based on their income levels; with higher income levels, the patient contribution should also increase.

The goal of reforms should be to improve significantly the quality of health care services rendered, while ensuring access for everyone regardless of income. Costs can be held in check by improving efficiency and bringing in accountability and control. Only when staff, providers of services and suppliers have sufficient financial incentive to be involved in the rural health care market can we expect long-term sustainability of an efficient and effective program.

With clear mandate, proper organization and adequate funding, both the PHC and private models have the potential for success. In a brief time, these may be stories to write home about.

It is our hope that the new health care model offered through EDPS2000 will one day become an integral part of the government-run national primary health system, while the privately run Baldev would be a shining example to rural areas everywhere. Through a new "partnership for rural development," drawing on the strengths of different constituencies, we can solve this major human rights issue over the next decade or two.

Chapter 11

THE INTANGIBLES

ENVIRONMENT, FREEDOM OF THE PRESS, & THE ARTS

My journey in India took different directions. Each time, I faced a new humanitarian concern or a critical need that I attempted to address in a small way. I had returned to India to bring up a few children from poor homes, but I soon realized there are many interrelated problems for which I should seek to offer some solution. My interests led me to issues dealing with education, health care, empowerment of women, poverty eradication and social justice, for none of which I was properly trained. I was also drawn into environmental concerns, development of rural art and culture, and into journalism. Each one of these areas is related to the others, and I decided to take a comprehensive approach rather than dealing with them in sequence. These initiatives incorporated several concepts that departed from the traditional methods of implementing and operating rural poverty programs. The goal was to demonstrate successful models that could be adapted elsewhere by others to suit their specific conditions.

I have already discussed my experiences in some of these areas in earlier chapters. Now I will briefly touch upon three others: protecting the environment; promoting good governance through a free, independent and fair press; and encouraging rural art and culture to preserve the heritage of the country.

GLOBAL ISSUES

Global concern about the environment and climate change has brought both developed and developing nations together to find solutions that are acceptable to all. The Earth Summit on Sustainable Development held in Johannesburg in August 2002 tried to find common ground for developing and implementing projects in five major areas: water and sanitation, energy, health, agriculture productivity and biodiversity, and ecosystem management.[42] It has been more than a decade since the 1992 Earth Summit held in Rio, and yet questions involving funding still remain. Such stumbling blocks may be preventing countries from building sustainable economies and protecting the environment. While there was considerable discussion of issues and proposed solutions, no serious agreement has been reached yet that would channel new sources of funds or other assistance to poorer nations.

With passing time, the relationship between people and critical natural resources has become all the more important. By the year 2025, nearly three billion people could live in either water-scarce or water-stressed conditions; one billion people could be living in land-scarce countries unable to feed the population; more than four billion people could be in one of 40 countries, including India, that have less than 0.1 hectare of forest land per capita, the threshold low level of forest cover.[43] All these dangerous environmental trends are occurring while the world population is steadily increasing.

A series of disputes over international agreements has caused the Bush Administration to face severe criticism from many countries, including some of its allies. The United States government's rejection of the Kyoto Protocol that would have required countries to maintain greenhouse emissions within certain set standards appeared as a unilateral rejection by the United States of pursuing a clean global environment.[44] Regardless of the merits of the arguments put forward by the United States, the manner in which the issue was handled left much to be desired in the court of world opinion. In 2002, the United States took the unprecedented step of rejecting the jurisdiction of the International Court of Justice to try American soldiers for alleged war crimes during peace missions. In another dispute over the right to exploit the seabed's mineral wealth, the United States managed to nullify some of the provisions of a previous Sea Agreement that would have placed severe restrictions on such activities.

All of these, combined with the unilateral decision by the United States to terminate the Strategic Arms Agreement with the Soviet Union that had been in place for the past few decades in favor of its right to engage in a missile defense system, was seen as a sign of militarism. In each instance, there was an arguable case in support of the United States position, but the poor public relations in its unilateral approach left the United States open to criticism from many quarters.

America also faced criticism from many countries over its rejection of binding targets in the fight to reduce poverty and cut pollution. The United States countered by proposing a "new approach to development" that involves partnerships between industry and private foundations to address the developing world's pressing problems, including hunger, shortage of energy and clean water, AIDS and deforestation.

The United States contributes $10 billion each year in donations to developing countries, making it the largest provider of developmental aid, and President Bush recently announced an additional $5 billion. But sustainable development means more than giving money away to the poor, especially when the money is used for things that are short sighted or destructive. As a delegate from Kenya pointed out at the Earth Summit, most of the countries represented at the Johannesburg conference are a big burden to themselves.

To quote Caesar Wamalika, a delegate to the Summit, "Mugabe has rendered Zimbabwe a desert through his policies. The natural resources in Congo are being plundered by surrounding countries. Blaming industrialized countries or Mr. Bush for not attending [the Summit] is seeking a scapegoat. What we need is a regime change where poverty exists."

While such expressions are rare from delegates of poor countries, the indisputable fact is that bad governance has been the main reason for the failed policies and programs of the past. With corrupt and autocratic governments in power, most developing nations cannot find effective solutions to their long-standing problems. India is not an exception to this condition entirely, as its inefficient bureaucracy and corrupt system make it hard to implement ideas that would truly benefit the needy.

Developed countries have been attempting to get India and China to reduce their greenhouse emissions. The fact is that the per capita greenhouse gas emissions of developing countries are just a fraction of the world average per capita emission and much below that of developed countries. Countries like the United States are the largest contributors to emissions, and yet they have not taken substantive measures to reduce their share. According to a recent study, America stands 11th among 122 countries in its overall environmental efforts, mostly because it has done a good job in cleaning up its drinking water and the air in its cities. But the United States is also the worst culprit in producing greenhouse gases, and is dragging its feet on international negotiations to bring them under control.[45]

With only five percent of the world's population, the United States accounts for one-quarter of all greenhouse gas emissions. Europe has a better record on a per capita basis but is also a major contributor to the problem. The Kyoto Protocol with its target of reducing greenhouse emissions by six percent to eight percent below 1990 levels by 2012 may not be a realistic international framework, but it is not acceptable for the United States to be the worst polluter and not take the leadership to do something about it. When it comes to environmental protection on a global scale, those who do not want to do much can seize upon enough uncertainty to avoid doing anything.

The Kyoto Protocol also recommends that developed countries invest in the U.N.'s Clean Development Mechanism (CDM) projects in developing countries and obtain "carbon credits" which could be counted toward their compliance of the emission standards. The onus is on the developed nations to identify opportunities for CDM projects in developing nations.

Our foundation has recently begun discussions with a Swiss company toward implementing a biomass gasification project for generating renewable energy. It involves the burning of woody biomass in a limited quantity of air, yielding a mixture of combustible gases that runs a gas engine.

The product is cheap, clean and reliable power in the form of cooking gas, steam and electricity. When the technology is transferred to us, along with some initial capital, and we start using this form of energy, Switzerland obtains carbon credits through the Kyoto mechanism. In this case, the quantum of carbon dioxide emissions reduced is the credit received by Switzerland, which helps to lower the overall global greenhouse gas emissions.

Countries like India with large populations cannot use per capita emissions as a standard and instead, must try to work toward the goals set by the CDM. India must participate on a global level in the effort to reduce greenhouse gas (GHG) emissions and ozone depleting substances (ODS). However, India's major contribution to GHG does not come from its industries but from agricultural practices and hundreds of thousands of heads of cattle. This unique situation makes for convenient scapegoats and loopholes in GHG policy implementation. The recent discovery of the "Asian Brown Cloud" – the size of the United States and two miles thick over the Indian Ocean – has also raised questions about factors in addition to greenhouse emissions contributing to global warming.

Led by V. Ramanathan from the Scripps Institution of Oceanography in the United States, a team of 200 scientists has been studying for the past several years the dark brown blanket of soot, dust and smoke that may be causing climate change in the region.[46] According to many experts, the dark soot warms the upper air by absorbing sunlight and artificially cooling the surface of the earth. The burning of cow dung and firewood for cooking and the use of coal for power plants are believed to be the main sources of the soot.

Evaporation is reduced from the ocean from cooler conditions, resulting in less moisture for rain. Some scientists blame the dark cloud for the drought that India has been experiencing in most areas since 2001. The cloud could reduce sunlight hitting the earth by as much as fifteen percent and cut rainfall over much of Asia by up to forty percent.

How has India responded to this troubling discovery? As was to be expected, the government's initial reaction was to discredit the findings as faulty science and deny that India is responsible for the dark cloud. Certainly, there are several other Asian countries, such as China, that have been burning coal in large quantities in their power plants, but that does not absolve India's share of responsibility. Instead of trying to learn more about the formation of the cloud and its serious effects, India joined with Pakistan and Indonesia to block any funding by the United Nations Environmental Program (UNEP) for further research to cover all of Asia. Unfortunately, for political reasons, these countries prefer to remain ignorant and silence their critics instead of attempting to uncover the ramifications of this discovery to safeguard their countries.

Developing countries are encouraged to use alternate energy sources, such as wind and solar power, in reducing overall greenhouse emissions. India is one of the larger users of both solar and wind energy, and with further assistance in financing and technology, there is considerable potential for wider application in most parts of the country. However, the only form of renewable energy that currently works out economically for India is biomass – agricultural waste, and plantation wood. Wind and solar energy are presently far too expensive to be cost-effective as a national solution to power generation. Renewable energy projects in India are heavily subsidized, and are very local and limited in application. Hence, the energy deficit as a whole is not being addressed.

India urgently needs to improve the manner in which it harnesses and directs the use of all its natural resource stocks, and that includes the economic use of the plentiful bright sun in most regions and the strong wind in wide coastal areas. Technology and finance are key to wider application. There are no well-defined markets for these "public goods," and thus a non-optimal allocation, especially in a developing country, is inevitable. India does not need to follow the poor example of developed countries and instead, should pursue cleaner fuels and lower consumption of energy without sacrificing economic development.

While many developed countries have slowed down or halted the construction of new nuclear reactors for producing energy during the past two decades, India has entered into agreements with Russia and Germany for assistance in the construction of no less than four additional plants. All the currently existing six nuclear power plants are in heavily populated areas, and an accident similar to Chernobyl in 1986 would cause unimaginable loss of life. Further, the terrorism threats faced by India and other countries around the world make nuclear plants potential targets. The safe disposal of nuclear waste is another matter of serious concern. While it is rumored that the deserts of Rajasthan and Madhya Pradesh are the site choices for nuclear waste disposal, independent outside organizations have been unable to verify the safeguards already implemented as the authorities have been totally secretive.

CONSERVATION AND PROTECTION OF RESOURCES

As rural India is well suited for the use of both solar and wind energy, I decided to experiment with solar power in many of our social projects. The use of solar power for the applications we chose turned out to be rewarding in terms of cost savings and efficiency, though the initial capital costs were high. Both Shanti Bhavan and Baldev Medical Center were built with solar energy in mind; residential lighting that requires low-watt bulbs has been wired separately in all dormitories and connected to solar power panels on each roof. The hot water requirement for bathing is fully met with overhead tanks fitted directly to solar panels. Street and pathway lighting relies on rechargeable batteries connected to panels and time switches; these provide adequate lighting throughout the night.

Well water from depths up to 150 feet is pumped with solar submersible pumps, while above-ground collection tanks distribute water to fruit orchards and vegetable gardens with overhead solar pumps. All these non-industrial uses of solar power have cut conventional energy consumption at Shanti Bha-van by more than sixty percent. Staff and children are trained to be conscious of the need to use water efficiently. With proper maintenance of all solar equipment arranged with the supplier, our experience has been encouraging, and we are now considering working with the village officials to provide solar lighting at key locations within their residential areas.

Contaminated drinking water is a serious public health issue. Most people living in Indian urban areas are afraid to drink tap water from the public water supply system as it is known to contain bacteria and other harmful elements. According to a senior public health expert at the community medicine department of the Christian Medical College, Vellore, tap water in practically every city is unsafe for drinking. Human and animal excrement and other waste commonly wash into rivers and lakes that serve as sources for the public water system.

Excess chlorination of city water to counter bacteria has also made it un-safe for consumption. Despite excess chlorination, drinking water is not free of harmful bacteria, and germs that carry many of the serious illnesses, such as dysentery, typhoid and cholera, can be easily found in the tap water. For safety, many homes boil the tap water before drinking. Those who can afford to buy bottled water do so under the assumption that it is safe. But tests now show it might also contain harmful elements other than bacteria.

The Center for Science and Environment based in Delhi recently reported toxic pesticide residues in 34 samples of bottled water they studied, from different manufacturers. The samples included both packaged water that is treated to meet certain health standards, and packaged natural mineral water from clean sources that may not require any treatment. Deadly pesticides were found in all samples, except those brands which were imported. The pesticides detected include those commonly used in agriculture, as well as the banned HCH variety. In practically every case, the amount of pesticides exceeded safe levels, and in some, they were 45 times higher than what is declared safe by the European Economic Community's (EEC) directive on water intended for drinking.

The discovery of pesticides in bottled water has uncovered a much larger problem: contamination of open drinking water sources by pesticides. The root cause of the problem is irrigation and agricultural run-off. Pesticides are constantly seeping into groundwater and surface water used by both bottled water manufacturers and public water supply systems. There is no doubt that pesticides are essential for ensuring good crop output, but none of them are safe for human consumption. India still uses pesticides that were banned years ago in other countries due to their proven adverse effects on human health as well as the ecosystem.

Banning the use of highly toxic pesticides alone will not address the health dangers caused by other permissible pesticides. Farmers need to be educated on safe use of pesticides – something that manufacturers have deliberately avoided so far in the interest of larger product sales from wide and indiscriminate applications.

It also appears that most agricultural belts permit drain water containing pesticides and chemical fertilizers to run into feeder ravines and canals and subsequently into rivers and lakes. Also, it is not well known or understood how much water and soil pollution is caused by the pesticide industry in their manufacturing processes. While much study is needed to ascertain methods of prevention, common sense tells us that the sources of drinking water need to be protected, and that should certainly include rivers, lakes and reservoirs.

Where ground water is used for drinking, it should not be obtained from farm areas where pesticides are applied in significant quantities. Water contamination has become a serious problem for the rural population that relies exclusively on local wells and lakes that are usually close to farms that apply pesticides.

Strict government standards for bottled water may force manufacturers to find ways of removing pesticides from water or to obtain water from cleaner sources, but it does not deal with the basic problem of contamination of sources. Moreover, most people can afford to drink only tap or well water, boiled or otherwise, so it is imperative that sources be free of pesticides and other harmful chemicals and metals. If the present trend is allowed to continue, much of India's drinking water will soon become daily poison, widely causing many illnesses, including cancer.

Probably the biggest success story about India is its transformation from famine to self sufficiency in food in a short period of 40 years following the country's independence. The agriculture miracle (The Green Revolution) was brought about by the use of modern farming technology and superior grain seeds. Farmers were encouraged to use chemical fertilizers to obtain higher crop yields, without a clear understanding of the long term implications. Organic compost manure has been replaced in large measure by a range of chemical fertilizers that offer nitrate, phosphate and potassium.

As a result, high-density cultivation is possible for a few initial years with these new applications, but the soil is quickly being depleted of many other essential elements including micronutrients. The texture of the soil and its ability to retain water are adversely affected. Harmful residues from chemicals are settling in the soil, further damaging its content.

The problem is further complicated by the toxicity of the entire Indian river system relied upon by many farm belts. Alarming levels of arsenic, cadmium, mercury, nickel and chromium from industrial pollution get into rivers, and they finally end up in the soil and in underground water for drinking. Persistent Organic Pollutants (POP) that resist photolytic, chemical and biological degradation, such as DDT, dioxins and furans, are banned by most nations, but India continues to use many of them. The results are the constant degrading of farmland, the entry of dangerous heavy and trace metals into the food chain and the introduction of chemical poison into underground drinking water. Many people now carry enough toxic substances in their body fat to cause serious health problems, including reproductive and developmental damage, cancer and immune system disruptions.

Soil damage from the application of chemical fertilizers is further aggravated by topsoil erosion from wind and heavy rains. Poor drainage has caused excess water during monsoons to wash away fertile topsoil in many farms across the country. Conserving soil and moisture is of great importance in the extensive regions with low and uncertain rainfall. These areas are often characterized by scanty, ill-distributed and highly erosive rains, undulating topography, high wind velocity and generally shallow soils.

Poorly planned and carelessly constructed dams and deforestation have further contributed to the environmental damage in local ecosystems and to communities, while wind erosion has been responsible for destroying valuable topsoil in many areas. The constant march of the desert in Rajasthan and the Saurashtra region of Gujarat are examples of major sand movements. In addition to the erosion of cultivated fields, poor drainage along roads and highways and water-logging are both causing serious damage to the large areas where cultivation would have been otherwise possible.

In India, there is very little land not subject to soil erosion. It is estimated that 145 million hectares, or nearly half the agriculture land, is in need of conservation measures. Further, after decades of heavy use of chemicals, we are now beginning to witness lower crop output in many areas. Farmers who had relied on chemical fertilizers in past years are now forced to add more chemicals with little improvement in output.

With an increasing population to support every passing year, India cannot afford to see a declining agricultural sector. Farmers need to be re-educated on the use of organic fertilizers and effective micro-organisms, and there has to be a determined effort to make these available at affordable prices. The danger signs are all too evident, and time is running out for reversing the course.

Recognizing these environmental hazards, our foundation initiated several conservation measures at all our projects, especially Shanti Bhavan and Baldev Farms. All cultivated sloped land has been graded at different levels to avoid soil erosion during heavy rainfall. Proper drainage has been made to avoid run-offs during the monsoons. To avoid contamination of the nearby lake by chemical fertilizers and pesticides, we do not permit drainage water to flow into nearby ravines. Instead, it is diverted into large pits where agriculture waste is kept for making compost. The waste is kept moist with water from the drainage system, and is allowed to decompose with the help of effective micro-organisms (EM and Bokashi) that are added periodically.

Our farm is one of the largest buyers of organic compost from the government-run garbage processing factory near Bangalore. Lately, we have been obtaining truckloads of lake-bed soil while the dredging is taking place in Ulsoor Lake in Bangalore. In Shanti Bhavan, we recycle the entire sewage and laundry wastewater of the campus through a series of chambers, filters and aeration processes to obtain more than 50,000 liters of clean water every day for irrigation. All these environmentally friendly measures are noted by our children at Shanti Bhavan and the villagers as good examples of protecting nature. In the process, we have reduced our groundwater consumption, introduced extensive use of organic manure and are saving considerable money on expensive alternatives.

POLLUTION

Industrial pollution is rampant in India. A World Bank report estimated that pollution-related ailments kill more than 40,000 people annually in the six Indian cities it has surveyed. With each passing day, the problem is compounding. While larger industries are the focus of attention, the bigger culprits are the medium- and small-scale companies.

In Delhi residential areas, there are some 100,000 smaller companies involved in highly polluting industries, such as electroplating, metal buffing, battery recycling, dyeing, powder-coating and asbestos brake manufacturing.

In a 1996 landmark case, the Supreme Court ordered the government to relocate these companies, but as of today, the infrastructure to relocate them has not been developed. Similarly, there are more than 7,000 chemical companies in Gujarat state producing dyes, pesticides and other dangerous substances, all operating with little safeguards. The larger companies, on the other hand, have shown some inclination to abide by the environmental regulatory laws, but they, too, are slow in their responses.

Experts now believe that the single largest cause of death for children globally – estimated to be nearly five million a year – is from acute respiratory diseases that arise from or are exacerbated by constant exposure to highly polluted indoor and outdoor air. India is experiencing its share of deaths and illnesses from air contaminated by automobiles and industrial emissions and from indoor air tainted by smoke from cooking in poorly ventilated homes.

State Pollution Control Boards are in a better position to enforce compliance of regulatory laws by companies that are setting up new manufacturing facilities. However, in the case of small-scale industries and existing manufacturing facilities of larger companies, the problem is much more complicated. Most of them continue to use outdated and inefficient technologies that generate large amounts of waste, which in turn are improperly disposed of. The authorities are quick to point out a few success stories, but there is no doubt that a great majority of industries throughout India still operate with little or no environmental controls.

It is estimated that more than ninety percent of the asbestos manufacturing and fabricating units do not have any pollution abatement equipment. Hazardous liquid waste is usually dumped into canals and rivers without any purification process. The regulatory agencies are unable or unwilling to enforce the laws. Pollution control officials do not provide the right guidance preferring to harass companies for bribes.

The country has not shown much concern about small harmful particles present in industrial pollution that cause lung and heart diseases. These are what they call Respirable Suspended Particulate Matter (RSPM), particles of 10μ or less in diameter, which deposit in the lungs. Combined with serious urban air pollution caused by automobiles and trucks, India faces an environmental crisis that is already leading to substantial increases in several pollution-related illnesses.

The victims of environmental hazards are the children who suffer from birth defects and retarded growth as a result of harmful environmental toxins. Neurological disorders occur especially during the fetus stage as well as in early childhood. Children absorb harmful metals, such as lead, from the environment, food and water at a rate several times greater than adults. Childhood cancer rates have been steadily increasing in India during recent years. Yet, asbestos and other hazardous industrial products that are banned in developed countries are commonly used in houses and other buildings throughout India.

Harmful chemicals are now increasingly used in processed food as preservatives and taste enhancers. Many fast foods that target children contain harmful substances, such as monosodium glutamate, but there is very little control or oversight by governmental authorities.

ADDRESSING LEAD POISONING IN INDIA

Environmental ruin in India is proceeding at a pace as rapid as the population explosion. Yet, until recently, the government paid very little attention to environmental issues. Until the mid-1990s, the Central Pollution Control Board and the Ministry of Environment and Forests at the central government did not pay any attention to the dangers of lead poisoning.

Although practically all developed nations had introduced unleaded petrol over two decades earlier and made its use mandatory, none of the government-owned oil companies in India had even a single facility to remove lead in their refining process prior to 1995. In the meantime, the number of cars and two-wheelers running along urban roads had multiplied several-fold, heavily polluting the air with lead exhaust. Though the neurological damage caused by lead intake, especially in children, was well established in many authoritative scientific studies, the government was not interested in addressing the problem. The "silent" nature of the damage caused by lead poisoning, and the absence of public awareness about it, made it politically feasible for the authorities to ignore a health hazard affecting more than 300 million urban residents.

My involvement in the effort to reduce lead poisoning in India started upon my return to India in early 1995 when I found every major city highly polluted. Delhi air was so dense with pollution that even visibility was restricted. Bangalore air was also much polluted, and its gardens were more brown and gray than green. By the end of any day spent in the city, my hair would be thick with some black substance from vehicle exhaust. I soon developed a serious eye allergy and breathing difficulty.

It was clear to me that the health problems I had acquired in India were related to air pollution. I found that petrol was leaded, and vehicles did not use catalytic converters to make the exhaust cleaner. My inquiry with the state Pollution Control Board revealed that there was no immediate plan to deal with vehicular exhaust or for removing lead from petrol.

When I returned to the United States, I checked with the New York city Environmental Protection Agency on the dangers of lead in vehicle exhaust. I was provided with extensive information and was introduced to Steve Null, a crusader for a lead-free environment. Steve was already doing considerable work in the Dominican Republic trying to create awareness about the dangers of lead poisoning and testing the blood lead levels of workers in the battery recycling industry. His energy and commitment were so contagious that I soon joined him in the campaign to deal with the problem.

We met with India's ambassador to the United States in Washington and the consul general in New York to seek their help in bringing the subject to the attention of the Environment Ministry in Delhi. By then, we had arranged for blood testing equipment and other supplies to be brought to India. We sought their help to obtain duty waiver for the import, but were rebuffed. One of them told me, "What is this lead poisoning? We have so many other major problems in India. Why waste money on this? Why don't you help some poor people?"

We were both surprised and angered by their patronizing attitude. Steve couldn't contain his annoyance and responded, "Mark this day." We left the meeting with the realization that this battle was going to be a lonely one.

By the middle of 1996, I understood what needed to be done in a wide screening of the urban population in India. The Center for Disease Control and Prevention (CDC) in Atlanta was very supportive, providing their protocols for blood testing and guidance on how to proceed. Steve took me to some of the lead blood screening laboratories in the United States, and I met with ESA in Boston, the leading manufacturer of lead testing equipment. ESA promised to supply the testing equipment, reagents, calibrators and other supplies at steep discounts to carry out screening of some 25,000 individuals.

I needed someone to spearhead the national blood lead screening study. S. Dawson, a retired admiral of the Indian navy, was recruited in a voluntary capacity to head up "Project Lead-Free" and carry out blood screening of at least 15,000 children and 5,000 adults in seven major cities in India. He recruited several hospitals to take part in the study and launched a major awareness campaign to inform government officials and medical institutions on the dangers of lead poisoning. Most officials and institutions admitted they knew very little about the problem when they wrote back expressing their appreciation, yet were unwilling to offer any financial help.

In January 1997, Steve and I arrived with all the equipment and supplies needed to launch the training program in the eight hospitals that were going to screen their local populations. It was the largest blood lead screening study conducted anywhere in the world.

By the end of 1998, we had collected all the required data. Preliminary analysis indicated high levels of blood lead in children, but we would wait to announce the final results at an international conference to be organized in Bangalore in early 1999. Steve and I approached the World Bank and WHO for their support, both financially and otherwise, in holding the conference. I wanted this to be a three-day conference and workshop to discuss practical measures that all developing countries could implement with limited financial resources.

Our invitation was accepted by 24 foreign governments of developing countries and some 80 experts in the field from developed countries. Most leading environmental organizations and health-related research institutions in India agreed to participate. The most exciting news was the willingness of the three leading oil companies in India to send their senior executives. We now had more than 500 scientists, academicians, senior government officials and representatives from major international institutions signed up to attend the conference. We booked all seven banquet and conference halls and several floors of rooms at Hotel Ashok in Bangalore.

Following the introductory formalities, the conference opened with my presentation of the results of our two-year-long study. We had kept the findings fairly secret all along, as I wanted to start the conference with some excitement and expectation. However, it did not come as a surprise to most experts to hear that more than fifty percent of the children in the seven cities we screened showed blood lead levels over 10 micrograms per deciliter, the upper acceptable limit set by CDC.

There are more than 100 million children below the age of 12 living in urban areas, and it is heartbreaking to imagine that half of them are already poisoned by lead. It is now established that even at much lower levels permanent neurological damage could occur, along with lowering of IQ and attention deficiency, among other problems.

The general adult population was affected slightly less, but there were many pockets of serious lead poisoning among certain types of workers, such as traffic policemen, and in industrial areas. The best estimate was that no less than 300 million adults and children, mostly living in urban areas, were then significantly affected by lead poisoning. The press covered the story fairly well on the front pages, and most television stations gave it a few minutes. Yet, it was not clear to me that the general public was prepared to accept its implications.

What followed were a series of discussions between experts and everyone else, especially those responsible for implementing lead poisoning prevention and treatment programs in their respective countries. It wasn't a conference about science alone; participants discussed every issue from how to eliminate sources and pathways to treatment choices and protocols. Blood screening, environmental monitoring and low-cost prevention methods were of major interest to most participants.

The conference ended with an announcement by the executives of the three oil companies that their refineries would start offering unleaded petrol within 18 months. The mood at the outdoor parting dinner was one of jubilation and satisfaction that a general consensus had been reached on many important environmental issues facing developing countries.

In the six months that followed the January 1999 conference, a concerted effort was made to compile its proceedings and to develop a consensus document on the priorities and actions to be taken by developing countries to prevent and treat lead poisoning. I wanted to be sure that the senior officials who attended the conference from the World Bank, WHO, United States Environmental Protection Agency, Indian Council of Medical Research, and other leading institutions signed on a single document outlining their recommendations. Revision after revision were made to the draft document to gain a consensus among the 10 signatories, and by the end of the year, everyone agreed to an unambiguous and action-oriented plan.

The World Bank and the WHO agreed to distribute the conference proceedings and the Action Plan to environmental authorities of every developing country. Many governments responded positively to the recommendations, and some appointed task forces and committees to study the problem. I met with the central minister for environment in Delhi, and he, too, agreed to appoint a committee to evaluate the problem and make regulatory recommendations. I was appointed as one of the committee members.

In April 2000, all three major Indian oil companies announced the introduction of unleaded petrol nationally. The national committee on lead poisoning met under the auspices of the Central Pollution Control Board and approved most of the recommendations presented in the Action Plan. Soon thereafter, regulatory recommendations on safe recycling of automobile batteries were put out. The central environmental secretary promised to persuade major paint manufacturers to make unleaded paint for most applications, especially offices and residences.

After the Bangalore conference, articles began to appear in newspapers on lead-poisoning cases and sources, and national awareness of the problem began to rise. Parents living in urban areas started inquiring as to how they could prevent lead poisoning of their children. We were elated by the quick initial success of our efforts to deal with a national problem that was already harming hundreds of millions of people and could seriously affect future generations.

Despite all the lead poisoning fanfare, it soon became obvious that very little was actually getting done on the ground. The Committee on Lead Poisoning formed by the Central Pollution Control Board produced a document that outlined its policy recommendations, but there was no follow-up to ensure proper regulatory enforcement. Contrary to the earlier announcement, lead was not being totally removed from all petrol, and further, it was being replaced with benzene, a carcinogenic additive. Moreover, even with low lead content in petrol, significant increases in the number of vehicles and the distances traveled by them have not permitted total lead exhaust to be sufficiently reduced.

Thousands of lead smelters and lead-based industries across India still operate with few controls. Neighborhoods surrounding most of these factories have already become highly contaminated, and without major efforts to clean up soil and waste, generations of children and adults face serious threat of poisoning. Workers are offered little or no safeguards in their jobs, and most come home every day in their work clothes and unknowingly poison other members of their families.

Paint companies, another major industry responsible for lead poisoning, have shown no genuine willingness to remove lead from their paints. With paint used more widely now, lead is becoming a part of the home and office environment. There are many other major sources of lead that have not received sufficient attention. Many homes use cooking utensils coated with lead; battery recycling is a major cottage industry; Ayurvedic medicines routinely use lead as an ingredient; toys and pencils are coated with lead paint.

Lead has already entered the food chain; a recent study of vegetables grown near Delhi showed dangerously high levels of lead in spinach. Without adequate enforcement of environmental laws, and the threat of class-action lawsuits and major financial penalties, culprits of lead poisoning continue undaunted.

Once again, we couldn't wait for the government to enact and implement regulatory laws effectively to deal with the many sources of lead poisoning. There was clear need for an active non-governmental organization focusing on creating national awareness, providing guidance on blood lead testing and treatment and persuading the government and private industry to implement environmental safeguards. The George Foundation joined forces with St. Johns National Academy of Health Sciences in Bangalore and funded the creation and operation of the National Referral Center for Lead Poisoning in India (NRCLPI) to carry out these important initiatives.[47] Under the able leadership of T. Venkatesh, the project director of NRCLPI, we launched an awareness campaign that generated great interest on the part of the private sector, especially from the lead-based industries and some paint manufacturers.

Subsequently, the State Pollution Control Board of Karnataka (PCB) offered some funds for blood screening and for distribution of informative leaflets. To assist implementation of environmental protection measures at private and public institutions, The George Foundation decided to finance a start-up company, AwenGaia, run by a group of young female entrepreneurs trained in environmental science. Gaia submitted numerous proposals to public and private companies on projects ranging from wastewater recycling and safe waste disposal to attractive ecotourism concepts.

Alas, Gaia's efforts have accomplished very little so far, but its failure to attract any business has provided valuable insight into the hurdles faced in bringing about environmental protection in India.

EXPERIENCES IN DEALING WITH ENVIRONMENTAL AGENCIES OF THE GOVERNMENT

Gaia's experience in dealing with the PCB over a two-year period was terribly frustrating. Each time a proposal was submitted, it soon became apparent that the only way it would receive serious attention was if Gaia tried to win the favor of a senior PCB official. Until then, the proposal would not be given genuine consideration, and all attempts to obtain access to key officials would be rebuffed. Unduly long waits, misinformation, disinterested staff and miles of red tape ensured inaction and inaccessibility. There were also frequent changes in PCB management, with each new chairperson of the board following his or her own agenda. This turnover ruled out the possibility of follow-ups, and again and again the consultant was required to resubmit the proposal and start from scratch.

Bureaucracy and red tape are so deeply entrenched in the system that there is no chance for improvement and efficiency in the functioning of the board without major organizational changes and accountability. There is an all pervasive colonial culture that does not allow for a professional work environment. PCB staff members spend most of their time going through compliance documentation submitted by companies, while assigning very few people for field inspections. It appears that state PCBs receive little attention from higher authorities, and they operate without sufficient accountability.

The board claims that it is so slow to respond because the department is understaffed and therefore overworked. Apparently, a competent staff is hard to come by, as many positions remain vacant. Having visited board offices on a regular basis for two years, Gaia has found a laid-back attitude among its staff; there is no sense of urgency. Corruption plays a big role, ensuring that one cannot do business without talking about "things other than business." State PCB officials usually work out deals with preferred consultants who keep corruption alive and well at all levels within the agency.

It is now abundantly clear that enforcement of environmental laws cannot be left to state and central governmental agencies alone, and citizens will have to resort to legal measures in their common interest. Despite all these drawbacks, most international agencies, especially the World Bank, continue to work mainly through state PCBs.

Gaia's experience in dealing with the private sector has been somewhat different. Most companies are interested in projecting a superficially clean appearance, and it is very hard to motivate them to implement real changes to meet environmental standards. Larger companies certainly want to avoid any negative environmental publicity, and they are prepared to spend considerable sums of money on advertisements and public relations activities to project environmental concern. However, translating this insincere motivation into real work is not usually on the agenda.

It is more convenient and cheaper for companies to pay bribes to corrupt government officials than to clean up their act once and for all. There are, of course, exceptions to the rule, but without persistent public pressure and major penalties for wrongdoings, there is not sufficient incentive to conform to environmental standards.

For small- and medium-scale enterprises the green image is not really a concern. Only money talks to them, and short-term goals completely block out any long-term changes. These companies receive the brunt of harassment by corrupt board officials, and they prefer to pay out small amounts as bribes on a regular basis than to make major capital investments in pollution-control technology and optimal resource usage.

For both large and small enterprises, environment is a "soft field" that demands very little management attention. Although proposals are accepted from environmental consultants like Gaia, companies are not willing to pay for their expertise or work unless they are already in trouble with the board or from negative publicity.

As a company run mostly by women, Gaia has found there is a prevailing mentality that men should do fieldwork, and women are suited only for administrative positions. Prospective clients, including the board, do not seem to accept the judgment of women advising them on what to do and how to do it. Further, environmental problems in India are largely dealt with by employing engineering solutions as opposed to management solutions. In other words, the focus is on "end-of-pipe solutions" that conceal the environmental damage, as opposed to preventive and control measures.

ENVIRONMENTAL IMPACT ON DEVELOPMENT

In a developing country like India, concern for the environment is considered a luxury, relative to the more pressing issues of poverty, health care, education, trade and investment. The general public has yet to recognize that environmental problems will sooner or later impede progress. Though lead poisoning prevention is off to a good beginning, there are many other serious environmental problems facing India that demand immediate attention.

Sustainable development, as proposed in the last two Earth Summits, is certainly the way to proceed. Economic prosperity cannot be achieved at the expense of fresh air and water, productive soil and bio-diversity, all of which are important to human survival. India must quickly incorporate an aggressive environmental policy into its developmental strategy. To do otherwise would simply be suicidal in the longer run. For example, the energy needs of a fast-growing economy are likely to multiply several-fold in the next decade or so, and hence, the country's reliance on coal and oil must be supplemented by non-polluting alternatives, such as wind and solar power.

No one disputes that the governmental agencies responsible for enforcing environmental protection have made some progress. But future development must take place without harming the environment, and that calls for a national policy giving equal priority to many of the pressing environmental challenges facing the country. The time has come in India for a national environmental movement, especially among the younger generation, similar to the one the legendary environmentalist Ralph Nader initiated in the United States several decades ago. Citizens must demand environmental safeguards in every developmental activity, and their national and local leaders must be pressured politically to support and carry out environmental initiatives.

The World Bank talks about sustainable development and incorporates ecological concerns into its sponsorship of economic development. However, until recently, environmental concerns in India have been ignored in favor of industrial growth. As Aleksandr Solzhenitsyn notes in *Bill Moyers' World of Ideas* (Doubleday Books, 1989), Homer's warning of the doom of Nemesis in the Greek epics might be an appropriate reminder about the dangers of ignoring nature in the name of progress. Driven by uncontrollable greed, Prometheus contravened the boundaries of the human condition. Mindless, he brought fire from the heavens and thereby brought doom onto himself. He was chained to a rock; an eagle preyed on his liver, and heartless gods kept him alive by regrafting the liver each night.

The encounter of Prometheus with Nemesis is a timeless reminder of the inevitable reckoning for the ecological damage being caused in the name of eliminating human suffering. Every man has become Prometheus, and Nemesis has become ubiquitous; it is the backlash of progress. We are hostages to a lifestyle that elicits doom. In the words of the Chilean poet Vincente Huidorbo, insight into alternatives not chosen and opportunities missed can be found by remembering "those hours which have lost their clock."

Even with the new opportunities that technology and business investment have produced, all of us need to exercise some caution and responsibility. We have now discovered that unlimited progress cannot occur within the fragile resources of our planet; nature needs to be supported rather than conquered. The concept of "ecology" is deeply rooted in the concept of "life." We cannot live a life in opposition to nature. We must use technologies not for conquering nature but to coexist with nature.

All hope cannot be pinned on science, technology and economic growth. While such progress could enrich us, it could also enslave us. As we struggle for material things, an inner voice tells us that we have lost something pure, elevated and fragile. We have lost site of the real purpose of our lives.

The joy of living itself is now threatened. Rapidly increasing consumption by the affluent without sufficient concern for the environment is endangering the healthy and productive lifestyle of everyone. The growing ecological crisis may alter the climatic zones, leading to shortages of fresh water and suitable land in places where they were once plentiful. Simultaneously, the demands on the rich for economic and social justice could lead to unprecedented social unrest. We must care for nature and share our plentiful gifts with those who are less fortunate. Otherwise, tranquility will not descend upon India.

PRESS FREEDOM AND INDEPENDENCE

Every oppressive government has curtailed press freedom. Most corrupt governments have allowed varying degrees of press freedom. The presumption is that a free and independent press contributes to democracy and good governance. Contrary to this expectation, corruption in India has only increased over the years, even in the face of a supposedly "free" and "independent" press. This outcome is surprising and disappointing, but there is no doubt that the future of India's democracy is heavily dependent on the future of the Indian press.

Many countries have enshrined press freedom in their constitutions but feel free to ignore or twist it to suit their political objectives. Governments restrict press freedom using many arguments that appeal to the ordinary citizen.

The argument based on patriotism insists that the nation cannot tolerate "destructive" criticism during times of crisis. The nationalism argument seeks to protect the traditional native culture and values from the "vulgarities" of Western culture.

The economic argument is that criticism of national policies undermines developmental efforts. The secrecy and subversion argument insists that it is not safe for the country to let the foreign media enter into sensitive domestic areas. Investigative reporting is resisted on the grounds that the press tends to be untruthful and vindictive.

The arguments in support of curtailing press freedom would appear sufficiently persuasive to most people. But in reality, the fight against a free press is nothing more than politicians seeking to hide their misdeeds and maintain the status quo. It appears India is no different when it comes to these invisible restrictions on the press. The Indian press may not, after all, be as free or independent as everyone is led to believe.

At the Hemisphere Conference of the Inter-American Press Association held at Chapultepec Castle in Mexico City in March 1994, political leaders, writers, academics, constitutional lawyers, editors and private citizens from throughout the Americas drafted a document containing 10 principles necessary for a free press to be able to perform its essential role in a democracy.[48]

Despite there being consensus that a free press is a fundamental prerequisite for societies to resolve their conflicts, promote their well-being and protect their liberty, no people or society has been completely true to these principles. The exercise of the freedom of expression is not something authorities grant but an inalienable right of the people.

While it is true that this declaration has now been signed by the heads of state of the Western Hemisphere countries and has become a barometer to measure the extent of true freedom of the press in all countries, we see that such freedom has not, in fact, progressed much. Politicians who proclaim their faith in democracy can become intolerant of criticism. Judges with limited vision order journalists to reveal their sources, while denying public access to records that are embarrassing to the government, in the name of national security or interest.

Following the September 11 terrorist attacks, several foreigners were imprisoned in the United States for fear that they could be terrorists. The Bush Administration also tried to conduct deportation hearings in secret whenever they felt the detainees might be linked to terrorism. The Justice Department had previously held many secret hearings, out of sight of the press and the public, and in some instances, the fact that the hearings were being held was also kept secret. The press tried to obtain information about the prisoners and their treatment, but the government refused in the name of national security.

In a case that challenged the constitutionality of secret trials, Judge Damon J. Keith of the United States Court of Appeals of the Sixth Circuit dismissed the government's argument for secrecy with a forceful and eloquent opinion: "Democracies die behind closed doors. " The judge noted that the First Amendment offers the constitutional right to free press and protects the "people's right to know" that their government is acting fairly and lawfully.[49]

This ruling echoes the comments made by John Adams nearly two centuries ago. "Liberty," said Adams, "cannot be preserved without a general knowledge among the people."

Both the press and the general public have the right to know what their government is doing, even with those who might be enemies of the state.

Is the Indian media truly free and independent? Certainly, there is no dearth of newspapers, magazines, and television and radio stations ready to report on whatever they wish. India also has some of the best writers anywhere, and many have produced great works on a wide range of issues that have appeared in magazines and books. But daily news reporting is another matter.

There is a strong tradition among journalists to rely on the pronouncements of government officials instead of doing their own investigations. Journalists may seek government records under the Freedom of Information Act that several states have legislated, but no one seems to take the trouble to make any such request, and if one does, the government is able to delay the process so as to frustrate the reporter and make the timeliness of the article less relevant for the reader.

Discussions we have had with editors in Bangalore indicate that not even one major newspaper has so far filed a single request for a government document under Karnataka's Freedom of Information Act. Reporters cannot simply rely on information put out by politicians and government officials, unless it is verified with alternate sources or confirmed with internal documentation and records. When the media allows itself to be used for propaganda, misinformation or distortions favoring the government's position, the public is deprived of the truth on matters of governance.

Stories appear every day in the media about official investigations of corruption, difficulties faced by industry, criticism on policies and other news unpleasant to politicians and the government in power. The problem lies in the fact that many of these reports are superficial in their coverage and often reflect the official version put out by the government. There is very little investigative reporting in the Indian media (except in a few instances such as the Bofors arms transaction, cricket match fixing, and the Tehelka military bribes) that has persisted beyond the initial day or two of coverage.

As though by some mysterious coincidence, many stories that delve into controversial government action or inaction, or those that are critical of powerful politicians, simply disappear from the front pages of newspapers and television screens in short order. Readers and viewers are given incomplete or unsatisfactory explanations. They are expected to believe what they are told and are presumed to have short memories. To any astute observer, it is obvious that the press has succumbed to the threat of reprisals or economic pressures from politicians, and there is little interest on the part of owners of media organizations to search for truth.

In my conversations with editors of major English language newspapers in India, some emphatically make the assertion that they are free to write what they wish. The question then is, do they? The government may not censor what newspapers write, but there is no doubt that newspaper publishers are reluctant to critique government policies on sensitive issues. Dissenting opinions within the country on a variety of topics are kept within limits, and coverage of adverse world opinion on government policies and actions (or inactions) receive only superficial exposure.

Editors cite their public and social responsibilities for not digging into certain stories or opposing government views. For example, critics of the government's Kashmir policy find it hard to debate their views on the real danger of escalating a military confrontation with Pakistan, or on the wisdom of testing nuclear bombs and long-range rockets. The press takes upon itself the "responsibility" to promote the government's position in such matters in the name of national interest and patriotism.

One could take comfort in the fact that the Indian press is free to cover news and critique policies, whether they are as complete and thorough as one would like or not. It is far better than having no press freedom or independence as is the case in many countries. In a few years, perhaps the Indian media will be strong enough to assert its legitimate role. With sufficient competition in the marketplace, the press will be forced to compete for truth.

Through a free, independent, investigative and fair press, citizens learn what is happening around them and are willing to express their informed views to impact policy in the right direction. We must not hesitate to discuss ideas that shape, sustain and challenge us; ideas we constantly test against experience and refine through the trials and errors of a true democracy.

Only through press freedom can violations of human rights be spotted and public opinion mobilized to stop them. Corrupt and inefficient governments that are arrogant enough to subordinate the interests of the people may one day be brought to account by a free and independent press. When governments control the press in any way, the voice of the people is suppressed. As Thomas Jefferson remarked, if he had to choose between the country's constitution and a free press, he would prefer the latter.

FAIR AND TRUTHFUL REPORTING

The general public is angry, cynical and mistrusting of practically all politicians. There is a belief that politicians simply want to get elected, and at once, are transformed into self-interested deceivers of the public and the puppets of power brokers who put them into office in the first place. Politics in India seems to serve the personal interest of the politicians. Politicians feed their contempt of the electorate's ability to discern with ugly election campaigns, discrediting the opponent with lies and accusations, while promising voters new benefits if chosen.

For example, despite the evidence that the recent economic reforms are mostly benefiting the middle and upper classes, politicians have managed to divert the focus of debates in the last three general elections to issues of caste and communalism. The press earns its low esteem by joining forces with one party or the other, often subtly but sometimes blatantly, focusing on personal lives and selfish political maneuvering, all at the expense of reporting on substantive issues that affect the people.

What is going on with the readers? My guess is that the anger, frustration and cynicism derive less from what public figures do or do not do than from the sense of mistrust about their conduct. There is a malaise about rising social dysfunction, corruption, bribes and special favors. What is most troubling is the hopelessness that people generally feel in bringing about any positive change through their own opinions or actions.

The practice of democracy has become a ritual and an end in itself, with elections, power politics, and poor governance. Most of it has no relevance to the welfare of citizens. The voice of the people as it is expressed through the media is muted. Media serves special and self interests, and the public has no tools to influence the decisions of those who own the media. As a result, democracy itself suffers.

Frustrated and disenchanted, Indians blame the government for most of the troubles the nation faces. The grumbling may be satisfying to the soul, but it is futile. Politics as practiced today in India cannot deliver what the nation needs, and only through transparency and accountability can we bring about reform. People's voices must be heard, and that is possible only if the press is truly free and independent.

The public must be able to engage in an honest dialogue through the press and actively participate in the effort to transform the legislative bodies and the judiciary into institutions that are responsive and accountable to the needs of the people. Until then, the spiral of despair will continue unabated.

The media has a public duty to inform citizens about the candidates running for public office. People cannot expect much out of their national leaders if they continue to choose the wrong ones. India has had a steady stream of politicians in high positions who do not have the needed background either by way of education or experience.

We need to elect politicians who have the intellect to grasp issues, the humility to seek expert advice and the ability to make wise choices. They must have the vision for what is needed, focusing on real concerns and not the phony ones of the past. They must speak the language of inclusion, not division, and must work for the betterment of all instead of their own constituency only. We must have leaders with character whose voices resonate with moral authority. As distinguished United States Senator Alan Simpson once said, "If you have character, that is all that matters. And if you don't have character, that's all that matters, too."

Given our political system, we may be asking too much from our present day politicians. As for the electorate, they must be able to distinguish the good from the bad. The hope lies with an honest and free press that is prepared to dig into what the candidates have to say, and their records. At the end of it all, the exercise of democracy places the burden of electing the right individuals squarely on the shoulders of citizens, and we have only ourselves to blame for our choices.

George Bernard Shaw once said, "Democracy is a device that ensures we shall be governed no better than we deserve."

The absence of serious participation by citizens in the formulation of national policies is evident in India's budget process. Each year around February's end, the finance minister unveils the union budget with great anticipation on the part of the press and the politicians. Industrialists who have been campaigning for financial concessions are equally interested, but the rest of the country is hardly excited. The budget presented by the government always attempts to offer some popular "path-breaking" incentives in the form of cuts in duty, excise taxes or other forms of taxation, combined with subsidies for one thing or the other.

As is customary, there is a great deal of talk in the document about the need to improve the lives of the rural poor in the depressed agricultural sector. The assumption and practice from the very first year of India's independence more than 55 years ago is that the government knows what is best for everyone, and there is hardly any need to have a meaningful dialogue with its citizens before the national budget is unveiled.

To get a sense of what the ordinary person thinks about the budget, I decided to ask a few people I knew during one of my recent visits to India immediately following the budget announcement. The city folks I talked to had read newspaper characterizations of it as an "ingenious balancing act" between keeping the fiscal deficit in check and offering something to everyone.

Their opinions reflected mostly what the newspapers had to say. The finance minister was praised for his "clever political sensitivity" in addressing the concerns of his party's major constituencies. There were also some criticisms in the media focusing on what concessions were not sufficient and what else could have been offered. The projected GDP growth rate of nearly seven percent for the next fiscal year was reassuring to those I talked to, but they could not articulate how that would benefit them. None said that the budget would have any real impact on his or her future.

The responses I got to my questions from the farmers of Baliganapalli were quite different. I talked to a couple of village heads whose families have been cultivating their small farms for generations.

"What budget?" one asked. "We have been hearing about it every year, but nothing happens."

The other responded, "I hope the government will give us subsidy for our crop this year. You know, the prices are low, and we cannot make any money."

Both wanted the government to give them free electricity for pumping water from the farm wells, but this exemption was recently discontinued.

"The officials want me to pay Rs.1 lakh to get free power. I don't have that much money."

Budgets didn't mean anything to them, and their only concern was to get government benefits somehow from their corrupt officials. They had read and heard enough of politicians talking about "improving the lot of the rural farmer."

It is not that people find the government worthless; most people agree that the government can help those who are unable to help themselves, but they also believe that the government cannot be trusted to do the right thing. What do people want from their government? Not much. There are no great expectations. Perhaps, what America's third president, Thomas Jefferson, suggested in his inaugural speech is what Indians also want: "A wise and frugal government, which shall restrain men from injuring one another, which shall leave them otherwise free to regulate their own pursuits of industry and improvement, and shall not take from the mouth of labor the bread it has earned. This is the sum of good government, and this is necessary to close the circle of felicities."

Most Indians do not believe that their government would implement any courageous measures, no matter how good they would be for the country as a whole, unless it would help them get re-elected. They do not expect the press to be sufficiently objective or truthful in what they say about politicians. The frustrated and disillusioned population whose anger today is toward politicians and government in general may someday be brought together by its intrinsic sense of despair. Then we all will be in for a difficult time, or conversely, something good might finally happen.

Most governments are instructed by their constitutions not to intrude on press freedom. The press is expected to be adversarial. Good media plays a watchdog role in public interest, as the main purpose of a free press in a democratic system, it is often said, is keeping the public informed about governmental activities.

Since the media often runs into a resistant government, not eager to disclose its failures, a natural conflict results. But the role of the press is to probe and reveal the facts behind the pronouncements made by government officials and politicians. This important adversarial relationship has a checking value wherein the press attempts to bring out the truth that the government is hiding from its citizens.

How will journalism improve in India? Part of the answer lies in the independence of media organizations and increased competition among them. To a larger measure, quality of the media is greatly dependent on future journalists. My plunge into journalism was an offshoot of my frustrations with the Indian media on how it had been covering daily news and issues of vital concern to a large majority of the people.

While I do not have any serious problem with the entertainment focus of newspapers for commercial reasons, my main criticism about news coverage by the English language newspapers in India is their apparent lack of independence and poor investigative journalism skills. The media has consistently failed to follow up and dig into stories of corruption and inefficiencies at high levels of government and to challenge the wisdom of the government's policies in economic and foreign affairs.

Issues that concern the rural poor are rarely covered in any depth. My dissatisfactions with the press were brought to a head during the Kargil conflict with Pakistani infiltrators in Kashmir in 1999.

India's attempt to dislodge Pakistani militants from the hills of Kargil was an expensive military operation in terms of human lives and wounded. The political leadership of India tried to cover up its failure to prevent the infiltration by making promises of quick victory, and the generals responded with swift military action, ordering soldiers to carry out frontal assaults by climbing the steep hills. The enemy was well entrenched in safe bunkers, looking down on anyone trying to approach from below. There was very little air or artillery support, and the result was several thousand dead and wounded.

As a former military officer in the Indian army, I felt the military tactic was unnecessarily expensive in terms of human lives. The Indian media, however, never questioned the military throughout the operation and continually played to the patriotic fervor of the public.

THE BIRTH OF THE INDIAN INSTITUTE OF JOURNALISM

One day during the crisis, I was discussing with two middle-level newspaper editors the coverage of war news by Indian media. It was reported that trains were filled with wounded soldiers, bringing them to military and civilian hospitals all across northern India. In my telephone call to my doctor friend in Calcutta, a city far from the battlefield, she mentioned that hospitals there were also receiving the wounded. There was no doubt that several thousand soldiers were injured, and the dead could easily number in many hundreds.

Yet, Indian newspapers were still reporting the government's count of only a couple of hundred dead and fewer than 1,000 wounded. While most journalists covering the war anywhere near the battle zone could easily verify those numbers were grossly understated, newspapers were prepared to go along with the official version. I questioned the two editors I had met that day on the likely undercount.

"Everyone knows that these published numbers are low. But it is our duty to support the government during times of war," one editor explained.

"Am I buying your paper knowing fully well that you are lying to me?" I asked.

"New York Times also does the same," was the retort. I felt no need to answer that.

That agitated exchange brought me to the realization that most journalists working for newspapers in India do not clearly understand their role, and are not vigorously trained in the high ideals of independent and truthful reporting.

There also appears to be a great deal of confusion about the role of the press in reporting government policies. Having spent many years in America, and witnessing the Watergate episode involving President Richard Nixon and other major events concerning senior government officials, I had developed a keen understanding of the adversarial role of the press, and have learned to appreciate that a vigilant independent press is essential for safeguarding the public against the excesses of governments and powerful institutions.

As Tom Goldstein, former dean of Columbia University Graduate School of Journalism, once told several journalists in Chennai, it is not the journalists' job to protect "national interest" except when military secrets are involved. "Leave that to the citizens to determine. Your job is to inform the public, to tell them what you know to be the facts," he said.

I thought I should start a journalism school in India along the lines of some of the excellent institutions in the United States. That was one way to make my little contribution to strengthening India's democratic values and institutions. If I could train a few young people each year on the great ideals of journalism, India would have many more good reporters and writers in a few years. In a competitive environment, the Indian daily press would be forced to provide something of greater value to the readers than what is currently being offered, I thought.

I made up my mind to start a new journalism school in Bangalore offering a postgraduate diploma in print and web publishing; broadcast media could come later. It would be totally independent of the government and the media establishment, but it would work with the latter to improve the stature of the journalism profession.

I was aware that journalism is a profession that could draw the wrath of the government and felt I needed an independent partner who could provide some protection. I thought of a religious leader with considerable stature as one choice. I was introduced to His Holiness Balagangadaranatha Swamiji, one of Karnataka's prominent Hindu religious leaders. I knew that he was already running several colleges, hospitals and charitable institutions, and a partnership with his organization would be a natural affiliation as long as I would be free to run the journalism college as I wished.

My first meeting with Swamiji was a memorable event. I told him who I was and then explained the importance of starting a good institution to train a couple of dozen young people each year on the ideals of the journalism profession so that they would go out into media institutions throughout the country and practice what they had been taught. Within a decade or so, these well-trained graduates would make a major difference in the way the media covers news in the country. Ultimately, it would have a positive impact on the governance of the nation.

At the end of my initial brief talk in English, which was simultaneously being translated into Kannada, Swamiji looked at me with a smile and said, "When can we start?"

I was elated and thanked him for his quick decision and support. It was the beginning of a close and rare association between a prominent Hindu religious leader and an NGO with a Christian name, under a newly created nonprofit trust (BS&G Foundation) to work toward improving the quality of the press in India.

In the next few months, Swamiji and I worked out an arrangement whereby I would have the freedom to run the new Indian Institute of Journalism & New Media. Upon my return to New York, I met with Tom Goldstein, then the dean of Columbia University's journalism school, to solicit his assistance in developing the curriculum. He was enthusiastic about my idea and assigned one of the school's professors, Sreenath Sreenivsan, to guide me. By then the architectural drawings were ready, and soon the construction began in full swing.

A 30,000-square-foot modern facility now sits on five acres of beautiful grounds overlooking hills and valleys. A media lab with individual workstations and high-speed Internet access is provided for both students and faculty. Television video editing stations are available for training broadcast media. Space for an adjoining broadcast studio is set aside for the future when radio and television news broadcast will be considered.

A hostel caters to the residential and dining needs of the students. An international advisory board consisting of well-known journalists, business executives and academicians was formed to advise the management of the institution.

In January 2001, the doors opened to our first batch of journalism students at IIJNM. For the time being, I was the self-appointed dean. Since then, to date, we have had three more classes of students, each one smarter than the previous. The school quickly gained a reputation as one of the best journalism institutions in India, and our graduates are now sought after by media organizations. *The New York Times* and Scripps Howard Foundation offered internships to two of our graduates to be trained in the United States, while several foreign journalists joined their Indian counterparts courtesy of Knight International Fellowships. One of our faculty members was selected by the Ford Foundation for doctoral studies abroad.

In 2003, the British Broadcasting Corporation (BBC) selected IIJNM among only two institutions in India for starting an i-Learning curriculum, for distance learning of journalism. While we want to develop these and other close affiliations with highly reputed private media institutions, we will also maintain our academic and administrative independence so as to be faithful to our stated mission of free, balanced and investigative journalism in India. Subsequently, I was invited onto the board of the prestigious International Center for Journalists (ICFJ) in Washington, D.C. IIJNM had made a good beginning.

At the start of each academic year, I address the students in a series of lectures designed to motivate and challenge them for their chosen profession. It is also a good opportunity for me to learn their viewpoints on their government, society and international affairs. With every batch of students, what strikes me most is their more or less uniform negative view of America and their reliance on government sources for information.

One after another, I hear comments like: "American multinational companies are in India to exploit our resources." "The CIA is helping Pakistan to send militants into Kashmir. Russia has always been on our side." "America is an imperialist country. Look at what they did in Vietnam, Somalia, and other places?"

But when I ask them to name a country America has conquered and kept, or to compare the Soviet occupation of Eastern Europe, there is silence. Most students recognize the need for American corporate investment in India, but they also want profits and repatriations to be limited. It was obvious that these young people are carrying the same views as their parents and grandparents, and their main source of information was the constant barrage of anti-American opinions expressed over several decades by the government and the Indian media. It is taking a concerted effort to expose them to other viewpoints that might still be critical of America, but more objective in tone. But it is not a lost cause, thanks mainly to the many alternate sources of news and information now available on the Web. Perhaps soon young people will learn to make their own objective judgment.

Over the past few years, my social and journalism work in India has been attacked in local and national papers and magazines. When Shanti Bhavan was set up, I was falsely accused in the press of converting poor children to Christianity. Similarly, each time I terminated the employment of a faculty member at the journalism college for poor performance or unprofessional conduct, newspapers would write about how badly the institution was carrying out its educational programs. I was personally accused in an educational magazine of charging high fees and taking the "profits" to America, when, in fact, the institution was experiencing substantial financial losses from offering quality education and modern facilities at a subsidized cost.

In all these instances, there was never an attempt by the media to contact me or the foundation to check the veracity of the information that was being published. It is common practice in the Indian media to quote undisclosed sources or no sources at all in covering a story, and the reader is left to believe that somehow the newspaper has verified the facts. We cannot allow the public thirst for scandals to be met by distorted and untruthful stories that only serve the divisiveness within the society. When the media becomes irresponsible and arrogant and fails to investigate stories before publishing, it harms both society and itself, as confidence in all institutions breaks down.

The adversarial culture forming in our societies thrives on controversy and ridicule. We are living in a time of accelerating social and economic changes, but with very little trust of government and most institutions. Too often, the only thing that draws attention is scandal. The general public is cynical and asks, "What else is new?" Indians expect politicians to be dishonest and deceitful, and they are not surprised to have their assumptions confirmed with scandalous published events.

The media senses that assaulting an individual's character or professional work is good news in the pretext of exposing and correcting the evils of the day. But the truth is that the media is less interested in serving public interest than in satisfying public curiosity. More often than not, reporters do not sufficiently check out the truthfulness of the stories they write, and editors do not bother to inquire about the individual being scandalized, unless they fear some reprisal. The consequence is a subversion of the moral authority of everyone.

How is the Indian media influencing morality and violence among people, especially young people? It was not too long ago that Indian television was limited to government-run channels, and radio stations were totally "Bharat-Vani" state radio. I recall my young days when my brother and I sat up late nights to follow the cricket test match on BBC radio or to enjoy some Beatles' songs on Radio Colombo. In the past decade, many private television and radio stations have sprung up offering Indian and Western entertainment and news around the clock.

English language movies and Western music and fashion are now readily available to viewers, including the pop culture MTV channel. Indian movies have incorporated many of the Western entertainment ideas of violence and sex that always capture a bigger audience. Many Indians are concerned about the impact these TV broadcasts have on the younger generation, and they question whether the increased violence seen in India in recent years is a result of the permissive nature of entertainment.

Once upon a time, filmmakers used to evoke sexual longing through eye contact or a passing touch of hands. Violence was nothing more than a quick culmination of a long sequence of suspense scenes. Today, movies resort to startlingly graphic ways of presenting sex and violence. Even talk shows and music videos are explicit in what they present. Many of the topics deal with extramarital sex, murder and mass killing. This might not be quite so bothersome if the kids weren't listening and watching. According to a number of surveys on Indian entertainment, children and young adults spend several hours each week watching mostly such shows. What is the impact of such programs on these young viewers?

For all the concern, we need to keep our cool and not look for scapegoats for the malaises in our society. In a free marketplace, where individuals make decisions about what they will buy, read or see, some choices will veer toward the vulgar, the profane and the excessive. The price that we pay for our cultural freedom is that a few unwanted weeds may thrive amid thousands of blooming flowers. Values are formed at an early age by the examples set at home and in interactions with others. Children are affected by the general decline of public morality and ethics, family breakdown and poor parenting and less so from television programming.

Adults will serve their children better by focusing on how they live their personal lives. We should encourage the media organizations to put out news and entertainment of value and hope that the marketplace of viewers will make the choice between what is good and bad. But we cannot allow politicians and bureaucrats to meddle in what we see, read or hear, just as we do not want them to restrict what we can eat.

AN INSUFFICIENT ADVERSARIAL PRESS

Has the Indian media done a good job since the country's independence in contributing to the nation's progress? Has it offered an independent view of national and international events by truthfully informing and educating the citizens of the facts? These questions require a critical examination of the many policies and events that have shaped India and how the media has responded in each instance.

The print press, especially English language newspapers and magazines, is considered by most educated citizens the main source of information and reflective of national opinion. The television media, on the other hand, could not play an independent role until the early 1990s as it was run by the government. Radio stations were also under the control of the government until recently, but no longer. However, for all these years, privately run newspapers in every language have been catering to the nation's diverse population mainly with local news. Mainly English language national dailies and magazines have been covering national and international events and policies.

It is not possible to come to generalized conclusions about the performance of all media institutions on all issues and events. But it is fair to say that, in the case of newspapers and magazines, editorials and opinions on key issues, especially foreign policy matters, have usually reflected the viewpoint of the government in power.

Consider the role of the press during the evolution of a socialistic economy in India following the country's independence in 1947. India's economic policies were initially shaped by Prime Minister Jawaharlal Nehru, who had very little training and understanding of developmental policies. He was a great patriot, but his policies, both national and foreign, were an offshoot of his personal dislike for America and the West, and his closeness to the leaders of the Soviet Union. The Cold War forced India to take sides while professing neutrality, and the country was led in a disastrous economic direction.

Centralized planning by governments since then offered one five-year plan after another that consistently relied on more government-run institutions to bring about economic development and social justice. The result was an inefficient and corrupt burgeoning bureaucracy that functioned through licenses and permits, controlling every aspect of daily commerce and personal life. Until the policies changed in 1991, the economy experienced very slow growth, offering little relief to the misery of at least two generations of citizens. And what was the Indian press doing? Did it seriously question the wisdom of the socialistic policies of successive governments even in the face of clearly visible failures for more than 44 years?

There might have been a few lonely voices in the press arguing against the Soviet model for India, but most of the media went along with the failed economic philosophy of the government. The press cheered the few successes of the Soviet economy during the early years of India's independence, while quickly pointing out the social inequities and excesses of the American capitalistic system. Even the rapid economic progress made by Western Europe and Japan from the ravages of World War II did not entice the Indian press to take an unbiased fresh look.

Corruption, inefficiency and absence of entrepreneurship inherent in a socialistic system were simply explained away in an "Indian context." The government justified its economic policies, and the press served as its mouthpiece. Reluctance on the part of the media to investigate and expose the financial misdeeds of political leaders further contributed to the failure of a doomed economic system.

Only when the Soviet Union fell apart, and the Indian economy almost went bankrupt at the start of 1991, did the government and the press set aside their aversion for America and accept the capitalistic medicine prescribed by the International Monetary Fund. In the meantime, millions of Indians had to suffer the consequences of a failed ideology and the mismanagement of the economy.

The wisdom and the moral correctness of India's foreign policy have scarcely been seriously challenged by the nation's media to this date. Since independence, the country's preoccupation with the Kashmir dispute with Pakistan, and the reluctance to involve third parties to mediate, led to the formulation of the doctrine of "non-interference in the internal affairs of another country" as its supreme foreign policy principle. India's reliance on the Soviet Union for military and economic support persuaded the country to take a pro-Soviet stand in almost all international disputes.

From the days of V. K. Krishna Menon, India's first foreign minister under Nehru, it is hard to find a single instance in which India did not vote in the United Nations in support of the Soviet Union, and now Russia, on any major international dispute. Despite all the proclamations of non-interference as a foreign policy doctrine, Prime Minister Vajpayee suddenly reversed 43 years of India's opposition to China's claims of sovereignty over Tibet during his visit to China in June 2003. There was no internal debate over this in India before the prime minister made the announcement, supposedly to "bribe" the Chinese to accept India's claims over Sikkim. This change has shocked both Indians and Tibetans alike, but the Indian press seems to have accepted these inconsistent applications of foreign policy doctrines as the last word, and not to be challenged in the "national interest."

India failed to condemn the Soviet invasion and occupation of Eastern Europe and Afghanistan and Iraq's invasion of Kuwait. When NATO intervened in Bosnia and Kosovo to protect the Muslims against ethnic cleansing and genocide by Yugoslavia under former President Slobodan Milosevic, India sided with Russia to argue against interference by the West. When America decided to topple the oppressive Taliban government in Afghanistan that had been harboring terrorists, India criticized America for its military action. But in the recent invasion of Iraq by America and Britain to free the country of a ruthless dictator and his weapons of mass destruction, the Indian government decided to express a far less vocal opposition for reasons it described as in "national self-interest."

In each of these instances spanning more than 50 years, the Indian press solidly stood by its government, justified by its "patriotic duties" and probably biased by its long-standing aversion to America. Arguments favoring world security, individual freedom and human rights have persuaded neither the Indian government nor the media. It is to be seen whether history will prove India right that non-interference in the internal affairs of another country, the impermissibility of the use of force in the face of serious threats to world peace, and lower concern for human rights elsewhere are still prudent foreign policy approaches. What surprises many outside observers is the general uniformity of opinion expressed in the Indian media on significant foreign policy matters, consistent with the views of the government.

The press helped to rally the Indian masses against America where America was involved, without offering balanced viewpoints and practical solutions to the inherent reasons for the conflicts. However, it now appears that, with closer economic interests, this hostile attitude toward America is no longer vehemently expressed publicly by the government or the press.

Soon after September 11, I had expected some sympathy for America from the Indian media. While most Indian newspapers and the media in general talked about the human tragedy and expressed words of concern for those affected, the same presentations would invariably conclude by morally equating the incident to the "crimes committed against the Palestinian people," or some other event where America was directly or indirectly involved, as though America well deserved this punishment.

Soon after the terrorist attacks on the World Trade Center buildings and Pentagon, I wrote an article on why America should still remain engaged in international affairs in the interest of maintaining world order. None of the leading Indian newspapers would publish the article, making the point that my views did not "fit our editorial perspectives." When the prestigious Christian Science Monitor in the United States published it soon thereafter, the Indian Express countered with an opinion column by one of its staff journalists saying that American policies are too devious, and my article to the paper should have been "returned unopened by the postman."

While no support came from India, the article drew favorable email from places as far away as Ireland, Poland and Australia. It is now obvious to me that, after many years of close relationship with the Soviet Union and now Russia, both the general public and the media in India are not yet prepared to give an objective hearing on American foreign policy. Even editors of book publishing houses in India are not generally receptive to manuscripts that support American foreign policy. I do not believe that this media bias has helped the nation's interests.

STATE INTERFERENCE IN AN INDEPENDENT PRESS

Quality journalism demands fair and unbiased reporting of news. When the state interferes with what and how news is covered, there is real danger to truthful reporting. While there is no formal censorship of the press in India, owners and managers of media institutions clearly know what can and cannot be said about those in power. According to the reports released for 2001 and 2002 by the Committee to Protect Journalists, Indian journalists continue to face physical threats, legal harassment and subtle pressure from both central and state governments.[50] Some state governments have engaged in deliberate measures to suppress dissent, cracking down on both political opposition parties and journalists. Journalists working for vernacular press and living outside major urban areas tend to be far more vulnerable to attack.

The government has used administrative tools to stifle the press; a clear example is the raid by tax authorities on the offices of Outlook magazine following a series of articles examining corporate influence in the prime minister's office.[51] The magazine has succumbed to government pressures and has toned down its editorial content since then. Similarly, the news Web site tehelka.com that carried investigative reports on corruption and bribes in the defense department faced continuing harassment and investigations by several government agencies. After three years of legal battles with the government, this Web news service has all but shut down and is now operating with a few unpaid employees.

Recently, the government of Tamil Nadu issued arrest warrants against six senior journalists, mainly of the national daily The Hindu, on charges of violating the special privileges enjoyed by parliamentarians. The vague definitions under the Indian Constitution relating to powers, privileges and immunity for Members of Parliament (MP) and Members of State Legislative Assembly (MLA) permit politicians to bring charges against the press when articles are published criticizing the government. All this is happening while the government trumpets the "vigorously free" character of the Indian press.

MEDIA'S ROLE IN SHAPING A SOUND DEMOCRACY

Media plays a major role in injecting the ideas of mutual understanding, tolerance and spirituality, as opposed to any particular religious philosophy or communal interests, in the affairs of the state. Regardless of background and economic status, citizens must involve themselves in the pursuit of the common good, seeking freedom and equal justice for all. People need to insist on the notion of a participatory public, as opposed to special interest groups and favoritism, to allow citizens to be responsible for their own destiny. We can only hope there will be increased public debate of public policy through the many media channels currently available, including the Internet. As Bill Moyers, a well-known American journalist, points out, a public emerges only when citizens take part in the decisions their government makes and not when they merely watch.

Citizenship is more than voting; it means participating in the dialogue of democracy. Participation does not end with elections, and wisdom does not belong only to those we elect. With an open exchange of ideas through a press that is respectful of individual rights, peaceful community activities, and political participation, we can bring about a real change in the way policies are formulated and executed. Only if we succeed in this endeavor can we hope for a brighter future for the country.

As such, a journalist's job is to present the facts, diverse views and opinions as compellingly as possible. The object of a newspaper is to be read, and hence, each story must be interesting – topics that matter to readers or stimulates their curiosity and concern. The media business has to work toward overcoming public mistrust of the press, balancing the focus between entertainment and news values, increasing readership among the younger generation and generating advertisement revenues. If each successive generation does not trust the press to deliver truthful information, a free press will be less significant to the working of democracy, civil society and free markets.

There is also some concern about the concentration of ownership of newspapers among a few powerful individuals and organizations. Commercial pressures and new communication technologies have already changed the way the press is now behaving. Yet, many media owners are attempting to curtail competition. Under the pretext of "national security" and "preserving Indian culture from foreign views," participation of foreign media organizations in the Indian newspaper business is still restricted to twenty-six percent ownership. Such protective policies only help those newspaper organizations that are trying to safeguard their market share and profits, at the expense of quality journalism.

Despite the apparent lack of adequate freedom and independence for the Indian press today, it still has a good foundation to go forward with further zeal. For example, almost all the major English dailies have been strong defenders of secularism in the country, and some have displayed courage in pursuing stories that were not complimentary of powerful politicians. Few English media TV stations now engage in aggressive debates on a wide variety of isues in their weekly programs. There is no doubt that competition among the news media will be beneficial, as each one tries to win a larger audience with better coverage of news and issues of importance.

An open society that permits free flow of news and diverse opinions will be vibrant and self-correcting, and India is well advised to embrace this reality instead of finding excuses for not encouraging transparency. Without a fair and open press, the exercise of democracy suffers. History has taught one nation after another that a free press is among the most important human institutions of the modern world and may be our best resource for a dynamic and just society.

CONTRIBUTING TO ARTS AND CULTURE

Though I do not possess any artistic talent, I have always greatly appreciated many forms of art, both Indian and Western. I was born into a family with considerable musical skills, and we often talked about ways to promote the arts and music among those who were talented but unable to make a start. As I learned more about rural arts and crafts in India following my frequent visits there, I became convinced that the arts are an integral part of rural life.

It was then that my parents made a proposal I could not refuse. After an illustrious career as a physicist both in India and America, my mother had taken up painting and sculpture in her retirement. It was her wish that I build an institution in India to promote fine arts. My parents offered a substantial part of their life's savings toward the initial capital needed for building an arts village, museum and gallery; yet, there are still many questions to be answered: What is the purpose of the proposed project? How do we accomplish the goals? Where should the museum be? How would we ensure its long-term sustainability?

Right from the outset, it was clear to all of us in my family that the aim of the project should be to empower poor and emerging artists and artisans, especially from rural India. There is a great need to preserve the different forms of earth, material, spaces and patterns of construction as applied by traditional artisans, and new art forms must also be given an opportunity to flourish.

To address current sensibilities and tastes, a new language of form and perspective must evolve from the traditional arts rooted in thousands of years of history and culture. There has to be an organic interaction between traditional and contemporary artists. The emergence of contemporary art is part and parcel of the modern creative form. However, all prior attempts to merge traditional Indian crafts and contemporary art have not materialized; they exist as isolated entities. Unfortunately, both the intelligentsia and contemporary artists and their patrons look down upon the craft tradition as inferior. There is much contemporary artists can learn from traditional artisans, while traditional artisans can find innovative progression for their skills by their exposure to new art forms.

Much of village life is rooted in traditions, religious festivities and expressions of spirituality. Through these, the poor find comfort even in the face of extreme hardships. Art work is a creative outlet for anyone with talent, regardless of income. According to Leo Tolstoy, the arts serve as a medium of spiritual communication, helping to create the ties of human brotherhood. Through art we express our history, our traditions and our thought. It helps us see the world around us in a way different from what our eyes see in our daily lives. Often art lets us see the real meaning of what we see and what we fail to see.

For any society to be complete, art must exist. It needs to be encouraged and supported. For the poor villagers, art could serve as a medium of expression of their isolated lives. Many talented artists in India are unable to project their skills because they do not have the financial means to support themselves. Or, they do not have the ability to market their work and earn a living. Consequently, art often fails to materialize and society is thus deprived.

Until recently, traditional Indian crafts were respected throughout the world for its fine sensibility and their relationship to the elements of nature. The beautifully interwoven relationship between humankind and nature found expression not only in crafts, but also in everyday community living. Floors, walls, doors, gates, and even the face and hand of the human body were decorated artistically as important expressions of the culture and traditions of the people.

Today, the survival of traditional crafts is on the edge of extinction. Many artisans have abandoned their centuries-old traditions and wealth of knowledge and skills to join the unskilled labor force. A few have continued in the arts believing their skill is a God-given gift and that it is their duty to hand it down to generations to come. The George Foundation will work toward halting the slippage of local traditions into the oblivion of history.

How will the foundation promote arts and crafts in a country where such works are usually not priced high enough to support an artist. Undoubtedly, it is a difficult task, unless works of art can be better integrated with commercial use, such as home and office decoration. People need to be reminded that, while fine arts and crafts are not normally thought of as necessities of life, they are an essential part of human pleasure. Like science and moral action, art belongs to the human mind and involves imagination, thought, expression and experience. Fine art is the product of "genius." It arises only from a talent unbound by rules.

The great artist Pablo Picasso once said, "Art washes from the soul the dust of everyday life." In the rural setting of the rustic landscape where everyday life is a struggle against odds, art brings solace to the soul. In the midst of village communities, there is no dearth of human creativity. What is lacking in people is the means to express their artistic yearnings. An arts village and museum would represent a meeting ground – a home for talented upcoming artists who deserve encouragement and support for their expressions. It is our hope that their creations will be exciting, and art lovers around the world will discover and pay for them. With better recognition of the value of art, even ordinary people will display art in their homes.

THE BIRTH OF TILLANY

Tillany Fine Arts Museum & Gallery, as it was to be named, would address this need by assisting artists and artisans who possess exceptional talent but lack the means for furthering their creative expression. It was decided that both the museum and the arts village would be built close to Shanti Bhavan in the village of Baliganapalli to symbolize the fact that the project is meant to support rural arts and crafts. Instead of the rural folks going to the city to see their own arts and crafts, the city folks would come to the rural place where they originated.

The foundation would offer support in the form of materials and tools, both indigenous and modern, and through workshops and videos conducted by reputed, established Indian and international artists and artisans. These and other facilities would be provided in the artists' colony adjoining the museum and in their own homes and workplaces. Outstanding works of art chosen by a committee of respected artists would be displayed in the museum and subsequently put up for auction or sale. The foundation plans to connect the Tillany museum to other museums and galleries in India and abroad to reach discerning collectors and connoisseurs. Tillany would assist in marketing the works of art to enable the artists and artisans to gain recognition in their field, and to generate the revenue needed to continue such outstanding work.

Time was running out. My father had crossed 90 years of age by 2000, and my mother was in her early-80s. If they were to come from the United States and see the beginning of their new dream, I needed to build either the museum or the arts village soon. The decision was quickly made to put the cart before the horse by constructing the museum first, as it would be a more impressive structure. I visited several museums in New York and Italy and a few arts villages in South India.

The design called for a three-story 15,000-plus square-foot modern structure, replicating some of the concepts and shapes incorporated in the Guggenheim Museum in New York. With the help of V. Kiran, a young and talented architect trained in the United States, Tillany was designed and built in a contemporary style, with glass and skylights to let in natural light, air-conditioning, wood flooring, strip and spot lights, and water bodies to reflect the building. The museum structure and the grounds were ready for the first exhibit and inauguration in January 2001. Some called it the finest building in India for a museum.

With the involvement of the artistic community, Tillany museum can bring about an explosive energy, as the word Tillany evokes, to all forms of fine art. In doing so, we hope that the communities around Tillany will come together to showcase their works and enjoy the harmony and spiritual fulfillment that art brings. A selection committee appointed by the foundation will identify artists and artisans who deserve assistance. Those who are selected will be exposed to artwork from other parts of the world through pictures, videos and samples to help broaden their creative ideas.

Those requiring tools and supplies, such as canvas, paint, brush, granite and cutting tools will be given free of charge. Completed works will be evaluated for their suitability for display in Tillany during organized exhibits that will be held every month. After three months of display, the work will be put on sale and auction. Indian and foreign galleries will be invited to participate with Tillany to exhibit and purchase the arts and crafts created by our artists and artisans. Up to forty percent of the net proceeds from the sale will be paid to each artist and artisan, and the balance will be used for creating and promoting new work.

Unfortunately, plans for the construction of the arts village were put on hold. The world financial markets tumbled, and my personal investments suffered losses. I had to allocate the available resources toward the continuing operation of other projects that were already in place. As is always the case, with great regret, I, too, put the promotion of arts behind other human necessities. But I am sure that one day when my finances look brighter, I will return to Tillany to complete the mission that my beloved parents initiated. Until then, Tillany is a place where the children of Shanti Bhavan come occasionally to dance and put up their shows. Their beautiful voices and creativity fill the vacuum that is left behind.

Chapter 12

IN SEARCH OF MORAL AND ETHICAL CONDUCT

THE COST OF UNETHICAL CONDUCT

The unraveling of the fraud surrounding the Unit Trust of India, a state-owned mutual fund, in July 2001 shook up the public in general and some 20 million Indians who had invested in its United Scheme 64. UTI managed money for about 41 million people and controlled assets of approximately Rs.600 billion or $13 billion.[52] A sharp rise in withdrawals triggered by revelations of serious financial losses and underperformance forced UTI to freeze redemptions to stem the exodus. This case is a classic example of a state-owned financial institution whose investment decisions were dictated heavily by political objectives and corruption, with very little accountability and transparency.

UTI made equity investments in dubious companies as favors to many politicians and corporate chieftains, and with the sharp decline of financial markets after 2000, the mutual fund lost substantial money. The government had also used UTI as a vehicle to prop up the financial markets during times of market declines by buying up shares of other companies as investments. All these appear to be legal, though highly unethical, and with little regard for investors' interests. All major political parties hid their misdeeds by avoiding finger pointing at each other. The government quickly offered an expensive rescue package in the "interest of the public" that is to cover the losses using tax revenues.

This UTI episode and the Home Trade scam of 2002, involving politicians, bankers and brokers who swindled some Rs.6 billion ($125 million) from banks and Public Provident Funds, are just two recent examples of illegal and unethical conduct by individuals in power, and they reflect countless other infringements of lesser magnitude.[53]

Poor governance in both public and private sectors is cited by many as the major reason for the failure of nations to achieve their full potentials. The problem lies not just in inefficiencies but equally or more in illegal and unethical conduct. According to a study conducted in 1985 in the United States, unethical or illegal conduct in Corporate America resulted in an estimated $200-$300 billion a year in lost revenues to the government and in higher costs for consumers. By the year 2000, the cost of unethical conduct to the nation is estimated to have exceeded $1 trillion.

In India, some estimate that thirty to forty percent of all financial transactions go unreported in the form of bribes, and other illegal activity and to avoid taxes. India is rated by several international corruption watchdog institutions as among the top 10 most corrupt nations in the world and second within Asian countries. Most people in India place no trust in businesses to keep their commitments or to perform as agreed upon, and in turn, businesses do not trust individuals either.

As India aggressively seeks global business opportunities, professional ethics will play a decisive role in the degree of success. Without strong ethics in all spheres, it is all but impossible to build an economic system that serves the interests of all people, especially the poor.

ETHICS IN THE PRIVATE SECTOR

According to Azim Premji, the chairman of Wipro, one of the leading information technology companies in India, the economic impact of the recent corporate scandals in the United States and elsewhere was worse than the impact of the terrorist attack of September 11. Studies have shown that markets and investors take notice of well-managed companies, respond positively to them and reward good companies with higher valuations. A common feature of such companies is that they have proper systems in place, which allow the board to keep management tightly within a framework of effective accountability.

While common accounting standards and independent boards could help deal with problems in corporate ethics, Premji notes companies need to have well-articulated values.

"The first thing any business organization needs to have is a set of values to be uniformly adhered to under all circumstances. There should not be any exception. These should be consistently communicated to the employees from the day they join the organization," Premji says.

Others point to the professionalism that all employees must cultivate. A prominent industrialist, Rahul Bajaj, chairman of Bajaj Auto, India, concludes that transparency and full disclosure are not just ethical issues, but essential requirements for the survival of large corporations. He warns that, with a few exceptions, adherence to the prescribed codes is in form and not in spirit in India and in most other countries. He emphasizes that, while guidelines are necessary, there is no substitute for good character.

There is no denying that professionalism and ethics in Indian businesses leave much to be desired. Too often, business commitments are not adequately met, and legal contracts are violated. Transparency in transactions, especially in the dealings between ordinary individuals and businesses, is not sufficient to protect the interests of the consumer. Regulations are either weak or not properly enforced, both individuals and businesses conveniently misuse the legal process to circumvent contracts, and the judicial system is presently incapable of offering timely remedy.

Because India generally does not project sufficient professionalism and ethics to generate trust between parties, business efficiency is compromised, and transaction costs are raised, resulting in considerable economic loss to the nation from lost opportunities. While increased competition and interaction with foreign companies have brought about some improvement in the way business is conducted in recent years, Indian companies, for the most part, have not yet adopted globally shared values to truly succeed in the world market.

Much of business ethics today is focused on questions of law and policy, regulations, business practices and legal requirements. All these, while important, are considered as either legal or regulatory requirements and most Indian companies are constantly trying to circumvent them, because government officials do not enforce them enough. What gets left out in this thinking is an adequate sense of or an emphasis on personal values and integrity. Business does not operate in a vacuum; its conduct is a reflection of the social order.

Business ethics is more than a public policy or a legal contract. It encompasses honesty, forthrightness, reciprocity, fair play and commitments – virtues that may be too much to ask for in today's world.

The real problem facing corporations today with respect to ethical behavior is a management problem. The corporate culture, its planning process and the way it implements and controls its actions are all critical factors that have a significant impact on whether a business will conduct its affairs ethically. Companies need to formulate core values that dictate their conduct internally as well as with customers, suppliers and society in general. Employees may need to be "indoctrinated" on codes of conduct.

To argue, in the manner of Machiavelli, that there is one rule for business and another for private life is to open the door for an orgy of unscrupulousness. On the other hand, to argue that there is no difference at all is to place morality itself under an almost intolerable strain.

Competition involves trying to do things better than anyone else – making or selling a better product at a lesser cost or otherwise giving better service. Competition is not about gaining advantage over someone else through illegal or unethical means. When the government involves itself to offer unfair advantage to one party or the other, there is no longer any public confidence in the economic system. When the judicial system operates in a fashion that constantly favors the government or certain institutions, citizens lose their trust in fair play and justice.

An example of this is the banking system in India for which the normal judicial processes are circumvented in special courts, Debt Recovery Tribunals, that handle disputes on non-repayment of loans. As the name "recovery" suggests, these special courts are notoriously known for consistently rendering judgments in support of financial institutions.

The cynical view of doing and succeeding in business plays up to unethical behavior. "It is business, and we just have to do it this way to make a buck," or "Who is to say what is right or wrong; it is a matter of opinion," or "After all, that is the way things are done here." The perception is that there are many easy paths to quick riches in business through cold-hearted and unscrupulous schemes.

In our age of cynicism we seem to have developed a disdain for old truths and simple stories of honesty, loyalty, friendship and fairness as a guide in how we live. Nevertheless, these visions of greatness are available to everyone regardless of social and economic status.

In today's highly competitive world, it is hard to be ethical always. There are times when the temptation is too strong or the fear of failure is considerable. While such emotions can at times be overwhelming, they are not sufficient justifications for acting unethically. People tend to justify their improper conduct with arguments of self-interest.

I am reminded about the story of two great friends who went backpacking. In the thick of the jungle, a tiger confronted them. One of them prepared to scare the tiger away and turned to his friend for help, when he noticed that his friend was unloading his backpack and getting ready to run. He asked: "Why are you getting ready to run? The tiger is faster than us." His friend replied, "I've only got to run faster than you."

We need to embrace the Aristotelian approach to business ethics in that every professional conduct and every business action must be seen as part of living a good life; getting along with people, having a sense of self-respect, and being part of something of which one can be proud. But the point is not that we should stop thinking about money; in fact, we all should work hard to earn it. But we should also not forget that the pursuit of happiness involves a lot more than the pursuit of money. Happiness is an all-inclusive holistic concept. It is ultimately about character, integrity, and accomplishments. This fact is as true of giant corporations as it is of the individuals who work for them.

PERSONAL ETHICS

Ethics in business and government is a reflection of ethics in individual life. Ethical problems are "people problems." To quote Peter Drucker, the leading management guru of modern times, "The root of confusion is the mistaken belief that the motive of a person – the so-called profit motive of the businessman – is an explanation of his behavior or his guide to right action. The concept of profit motive is in large part responsible for the prevailing belief that there is an inherent contradiction between profit and a company's ability to conduct itself ethically and make a social contribution."

Implicit in many self-described pragmatists' conceptions of the profit motive is the idea that notions of "virtue" or "integrity" in business are simply idealistic. The dangerous assumption is that the quest for profits justifies unethical personal conduct.

Very few people aspire to greatness or pursue excellence. People generally accept mediocrity. Mediocrity is a great leveler; it raises up the low average and sinks the high average. When one accepts mediocrity, the desire for excellence is also lost. The familiar line "Everybody else is doing it this way" is nothing more than accepting a general behavior. If everyone believes that every real-estate broker is dishonest, every salesman is a crook, every government official is corrupt, then the society as a whole turns into one with low values.

Few people will quarrel with the proposition that success in any field requires honest hard work. But it is difficult to accept the fact that hard work does not guarantee success. It simply improves the odds. There are other factors that determine the outcome – idea, timing, execution and even luck. The temptation to get rich quick by any means leads one to abandon hard, ethical work. The result of such behavior is usually failure; one has simply lowered the odds for success.

Today, most Indians have become cynical about ethics in government and business, and do not believe the situation will improve any time in the foreseeable future. People generally are used to conducting their daily lives in an unethical environment. There is a growing degree of moral sophistication in society, a sense that all things are relative and that nothing is absolutely right or wrong. This sense of artificial relativism suggests that absolute notions of good and bad, right or wrong, no longer apply.

Also contributing is what many see as a breakdown of moral and ethical teachings in the family and religious institutions. Too often, young people are not being taught the virtue of telling the truth and other forms of ethical behavior, especially through the examples of their parents, and these children in turn do not see any advantage in being ethical in an unethical society.

ETHICS IN GOVERNMENT

Corruption in the form of bribes, kickbacks and favors has become so well entrenched in government that most Indians accept the need to bribe officials to get government consent for anything of significance. Furthermore, one of the main reasons for the country's failure to tackle poverty is the misuse of government funds. Limited available resources are wasted on worthless projects, and the beneficiaries are mostly those who are able to win the favor of government officials.

Many business ventures have received special considerations by way of licenses, permits and monopolistic market privileges to which they would otherwise have not been entitled. No large government contract can be won without exerting special influence on officials through underhanded financial dealings. Politicians are pretty open about what they want by way of kickbacks, even when the application is for something very legitimate. Honest business practices will only find delays and frustrations when government approvals are needed. At present, there is no practical remedy as the system does not easily permit investigations into allegations of corruption against politicians and powerful officials in India.

Corruption in India is not confined to the commercial world. I had originally thought that government officials would be more considerate in their demands on The George Foundation because of the charitable nature of our work. But anything we had ever asked of the government – electricity connection to the rural hospital, improvement of the access road to the school, duty free customs clearance of items designated for the poor – was either held up at one official level or the other or returned for more paper work. In each instance it became obvious that, without paying a bribe, the process would never be declared complete.

Procrastination is the preferred technique used by officials, with expectations raised periodically, followed by new obstacles introduced when one thinks progress is being made. There were times when the entire application file would mysteriously disappear after several months of follow-up, and we would be asked to restart the process. Politicians have very little interest in taking any trouble for us as they find it delicate to demand large sums of money as bribes; after all, their needs are much greater than what a charitable organization can offer.

The fact that The George Foundation is a charitable organization does not stop some powerful officials from making monetary demands on us. When I first started my work in India some years ago, I was told that no donations could be made by a foreign organization to any Indian institution without prior clearance from the Home Ministry in Delhi. For tax reasons in the United States, all my contributions were to be channeled through a public charity organization in the United States. I was also told that the Home Ministry was concerned about foreign funding of terrorist organizations in India, but given the genuine nature of our charitable activities, I thought the approval from the Home Ministry would be quick and permanent.

After I waited for more than six months after submitting the application, it became apparent that, without the intervention of someone with influence, the process could drag on for years, and my planned work in India would be held in abeyance. It was then that we were introduced to a union minister from Karnataka constituency who expressed her willingness to help. But soon her personal assistant informed us that she would require twenty percent of any funds brought into India by us for her own "charitable work" in return for her obtaining speedy approval of our application. We then had to figure out a way to abandon that effort without annoying her.

Again, concerns about terrorist activities "compelled" the government to block many foreign donor contributions, especially from Christian organizations, designated for charitable and developmental activities. The Foreign Contributions Regulations Act (FCRA) was enacted nearly two decades ago by Prime Minister Indira Gandhi to prevent foreign funding of opposition groups. The net result of this unworthy legislation today is that corrupt government officials have discovered another convenient mechanism for extracting money from recipients of foreign contributions, while terrorists probably utilize other means of financing their criminal activities.

If and when the government abolishes the FCRA, and also makes it possible for NGOs to accept material donations without the harassing scrutiny and duty assessments of the customs department, the generosity of the world community will translate itself into a flood of direct foreign assistance to the nation's poor. It is terribly unfair to deny the poor the help that foreigners are prepared to offer, when Indians have so far failed to demonstrate any meaningful philanthropy.

One time, I shipped from the United States enough wheat flour to fill a 40-foot container, thanks to the generosity of the Mormon Church in Utah. It was intended for the children of Shanti Bhavan; we had thought that their needs for chapatti, a wonderful Indian bread, could be met for more than a year. Upon its arrival at one of the Indian ports, the customs officer in charge told us that the flour had to be tested for human consumption, unless of course, he received a substantial amount of money from us. There was the danger of rejection by the customs laboratory, but I did not anticipate a problem as the flour was prepared and stored under very hygienic conditions. The officer's request for a bribe was turned down, and soon we were told that the flour was not fit for human consumption as it contained "too much alcohol."

It is well known that there is always some fermentation of flour material during overseas shipping, which is by no means harmful. The only choice left for us was to send the sample to another approved laboratory, a process that could take several days, if not weeks, and in the meantime, we were incurring demurrage and other port charges. As a matter of principle, I would not allow the bribe to be paid, and after several further attempts to appeal to the good senses of the customs officials, we proceeded to obtain the approval to burn the wheat flour at the port itself.

This instance is one of several dozen over the past few years in which our foundation has encountered demands from government officials for bribes, despite their full knowledge that our work is entirely humanitarian. As one customs inspector told one of our staff, "We are also poor." Looking back on this incident, I am no longer certain that my decision was the correct one. On an ethical principle, I had made the decision to sacrifice the welfare of several hundred children and poor people.

The corrosive nature of corruption runs from top to bottom in government. There may be a sprinkling of officials in government who are not corrupt, but they are usually overwhelmed by their superiors who constantly attempt to amass wealth through bribes. Most Indians would agree that there is no permit or license that can be obtained without payment, no factory that can be run without satisfying the illegal monetary demands of government officials, and no business that can expect to obtain a contract from the government without satisfying the politician with "special favors. "

Our own experience as a charitable foundation has taught us that there is no way to escape government involvement in what we do, and while we try to minimize it, we cannot avoid having to overcome unnecessary hurdles and demands placed by officials. Unlike most other NGOs, we have all along chosen not to accept government funds in any of our work, and yet, the few services we need from government-run institutions constantly expose us to the corrupt practices of officials at all levels.

Consider the simple usual request to the electricity department of the state to connect the power line to our property. The George Foundation, in its farming project to empower poor women, needed an electricity connection to pump water from wells. The first thing to do was to apply in person to the electricity department of the district, and bring along a substantial deposit. As was always the case, we were assured of the connection in no less than 30 days and encouraged to go ahead with cultivation.

When there were no signs of any work in progress, we began to call and inquire, only to find that our paper had been temporarily "misplaced." On further inquiry, we were told that the papers were somewhere at the bottom of a long list of permits to be issued. After a considerable number of visits to the department, and after satisfying the subtle demands of senior officials for bribes, we managed to obtain an "order" for inspection.

The next step was to somehow get the inspectors to come to the farm to determine what work needed to be done for the power connection. Then a work order based on the inspection had to be issued. None of these steps could be accomplished within a reasonable time period without paying bribes to everyone involved in processing the paperwork.

When the time finally came to make the connection, we were informed that there was a shortage of electricity poles and other parts. We were advised to buy them at our expense so that work could begin; otherwise, there was no certainty about when these supplies would be available. Even after their purchase, the delivery was delayed for want of government transport. Again, we hired a truck at our expense and got the supplies delivered to the site. It goes without saying that there was no refund of any of these expenses, as they would be shown as departmental expenses, and the proceeds shared among those involved.

By now, you can well imagine how many more hurdles we had to cross before power was finally made available. There is no point in complaining to anyone in the government, as almost every other official is involved in these practices or fully aware of them. Moreover, the repercussion for complaints can be periodic blackouts.

There is no doubt that anything can get done quickly and efficiently if you are prepared to bribe powerful politicians, senior officials and junior staff – all at the same time. There are politicians who are capable of getting things done. However, the ethical issue faced by citizens everywhere is the paradox of corrupt yet effective leadership in the society. In the early 1800s, a Virginia congressman, John Randolph, coined the phrase "shining rotten mackerel in the moonlight" to describe two of his brilliant colleagues who, he complained, were very corrupt. In recent years we have seen many such men in government and in the private industry.

There is no shortage of unethical and immoral political leaders in Indian society, but they all seem to be judged for their contribution to their political constituencies, with little importance given to their improper private lives and their misuse of official power. What is most disturbing is that a majority of Indians do not seem to care about these "distractions" and repeatedly vote many such moonlight mackerels into power to lead their states and the country.

ETHICS AND SOCIETY

Businesses have a role to play in directly impacting the ethical standards and in contributing to the social order of the nation. Frequently, they fail in some areas, such as in product safety and reliability, proper and sufficient disclosure of information in contracts with consumers, truth in advertising and lending, environmental protection and others.

N.R. Narayana Murthy, chairman of Infosys which is one of the largest software companies in India, stated in an article for *India Abroad* newspaper recently that Indians lack a sense of public good and rationalize their failures to the point of justifying incompetence. He argues that the value system as exemplified by ethical conduct and commitment to the community is lacking in India, and everyone is concerned only about himself and his family. As compared to the West, he notes that Indians lack civic sense and the desire to do anything for the common good. Decision makers, especially in government, are not inclined to solve difficult problems, as each one wants someone else to take on the responsibility. Consequently, there is nobody to look up to for honest solutions.

Murthy notes that, while Indians generally keep their homes clean, they would have very little reluctance to litter the streets, spit on sidewalks and dirty public toilets – all a reflection of the disregard for the common good. Unlike the West, where it would be difficult to bribe a police officer to avoid a traffic ticket, in India such bribes are the norm. Corruption, tax evasion, cheating and dishing out undeserved favors are just a few of the well-entrenched and condoned practices in the society.

The result is money wasted on undeserving projects, substandard products, poor infrastructure and badly delivered social services. Murthy makes the distinction between the interests of the public sector and the interests of the general public. When the government fails to focus its policy for the benefit of all people, the society continues to lose terribly.

It is interesting to see that Murthy did not hesitate to express his contempt for the intellectual arrogance on the part of many educated Indians, especially those who had previously held or currently hold high positions. He notes that Indians generally express contempt for other societies, especially the West, though their own country has failed to make much progress when compared to developed nations. Yet Indians rationalize their failures and refer to the country's ancient past to prove their point about India's glory, just as the politicians pronounce every day that India is the greatest nation in the world, with superior values and culture. He finds this arrogance nothing more than hypocrisy.

I have quoted Murthy at such length because I find it very refreshing to see in a businessman of his position in India the rare courage to speak the truth candidly. Most Indians do not like to be told of their weaknesses, especially by outsiders. Perhaps voices from within can make an impact. I share

Murthy's sentiments and hope that others will emulate the example that he is trying to set through his company. Only through correct practice, and not with words alone, can we make progress. As Aristotle once said, it is "settled habits" that determine who we are.

In India, public service or working for the government is now deemed to be only for the crooks, the dishonest or the lazy. Everyone understands that bureaucracy is inefficient and arrogant, and the only comfort in working for the government is the steady or "permanent" nature of the job and the opportunity to "make money on the side." Most politicians in India now rate at the bottom in public opinion, while the people who command the heights in large companies are worshipped for their successes. Once upon a time, national leaders like Nehru and Shastri were respected for their honesty and commitment to the country, and the bureaucracy was also seen as working in the interest of the people. So much has changed since then.

In America too, politicians were once the giants of public life, respected for their integrity and dedication, but today, they are not held in high esteem. One of the saddest outcomes of this change is that many young people want to avoid politics. Bob Rubin, the secretary of the treasury under President Bill Clinton, was an exception to this general rule about public figures; he was one of the most trusted officials within the country and recognized internationally for his stewardship and integrity. He left his lucrative job as head of Goldman Sachs, one of the largest investment banks in the world, to offer public service, and when he resigned after eight years of exemplary service in government, he told graduates at the Harvard Business School to go out and make money but to save time in their careers for when they could give something back.

He said, "In some fair measure our country's future will depend on enlisting its most gifted and best trained in the great issues of the nation."

This wise counsel from a man who gave up Wall Street to offer public service may be the best hope for America's future.

Every country is led by politicians, and politicians are ordinary people whose actions have a major impact on other ordinary people. Hence, any moral demands that civilized societies impose on individuals, such as understanding the differences between honesty and deception, between goodness and evil, must to a large degree be expected from the politicians, governments and parties.

When we abandon such expectations from each other as individuals, we might as well relinquish any noble expectations from politics and politicians.

If economic and social policies will not seriously consider morality, then mankind has no future. The converse is also true; when individual and government conduct is guided by a moral compass, it will lead the society into more humane and prudent actions in everyday life.

Does ethics pay? One popular assumption that is prevalent today is that success in business rests on greed, deceit and unfeeling ruthlessness. Accordingly, living a virtuous life is seen as incompatible with profitable commercial activity. Plainly put, many believe that a truly good person cannot succeed in business. Although this perception of morality in the realm of business is widespread and goes largely unquestioned, a careful study of truly successful people engaged in commercial activity shows that it does not tally with reality. Instead, longer-term success in business, as in all other honorable human endeavors, depends largely on adhering to the highest moral ideals and ethical standards our civilization honors. While the short-term returns of unethical behavior may appear attractive to both individuals and organizations, a mounting body of evidence suggests that they are at longer-term risk.

Merely avoiding illegal or improper actions may meet the law, but those who are recognized for their integrity meet higher standards. These standards are well above the bottom line – above profits. People with integrity often struggle with the question: "What is the right thing to do?" The problem with such questioning is that the benefit of doing the right thing cannot be measured easily. Some would say, if it cannot be measured, it does not exist. Such people will tell us that one needs to be practical and deal with what is real – what we can see, touch and measure.

Intangibles have, in their view, very little value. Such an argument is simply faulty. It is the intangibles, such as loyalty, commitment and integrity that often make the difference between success and failure. In the words of Socrates, "He has only one thing to consider in performing any action: that is, whether he is acting rightly or wrongly, like a good man or a bad one." If the society does not value these intangibles, there will be no order.

Unethical conduct is not without consequence. There are many examples of unethical behavior in American history that have proved very costly to those who engaged in such activity. Richard Nixon, who was elected by a landslide for a second term as the president of the United States, was forced to resign in disgrace for unethical and illegal acts two years thereafter. Ivan Boesky was an immensely successful stock trader who amassed nearly half a billion dollars through unethical and illegal transactions before he was caught and punished. Michael Milken was one of the most successful investment bankers with Drexel Burnham & Lambert, a well-established and reputed financial powerhouse during the 1980s. He accumulated nearly $10 billion for himself and a lot more for his firm, but soon ended up in jail and was forced to return a good portion of what had been illegally obtained. As for Drexel Burnham & Lambert, Milken probably brought the firm to bankruptcy as a result of public lawsuits.

In modern day American business, there are numerous cases of unethical and illegal activities that financially deprived hundreds of thousands of employees and investors: Enron, WorldCom, and Global Crossing, to name a few. Today, these firms either do not exist or have been practically destroyed. In recent U.S. government, the vice-president of the United States and the attorney general under George W. Bush are accused of affecting policy for the benefit of energy companies and the gun lobby. Politicians and government officials at high levels have been involved in conflict-of-interest situations, influenced by large donations to their parties during elections by large contributors. These alleged actions and perceptions tend to lower their moral authority. Paying money to get favors erodes confidence and trust in government, but the good news is that there are enough individuals and groups in America to represent the consumer in trying to unravel these abuses through the media and the courts.

RELIGION, PHILOSOPHY AND ETHICS

In recent years, another disturbing trend that has been evolving is the convergence of religion and public governance in the name of social good. Several religious leaders, each with millions of devotees, have embarked on socially favored business enterprises, such as schools, colleges, hospitals, and meditation centers with the assistance of government funding. While traditional NGOs struggle to get funding on their proposals to serve the poor, religious leaders do not seem to have much difficulty in obtaining millions of rupees from state and central governments. With such government funds, many of these institutions propagate their individual religious beliefs and philosophies and cater mainly to their own religious sects.

Some have gone beyond education and health-related activities into public works programs, such as road construction, water systems and farming. There is no doubt that many religious leaders are genuinely committed to social causes and are doing excellent humanitarian work. While the social service organizations run by religious institutions are admittedly more efficient than those of the government, there is little scrutiny and accountability for their activities though government funds are used. Politicians are offered good cover behind religious leaders, as the public is reluctant to question these financial arrangements for fear that the religious groups involved would be offended. There are rumors of major kickbacks and waste, but this questionable arrangement goes unchecked. Religion, government and corruption all seem to converge.

Some people point to the modern-day interpretation of ancient religious teachings and scriptures for many of the unethical problems we face today in India. This argument deserves further scrutiny. There has never been a shortage of great philosophical ideas originating from India. The Vedic wisdom on all matters of life was given in a series of scriptures written as early as 2000 BC or even earlier. The word "Vedic" is derived from the Sanskrit word "Veda," meaning knowledge or wisdom.

The four Vedas known as Rig, Yajur, Sama, and Atharva are the original scriptures. Rig Veda contains prayers or *mantras* for the worship of universal forces; Yajur Veda teaches how to conduct ceremonies; Sama Veda tells how to chant the prayers; Atharva Veda describes different kinds of worships and invocations. Through these Vedas, one is made to understand that the individual is not an independent body but part of higher universal forces. Only by finding the connection between oneself and the divine forces through *mantras* and rituals can one attain material success, peace and harmony.

Vedic scriptures do not talk about any particular religion; they describe the steps one must go through to achieve the goals of living. Life is defined in terms of several lifetimes passed through many reincarnations. Each individual must find his path and live an ethical and correct life. Tolerance of all religions and emphasis on good deeds in Hindu culture stem from this great philosophy in the scriptures.

The Katha Upanishad is part of a larger set of literature known as the Upanishads, which means "sitting beneath" to obtain knowledge from a spiritual leader. These writings emphasize the need to seek beyond short-term material goals to attain eternal energy through prayers and rituals. It tells us that divine intelligence is present within all of us and it has the power to return us to the divine, and hence, we are part of the divine. The Vedanta-sutra define all the Vedic truths in the most general terms, while the Itihasas, the book of legends, tells the history of creation and of ancient India through the stories of

Ramayana and Mahabharata. The holiest scripture of all is the Bhagavad Gita or the "song of God," representing the words of God. The Gita is presented in the form of a dialogue between Lord Krishna and the mighty warrior Arjuna that emphasizes the central message that one should discharge one's duty bravely and with selfless dedication no matter how difficult and unpleasant it may be.

The practice of Vedantic "Sanatana Dharma" or eternal religion defines the four major goals of life as ethics, creativity, harmony and liberation from human constraints. Dharma is broadly interpreted as the underlying ethics of a stable social order. Hinduism does not profess to uplift or save others by its teachings; instead a Hindu attempts to make himself pure, while others who come in contact with him learn from his conduct. It is a religion of the individual. Prayers and rituals are intended to keep evil thoughts away from one's mind and not necessarily to get relief from suffering.

The way of Hinduism is not to grieve over suffering but to pray that evil thoughts may not enter our minds during moments of distress. By focusing on "purifying" oneself through prayer, meditation and other forms of discipline, the Hindu believes that God will dwell in his heart and direct his deeds. It is through action that a Hindu is expected to fulfill his duties. Whether *karma* or action is right or wrong depends on *dharma* or duty as established in the Vedas. Vedic dharma is different for each person and depends on one's caste, age and sex. Dharma varies with caste as one's duties are defined by the social hierarchy in the society; age matters as the obligations at different stages of one's life are different; and responsibilities of men differ from women. With these distinctions, according to Vedic teachings, it is possible to treat a bad karma by one as a good karma by another.

It is not just Hinduism that had its impact on the forming of Indian thought. Buddhism, which had its origin in India from 500 BC, advocates goodness, kindness and justice for all. Buddha taught that ignorance and desire invariably lead to pain and disappointment; to avoid these, one must practice right views and aspirations, right speech and conduct, right livelihood and effort, and right mindfulness and meditation. According to Buddhist teachings, everything is subject to change, although some things may last longer than others. Moreover, the law of causation assures that nothing occurs due to pure chance. Besides natural forces, it is karma that leads to the occurrence of all events.

Buddha advocated a "Middle Path" in which he offered a balanced, harmonious way of life, steering between the two extremes of self-indulgence and total abstinence. Buddhism rests upon four "Noble Truths:" suffering is universal; it is caused by desire and yearning; suffering can be prevented and overcome; and eradication of desires can lead to removal of suffering. To prevent suffering one has to conquer craving and desire, and this conquest leads to the attainment of *nirvana* or complete enlightenment. Buddhism and Jainism, both variants of Hinduism, reject the Vedic definition of dharma and the distinctions based on caste.

The great Indian philosopher, Swami Vivekananda exemplified the Vedic wisdom and the Indian religious traditions at the World Parliament of Religions in 1893 in Chicago when he said, "If you cannot see God in the human face, how can you see Him in the clouds, or in the images made of dull dead matter. I shall call you religious from the day you see God in men and women. Whatever comes to you is but from the Lord, appearing to us in various forms – our own soul playing with us."

Touching on a more modern theme, the great Indian poet and Nobel laureate Rabindranath Tagore wrote in Gitanjali the following verses nearly100 years ago:

where the mind is without fear and the head is held high;
where knowledge is free;
where the world has not been broken up into fragments by narrow domestic walls;
where the words come out from the depths of truth;
where tireless striving stretches its arms toward perfection;
where the clear stream of reason has not lost its way into the dreary desert sand
of dead habit;
where the mind is led forward by thee into ever-widening thought and action –
into that heaven of freedom, my father, let my country awake.

Mahatma Gandhi, the father of the nation, wrote the following about service to fellowmen: "Man's ultimate aim is the realization of God, and all his activities – social, political, religious – have to be guided by the ultimate aim of the vision of God. The immediate service of all human beings becomes a necessary part of the endeavor, simply because the only way to find God is to see Him in His creation and be one with it. This can only be done by service of all. I am a part and parcel of the whole, and I cannot find Him apart from the rest of humanity. My countrymen are my nearest neighbors. They have become so helpless, so resourceless, so inert that I must concentrate myself on serving them. If I could persuade myself that I should find Him in a Himalayan cave, I would proceed there immediately. But I know that I cannot find Him apart from humanity."

In this land of such incredible spiritual traditions and noble values, why have the modern-day people abandoned the ethical foundations that have nurtured the country? Present-day Indian society has discarded many of these values and concepts in embracing science and technology for progress and prosperity, and at best there is now only a distorted understanding of the ancient teachings. The influence of Mughal and British rulers for centuries is commonly attributed in part to this deterioration.

While the urban society is engaged in scientific developments, the rural poor are immersed in a swamp of superstitions and rituals. Consistent with the religious thought of purifying oneself, most Hindus worship their gods every day for their own enlightenment, inner peace and harmony with everything around. This has become little more than a ritual for most individuals, regardless of their religious orientations, with little thought given to living a life of high moral and ethical values.

Religious ritual is good tonic for the soul, even for the one who is living an untruthful life. Like ancient Greeks, many Indians believe that gods will forgive their wickedness if they offer enough sacrifices. I remember my meeting with a prominent real estate broker in Bangalore, soon after my return to India some seven years ago, to conclude an arrangement that would lead to the purchase of a land to start Shanti Bhavan. I was assured by my good friends of this broker's honesty and involvement in numerous other construction projects with reputed commercial institutions.

The meeting started with this broker telling me of his appreciation for what I was attempting to do and his genuine interest in helping a noble cause. He had demanded an advance of nearly Rs.100,000 to "motivate" the sellers to part with the valuable land. While I was hesitant to provide any such deposit, assurances from my friends prompted me to take the chance. As I handed over the money, the broker paused for a moment and politely asked permission to leave us for a few minutes to do *puja* or worship in a room behind that was already set up with an idol and a lamp. He returned after five minutes, thanked me for my understanding of his religious obligations and proceeded to lock up the money in the drawers. Barely one month after this interesting episode, I discovered that the land that was being transacted was never there for sale in the first place and that he had forged the documents he had produced.

Students of Eastern religions and traditions get the impression that present-day Indians must be very religious and hence, ethical. Many Westerners, disillusioned by what they consider as the moral decay in their societies, are charmed by what they hear from Indian spiritual leaders, some of whom travel to America and Europe to give lectures on how to lead a happy life. They offer complex philosophies and alternate lifestyles to finding inner peace, reducing stress, improving personal relationships in marriages and becoming wealthy. Even ordinary Indians often talk in religious and spiritual terms to explain events that take place in their daily lives.

Somehow the impression portrayed is that, in the West people are busy making money but are generally unhappy, while Indians are happier people with far less. Many foreigners come to India to experience *nirvana* and to discover the "truth," as Indians put it, only to find a country that treats a great majority of its people with contempt. As they get to know more about Indians, they find a great contrast between what they have read and what they see. It surprises most foreigners to realize the contradiction in what many Indians say about living a correct life and what they practice.

How is it that many people who make pilgrimages to holy places each year, or go to church every Sunday, or perform *puja* every morning, or pray several times a day, frequently conduct their daily lives dishonestly? This situation is not something peculiar to Indians alone; it is universal. The answer probably lies in the fact that, when religion is practiced for self-fullfillment but does not define the conduct toward another, it is easy to be spiritual in one's relationship with God and not with fellow human beings. There becomes a clear separation between trying to attain *nirvana* by serving God and caring little about others, especially those who are not part of one's immediate family. The act of going to temple or church, in itself, seemingly gives the license to lead a selfish or dishonest life, as one has already fulfilled one's duty to God.

Expressions of spirituality through spoken words become the means to connecting with God. Conduct and actions have taken a secondary role, where end seems to justify the means. Almost everyone tells me that it is not possible to live in India and not bribe anyone, if one wants to get daily needs met. Trusting others with money is a perilous act, both in business and in personal transactions.

In one of my recent talks to graduating students at a prestigious Indian management institute, I asked the students whether they could see themselves following the code of ethics in their future business careers. The unanimous reply was an emphatic no. My own experience in India for the past eight years, which has required me to interact with people of all classes and castes, has taught me one invaluable lesson – go not by words but by action alone. At the end of the day, I wonder how religion has impacted people's conduct and living.

HOPE FOR A MORE ETHICAL SOCIETY

How do we then improve the professional ethics in India? Or put differently, how can we reduce unethical practices? Here are some thoughts.

First, bring about vigorous competition in business. Make practically no exception; every field, every profession, every industry and even government should be made competitive. The free enterprise system, when practiced properly and with sufficient safeguards, assures fair competition. When consumers have alternatives, producers, sellers and those who offer services will have to live up to higher standards. The costs associated with corruption, bribes and unethical practices that are borne by the seller will not easily be passed on to buyers. In the longer run, ethical businesses will be more cost efficient and successful.

Business activity is as much social as it is economic. Most business relationships involve some exchange between individuals, often strangers, for the benefit of both parties. When one party feels that he has been ill-treated or has received an unfair bargain, he takes steps to avoid future interaction. The free-market system has ways of permitting parties to work out their differences, to discover cheats, to follow alternatives to obtain satisfaction. Just as in social situations, reputation obviously carries considerable weight in determining whether one chooses to enter into a business relationship with another. Word travels fast in business, faster than money.

Second, eliminate all unwanted controls, subsidies, license requirements, and permits. These are the sources of power for bureaucrats. Power corrupts, and absolute power corrupts absolutely. That is not to say the government has no role in regulating industries or commercial transactions. But where market forces can assure effective controls, we don't need another layer of intermediation. The government must simply enforce the laws regarding monopolistic practices, price fixing and untruthful advertising or misinformation.

Third, provide clear, fair and practical laws governing business and professional activity; for example, laws concerning pollution standards, non-competitive or monopolistic practices, illegal transactions, such as bribes, and so on. The government has a key role in detecting dishonest acts and enforcing the laws evenly, and the judiciary must be equipped to handle them expeditiously. The penalty for illegal activity must be sufficiently high to deter misconduct and to set examples for others.

Fourth, teach ethics in schools and colleges from an early stage. Children learn from examples of successful and noble people who have pursued a high level of ethical standards. Children need to learn that personal and professional success go hand in hand with correct ethical and moral conduct. Everyone who interacts with children, especially teachers, must be role models and counselors for the students.

Fifth, strengthen the family. Honesty, integrity, kindness, unselfish conduct, generosity and other virtues are best taught in the family. Children learn from their role models – mostly parents – who must set standing examples for children with their day-to-day conduct. Family has the biggest influence on the character of the child, and hence, parents who wish to bring up their children correctly must lead the way.

Sixth, television, radio and printed matter must elevate the importance of ethics in professional and personal conduct. Media should become aggressive in investigative journalism to reveal inefficiencies, waste, corruption and misuse of public funds. There has to be a deliberate effort on the part of media to communicate the importance of ethics. Given the privileged or special status of radio and television, they have a social responsibility to do so.

Last, seven, people who practice high moral and ethical standards must speak out. There are a sufficient number of idealists among us who want a just society. Grassroots movements against corruption, bribes, illegal activity and the misuse of power can be effective in dealing with wrongdoings in society. Citizens may boycott or bring class-action suits against businesses that continue to behave unethically. People must demand a higher standard than mediocrity in the public services they receive. Citizens must use the power of vote to elect honest politicians. One cannot expect an ethical government in an unethical society at large and vice versa. It must begin with each individual trying to practice ethical conduct.

There is more to ethics than living a life by the rules of society. In fact, we need fewer rules when everyone is ethical. Everyone should do the right thing for the right reasons. People's motives should be pure and guided by idealism. But with the world as it is, there is no getting away from the reality that people act in self-interest. Hence, the trick is in finding out what is the interest of the people and then motivating them to do the right thing.

People are conditioned by their past experiences. They have to be provoked to find their rightful place in the present. It is the past that is still alive in our present. We carry the burdens of our past and remain deep in the mud of our beliefs. Gustave Flaubert once said, "The thought of the future torments us, and the past holds us back. And that is why the present is slipping away from our grasp."

The definition of "good life" should encompass not just the material, but also the deeper commitments of virtue, moral order and spirituality. It has to do with how people live their lives and what politics and governance do for them. It has also to do with how compassionately we deal with each other —ethics and morality demand that. It is not enough to think of oneself only as a professional, when humane values, such as compassion, kindness, generosity, and caring toward the poor, are not cultivated. There is so much avoidable suffering in this world from hunger, poor health and disease, cruelty and the indignity of social deprivation.

The tremendous disparity between the rich and the poor is unacceptable, and the bond of our common humanity cannot permit despair and suffering to go unanswered. After all, those of us who have been "successful" cannot claim it all on our skills, intelligence and hard work alone. The truth is that we are a product of the opportunity we had from the accident of our births. The fortunate among us cannot ignore the plight of others who are victims of misfortune.

There are many measures of poverty, but the most commonly applied one is in terms of a minimum income required for subsistence. In practice, the poverty line is drawn by the income needed for the barest minimum desirable nutritional standard of calorie intake. But human needs are not confined to food intake alone. A more meaningful definition of poverty should also include minimum levels of access to and affordability for health, housing, education and recreation. Access to the basic necessities of life is more fundamental to human rights than any other, and yet, this right is denied to more than fifty percent of the population in India as well as the world.

Under varying definitions, the number of people classified as poor in India ranges from 350 million to 500 million. The absolute destitute are around

50 million to 60 million. It is not acceptable for the rest of us to rationalize and explain away the reasons for such large poverty, while leaving the entire responsibility to the government to solve this inhuman problem. Every one must participate in the solution, either by contributing money or by volunteering time; indifference will one day demand a higher price from all.

Each one of us has a moral responsibility to study what is going on around us, especially about how others live. One cannot just shut the window, close the door and be oblivious to the plight of the poor. Well-to-do people have to become more sensitive to the hardships faced by the poor, and do something about it; to be callous is simply immoral. It is not morally acceptable to remain a bystander all through one's life, and not demonstrate compassion for others. It is both a social and moral responsibility to come to the aid of those in need. Charitable giving is a part of ethical living. People must cultivate the habit of giving, sharing some of the "excess" wealth for good causes.

It surprises me to see many Indians who claim they are not rich enough to offer even a small charitable donation, engaging in lavish wedding parties and cladding their daughters in gold ornaments. Most NRIs who have amassed considerable wealth in the United States and elsewhere have also been far less generous than they could easily be. Indians are generally more receptive to giving to their religious institutions, and at times to their local communities, but most have not yet learned the value of brotherhood and compassion toward strangers anywhere. They have to transcend their communal inclinations and reach out to those in real need, regardless of religion, caste or ethnic origin.

None of which takes us away from the need to make money. We have to avoid the hypocrisy about money; people need to accept it as a force that affects our lives significantly. One can be philosophical about money, but philosophy bakes no bread, builds no shelter and covers no naked bodies. The art of living is in the pursuit of wealth without being devoured by it. The ability to use the power of money without arrogance for the right causes is paramount.

The trick is, I think, to make it and give it away for worthwhile causes – for the benefit of others who need it badly. It is like the leisure fisherman who catches the best fish only to throw it back into the water. The use of money in the service of others is among the noblest of acts. In the words of Ben Franklin, the great philosopher and diplomat who made major contributions to the cause of the American Revolution of the 1770s, "The most acceptable service to God is doing good to man."

Fortunately, there are some well-to-do people around the world who are willing to help. In the West, there is growing excitement around the potential of private philanthropy, as a source of funds as well as ideas and action-oriented strategies. In 2000, international NGOs contributed development-related grants in the range of $6 billion, of which some portion came from private philanthropy. In 2002, private contributions to charity in the United States exceeded $240 billion, 2.3 percent of the country's GDP.[54] Other Western countries and Japan contribute far less to charitable projects internationally.

The few individuals who have made serious commitments to global issues include Ted Turner, who has given $1 billion over 10 years to the U.N. Foundation; George Soros, who has contributed several hundred million dollars for each of the past five years; Bill and Melinda Gates, who have set aside several billion dollars for global health-related issues and other causes. The Ford Foundation and the Rockefeller Foundation are among the leading private institutions contributing internationally to charitable causes. Some major Indian companies have also set up foundations for charitable giving. These and other social investments illustrate the potential of private philanthropy. One can only hope that, as people become wealthy from the economic prosperity being experienced in certain business sectors in India, many more Indians will also take part in the endeavor to assist others.

For George Soros, the first prerequisite for giving away money is to make the money. While markets are eminently suited for wealth creation, they are not designed to take care of social or moral objectives. It cannot be left to markets to allocate wealth among all people, even in the very long run. Individuals and donor institutions have to make the distribution happen in a way in which the resources are used in capacity building for the poor to sustain themselves long after outside help has ended.

Governments have to participate with private donors without necessarily taking charge of projects. The main cause of misery and poverty in the world is bad government, but donor institutions have to work with officials to move them in the right direction. Given the sovereignty of states, it is very difficult for outsiders to impose conditions for giving, but by offering incentives and encouragement positive changes can be brought about.

It is not enough to be concerned about the predicament of others, and do nothing about it; true compassion is displayed in action. Compassionate feelings might make one feel good about oneself, but what really matters is generosity and the willingness to be helpful to others. Many think of compassion only in terms of physically caring for the sick and the destitute, but everyone is not capable of being like Mother Theresa. Compassion can take many forms; sometimes you remain outwardly detached from those who stand to benefit from your efforts. For me, it is about helping the poor solve their own problems. I try to concentrate on what needs to be done to make their lives better and in getting the job done as best as possible for the community as a whole, instead of any specific individual. I derive my satisfaction from my work and from their accomplishments. Each time I face a major setback or a disheartening event, I try to insulate myself from the emotional hurt by simply concentrating on the next task at hand.

Many of the social projects carried out by our foundation are deep in rural areas and hence, do not allow for our staff to attend church regularly on Sundays or conduct *puja* every day in a temple. The distance and schedules simply do not permit it. Initially many complained about the absence of spirituality in their lives, confusing it with their perceived duty to participate in religious rituals. It took me considerable effort and talking to make some of them understand that what they are doing each hour of their work is noble in itself, and their service to humanity is their service to God.

For me, there is nothing more spiritual than trying to lead a correct and compassionate life in the service of those who need my help. At the same time, I do recognize and appreciate the desire many have in experiencing their spirituality through prayers and rituals. Each one of us may find inner peace in our own way, but at the end of it all, there is no escaping the responsibility to be compassionate toward those in need.

In this age of preaching values and living with fewer of them each passing day, one wonders how people reconcile between what is professed and practiced. "Watch what we say not what we do" seems to be the practical way of today's living. It should not come as a surprise to anyone to observe that the young generation is disinclined to take all the preaching and professing seriously.

Adults are quick to blame the television and modern-day movies for what they consider to be the objectionable ways of their children. The West has brought in too much negative influence, they say, but in the name of modernity and progress, even bad behavior has to be tolerated. Finding scapegoats is convenient, but does anyone stop and think what has caused all this perceived deterioration in the ethical and moral conduct among the new generation?

To conclude that young people have lower values than their parents would be erroneous, if the yardstick for comparison is what is practiced. When children from a very early age constantly see their parents negotiate their day-to-day problems with half-truths, blatant lies and cheating, they naturally believe that dishonesty is acceptable. Many people genuinely believe that telling the truth would only get them into trouble, especially in their jobs, when a mistake has been made. The act of bribing or cheating someone or taking a bribe is discussed openly within the family, as though it should be quite acceptable to every member, justified by common interest. Most people seem to interpret whatever they are doing as fitting within their high values, and the problem lies in the other guy's behavior.

When such conduct is the norm within society, we cannot expect the younger generation to be any better. What the society needs are real heroes and role models, not the powerful politicians and officials of today who, by virtue of their positions, have national visibility but little courage to take major personal risks for the common good. Instead, individuals we can call today's role models and heroes are visionaries like Verghese Kurien, who brought about the "white revolution" by creating the largest dairy development program in the world, and G. Venkataswamy, whose innovative eye-care delivery system has helped millions of poor people suffering from vision problems. They belong to a rare breed who have endured tremendous hardship, and taken great personal risks to achieve what they have set out to do for the benefit of society. The young are moved by greatness, and inspired by those who suggest a future they can be hungry for. They must have the right heroes to motivate them to do good beyond doing well.

America, too, has its problems with young people, but with a more conservative attitude, things have improved in recent years. In 1980, over seventy percent of high school seniors said they had been drinking alcohol, but that figure dropped below 50 percent by 2000.[55] Drug usage has also fallen over the past two decades; homicides remain high among teenagers but have fallen in several major cities. While many of society's ailments are reflected among the young, there are some positive signs that point to higher social responsibility. In the five years ending in 2000, more than 100,000 young people have enlisted in AmeriCorps to do volunteer work with young children.

Most young people are not rude and irresponsible; on the contrary, they have high ideals and want to make America a better country. They voice their opinions and protest when they do not agree with government policies, especially on issues of war and peace. The freedom for peaceful dissent is what brings about positive policy changes by governments. What the young people need are role models; adults whose conduct they can emulate, and they need parents who are compassionate, caring and honest.

V.H. Krulak was a three-star general in the United States Army who aspired for one more star, but President Lyndon Johnson passed him over for someone else. His son Chuck Krulak made it as a commandant, and President Clinton surprised both of them at a White House ceremony when he pulled out the set of four stars from the handbag belonging to Chuck's mother. She had once carried them for her husband, hoping that he would one day need them. Now it didn't matter to both of them, and this was their proudest moment. Chuck served his term well, having accomplished many things for the Marine Corps.

On the day he was to retire, his father wrote to him: "The greatest contribution you have made, the best and the most valuable by far, is not even visible. … Call it what you will – honesty, truthfulness, character, morality, reliability, integrity, dependability. Any one will do. … In each and every case, it creates respect, not just for you, but for the entire Marine Corps. That is one hell of a legacy to leave."

Undoubtedly, the ethical way of life has no equal substitute; it is rooted in very profound philosophical ideas, both moral and spiritual. A good person is one who always tries to do what is right. Others will definitely follow the good example.

Chapter 13

GLOBAL PERSPECTIVES AND PERCEPTIONS

ETHICS IN INTERNATIONAL RELATIONS

Just as we want individuals and businesses to be ethical, we expect governments also to deal with each other with some redeemable principles and morality. Foreign policy pursued by a country affects its relations with other countries, impacting the entire spectrum of political, social and economic activities between them. Even perceptions that ordinary individuals in one country carry about another are influenced by what they hear about each other's foreign policy.

Countries that are perceived to stand up for noble principles, such as human rights and non-violence, command higher respect and find it easier to seek cooperation and assistance from others. All these lead to improved trade and investment, higher financial and humanitarian assistance, and better human relations between the peoples of different countries.

Has India's foreign policy strengthened its relations with other nations to the benefit of its own people? For more than half a century, the Middle East has been the center of conflict between Israel and its Arab neighbors, including the Palestinians who are trying to establish a state of their own. Without getting into the merits of the dispute, it is worth noting that one of the underlying reasons for not being able to find a peaceful resolution so far is the ethical and moral mind-set of all parties. A recent poll of 1,600 respondents by an Arab political scientist found that by a margin of four to one, Arabs denied the Holocaust and rejected the idea of doing business with Israel even after a peace settlement is reached.[56] Arab contention that Israel is an alien growth in the Middle East, a post-Holocaust creation born of Western guilt, is nothing more than an extension of the belief that Islam is the master of this land. Just as Jews believe rather absurdly that they are the "chosen people," Arabs now claim to be God's chosen faithful.

When such beliefs dominate the minds, how can negotiations lead to a fair and just resolution of the conflict? Real peace will come only when Israel's Muslim neighbors get rid of their religious hatred toward the Jews. By the same token, Jews must rid themselves of their contempt for the Arabs and respect the legitimate rights and aspirations of Palestinians to a homeland free of Israeli occupation and interference. Real peace will be visible from the way leaders address their nations, teachers teach students and religious leaders direct their followers. Real peace will come when there is an end to the threats of violence, an end to disdain and defamation.

India's foreign policy stand in this and other recent major international disputes raises some serious ethical and moral questions. India had recognized the state of Israel as early as 1950, but relations between the two countries deteriorated following India's support of the Arab position subsequent to the 1967 Arab-Israel war. The Israeli consulate in India was closed down until Egypt again recognized the statehood of Israel in 1979 with the Camp David agreement. India, a country that has long claimed moral superiority in its external dealings, succumbed to economic boycott pressures from Arab countries and continued to keep its distance from Israel.

Subsequently, India found itself on the wrong side of history and opportunism and decided in 1992 to renew its full relationship with Israel, and allowed it to open its embassy in Mumbai. Since then there has been flourishing commerce between the two countries, including the purchase of sophisticated military gear from Israel. It now appears that India sought the military assistance of Israel during the Kargil conflict with Pakistan and later invited Prime Minister Ariel Sharon as a national guest in 2003. Obviously, India's foreign policy on the Israeli-Arab conflict is now dictated more by its self-interest and less by what it has all along been claiming to be its just position.

Kosovo represented another world event during which India's foreign policy showed its self-serving position, and moral insensitivity. When Slobodan Milosevic and his thugs in Serbia started the atrocities in Kosovo in the fall of

1998, the world stood watching. At the time of the Dayton accord on Bosnia four years before that, experts on a Balkans commission warned of a coming inferno unless Serbian military presence was reduced in Kosovo.

When Milosevic gathered his troops for an ethnic cleansing campaign in Kosovo, the world let him do as he pleased. It took almost a year of inaction before the world community, under United States leadership, decided to act. By the time NATO finally began its air assault, the conditions on the ground had already deteriorated terribly, and atrocities were being committed at high speed.

This inaction or delayed action resulted in the murder of hundreds of thousands of innocent Kosovans at the hands of the Serbs and the exodus of more than 500,000 refugees into neighboring countries.

Machiavelli had it right when he wrote, "In the beginning of the malady it is easy to cure but difficult to detect, but in the course of time it becomes easy to detect but difficult to cure."

The reluctance on the part of the West to act on time in defense of the people of Kosovo is one of the major foreign policy failures of modern-day history and a shameful chapter on the absence in moral courage. Throughout the genocide and during the NATO air attack that led to the liberation of the Kosovons, India maintained its foreign policy position that any interference by outside countries represented a violation of the sovereignty and territorial integrity of Yugoslavia.

India argued that the NATO action went against the U.N. Charter as it was being carried out without the authorization of the U.N. Security Council. India joined with Cuba and Belarus to prepare a draft resolution condemning the NATO attack, but they failed to win the support of a minimum of nine nations in the 15-member Security Council. The resolution was rejected by 12 votes to three, with only Russia, China and Namibia voting in favor. India's stand in this matter was supported only by a handful of states within the 114-member Non-Aligned Movement (NAM), and it represented a very minority opinion among all others.

Kosovo military victory was finally a moral triumph in insisting upon civilized conduct among nations. NATO air attacks on Serbia that ended the carnage displayed the effective use of limited military power for limited ends. The war was fought not for territory but for basic human values and moral principles. It transcended religious affiliations – stopping a Christian Serbia's military atrocities against Muslim Kosovans – and claims of domestic conflicts as a reason for precluding outside interference. The question of whether it was lawful to attack a sovereign country for actions in its own territory was answered. It was an historic lesson for all rogue nations and brutal regimes.

Even in the face of atrocities, why does India elevate the principle of "non-interference in the internal affairs of another country" as the supreme guide in the conduct of international relationships? How did it come to pass that India found its strongest supporter for its position in China? Has India always been consistent in its own application of this principle? The answers to all three questions are readily available in history.

Since independence, India rejected plebiscite in Kashmir as a means of determining its future status and has resisted any involvement by third parties, even as mediators, in settling the dispute with Pakistan. In recent years, India has also faced worldwide criticism for alleged human rights violations in its handling of the opposition in Kashmir. India has always maintained that Kashmir is an internal matter, and no other country has any right to interfere. China also faces world condemnation for its oppressive rule over Tibet and the handling of Muslim agitations in its Sinkiang province, and it does not wish to see any foreign involvement in settling these disputes. As for Russia, its continuing brutal military involvement in Chechnya inspires worldwide criticism, but it too wants a free hand to suppress the liberation struggle. The self-interest of all three nations in preventing the involvement of other countries in their conflicts has brought them together at the cost of sacrificing moral principles; even the two strange bedfellows, India and China, share similar views.

Many question India's consistency in upholding the supremacy of this foreign policy doctrine. Its 1971 military invasion of former East Pakistan, and now Bangladesh, is cited as an example of India's deviation from this doctrine; other cases include its involvement in Sri Lanka, Nepal, and Sikkim under somewhat different circumstances that are probably less controversial. India's support of Iraq following the invasion of Kuwait and its subsequent silence on the matter when the U.N.-sanctioned allied forces liberated Kuwait are seen by many as foreign policy positions lacking moral footing.

Since September 11, 2001, when America sought India's assistance in tracking down Al Qaeda and pressured Pakistan to hunt for terrorists in their country, closer ties began to develop between the United States and India. India welcomed American pressure on Pakistan to stop cross-border terrorism by mercenaries, and when both India and Pakistan came dangerously close to war in 2002, which could have resulted in a nuclear confrontation, it was probably the personal involvement of President Bush that discouraged a military confrontation.[57] India has since taken a more positive posture toward America, one that was quite evident during the months leading up to the invasion of Iraq by America and Britain in March 2003.

While India expressed its desire for a peaceful resolution of the Iraq crisis, it chose not to take any aggressive diplomatic stand in the United Nations or elsewhere against the American invasion, arguing, in the words of its foreign minister, "India's foreign policy is dictated by its self-interest." After more than 50 years of diplomacy affected by a dislike of America, and following the past declarations of non-interference in the internal affairs of another country as its supreme foreign policy doctrine, India's foreign policy finally gave way to the admission that it cares less about morality in these matters and more about what it perceives to be in the national interest.

All of us want our country to stand up for what is morally right, especially when innocent people are oppressed and killed anywhere. We cannot hide behind outdated principles that do not give sufficient credence to civilized conduct. In today's context, the validity of the foreign policy doctrine of non-interference is questionable for a variety of reasons. But the simplest and most powerful reason is one in defense of human rights everywhere. It is the manifest responsibility on the part of the civilized world community to come to the assistance of those anywhere who face atrocities on political, religious or ethnic grounds at the hands of oppressive governments and rulers.

Look at most of Africa and countries like Cambodia and Yugoslavia over the past 50 years. The cardinal principles of non-interference and the sacrosanctity of national boundaries allowed many despotic rulers to go unchecked at the cost of millions of lives and economic ruin.

In conflicts between nations, it may not always be possible for the international community to wait until a general consensus among most nations is reached. The world faces extreme dangers from terrorism, weapons of mass destruction and rogue governments. Even small groups of people who are unhappy with one thing or the other can now cause extensive damage and destruction of human life anywhere. It is a futile effort to appeal to the good sense of these groups that have taken up violence as their means of remedy; it may not be possible to appease them peacefully. Many governments have offered refuge for such groups in their countries, to organize, plan and execute terrorism. There may be little or no value in taking action after the damage has been caused.

While the world has undergone significant changes in the past 50 or so years, many of the global institutions designed to help maintain world peace and security and promote economic prosperity in poor nations have hardly changed. There is a need for leadership among nations, the policing of dangerous regions, and mediation of conflicts with authority and strength. America has taken on that role for now, but sooner or later, a reformed United Nations must assume the responsibility.

Until then, America may have to act on its own on rare occasions when national or world security comes under imminent threat, without waiting to obtain the consent of those governments whose decisions may be dictated by their commercial interests. After all, as per the mandate of the United Nations, it is mostly American military force that has been asked to resolve every major conflict during the past several decades. That is not to say that America may act unilaterally without sufficient regard for world opinion.

The world is a community of nations for which the protection of basic human rights ought to be the concern of all. This concept is not one that needs complex intellectual rationale and geopolitical considerations. Granted, it may not be always possible or desirable to use external military force to stop atrocities being committed within some countries as was done in the case of Kosovo. In such instances, economic and diplomatic measures might be the way to exert sufficient pressure to encourage proper behavior.

Specific situations will dictate appropriate responses, but there should be no question on the rights of the international community to come to the help of innocent victims of oppression. All countries must be required to treat their citizens within civilized norms and principles set by the U.N. declarations. The moral clarity of this universally recognized principle must be communicated between nations with diplomatic certainty.

The mission of shaping the world's future is too important to be left to politicians. It is our task as individuals to create a definition of the good life – one on which all societies can agree. To search for that answer is to ask a harder question: If we can't agree, how do we co-exist with different values and interests?

"If you really push people," says Martha Nussbaum, a modern-day American philosopher, in *Upheavals of Thought* (Cambridge University Press, 2001), "they'll agree that virtue is more important than money. What virtue means to people whose interests are as different as women from men, young from old, rich from poor – that is what we're trying to understand."

But we have to be careful about "imposter virtues" that appeal to emotions but are not necessarily right. For example, courage is a virtue different from fearlessness, especially when one is devoid of fear to commit wrong. Similarly, patriotism is not to be confused with standing up for your country when it is on a wrong path. Failure on the part of the people of Nazi Germany to resist Hitler's terrible crimes against humanity cannot be justified by arguments of patriotism. In India, tradition is taken as a virtue and has been used as an excuse by many to socially and economically oppress large sections of the society for centuries.

According to Nussbaum, at the heart of the inquiry into values is a quest for a working definition of leadership. Enlightened leaders have been wrestling with core values since the Greeks invented the idea of the good life as something that only institutions can provide. Rational thought, they argued, can settle any dispute. After all, everyone is human, so, of course, everyone wants the same things. But that was only true as long as "everyone" was a free Greek citizen. History reveals a long and troubled conflict about core values.

Christianity dominated much of Europe and beyond in the early Middle Ages, but by 715 AD, nascent Islam had taken hold of areas south and east of the Mediterranean and even most of Spain. With little warning, the world order had changed, and every new challenger carried an entirely different sense of how things did – or should – work. In the midst of conflicts between civilizations and cultures, common core values were unheard of. Beliefs and values not only conflicted, they also called for battle. Unfortunately, history is the story of people who seem happier to be defined by their differences than to be joined by what they share. We are divided from one another by our beliefs, and there will never be peace in the world as long as we seek others to share our beliefs.

Today, the world faces many grave dangers. Every country has the obligation to help bring about a better and more secure world, and that effort must begin with what nations do for themselves. As the second most populous country in the world, India will face many difficult challenges in the years to come. It is for its people to ask the hard questions and seek the answers. Do we elect national leaders worthy of our trust? Do we pursue a foreign policy that also reflects a correct moral position? What is the standard of honesty in public discourse? Can we carry out normal commerce without fear of being cheated? Can we expect the government to provide services without being subjected to indignity? Answers to these and other critical questions will shape the nation's future.

All the preaching and professing is not worth a thing when there is a split-screen moral picture: the pretentious and the real. The words may be soothing to the heart – brimming with the nobleness of values – but what counts is simply what we do with all those platitudes. What our children need is not all that advice we adults shower on them but what we have to show them by our actions every day.

As Ralph Nader, the third party United States presidential candidate in 2004 said, "It is easier to fight for one's principles than to live up to them."

It is for all of us as individuals to live up to correct principles, and insist that our leaders do the same in formulating and conducting policy. Similarly, when a nation is respected globally for its moral standing on issues, it is likely to bridge strong relationships with other countries in areas of diplomacy, investment, commerce, technology, cultural exchange and other arenas. With good governance and the right moral standing, India stands to achieve greatness in the future.

LIVING IN PEACE AND HARMONY

Maybe what society needs more of is "reverence" that we can all share and less of the religious beliefs that divide us. Today, the world seems to be increasingly captivated by men who believe they know what the gods want. The poet Lucretius ends his master work in philosophy with the strong line, "so great is the power of religion to lead us to evil."

Paul Woodruff in his recent book, *Reverence – Renewing a Forgotten Virtue* (Oxford University Press, 2002), tells us the Greek story of Agamemnon who set out to capture Troy. As he waited on the beach to launch his ships and chariots, the winds turned hostile. He asked his trusted diviner what he should do, and the diviner, who had faith in his powers to speak for the gods, told Agamemnon that the gods desired the life of the king's daughter. And so his beautiful daughter Iphigenia was summoned to her wedding in all the veiled finery of a bride. But there was no handsome young husband to be found, only a sharp knife poised to end her life.

Instead of trying to act like or speak for gods, we must understand our human limitations. We must develop reverence instead of beliefs in our minds to seek justice. We must develop reverence to act correctly at all times, to respect what is good, to face adversity with courage, and to feel shame for wrong-doing. With reverence, we can develop warmth in friendships, respect in diversity and compassion in the face of suffering. Without reverence, rituals are empty, and virtues are forgotten.

Reverence gives us the ability to shudder at doing wrong. The capacity for virtue rests in all of us, and it is for each one of us to bring it out in our actions. Reverence gives us the capacity for certain feelings that drive us to do what is right. Unlike belief, reverence is a uniting feeling – a joining force – that brings us all together. When the leaders of every community and the nation demand reverence from their peoples, and vice-versa, society finds peace and harmony.

In a world of conflicting interests, what would a moral global system look like? It could be a set of universal values that includes the right to live free from hunger, the right to physical health and dignity, the right to participate in political affairs and free speech and the right to hold property.

"We may reasonably disagree about many matters," Nussbaum says. "That is why freedom of religion and freedom of speech and association are so very important. Each person ought to search for the meaning of life in his or her own way, using the resources of whatever religious or philosophical tradition he or she likes. For political purposes, we can also agree to endorse a common core of basic principles of justice. But I do not think that political philosophers should be in the business of recommending a fully comprehensive account of the human good."

Most people think that as far as virtues and ethics in India go, it is not going to change in the foreseeable future. Bad governance is blamed for most problems faced by the country. I have often heard words of cynicism and expressions of hopelessness. But we have to start somewhere, with each one of us making a small difference. It is like steering large oil tankers with huge rudders in congested waters. These rudders are awkward and hard to use to make minor corrections in the open sea.

Consequently, these ships are equipped with a trim tab – a very small rudder – attached to the large rudder. The tab, while small, can change the course of the ship by exerting a little pressure over a long stretch of ocean. Each one of us practicing ethics in India is changing the direction of a mighty ship in a small way.

As Aristotle implied in his writings, the concept of ethics and excellence is to put hard work, good ideas and integrity together for a good, stable, harmonious and successful corporation with happy employees striving to satisfy clients. This concept may sound a little like fantasy in today's world, but it is certainly a promising alternative to the bloodletting that is presently going on.

Societies succeed by producing responsible individuals. Economic excellence is achieved not by capital alone but character as well. In today's global economy, professionalism and ethics play a major role in picking winners. If the economic environment is such that the cost of unethical behavior is high, businesses will be more careful. If the laws are fair and enforced vigorously, and the penalty for serious violations is steep, individuals will be more careful. If the public participates in the exercise of democracy, governments will be held accountable.

Citizens must demand transparency in government, and the press must work to uncover the abuse of power by their leaders. Over time, maybe in several years, we will then see a remarkable improvement in the way people interact with each other, how companies do business, and what governments follow by way of policies. Ethical conduct improves the economic system, increases productivity, and assures social justice, peace and harmony among all people.

✳ ✳ ✳

The ideas presented in this book are founded on principles of good private and public governance, creation of economic opportunity for all, fair market competition, a redefined supportive role for the government and effective enforcement of laws and dispensation of equal justice. The practice of these concepts would take India to far greater heights.

There is hope as long as goodwill and determination prevail. The nation must commit itself to eliminating poverty within the next half century and follow through with sound policies that can accomplish this mission. India must strive to build a fair and ethical society that offers equal opportunity and justice to all its people. Peace and communal harmony will be assured only with religious tolerance and acceptance of diversity. Good governance in public and private enterprises is essential for improving productivity and in achieving fair distribution of income, wealth and public services.

In conclusion, national policy should focus on enhancing economic opportunities for those who are left behind in the recent industrial expansion, especially the rural poor who comprise a great majority of the nation's population. Government must embrace its rightful role as the servant of the people and permit private businesses to operate without unwanted interference. When democratic institutions, such as the press and the justice system, are strengthened, they will serve as effective checks and balances against the excesses in both public and private sectors.

India must actively participate in the global effort to solve international conflicts, advance security free of terrorism, and promote human rights everywhere. With moral political leadership, a participatory public in the exercise of democracy would assure the formulation of sound national policies. If these and other critical issues can be adequately addressed, India stands to achieve social tranquility and great economic prosperity for all its citizens within the next few decades and to set an example for other developing nations.

END NOTES

CHAPTER 1: A LONG AWAITED JOURNEY

1. *This was the birth of The George Foundation, a nonprofit charitable trust that would work toward the goals of addressing some of the most persistent problems in Indian society, especially with regard to the poor:* The mission, goals and activities of The George Foundation are described in www. tgfworld.org.

CHAPTER 2: GETTING TO KNOW INDIA

2. *By some accounts, there are more than 22 million people of Indian origin living in over 120 countries, of which 2.2 million are in the United States:* The estimate on the number of people of Indian origin in the United States is based on the 2000 United States Census that shows that 1.02 million people presently living in America were born in India. The balance of 1.2 million of Indian origin was born in America or outside India.

CHAPTER 3: THE "LITERATE" CHILDREN OF RURAL INDIA

3. *On the other hand, India has neglected basic education, spending only about 1.7 percent of the country's gross domestic product on primary education and 3.8 percent for education overall, compared to more than 5 percent for an emerging country like Brazil. Up to 40 million children are now estimated to be out of school in India:* The statistics on India are derived from extrapolating the official data available for 2000-2001, compiled by IAMR, Ministry of Education, Government of India.

4. *United Nations identified universal primary education by 2015 as one of the goals that the world should attempt to achieve, but it appears that the diversion caused by terrorism makes it far less likely even by year 2025:* The goal for education was set at the United Nations Millennium Summit, New York, September 2000.

5. *Less than 30 million people had phone lines in use, while the Internet was accessed by some 5 million in 2000. Very few educational institutions offer Internet access to their students; less than 5 percent of India's 100,000 secondary schools use computers in education, and only a small fraction among them have Internet access:* The World Economic Forum report, January 2002, New York.

CHAPTER 5: BEYOND PROSPERITY FOR THE FEW

6. *'Within less than two years, the government fiscal deficit fell from 8.4 percent of GDP in 1990-91 to 5.7 percent in 1992-93, and foreign exchange reserves rose to $20 billion from barely $1 billion:* The International Monetary Fund report by T. Collen, P. Reynolds, and C. Towe., "India at the Crossroads – Sustaining Growth and Reducing Poverty," attributes much of India's economic strength during the early and mid-1990s to the broad-ranging fiscal and structural reforms undertaken following the 1991 balance of payments crisis. These included reforms to the tax system, substantial cuts in the deficit of the consolidated public sector, liberalization and deregulation in the industrial sector, trade and tariff reforms and measures to recapitalize and strengthen the supervision of banks and other financial intermediaries. These policies helped spur a strong recovery, with real GDP growth accelerating to an average of 7.25 percent in the mid-1990s from as low as half of 1 percent at the beginning of the decade. Following the 1991 crisis, India's balance of payments also strengthened. Indeed, in the latter half of the decade, despite the effect of the regional crisis on merchandise exports, the current account deficit began narrowing. The deficit fell to less than 1 percent of the GDP in FY1999/00, partly reflecting the impact of India's growing exports of information technology-related services.

7. *Annual gross domestic product (GDP) growth has averaged more than 5 percent, industrial growth around 6 percent and services growth nearly 7 percent, while export growth has been in excess of 20 percent annual in recent years. According to some estimates, the country is expected to be the next trillion dollar economy in the world. Some claim that India is poised to become the third largest economy in the world by 2050:* Barron's, the United States financial weekly, reported in October 2003 on a Wall Street study by the leading investment firm, Goldman Sachs, showing that China, India,

Russia and Brazil will, as a group, overtake the dominant United States-Europe-Japan economic bloc by 2050. It also predicts that the Chinese economy will become the world's largest, supplanting the U.S. economy, with India's third.

8. *India's cumulative borrowings from the World Bank alone were nearly $50 billion, over 15 percent of the bank's total lending in the past 50 years:* India is now World Bank's largest borrower with more than $47 billion as of June 2000 in market-based loans. India began massive borrowing from the World Bank in 1991 and was forced to accept conditions that included cuts in social spending, privatization of natural resources and agriculture, and free trade to allow multinational corporations to compete against local businesses. However, India also maintains good credit ratings, and with nearly $100 billion in foreign exchange reserves at the end of 2003, its annual borrowing power has nearly doubled.

9. *Further, despite all the predictions of a boom in offshoring by foreign companies, the best bet is that only 3 million or so jobs will move out of the United States in the next decade.* According to a New York Times report (December 22, 2003), Forrester Research, an independent technology research firm based in the United States, predicts a figure of 3.3 million services jobs moving offshore between 2000 and 2015. The projections show that half of the 3.3 million jobs will be in traditional office services, like bill processing, order handling and the like. Only 14 percent of the total is in computer services, according to Forrester.

10. *For example, the subsidies on the average toward maintaining a cow range anywhere from $3 in Europe to $7 in Japan, while a great majority of the people in most developing countries live on less than $2 a day. Their collective $50 billion in foreign aid barely offsets 20 percent of the damage from this protectionism:* WTO trade talks held in Mexico in September 2003 designed to change the face of farming around the world collapsed amid differences between rich and poor nations, the second such failure for the organization in four years. Many of the poor nations were frustrated that officials avoided serious discussion of agricultural reform. Delegates had hoped to slash the subsidies rich nations pay their farmers and lower the tariffs many countries charge for importing farm goods.

11. *The central government expenditure on defense (20 percent), debt service (50 percent) and payments to central government employees (7.5 percent) is in excess of 78 percent of the total government expenditure, leaving barely 22 percent of the budget for all other items, including programs for poverty eradication:* India's budget for fiscal year 2003-04 forecasts central and states combined deficit of 9 percent to10 percent of the GDP, one of the highest in the world for a major country.

12. *In 1970, United States per capita income was 31 percent higher than that of other major industrialized countries. By 1991, the difference had narrowed to only 10 percent. But with the dawn of the Internet Age, the gap started to widen to more than 22 percent by 2000. This situation is historically unique and shows the power of technological improvements:* Data & Statistics, World Development Indicators, World Bank Group Publications, appropriate years.

13. *For example, when the government opened the door to foreign investment in automotive manufacturing and relaxed licensing requirements for carmakers, overall productivity increased by more than 250 percent during an 8-year period from 1992, and employment increased in the industry by 12 percent:* According to McKinsey & Company studies published in its quarterly reports, liberalization of the automotive sector in India since 1983 contributed to rapid growth in output, productivity and employment. Growth rate in passenger car segment alone reached nearly 25 percent per annum by 2000.

14. *As of year's end 2001, there are an estimated 22,000 cases pending with the Supreme Court of India, while state courts have some 30 million outstanding:* In reply to a question in the Rajya Sabha on the pendency of cases in various high courts, Law Minister Jana Krishnamurthy stated that The Allahabad High Court had 8.68 lakh (860,000) cases of arrears, the highest number of any High Court, as on March 1, 2002, followed by the Kerala High Court with 4.05 lakh cases and the Madras High Court with 3.5 lakh cases. The other High courts with huge pendency are Bombay, 2.95 lakhs; Calcutta, 2.83 lakhs; Punjab and Haryana, 2.33 lakhs; Delhi, 1.78 lakhs; Andhra Pradesh, 1.46 lakhs; Gujarat, 1.41 lakhs and Rajasthan 1.32 lakhs. In the Supreme Court, the outstanding number of cases as on May 31, 2002 stood at 23,012. (The Hindu, December 3, 2002).

CHAPTER 6: FOREVER LEFT BEHIND

15. *Depending on the yardstick for defining poverty, there are as many as 350 million to 500 million people below the poverty line in India today. More than 50 percent of the rural population is poor by practically every definition:* According to the Millennium Indicators published by the United Nations Statistical Division, 34.7 percent of India's population (approximately 360 million) is below $1 per day of income in 2003. By a slightly broader definition of $2 per day, the estimated number of poor people is at least 500 million. Poverty imposes an oppressive weight on India, especially in the rural areas where almost three out of four Indians and 77 percent of the Indian poor live.

16. *Agriculture and its related products and services contribute 24 percent of the GDP and employ about two-thirds of the country's labor force:* In its State of the Economy review of the economic situation, the Confederation of Indian Industry (CII) has revised its prediction for growth of the GDP to 7.2 percent during the fiscal year 2003-2004, with the agricultural sector contributing 24 percent to the GDP.

17. *India has the largest stock of food-grains in the world, but it also has one of the highest prevalence of malnutrition; 40 percent to 60 percent of the children in India are undernourished:* According to a new World Bank report, Wasting Away: The Crisis of Malnutrition in India, malnutrition remains a silent emergency in India, where more than half of all children under the age of four are malnourished, 30 percent of newborns are significantly underweight and 60 percent of women are anemic. According to the report, malnutrition costs India at least $10 billion annually in terms of lost productivity, illness and death and is seriously retarding improvements in human development and further reduction of childhood mortality.

18. *The literacy rate in India is presently around 60 percent:* According to the government, the literacy rate in India has risen from 52 percent in 1995 to 60 percent in 2001. The gap between male and female literacy rates fell from 29 percent in 1991 to 21 percent in 2001. Many question the accuracy and validity of these figures, especially in the context of functional literacy.

CHAPTER 7: HOLY COWS, UNTOUCHABLES, AND NON-BELIEVERS

19. *In the communal riots and killings that took place in Gujarat in 2002, India's National Human Rights Commission itself has "found substantial evidence of premeditation by members of Hindu extremist groups; complicity by Gujarat State government officials and police inaction in the face of these violent attacks on Muslims in which many persons were shot, stabbed, raped, mutilated and/or burned to death:* The highly critical report released in 2002 by The Human Rights Watch, an independent U.S.-based organization, alleges that state officials in Gujarat were directly involved in the killings of hundreds of Muslims and were engineering a massive cover-up. What happened, it says, was "not a spontaneous uprising. It was a carefully orchestrated attack against Muslims, planned in advance and organized with extensive participation of police and state officials." The 75-page report directly implicates police officials in all the incidents it documents. It alleges police personnel as telling Muslims that they have no order to save them and in many incidents even leading "murderous mobs," aiming and firing at Muslims. Amnesty International, another independent human rights organization that was denied access by the government of Gujarat for its own investigation, also made similar allegations.

20. *Nothing much has changed since Tagore translated Kabir's poem when he saw the failed promise of unity between Islam and Hinduism.* In Kabir: One Hundred Poems of Kabir, Trans. Rabindranath Tagore assisted by Evelyn Underhill. London: Macmillan, 1915. Tagore is acclaimed by many as a spiritual genius whose realization transcends all barriers of dogma, religion, country and civilization.

21. *Of the 1 billion people in the country, some 200 million to 250 million are Dalits (meaning "broken people," formerly called "untouchables,"), and another 300 million or so are among the lower castes. Brahmins, who are approximately 35 million in number, have claimed the status of uppermost caste, and everyone else is in between:* The number of Dalits in India is estimated differently by varying statistics, depending on which groups of people are included. Traditionally, Dalits, known as panchamas, bahyas and outcastes, were outside the Hindu caste order. Today, the Dalit movement argues for the need to break away from Hinduism for libera-

tion, which they allege to have given religious sanction to oppression and inhuman treatment by the concept of ritual pollution and legitimized it through the concept of karma.

22. *Minister Joshi wants the agenda of "Indianization, Nationalization, and Spiritualization" to be accomplished through educational and cultural organizations:* Among several arguments put forward by Minister Joshi in defense of his attempt to change the educational focus in India, he cites the UNESCO, "favoring value education and learning from within to promote social and moral values." Explaining the term "within," he said it meant there is to be some sort of spiritual content in the education and that is the value in education.

23. *Mao launched the Socialist Education Movement (1962-65) for the purposes of restoring ideological purity, reinfusing revolutionary fervor into the party and government bureaucracies and intensifying class struggle:* The Socialist Education Movement in China was inaugurated in September 1962 at the Tenth Plenum of the Eighth National Party Congress Central Committee as a mass ideological campaign for both party cadre and the general population. The movement was patterned along the lines of the Yan'an rectification campaign of 1942-45 and was intended to increase ideological "correctness" and consciousness, especially in regard to reversing "capitalist" and "revisionist" tendencies perceived in social and economic life. The Socialist Education Movement, which continued at least until 1965, is considered a precursor of the Cultural Revolution. The assertion that the BJP party is attempting to "saffronize" education in India as a precursor to a larger cultural and religious mobilization is debatable.

CHAPTER 8: UNEQUAL AND POWERLESS

24. *Reports published by WHO and other international agencies probably understate the number of violent deaths, as many people even in developed countries do not make a report to police when the assailant is a family member or someone they fear:* World Health Organization's 2003 World Report on Violence and Health, is the first comprehensive report to address violence as a global public health issue and to provide a thorough international review of the problem. Violence and Health compiles statistics from the 70 countries that report health data to the WHO, exploring all forms of violence, including violence against women, as an international problem of epidemic proportions.

25. *Domestic violence has for long been one of the major causes of death, especially among women.* According to the International Center for Research on Women (ICRW), Washington, D.C., violence against women in India has been increasing. ICRW's three-year research program on domestic violence in India, which began in 1997 in partnership with researchers from a range of Indian academic and activist organizations, reveals a disturbing trend. While statistical evidence on the actual prevalence of domestic violence in India is scant, the few studies available indicate that physical abuse of Indian women is quite high, ranging from 22 percent to 60 percent of women surveyed. Most of the available information consists of qualitative studies of very small sample size. The only large-scale indicator of violence against women is the data relating to crimes against women published by the National Crimes Record Bureau, Ministry of Home Affairs, Government of India. The records of the bureau reveal a shocking 71.5 percent increase in cases of torture and dowry deaths during the period from 1991 to 1995 and may reflect increased reporting of violence. In 1995, torture of women constituted 29.2 percent of all reported crimes against women. In another study, 18 percent to 45 percent of married men in five districts of Uttar Pradesh, a large state in northern India, acknowledged that they physically abused their wives. In another study of dowry abuse, it was revealed that one out of every four serious dowry victims was driven to suicide.

26. *In 1999 a National Policy for Empowerment of Women was formulated by the Indian government, which seeks to make reservation of seats for women in the parliament and state assemblies:* The principle of gender equality is enshrined in the Indian Constitution in its Preamble, Fundamental Rights, Fundamental Duties and Directive Principles. The Constitution not only grants equality to women, but also empowers the state to adopt measures of positive discrimination in favor of women. However, there still exists a wide gap between the goals enunciated in the Constitution, legislation, policies, plans, programs and related mechanisms on the one hand and the situational reality of the status of women in India on the other. The underlying causes of gender inequality are related to social and economic structure, which is based on informal and formal norms and practices. National Policy for the Empowerment of Women formulated in 2001 by the government is intended to create an environment through "positive

economic and social policies for full development of women to enable them to realize their full potential, enjoy all human rights and fundamental freedom by women on equal basis with men in all spheres – political, economic, social, cultural and civil – and equal access to participation and decision making of women in social, political and economic life of the nation."

27. *At the 1994 International Conference on Population and Development held in Cairo, governments agreed to undertake a series of steps for the advancement of women, especially in areas of reproductive health:* The Program of Action, adopted on September 13, 1994 at the Conference, endorses a new strategy that emphasizes the integral linkages between population and development and focuses on meeting the needs of individual women and men, rather than on achieving demographic targets. The key to this new approach is empowering women and providing them with more choices through expanded access to education and health services, through skill development and employment, and through their full involvement in policy- and decision-making processes at all levels.

28. *In addition to the disadvantages that women in India face, the nation is now confronted with a dangerous disparity in the female-male sex ratio that is estimated to be 927 females to 1,000 males as compared to the worldwide ratio of 1,050 females for 1,000 males. Several states are below the 900 level, while the national ratio has been steadily worsening over the past half a century. India has the lowest ratio of females to males among the 10 most populous countries in the world:* The Hindu reported on October 23, 2003, that in some states, including Punjab, Haryana, Gujarat, Himachal Pradesh, Delhi, and parts of Tamil Nadu, Maharashtra and recently Karnataka, the sex ratio has declined to about 900 girls per 1,000 boys in the 0 to 6 age group. In some districts, the ratio has plummeted to less than 850 girls to 1,000 boys.

29. *More than 60 percent of the child labor in India is employed in the agricultural sector:* It is difficult to get an accurate picture of child labor in India as the government has not taken serious efforts to gather this data. According to the Human Rights Watch, an independent U.S.-based organization, credible estimates range from 60 million to115 million of

working children in India, the largest in any country in the world. They are sweating in the heat of stone quarries, working in the fields more than 12 hours a day, picking rags in city streets, employed at low wages by jewelers and silk weavers seven days a week or hidden away as domestic servants. Apart from their miserable lives, they do not go to school, and by the time they reach adulthood, they may be irrevocably sick or deformed. Despite this serious violation of human rights and exploitation carried out on a large scale, the government has not taken adequate measures to curb the practice.

CHAPTER 9: BEYOND REDEMPTION? DISEASE AND HEALTH CARE IN RURAL INDIA

30. *Botswana, the thinly populated land of 1.6 million people in southern Africa, is often cited as the hardest hit by the AIDS epidemic for its infection rate of 39 percent of the adult population. More than 16 million combatants lost their lives in WWII, but already 17 million people have died of AIDS in Africa alone. In Southern Africa, at least one in five adults is infected. In Zambia, Zimbabwe and Botswana, as many as 70 percent of teenagers are expected to die of AIDS. AIDS has already caused some 2.5 million deaths in Africa in 2002 alone. It has left 12 million African children orphaned since the epidemic began:* According to the World Bank Group report at the end of 2002, more than 20 million Africans have now died, and those living with the virus number 29.4 million, the vast majority in the prime of their lives as workers and parents.

31. *The story of Botswana should serve as a warning for all nations, especially the larger ones, such as China, Russia and India, whose combined number of HIV/AIDS victims is expected to reach 75 million people by the end of this decade (25 million in India alone), according to a recent report published by the United States government:* The United States National Security Council released a report at the end of 2002 warning that AIDS cases in India could go up to 25 million by 2010 if urgent and effective measures are not taken. The validity of this report is challenged by both the Indian government and some U.N. officials.

32. *Until recently, the Indian government did not want to acknowledge the growing problem of HIV/AIDS; statistics were put out in 2000 indicating fewer*

than 100,000 cases throughout the country. But by 2002, several community leaders began to speak out, breaking the reluctance to discuss sex, drug use and the disease. The government also updated its statistics to 3.97 million people with HIV, the virus that could lead to AIDS, more than any country other than South Africa: It is difficult to obtain reliable estimates from the government on the number of HIV/AIDS cases in India. The estimates from non-governmental sources range from 3.5 million to 5 million cases as of 2002's end.

33. *The WHO 2002 report on world health details the top 10 preventable health risks globally: childhood and maternal underweight; unsafe sex; high blood pressure; tobacco; alcohol; unsafe water, sanitation and hygiene; high cholesterol; indoor smoke from solid fuels; iron deficiency and obesity:* The World Health Organization's annual report, World Health Report 2002 – Reducing Risks, Promoting Healthy Life.

34. *Poverty, hunger and malnutrition are interrelated silent realities for a majority of Indians. More than half of all children under the age of four suffer from malnutrition; 30 percent of newborns are significantly underweight; and 60 percent of women are anemic. According to a recent report by the U.N. World Food Program, 38 percent of children in India are below their normal weight and 36 percent are shorter than they should be due to malnutrition. Further, according to a recent World Bank report, malnutrition costs India at least $10 billion annually in terms of lost productivity, illness and death and is seriously retarding improvements in human development:* In recent decades, India has established several programs to combat malnutrition, including a Public Distribution System (PDS), an Integrated Child Development Services (ICDS) program, a National Mid-day Meals Program (NMMP) and several employment schemes providing food for work. But these programs have failed to meet the needs of the poorest, especially in rural areas, because of ineffective targeting, implementation and coverage.

35. *Despite the high level of malnutrition in the country and the resulting loss of productivity, direct spending by the Indian government on nutritional and micronutrients programs amounts to less than 0.19 percent of the GNP. This figure compares with the spending by Sri Lanka of 1 percent of the GNP on direct programs, and additional use of significant resources on health education*

and services, and anti-poverty programs, with successful results in the 1980s: According to the UNICEF April 2000 report, more than 60 million children under four-year-olds (53 percent) in India are moderately or severely malnourished. While 30 percent new-borns are significantly underweight, 87 percent of pregnant women and approximately 60 percent of young children are anemic. These rates of malnutrition in India are much higher than those in some sub-Saharan countries. A comparative study of the cases of Low Birth Weight (LBW) in Thailand, Indonesia, Myanmar, Sri Lanka, India and Bangladesh shows that India is second from the bottom, slightly better than Bangladesh. The incidence of LBW in India stands at 33 percent, way above Sri Lanka (18.4 percent).

36. *For the period from 1996 to 2001, life expectancy at birth in India was estimated to be around 63 percent, while the infant mortality rate (IMR) was estimated to be 74 per 1,000 live births:* Life expectancy at birth is defined as the average number of additional years a person could expect to live if current mortality trends were to continue for the rest of that person's life. The estimate in 2002 for females in India was nearly 64 years, while for males it was 62.6 years. These estimates for India are nearly 20 years less than that for Japan, according to Population Reference Bureau, an independent research organization based in the United States.

37. *The mean age at which women marry in India has gone up from the age of 13.1 in 1901 to nearly 20 in 2000:* According to the International Institute for Population Sciences (IIPS, Mumbai), while the average age for marriage is now above the legal marriage age of 18, a majority of women still marry before the legal age.

38. *For example, the fertility rate for the poorest 20 percent of the population in India is around 4.1, while for the richest 20 percent it is nearly half that at 2.1. 89 percent of the richest 20 percent get prenatal care, while only 25 percent of the poorest fifth get some degree of such care:* According to the Population Resource Center, a nonprofit organization based in the United States, the total fertility rate in India has declined from 6 in 1947 to 3.3 in 2000. It is expected to decline further to the level of replacement by 2020. A major contributor has been the increase in the average age at marriage. However, fertility rates for the poor and uneducated

are significantly higher than that for the rich and educated. Unless both income levels and literacy rates rise across all segments of the population, fertility rate for the country as a whole may still remain above the level of replacement even after 20 years.

39. *Today, public spending on health is about 1 percent of GDP, which puts India among the bottom 20 percent of countries:* Though the World Health Organization recommends that 5 percent of the GDP should be spent on health, the expenditure of the central and state government has come down from 1.25 percent (1993-94) to only 0.9 percent (2000-2001) of the GDP on health. Given the large rural population and the pivotal role of the state in providing them adequate health care, the current spending by the public sector is exceptionally low by any standard. Private spending on health care of 5 percent of the GDP is mostly targeted to the urban population, according to a 2002 McKinsey & Company report.

40. *In India, there are nearly 500,000 doctors by some estimates, of which 80 percent are engaged in private practice or working for private medical institutions. The balance of 100,000 doctors is mostly employed in government hospitals in urban areas:* A national consultation on A Vision for India's Health System, jointly organized by the Administrative Staff College of India, Ministry of Health & Family Welfare and the World Bank in November 2001 in New Delhi, outlined several health priorities for the country. This conference noted that the poor tend to depend on public hospitals more than the rich, but yet, 40 percent of the hospitalizations among the poorest 20 percent of the population take place in private clinics and hospitals. The private sector accounts for 82 percent of outpatient care and 56 percent of hospitalizations, while the public sector provides 90 percent of the immunizations.

41. *Most PHCs are overstaffed at lower levels, and have excess capacity to provide better care for a lot more patients if run properly. 80 percent of allocated funds are spent on salaries, and only the balance is available for medicines, equipments and other necessary supplies:* This ratio in allocation of financial resources has led to serious shortages in medicine, poor lab conditions and deteriorating physical infrastructure at PHCs.

CHAPTER 11: THE INTANGIBLES: ENVIRONMENT, FREEDOM OF THE PRESS, AND THE ARTS

42. *The Earth Summit on Sustainable Development held in Johannesburg in August 2002 tried to find a common ground for developing and implementing projects in five major areas: water and sanitation, energy, health, agriculture productivity, and biodiversity and ecosystem management:* Johannesburg Summit August/September 2002 brought together tens of thousands of participants, including heads of state and government, national delegates and leaders from non-governmental organizations (NGOs), businesses and other major groups to focus the world's attention and direct action toward meeting difficult challenges, including improving people's lives and conserving our natural resources in a world that is growing in population, with ever-increasing demands for food, water, shelter, sanitation, energy, health services and economic security.

43. *By the year 2025, nearly 3 billion people could live in either water-scarce or water-stressed conditions; 1 billion people could be living in land-scarce countries unable to feed the population; more than 4 billion people could be in one of 40 countries, including India, that have less than 0.1 hectare of forest land per capita, the threshold low level of forest cover:* According to a 2002 report by Johns Hopkins School of Public Health, over the past 50 years nearly half of the world's original forest cover has been lost. Current demand for forest products may exceed the limits of sustainable consumption by 25 percent. By 2025, when world population is projected to reach 8 billion, 48 countries with a total population of 3 billion will face chronic water shortages. In 25 years, humankind could be using more than 90 percent of all available freshwater, leaving just 10 percent for the rest of the world's plants and animals.

44. *The United States government's rejection of the Kyoto Protocol, which would have required countries to maintain greenhouse emissions within certain set standards, appeared as a unilateral rejection by the United States of a clean global environment:* The Kyoto Protocol on Climate Change is an international framework to reduce greenhouse gas emissions in an attempt to mitigate global climate change. The United States administration rejected the protocol on the grounds that it is fatally flawed, that its adherence would cause economic crises and that the 130 developing nations should

not be exempt from the current emissions reduction requirements. In November 2003, Russia also rejected the Kyoto Protocol on the grounds that it "would harm the country's economic development."

45. *But the United States is also the worst culprit in producing greenhouse gases, and it is dragging its feet on international negotiations to bring them under control. With only 5 percent of the world's population, the United States accounts for one quarter of all greenhouse gas emissions:* Total United States greenhouse gas emissions, led by a decrease in carbon dioxide, fell by 1.2 percent in 2001, from 1,907 million metric tons of carbon equivalent (MMTCe) in 2000 to 1,883 MMTCe in 2001, according to Emissions of Greenhouse Gases in the United States 2001, a report released by the Energy Information Administration (EIA). The 2001 decline of 1.2 percent is in contrast to the average annual growth rate of 1.3 percent observed from 1990 to 2000, and it was enough to reduce the growth from 1990 to 2001 to an average of 1.0 percent per year.

46. *Led by V. Ramanathan from the Scripps Institution of Oceanography in the United States, a team of 200 scientists have been studying for the past several years the dark brown blanket of soot, dust and smoke that may be causing climate change in the region:* According to the press release by the National Science Foundation, USA, of June 8, 1999, an international group of scientists has documented widespread pollution covering about 10 million square kilometers of the tropical Indian Ocean – roughly the same area as the continental United States. This finding by scientists participating in the Indian Ocean Experiment (INDOEX) raises serious questions about what impact the extensive pollution is having on climate processes and on marine life in the ocean below.

47. *The George Foundation joined forces with St. Johns National Academy of Health Sciences in Bangalore and funded the creation and operation of the National Referral Center for Lead Poisoning in India (NRCLPI) to carry out these important initiatives:* Information on the activities of NRCLP can be found at www.leadpoison.net.

48. *"At the Hemisphere Conference of the Inter American Press Association held at Chapultepec Castle in Mexico City in March 1994, political leaders,*

writers, academics, constitutional lawyers, editors and private citizens from throughout the Americas drafted a document containing 10 principles necessary for a free press to be able to perform its essential role in a democracy.": The Inter American Press Association (IAPA) is a nonprofit organization dedicated to defending freedom of expression and of the press throughout the Americas. The 10 principles drafted at the conference have since been endorsed by heads of state throughout the hemisphere, as well as by human rights activists, judges, lawyers, journalists and editors, political leaders, local citizens groups, international organizations and thousands of private individuals.

49. *In a case that challenged the constitutionality of secret trials, Judge Damon J. Keith of the United States Court of Appeals of the Sixth Circuit dismissed the government's argument for secrecy with a forceful and eloquent opinion that said, "Democracies die behind closed doors":* The federal appeals court in Cincinnati declared on August 26, 2002 that the Bush administration acted unlawfully in holding hundreds of deportation hearings in secret based only on the government's assertion that the people involved may have links to terrorism. The decision questioned the administration's commitment to an open democracy, and on the government's legal tactics concerning September 11.

50. *According to the reports released for 2001 and 2002 by the Committee to Protect Journalists, Indian journalists continue to face physical threats, legal harassment and subtle pressures from both central and state governments:* The report by the Committee to Protect Journalists pointed out that in Gujarat, police and political activists were responsible for assaulting journalists covering the riots. The journalists faced harassment and assault by the police who did not want their complicity in the attacks publicized. Similarly, the CPJ report noted that journalists working in Jammu and Kashmir continue to endure physical assault, threats and harassment, and the number of attacks against the press has only increased.

51. *The government has used administrative tools to stifle the press; a clear example is the raid by tax authorities on the offices of Outlook magazine following a series of articles examining corporate influence in the prime minister's office:* According to The Hindu newspaper, income tax raids conducted on

May 29, 2001, on the Raheja group of companies which owns Outlook magazine was not only an attempt to silence the voice of an independent publication, but they also constituted a frontal attack on the Indian press by the NDA government.

CHAPTER 12: IN SEARCH OF MORAL AND ETHICAL CONDUCT

52. *The unraveling of the fraud surrounding the Unit Trust of India, a state owned mutual fund, in July 2001 shook up the public in general and some 20 million Indian investors in its United Scheme 64:* Following the crisis, the government was quick to announce a reform package and financial assistance of over Rs.14,600 crores to "help meet investors' expectations, reinforce confidence in the largest fund manager and provide a positive trigger to the stock market." The general public seems to have been pacified by the financial rescue, though substantial tax revenues have been wasted in the bailout.

53. *This UTI episode and the Home Trade Scam of 2002, involving politicians, bankers and brokers who swindled some Rs.6 billion ($125 million) from banks and Public Provident Funds, are just two recent examples of major illegal and unethical conduct by individuals in power, and they reflect countless other infringements of lesser magnitude:* The so-called "Home Trade Scam," involving several cooperative banks in various states, resulted in financial losses to the public of nearly Rs 500 crores, to be paid for from government funds.

54. *In 2000, international NGOs contributed development-related grants in the range of $6 billion, of which some portion came from private philanthropy. In 2002, private contributions to charity in the United States exceeded $240 billion, 2.3 percent of the country's GDP.* According to the report by the Foundation Center, Giving USA 2003, total giving in the United States in 2002 was $240.92 billion, almost the magnitude of India's GDP in that year. This amount consisted of 76 percent from individuals ($184 billion), 11 percent from foundations ($27 billion), 5.1 percent from corporations ($12 billion) and the balance from other sources. Disappointingly, just over 1 percent of the donations were earmarked for the rest of the world, despite the fact that poverty in America is negligible when compared to other developing countries.

55. *In 1980, more than 70 percent of high school seniors (in America) said they had been drinking alcohol, but that figure dropped below 50 percent by 2000:* According to the National Institute on Drug Abuse, the percent of high school seniors who have used alcohol has decreased in the past 25 years; still 80 percent of high school seniors have used alcohol.

CHAPTER 13: GLOBAL PERSPECTIVES AND PERCEPTIONS

56. *A recent poll of 1,600 respondents by an Arab political scientist found that by a margin of 4 to 1, Arabs denied the Holocaust and rejected the idea of doing business with Israel even after a peace settlement is reached:* The effort to deny the basic facts of the Holocaust has its roots not in the Middle East but in Europe and the United States, and it stretches back, if not to the Nazis themselves, then to the years immediately following World War II.

57. *India welcomed American pressure on Pakistan to stop crossborder terrorism by mercenaries, and when both India and Pakistan came dangerously close to war in 2002 that could have resulted in a nuclear confrontation, it was probably the personal involvement of President Bush that avoided a military confrontation:* The role played by the Bush administration during the period of December 2001 to July 2002 in persuading Pakistan to stop militants from crossing over into India, and the eventual withdrawal of military forces by both parties from the border, avoided the start of a conventional war that could have led to a nuclear one. During this crisis period, President Bush made repeated personal appeals to the leaders of India and Pakistan, and sent United States Defense Secretary Donald Rumsfeld, United States Secretary of State Colin Powell and Deputy Secretary of State Richard Armitage to both countries to diffuse the situation.

BIBLIOGRAPHY

This book is a personal account of my experiences and views about India's policies and programs based on the humanitarian work being carried out by The George Foundation since 1995. As such, I have not cited in the text many published works from which I have drawn several ideas. The following, however, is a list of publications that I have studied in formulating my opinions expressed in this book.

M. Francis Abraham, *The Agony of India*, EastWest Books Pvt. Ltd., Chennai, 1998.

Ram Ahuja, *Social Problems in India*, Rawat Publications, New Delhi, 2001.

Dinesh N. Awasthi, *Short Steps Long Leaps*, Tata McGraw-Hill Publishing Company Ltd., New Delhi, 2001.

Peter Bauer, *Development Aid*, ICS Press, San Francisco, 1993.

Lynn Bennett and Mike Goldberg, *Providing Enterprise Development and Financial Services to Women*, World Bank Technical Paper Number 236, 1993.

Elisabeth Bumiller, *May You Be The Mother of A Hundred Sons*, Penguin Books, New Delhi, 1990.

N. Burra, *Born to Work: Child Labor in India*, Oxford University Press, Delhi, 1995.

Robert Chambers, *Rural Development*, Longman Scientific & Technical, Essex, England, 1983.

Gurcharan Das, *India Unbound*, Alfred A. Knopf, New York, 2000.

John L. Esposito, *Unholy War*, Oxford University Press, London, 2002.

Milton and Rose Friedman, *Free to Choose*, Hartcourt Brace Jovanovich, New York, 1980.

Nathan Gardels, ed., At Century's End, Alti Publishing, La Jolla, California, 1996.

Dipankar Gupta, Interrogating Caste, Penguin Books, New Delhi, 2000.

Chris Hedges, War is a Force That Gives Us Meaning, Public Affairs, New York, 2002.

The Heritage Foundation, 2003 Index of Economic Freedom, Washington, D.C., 2003.

David Hume, An Inquiry Concerning Human Understanding, The Bobbs-Merrill Company, New York, 1955.

Human Rights Watch/Asia, The Small Hands of Slavery: Bonded Labor in India, Washington, D.C., 1996.

Anees Jung, Unveiling India, Penguin Books, New Delhi, 1987.

Elizabeth M. King, Women's Education in Developing Countries, The Johns Hopkins University Press, Baltimore, 1993.

James Kistorti and Fadi Doumani, Environmental Health, World Bank Discussion Paper, Washington, D.C., 2001.

Robert Van Kriekan, Norbert Elias, Routledge, New York, 1998.

Lead India, Rio, Johannesburg and Beyond, Orient Longman, Hyderabad, 2002.

Bernard Lewis, The Islamic World, Darwin Press, Princeton, New Jersey, 1988.

Oscar Lewis, Village Life in Northern India, University of Illinois Press, Urbana, Indiana, 1958.

John Madeley, Hungry for Trade, Penguin Books, New Delhi, 2001.

Adrian Mayer, Caste in an Indian Village, Oxford University Press, Delhi, 1997.

Gota Mehta, Snakes and Ladders, Martin Secker and Warburg Ltd., London, 1997.

Bill Moyers, ed., A World of Ideas, Doubleday, New York, 1997.

Martha Nussbaum, Upheavals of Thought: The Intelligence of Emotions, Cambridge University Press, London, 2003.

Albert Nyberg & Scott Rozelle, *Accelerating China's Rural Transformation*, The World Bank, Washington, D.C., 1999.

National Council of Applied Economic Research, *South India: Human Development Report*, Oxford University Press, 2001.

Wendy Kay Olsen, *Rural Indian Social Relations*, Oxford University Press, Delhi, 1996.

Octavio Paz, *In Light of India*, Harcourt Brace & Company, New York, 1997.

Louis Y. Pouliquen, *Rural Infrastructure from a World Bank Perspective*, World Bank, Washington, D.C., 1999.

The Probe Team, *Public Report on Basic Education in India*, Oxford University Press, New Delhi, 1999.

John Rawlins, *Justice as Fairness*, Harvard University Press, Cambridge, Massachusetts, 2001.

Vincent R. Ruggiero, *Beyond Feelings*, Mayfield Publishing Company, London, 1990.

Salman Rushdie, *The Satanic Verses*, Penguin USA, New York, 1992.

P. Sainath, *Everybody Loves a Good Drought*, Penguin Books, New Delhi, 1996.

Arun Sinha, *Against the Few*, Zed Books Ltd., London, 1991.

Joseph Stiglitz, *Globalization and its Discontents*, W.W. Norton, & Company, New York, 2002.

Amartya Sen, *Development as Freedom*, Anchor Books, New York, 1999.

Mira Seth, *Women & Development*, Sage Publications, New Delhi, 2001.

Katar Singh, *Rural Development*, Sage Publications India Pvt. Ltd., New Delhi, 1999.

Shashi Tharoor, *India: From Midnight to the Millennium*, Arcade Publishing, New York, 1997.

Mark Tully, *India in Slow Motion*, Penguin Books India, New Delhi, 2002.

S. Venkatesh and Sunita Bhadauria, *Diary of the Dispossessed, Books for Change*, Bangalore, 2000.

A.R. Vasavi, *Harbingers of Rain*, Oxford University Press, New Delhi, 1999.

Mahadevi Varma, *Sketches from My Past*, Northeastern University Press, Boston, 1994.

Robert Wade, *Village Republics*, ICS Press, San Francisco, 1994.

Leon Wiesltier, *Kaddish*, Knopf Alfred, New York, 1999.

Stanley Wolpert, *India*, University of California Press, Berkeley, California, 1991.

Paul Woodruff, *Reverence: Renewing a Forgotten Virtue*, Oxford University Press, London, 2002.

World Bank, *India: Achievements and Challenges in Reducing Poverty*, Washington, D.C., 1997.

World Bank, *Rural Development*, Washington, D.C., 1999.

World Bank, *India: New Directions in Health Sector Development at the State Level*, Washington, D.C., 1997.

World Bank, Primary Education in India, Washington, D.C., 1997.

INDEX

ABOUT THE AUTHOR

Abraham George was a successful entrepreneur in the United States for more than 25 years before he embarked on a number of humanitarian projects in South India. A former artillery officer in the Indian army, he went on to receive a Ph.D. in Business Administration from New York University and wrote three books on international finance. His business accomplishments include heading a software company he founded, serving as a managing director at a global investment bank and as a vice-chairman at a New York Stock Exchange-traded firm, and consulting for more than 100 of the Fortune 500 companies. Today, he shuttles between Bangalore and New Jersey several times a year and spends much of his time directing the activities of The George Foundation in India.

The author can be contacted by email at amgeorge@optonline.net.

For information on his charitable projects, visit www.tgfworld.org.

The George Foundation

210, 5th 'A' Cross, HBR Layout, Kalyananagar, Bangalore-560043
Karnataka, India. ☎ 91-80-25440164/25444170 🖨 91-80-25440210